The Making of a German Constitution

The Making of a German Constitution
A Slow Revolution

Margaret Barber Crosby

BERG

Oxford • New York

First published in 2008 by
Berg
Editorial offices:
First Floor, Angel Court, 81 St Clements Street, Oxford OX4 1AW, UK
175 Fifth Avenue, New York, NY 10010, USA

Berg is the imprint of Oxford International Publishers Ltd.

Library of Congress Cataloging-in-Publication Data

Crosby, Margaret Barber.
The making of a German constitution : a slow revolution /
Margaret Barber Crosby.—English ed.
p. cm.
Includes bibliographical references and index.
ISBN-13: 978-1-85973-812-2 (cloth)
ISBN-10: 1-85973-812-5 (cloth)
ISBN-13: 978-1-85973-817-7 (paper)
ISBN-10: 1-85973-817-6 (paper)
1. Constitutional history—Germany. 2. Civil law—Germany—History.
3. Civil law—Germany—Codification—History. 4. Nationalism—
Germany—History. 5. Germany—Politics and government—1848–1870.
6. Germany—Politics and government—1871–1933. I. Title.
KK4455.C76 2008
342.4302'9—dc22
2007043705

British Library Cataloguing-in-Publication Data

A catalogue record for this book is available from the British Library.

ISBN 978 1 85973 812 2 (Cloth)
978 1 85973 817 7 (Paper)

Typeset by Apex Publishing, LLC, Madison, WI, USA.
Printed in the United Kingdom by Biddles Ltd, King's Lynn.

www.bergpublishers.com

Joe B. Crosby

Dedicated to my Dad and best, good friend

Contents

Preface

Most of the lessons I have learned about the merits of peace and nonviolence I learned from my father, Joe B. Crosby. Although scholars often associate the experience of war with continuing violence back home, his life is a testament to how the experience of war often produces the opposite effect. In 1962, my father could not vote in Alabama or participate in the governance of the nation, but he could be drafted and he was. From a big farm family and with fifteen brothers and sisters, he had to go. He still laughs when he tells that the first time he got on a plane, he had to parachute out. As amusing as this is, he also had to graduate early and miss the graduation celebration with his friends and classmates. Instead, he went off to do his duty for a nation that, at that time, rigorously obstructed all avenues to his liberty and pursuit of happiness and then had the gall to place his life in harm's way. We have pictures of him walking through rice fields in Vietnam, with a machine gun strapped across his chest. There came a time also when he had to choose between going back to a war zone himself and having his younger brothers pull this duty. He chose to go back, underscoring the fact that sometimes the reason men go to war has little to do with the state's ideological justification of it.

What he does not talk about is the experience of Vietnam itself. The other members of my immediate family, however, know its impact well. Everything, as my father will always say, has a right to live and every life has value. I was taught this lesson as a youngster, one day, when I went to stomp on a spider. He stopped me and explained this lesson as he gently protected the spider in his hands and placed it outside.

Paradoxically, getting drafted turned out to be a blessing in disguise. The U.S. Army offered advancement to any citizen on the basis of merit, regardless of 'race'. After getting out for bit, my father re-enlisted. He retired from the U.S. Army after twenty-four years and was awarded the Legion of Merit. His service offered him and his family opportunities around the world. Indeed, my first of many tours to Germany was taken at three months, and I grew up between Germany, Japan and the United States. After retirement, he returned to Alabama, started a business and prospered in a state where, although old problems persist, there has been a remarkable transformation. As he takes in the news of violent conflicts from around the world these days, he will often remark on the senselessness of young men and women dying and wonders why people just don't find ways to get along. This is not the academic wisdom of a think tank scholar or foreign policy maker, but rather that of a man who, as a young man, watched other young men die next to him. He has taught me that there are times when it is absolutely necessary to fight, but they should be absolutely necessary. From my father I have learned to seek amicable resolution to the last and to reject unnecessary and unjust use of violence, but also not to stand on the sidelines lest those who would engage in illegitimate acts that cost lives get the upper hand. To have a father that you can be so proud of is a wonderful blessing. I am thankful for all that he has given and taught me over the years. I am still learning from him, and this book is dedicated to my father, who is my Dad, teacher, hero, and loyal, best, good friend.

Early lessons learned while just hanging out with my Dad first developed my ability to see that there are peaceful and nonviolent alternatives, and that, in all times, there are people seeking them in the face of conflict and injustice. Aside from the larger historiographical debates that this book takes on, at rock bottom, it is about a German generation that experienced the French revolutionary wars, sword-point democracy, conscription, unprecedented violence, bloodshed and loss of life, and, in the aftermath of such, determined to resolve their own domestic, sociopolitical conflicts through nonviolent means. These voices, the voices of men who fought in the *Freiheitskriege* against Napoleonic France, were making themselves heard even before fresh grass could grow to cover the blood on the battlefields. The nonviolent approach to sociopolitical revision was flawed, but it worked. The history of the German generation of war veterans who were committed to nonviolence, unfortunately, has been obscured by the focus on the horrific violence of the First and Second World wars. It is in the face of rising violent conflicts, however, that we might learn something from the earlier generation.

There are many people that I want to thank, not only for academic reasons, but for sticking by me and supporting me through very trying times. First, there is my father, who has supported and has loved me, unconditionally, my whole life. It is also due to his service that I was able to grow up in and experience a good bit of the world, including Germany. My mother, Callie, a student of history herself, appreciated our surroundings. She didn't just live on army bases in Germany and Japan, but endeavored to learn something of the culture and language. Thanks, Mom, for dragging me to every castle, cathedral and museum in Europe, most often against my will, and making me behave. I have learned different and valuable lessons from you that have made me smarter, and it is only because of your influence and insistence that I possess the manners and broad cultural tools that are so vital in the new global world. To my sister, Daphne, thanks for all the made-up fairy tales during our childhood travels. The cat, Kim, is still the greatest imaginary character ever, and you inspired in me the creativity that one needs to write a book of this kind.

Next, there is my *Doktorvater*, Volker Berghahn, who nurtured my scholarly growth and never once wavered in his support and encouragement. Thanks for everything, especially for being willing to pound your big German fist on the table to make me sharpen my arguments. Thanks also to the Berghahn family, especially Marion, for sharing him with so many of us. I also owe much to the support I have received from Tom and Sarah Gleason as well as Carolyn Dean over the years. Tom, as a young college student, went south into Mississippi, during the very dangerous summer of

1964, to protest segregation and do something about it. The opportunities I have today are, in part, owed to the courage of men like Tom Gleason. Carolyn Dean opened my eyes to understanding the importance of seeing how construction works and happens. It also should be understood that in the Ph.D. apprenticeship, your advisor and committee members do not just advise you in a professionally distant manner. They have to take you and your life on board for better or for worse. In my case, it was not always easy going, and my committee could not have been more supportive.

In the Brown University community also, I want to thank Joan Lusk, who stepped into the late dean, Bernard Bruce's, shoes. Through academic fellowships, they funded my entire graduate school career and Joan Lusk procured the money that funded my research trips to Germany when I was at Brown. On this note, I want to thank the Corporation of Brown University for maintaining such a fantastic institution, which opened its doors to me and opened new doors for me. The History Department's graduate program is tough, because excellence is a demand and not an option. For this, I am grateful.

On a purely professional note, I want to thank Dr. Jan Palmowski and Dr. Christopher Thornhill for giving me my first job in London and the United Kingdom's Arts and Humanities Board for their considerable financial support. Chris and Jan really helped me to see the link between my dissertation's focus on private law and the later development of German public law scholarship. I also want to thank the *Max-Planck-Institut für europäische Rechtsgeschichte* in Frankfurt am Main for their guest scientist appointments, housing, and considerable financial support and resources. Here, I must thank not only the Institute's scholars, but also its staff for their immeasurable kindness and help. I want to make special mention of Prof. Dr. Dr.h.c.mult. (em.) Michael Stolleis, Prof. Dr. Marie Fögen, Prof. Dr. Barbara Dölemeyer and the entire staff, but especially, Herr Gerhard Gräber. Similarly, I want to thank the staff of the *Bundesarchiv Berlin,* some of whom even showed up with little, wooden German toys for me to take back to my daughter, Erin, in the United States. Thank you also to the staff of Harvard University's International Law Studies Center. In particular, I want to thank Stephen Helfer for his many trips to the basement. I also want to thank the staff of the *Brandenburgische Landeshauptarchiv Potsdam-Bornim* for giving me access to primary sources, which they had not yet even catalogued. Finally, the staffs of the *Geheimes Staatsarchiv Preußischer Kulturbesitz, Landesarchiv Berlin,* the Göttingen University and Hesse-Darmstadt archives were consistently professional and as helpful as possible.

Thank you also to Daryl Michael Scott and Howard University's History Department faculty for giving me the opportunity to be a part of its strong research tradition. I am looking forward to many years at Howard and hope, as a scholar, that I am able to live up to this University's legacies.

In terms of this book, Michael Stolleis and Volker Berghahn patiently read the very rough first draft and offered their invaluable, scholarly advice. In terms of the final product, the interest and support of one's publisher is most important. Here,

I want to thank Berg Publishers and Apex Publishing for the attention and outstanding job they have done in refining the final production of this book. Special thanks to my editors, Hannah Shakespeare and Ken Bruce of Berg and Julia Rosen of Apex CoVantage. The fact that Apex maintains a nonprofit, Apex Foundation, which has supported amongst other worthy causes and organizations, the Vietnam Veterans of America Foundation, has added to my pleasure in working with them.

There are also many additional family and friends who are my support system. Here, I am grateful for all of my aunts, uncles and 51+ first cousins, not to mention a sizeable clan of extended family beyond this and on both sides. My aunts Eva Mae (d.), Sadie, Princella, Willow Dean, Cora, Doris, Sue, Mamie and Patricia and my uncles Henry, Isom, Walter, James, Andrew and Gerald all of whom are my father's siblings, have offered me warmth, guidance, kindness and love my entire life. Through marriage, my aunts and uncles expanded our family support system to include other people who have nurtured me. These are my uncles Robert (d.), Clinton, Hercules, Murphy, Gilbert and Ray, and aunts Margery, Vivian, Lula, Juliette, Carolyn and Clarice. On my mother's side, the same is true of my aunts Johnnie (d.), Callie, Doris, Georgia (cousin), Mattie (d.), Emily (d.) and Dorothy and my uncles Tom, James Earl, Edward (d.) and Samuel. Their spouses, George (a WWII veteran), John Lewis (d.), Henrietta (d.) and Cassandra have been kind and looked out for me over the years. Although my cousins are all like brothers and sisters to me and I love them all, special mention is in order for some of them who facilitated my research and writing namely Gilbert, Te'Sha, Devon and especially Paris, who gave up her room to me for several months. My cousins, Leonard (who has served in Iraq), Kimberly and Kiante, who were stationed in Darmstadt, took me in every summer, making it possible for me to visit different archives on my long summer research trips. Elvira Pritchett has been like an aunt to me as far back as I can remember, and because her husband was also military, I was lucky enough to have her in Germany also.

As a single parent, I could not simply pack off to Germany for a few years. I had to take short research trips, and this was only possible because of the extraordinary kindness of many German friends. In Berlin, the staff of the Hotel Ravenna gave me one great discount deal after another, and there was always a table for me at the restaurant, La Fattoria. Also, in Germany, Henning von Stechow and Marguerite ultimately gave me their extra apartment in Berlin as a place to stay on my many, many research trips. Mathias and Katja Hueske also have been good friends over the year and are always a joy to see.

In the Rhode Island community, there are many, but special thanks to Brad Shipp for his friendship, open door, great meals and good times. In New York, I look forward to more good times with Roger and Jenny Lyn Berkowitz and, with Roger, more intellectual sparring. Thanks to L. E. Hartmann-Ting and Vanessa Bobb for being such great friends since graduate school and to L. E.'s big Italian family for great holidays when I didn't travel to Alabama. I also need to thank many of my husband's friends, especially Russell Malbrough for his many trips to the library on my behalf. Now, in California, I also want to thank old friends Andy and soon Meghan Bell and Kevin and Anna Cloud for their unwavering friendship since graduate school and coming to my aid many times. Andy's parents were also gracious enough to take me in on many of my trips to London. In Australia, I want to thank Andrew Gentes also for his many years of friendship. Now in Texas and soon Iraq, Ryan Remley and his wife, Tammy, are fine, upstanding Americans and have been wonderful friends. In Alabama, the blessing is that there are too many people for me to mention them all individually. However, Anne Pearson is one of the best people I have ever had the pleasure of knowing and is always at the top of any list. I also want to make special mention of Laura Crum, Patrick Jansen, Cindy Harris, Richard Kohn, and the wonderful Terry Mitchell family for their friendship to Erin and to me. Finally, the many, many philanthropically engaged women I had the pleasure of knowing in Montgomery, Alabama are some of the most enlightened, forward thinking, savvy and fun women I have met anywhere.

I have saved the best for last. To my dear daughter, Erin, I love you more than I can say in words. You are a blessing and one of God's angels to be sure. I miss you and think of you every minute. I continue to struggle to break down old glass ceilings, social and otherwise, so that you might be friends with whomever you wish and live freely with the equal opportunity to live up to your potential happiness, unobstructed by gender discrimination, racism and/or anti-racist racism alike. To my wonderful husband, Artis, who recently married me, I'm so lucky to have met you. You are my knight in shining armor and the rock upon which I lean. I love you always and am looking forward to many, many, growing old, blessed years together.

Finally, I come from an old southern family, from the same town for generations. I had the joy of knowing my grandparents and great grandparents and knowing of their grandparents and great grandparents. The land in my family has been with us since Reconstruction, so I can see and know where they walked. This has given me a strong sense of identity, security, and knowing who I am.

Margaret Barber Crosby-Arnold

Coosada, Alabama (in spirit always)

Introduction

Transforming the Reich
Toward a New Political History of Modern Germany

> In its beginnings and origins, the Code reaches back to past times before our generation. From its roots in the century in which the modern state was born, one is able to say that it constitutes the rainfall of those legal, ethical and political ideals that under the currents and cross-currents of the previous century gradually have slipped into the consciousness and possession of the German people ever since the *Freiheitskriege.* It may be stated unequivocally that not only has our generation work on this Draft, but the German people before us also have thought on it and the spiritual power of the nation worked on it long before our time.[1]
>
> —Rudolf Nieberding, Minister of Justice 1896

> If anyone had foreseen that in a span of only thirty years, the German Reichstag would debate a law proposing the modification of the whole of private law for the whole of Germany ... they would have been laughed at as a fanatic dreamer ... Yet, before us lays the conclusive constitutional decision *(verfassungsmäßige Beschlussfassung).*[2]
>
> —Gerhard von Buchka, Reichstag Deputy, 1896

> Through unification, a majority of monarchs can also form themselves into a republic. Therefore, the *Deutsche Reich* also qualifies ... as a type of republic. Many leading *Reichsstaatsrecht* scholars have reflected on the question of the *Deutsche Reich's* form of state. Many have labeled it as a *Pleonokratie*, but this is nothing other than a new term for an old thing. A republic is the equal sovereignty of the majority in contrast to the sovereignty of an individual. That the *Reich* is a republic has been stated by no less a figure than Bismarck.[3]
>
> —Georg Jellinek, Professor of *Staatsrecht,* 1900

This set of comments spanning the years between 1896 and 1900 offers circumstantial evidence of a reorganization of political power in late-nineteenth-century Germany. In his opening speech to the Reichstag's deliberations on the *Bürgerliches Gesetzbuch für das Deutsche Reich* (BGB), Rudolf Nieberding, a long-time National Liberal and the sitting Minister of Justice, betrayed the liberal political basis of the code's origins. On the other end of the political spectrum, even the

Conservative deputy and lawyer, Gerhard von Buchka, in his opening comments to the Reichstag debates, alluded to the far-reaching constitutional implications of the proposed BGB. Only private law, as he stated unequivocally to the Reichstag, had been *'stiefmütterlich behandelt'* (step-motherly handled) in the slow course of legal development from the *Zollverein* (1834) to the 'surprisingly speedy' production of the *Wechselordnung* (1848) to the *Reichsjustizgesetz* (1879).[4] Finally, the well-known jurist Georg Jellinek's comments, published in the very year that the BGB was introduced as the law of the land, also serve to indicate that a fundamental political transformation of some kind had taken place. After a lengthy examination of the character of republics, Jellinek suggested that a constitutional transformation of Germany into a *Republik* had occurred, and he implied that it was linked to the legislative process.[5] Collectively, these comments spanning the important constitutional years between 1896 and 1900 indicate that contemporaries felt that a major political transformation was underway in Germany, and it is this transformation that I hope to begin making visible here.

Although the idea has not circulated for some time, the notion of constitutional transformation is not altogether novel and was a main subject of inquiry in early-twentieth-century *Staatslehre* scholarship. Jellinek's *Verfassungsänderung und Verfassungswandlung* (1906) is the most obvious example of this type of constitutional thought.[6] Paul Laband also explored a slow process of constitutional transformation in his *Die geschichtliche Entwicklung der Reichsverfassung seit der Reichsgründung* (1907).[7] That same year, Heinrich Triepel associated this process with political elements, and by 1917 he concluded that legislation, which had acquired the character of customary law, had produced alterations to the German constitution.[8] What is most striking about this body of scholarship is the expression of a sense that not only could a constitution undergo transformation, but that the German constitution had undergone such a transformation. As the legal scholar Michael Stolleis has pointed out, even in Bismarck's time it had become clear how politically dependent and changeable the material law of the constitution was and that it in fact was changed over time.[9] Historians, therefore, also need to consider the 'nearly unexamined phenomenon' of what Wilfred Fiedler long ago saw as 'tacit change in the constitution'.[10]

While the idea of constitutional transformation reached an important high point in early-twentieth-century scholarship on public law and in the political science literature, in fact it is argued here that the notion of constitutional transformation had its roots in the early-nineteenth-century development of German private law scholarship and the historical scholarship that supported it. Here, particularly in the writings of Friedrich Karl von Savigny, Barthold Niebuhr, Karl Eichhorn, Jacob Grimm, Karl Mittermaier and others, a programmatic political discourse saw development, which emphasized not only that political or constitutional transformation could occur through legislative means, but that such a transformation was the best course for German-speaking Europe. Deeply political, nineteenth-century scholarship on private law became the mainstay of German political science during the Restoration years, when the discussion of public law and constitutionalism was virtually banned and invited unwanted persecution from state authorities. This vitally important body of primary source material on German political ideals should be seen as a kind of *Privatrechts-Staatslehre* or political science of private law. What my examination of some of this literature suggests is that the understanding of 'constitution' needs to be broadened to encompass a legal regime far broader than formal constitutions. *Privatrechts-Staatslehre* was the dominant mode of political discourse in the first half of the nineteenth century. Thus, when constitutional transformation began in Central Europe, it occurred through the legislation of codes and measures of rationalized German private law, or, in technical language, civil law. This was a constitutional transformation that sped up from the middle of the century at the state level and reached its apex after unification with the enactment of the BGB in 1896, which I argue was modern Germany's bourgeois revolutionary moment.

A history of nineteenth-century German constitutional transformation, focusing on the role of private law, is also important because it offers an example of an historical precedent of what Joseph Weiler identified, relative to the European Union (EU), as an inverted process of constitutionalization, which spanned from Rome in 1950 to the Treaty of Maastricht in 1992.[11] The European Coal and Steel Community (ECSC) that resulted in 1951 was a first step in a long-range strategy of political transformation and, as Weiler argues, that transformation has been continuous since that time even if it was not perceived by the people and the world at large.[12] Weiler also pointed toward the critical role of the European Court of Justice, founded in 1952, in this transformation. The community, he suggested, used the rule of law to achieve its ends of European unity, and it was between 1958 and the early 1970s that the EU assumed its basic legal and political characteristics.[13]

Accordingly, this book is about constitutional transformation, specifically in the form of inverted constitutionalization, and its political significance for twentieth-century Germany. It contributes to the growing body of research that challenges the postwar scholarship, which located the rise of Nazism in a purported failure of the German bourgeoisie to effect a reorganization of law and politics. Focusing specifically on the BGB, I argue that its enactment represented the apex of a deliberate liberal programme of nonviolent, slow constitutional transformation, which was designed to bring about a bourgeois revolution in German society through legislation.

Several important points should be emphasized from the outset and kept in mind by readers. First, while the notion of constitutional transformation emerged against the backdrop of the unprecedented violence Europe experienced as a result of the sudden shocks of the French Revolution, the origin of this idea had deep roots in the particular legal history of German-speaking Europe. Once the idea of slow revolution as an alternative to sudden revolution was rationalized after the *Freiheitskriege,* constitutional ideology, as it saw unique expression in German-speaking Europe, emphasized nonviolent methods through the development and use of modern legal infrastructures and procedures. Second, constitutional theory in Germany developed in scholarship on private law, because the realities of the Restoration in post-*Freiheitskriege* Central Europe severely restricted the ability of intellectuals to openly develop constitutional and public law discourse. Thus, there developed in Germany the political expedient of inverted constitutionalization. Where the order of development in England and France saw the arranging of constitutions or public orderings followed by civil arrangements, in Germany the civil arrangements were constructed first with the goal of transforming and creating a de facto reordering of the public constitution.

Constitutional transformation, as it occurred in the nineteenth century, was bound up with German liberalism, and it began nearly before the ink dried on the Reich Constitution of 1871 if not before. Indeed, the 1873 *Lex Miquel-Lasker* constitutional amendment was almost as politically significant as the constitution itself. It extended the legislative competency of the Reich to the entire range of civil law and, increasingly, gaps in the constitution were filled with supplemental legal measures. Constitutional transformation was effected slowly through the legislation, not of public laws, but indeed of civil laws that held significant ramifications for public relationships of power. The enactment in 1896 and introduction of the BGB and its often overlooked *Einführungsgesetz* of 1 January 1900 were the capstone of a much longer process of inverted constitutional transformation, which ruptured and reordered power relations in Germany. Accordingly, this study locates Nieberding's beginnings and origins in 1814, seeks to put together a political picture of von Buchka's puzzle of laws, and offers evidence of Jellinek's *Deutsche Republik.*

From here, this study will flow into an analysis of post-1896 indicators of a nonviolent *Bürgerliche Revolution.* First, it is suggested that the Prussian monarchy's increased focus on foreign relations and military matters after 1896 was in large part due to the fact that its authority in domestic affairs faced severe restriction after the enactment of the BGB. Only relative to matters of national defence and security did the Kaiser still possess enough unencumbered power to act beyond the reach of judicial and parliamentary checks. While there has been little historical research on this phenomenon, Stolleis has pointed out that the 'Kaiser's civil authority, once defended as part of the "monarchic principle", had been stripped of its legitimacy ever since the Daily Telegraph Affair (1908), at the latest'.[14] It is suggested here that the severest clipping of the Kaiser's domestic wings came with the enactment and introduction of the BGB and *Einführungsgesetz.* As a result, Kaiser Wilhelm II was searching for avenues to regain lost domestic power after 1896, and this contributed to the crisis of 1914.

Thus, in considering possible domestic origins of the First World War, we might view the lead-up to war as part of an attempt by Kaiser Wilhelm II and his supporters to rebalance domestic power in favor of the Prussian crown. This was an old absolutist trick. In a letter to his young son-in-law Prince Frederick of Prussia in the early 1860s, Prince Albert of England warned that 'an *external* war for the elimination of *internal* dissension and evils is always a morally unjustified undertaking'.[15] 'The very evils, personal weaknesses, internal contradictions etc. which form the obstacles to the solution of internal difficulties', Albert cautioned, would be 'just the ones' that would most impede the required 'success in war'.[16] Nonetheless, with his domestic authority in decline and hemmed in by the impact of civil law, Wilhelm II resorted to the ruse of an imminent foreign threat and 'defensive' war to push through amongst other measures the *Ermächtigungsgesetz* of 4 August 1914. Rushed through a Reichstag led to believe that the nation was encircled, it gave the Bundesrat dubious wartime powers and inaugurated an era of what Stolleis has called extra-parliamentary legislation.[17] Some 825 decrees were handed down by the Bundesrat, covering key areas of domestic law, that attempted simply to swallow up the laws and political arrangements of the *Bürgerliche Republik.* As one legal scholar has noted, 'the chief effect of the state of war that was created as part of the "judicial mobilization" was a drastic curtailment of the basic rights granted by *Länder* constitutions or by simple Reich statutes'.[18] The war also declined the rights of persons by removing them from the jurisdiction of civil law and placing new recruits under military law, which, despite reform, remained within the personal rule of the King of Prussia. Securing counter-revolution through external war, however, depended on military victory, and when the war was lost, so was all hope of reviving the already obsolete monarchic principle in the German political system.

The failure of this attempted external war for domestic counter-revolution did not result in an immediate reconsolidation of bourgeois power, but rather it is suggested here that the social democratic character of the 1918 revolution reflected the German Left's formalized reaction against the emergence of bourgeois rule in 1896. Like the attempted counter-revolution, the reaction from below also associated the rise of bourgeois power with the consolidation of civil law. In 1896, the leader of the Social Democrats, August Bebel, referred to the draft BGB as the '*Götterdämmerung* of the bourgeois world'.[19] Nevertheless, beyond the document of the Weimar Constitution of 1919, social democratic revolution failed to penetrate the deep structures of German society. The BGB and other key juridical arrangements that formed the backbone of bourgeois rule remained on the books. The key failure of the Weimar government, particularly evident during the Ebert presidency, was that it did not nullify the methods of the *kaiserliche* wartime dictatorship, but adapted those methods to its own political agenda in the desperate hours of its political struggle for survival.[20] Interestingly, even Eckart Kehr's 'The Dictatorship of the Bureaucracy' expressed concern over what he viewed as the emergence of a social democratic dictatorship.[21] Accordingly, this study closes by suggesting that the attempted counter-revolution of 1914–1918, as well as the social democratic Revolution of 1918, may be seen as post-1896 indicators of *Bürgerliche Revolution* in late-nineteenth-century Germany. While this study acknowledges that there was instability in the German constitution, it argues that such instability was not connected to any long-term pattern of developmental deviation or failure of a depoliticized bourgeoisie.

Historiographical Background

After the Second World War, the need to explain the rise of Nazism in Germany contributed to the consolidation of a rather pessimistic view of German history, which suggested that the Germans took a special path to modernity, diverging from the 'normal' course followed by the great nations of the Atlantic rim. Friedrich Meinecke first looked deep into German history and identified a purported failure of liberals to fully execute reforms in the 1820s as having led Central Europe on the slippery slope to National Socialism.[22] On the whole, however, the writing of German history belonged to the victors, and it was amongst historians in the United States that the *Sonderweg* thesis came to prominence.[23] Research that followed put together a story of the German bourgeoisie's historical failure to effect a proper revolution against the feudal aristocracy like the English (1649 and 1689), French (1789) and American colonists (1776) as the source of divergence. Germans were charged with reaching the turning point in the European revolutionary years of 1848 and failing to turn.[24] If revolution was obtained at all, it was a bureaucratic revolution from above at best.[25] The German middle class was deemed weak in comparison to the English, and instead of defining itself, was accused of capitulation and aping the norms and values of the agrarian, Junker elite. It was said to have undergone a process of feudalization.[26] Others identified a pathological element in the growth of German nationalism.[27] Although one must acknowledge that he has modified his opinions in recent years, as the earlier leading spokesman for the *Sonderweg* thesis, Hans-Ulrich Wehler went so far as to polemically assert that 'in the beginning there was no revolution', and thus only a 'consolation analysis' of German history could be offered.[28] Later critics of this pessimistic assessment recounted that the argument held that the old agrarian elites were able to maintain political power through the Empire and Weimar years and that it was 'they who helped Hitler into the saddle'.[29] It suffices to say that the notion that Germany deviated from the 'normal' course to modernity found considerable support in the aftermath of the Second World War.

While no specific treatments of a 'special legal path' were produced in these years, studies by Leonard Krieger, Mack Walker, Reinhard Koselleck and Otto Pflanze situated legal development within the story of the failure of civic culture in Germany.[30] The seminal interpretation was offered in Leonard Krieger's *The German Idea of Freedom* (1957), and it set the standard view of German legal divergence. His story of political liberalism after 1871 is one of failure and decline. 'Buttressed by the free gift of an elective Reichstag with subordinate legislative functions', the initiative of the Prussian monarchy and support of local dynasties, the 1871 Constitution 'organized the new nation along lines which extended the tradition of the state in Germany to the national level'. Political liberalism 'calcified into an institutionalized party existence', which robbed it of its original radicalism. National Liberals were charged with leading 'important sections of the German bourgeoisie into a political alliance with the authoritarian state and a social alliance with the landed aristocracy whereby the bourgeoisie gave their support to the established order in exchange for protection against competition and against social democracy'. Krieger's evidence for this bourgeois sellout came in the form of German juristic theory, which he charged, 'doubled for the official political philosophy of the Empire'. He specifically pointed toward Rudolf Gneist's doctrine of the *Rechtsstaat.* It, according to Krieger, gutted the oppositional element in liberalism and instead set the tone for the adaptation of earlier liberal activism to the legal reality of Bismarck's vision of the nation-state. Finally, German liberals failed to effect the reorganization of law and politics that created in public institutions a respect for the rights of individual persons as seen in the states of the Atlantic rim; in contrast, *Recht* became 'a formal attribute of the state'.[31]

In the mid 1980s, David Blackbourn and Geoff Eley began to question the idealized yardstick of the English example against which the Germans were said to have failed to measure up.[32] In particular, these two scholars rejected the Prussian-centred focus of German historiography and called for more work on the role of other regions in shaping German identity. Since then, historians have offered a broader picture of German society marked by the cultural ascendancy of the bourgeoisie and showing that it was far more independent and influential than the older interpretations allowed.[33] Research on German liberalism challenged the idea of the unpolitical German and showed the strength of the liberal tradition in nineteenth-century Germany. Particularly informative, here, were a number of studies on liberalism at the local level.[34] In the last few years, the historiographical trend has been toward a 'normalization' of German political history.[35] Some scholars now suggest that the *Sonderweg* interpretation has been replaced altogether. Clearly, I have offered little more than an overview of the historiography, but it would not add value to offer a more detailed historiographical sketch here. Instead, relevant research has been integrated into the interpretation offered in this work.

On the whole, while the last twenty years witnessed the considerable expansion of economic, political and cultural history, less research on legal development in modern German history was undertaken.[36] Rejecting the methods of the 1950s consensus school of intellectual history, social and cultural historians inadvertently relinquished the historical interpretation of law to legal scholarship and other disciplines. An example of this may be seen in the edited book, *Bürgertum im 19. Jahrhundert,* in which the editors, Jürgen Kocka and Ute Frevert, turned to a legal scholar, a political scientist and a sociologist to offer the examination of law.[37] For the most part, where legal development has required mention, there has been an almost habitual reliance on Franz Wieacker's work on private law or Ernst Rudolf Huber's work on public law, both of which were published more than forty years ago.[38] In recent years, there has been a greater reliance on Michael Stolleis's work on German public law, but historians have continued to steer clear of offering historical interpretations that contextualize law within German historiography. With the exception of Thomas Nipperdey's volume, there is little if any mention of legal development in the larger comprehensive texts on German history.[39] This seems puzzling because Blackbourn and Eley clearly identified legal development as a pillar of the 'discreet charm of the bourgeoisie'.[40]

This is not to say that there have not been any historical studies of law in modern German history. Michael John's *Politics and the Law in Late Nineteenth Century Germany* offers the main interpretation of party factionalism surrounding the enactment of the BGB.[41] The primary data he provides remains invaluable. However, while John's work made the BGB visible in German historiography, his interpretation offers a pessimistic view. On the one hand, he took account of the legal historian Joachim Rückert's research and conceded that Friedrich Karl von Savigny was too close in his views to Freiherr vom Stein to be seen as a reactionary conservative.[42] On the other hand, although he makes it clear that the BGB was part of the National Liberal Party's agenda, he concluded that the BGB was 'unpolitical' and that its enactment represented the depoliticization of liberal politics in the Wilhelmine era.[43] In other words, in his view the BGB represented yet another manifestation of German peculiarity. He confirms his pessimistic position on German legal development again in his analysis of the German legal profession. Here he argues that 'lawyers failed to achieve the much-envied organizational successes of their counterparts in England or France' and that the state 'allowed the continuation of a typically German blend of *ständisch* and professional aspirations'.[44]

Perhaps more than any other historian, Kenneth Ledford has worked to integrate legal development into social history. He has been concerned to show that law is integral to the cultural workings of the modern social polity. 'A grasp of its meaning' and the behavior of its practitioners can help to decode the social thought and goals of social actors.[45] He also has emphasized the need 'to recapture law and legal thinking as an historical artifact and a suitable object of study for social historians'.[46] In contrast to John's pessimistic interpretation of late-nineteenth-century legal developments, Ledford offers a more sceptical view. He has given more credence to the success of liberal legal politics. The successful passage of the *Reichsjustizgesetze* of 1879, which both reformed and consolidated the German court system and court procedures, secured many of the demands of *Vormärz* liberals for judicial reform, including jury trials in serious cases.[47] In contrast to John, Ledford has found that 'lawyers and liberals achieved almost all of their aims for the legal profession in 1878, carving out space for the bar to create its own institutions, to govern its internal affairs, and to assume the important public role that theory ascribed to it'.[48] Nazi success in obtaining quick control of the *Deutscher Anwaltsverein* (DAV) did not result from a failure of liberals to entrench their legal programme in German society, but rather from the DAV's inability to manage conflicts for control of the professions' institutions, which had resulted from the crisis produced by a significant demographic shift in the composition of the legal profession by the 1920s.[49]

In his most recent study of the Prussian *Oberverwaltungsgericht* (Supreme Administrative Law Court), Ledford has taken a less optimistic position. Here he was interested to show 'how Krieger and the rule of law pessimists on the one hand and the legal history celebrators of the rule of law on the other, both fall short of a nuanced account of what the administrative law court reforms in Prussia actually accomplished'.[50] A series of laws passed by the Prussian Parliament between 1872 and 1883 reformed local administration and created a system of administrative law courts 'whose object was to protect the rights of the individual against abuses by government administration'.[51] At the top of this system stood the *Oberverwaltungsgericht,* and the establishing laws provided not only for the independence of the judiciary, but for the review of administrative decisions 'upon complaint by a citizen that his or her rights had been violated'.[52] A 'lively and energetic jurisprudence' emerged from this framework between 1875 and 1914, and Prussian citizens 'showed no shyness in asserting their rights' against state tax authorities in particular.[53]

At this point in his analysis, Ledford re-examined court decisions singled out by the rule of law celebrators. In the Kreuzberg matter of 1882, a property owner in Berlin filed suit against authorities who attempted to deny him the required permits to construct an apartment building on his private property. The plaintiff *(Kläger)* pled his case under Article 9 of the Prussian Constitution of 1850 and §65, Title 8, Part I of the *Allgemeines Landrecht* of 1794. Not only did the *Oberverwaltungsgericht* decide in the plaintiff's favor permitting him to develop his private property as he saw fit; in its decision, the court also expanded the definition of property rights under both the constitution and the *Allgemeines Landrecht.* As Ledford pointed out, this decision and other decisions that cited it as the establishing precedent 'carved out a wide sphere for judicial review of administrative actions that [tried to restrict] the rights of property owners'.[54] A string of court decisions also protected the association and commercial rights of Polish minorities in eastern Prussia against discriminatory police practices that aimed to block associations and businesses that used the Polish language. Social Democrats were also able to find judicial remedies against discrimination before the *Oberverwaltungsgericht.*[55]

While Ledford concluded that the 'body of case law suggests that the Supreme Administrative Law Court restricted arbitrary acts of the bureaucracy more independently than Krieger conceded', at the same time, he felt that the accounts of rule of law celebrators 'ignore decisions that upheld police power'.[56] As evidence, he pointed toward limits set by the court on the ability of Poles to use their native language in official relations with the Prussian state by forcing them to file double versions of their by-laws in Polish and German. He also criticized the court for handing decision power on the language of religious instruction in public schools to school authorities rather than the church.[57] Additional evidence of the upholding of police power came in the form of the *Oberverwaltungsgericht's* failure to overturn measures that allowed the police to break up Social Democratic meetings 'at which women would be present, in violation of the law on political associations'.[58] Finally, Ledford frowned upon the court for intervening 'only *after* the police acted, meaning that the exercise of right had already been abridged and that the Court found the abridgement illegal only after the fact'.[59] 'Regardless of how effective the ultimate protection given to individual rights by the supervision of the administration by the Supreme Administrative Law Court was', he therefore drew the sceptical conclusion that 'Prussian citizens remained vulnerable to the immediate effects of arbitrary actions of officials high and low'.[60]

Scholarly circumspection not withstanding, Ledford's scepticism is based on a questionable view of legal procedure and judicial process. His finding of the development of some measure of 'case law' is interesting, but the German judicial system was not that of Great Britain or the United States, and courts simply did not possess wide discretion to produce judge-made law, particularly after 1900. In Germany, the separation between the judicial and legislative functions was far more rigid than in the United States, and courts were confined to issuing findings of law on the basis of what was on the books. This lack of judicial latitude was at the heart of Hermann Kantorowicz's and the *Freirechtsbewegung's* (Free Law Movement) criticism of the German system after the consolidation of bourgeois law in 1900.[61] This critical distinction means that interpreting the politics of court decisions must be taken up, not with concern for whether they deviated from the law on the books, but whether they upheld it. Since the *Eindeutschung* of 'Poles' in the East was a part of the liberal agenda, the *Oberverwaltungsgericht's* decisions relative to language could be read also as an indicator of the bourgeois consolidation of power. However unpalatable it may be according to contemporary standards, the same conclusion is valid relative to the court's decisions to uphold the barring of women from political association meetings, which merely upheld the law of the land as it existed before the passage of the *Reichsvereinsgesetz* of 1908. Indeed, the fact that the court used its authority to uphold the *bürgerliche* laws that confined women to the private sphere by blocking their access to the public sphere only serves to underscore that a constitutional transformation had taken place.

In addition, Ledford's suggestion that the *Oberverwaltungsgericht* should have been able to preempt the abridgement of people's rights runs counter to the nature of modern judicial process. It is the violation of right defined by law itself that makes an offence actionable. Only at this point would a complainant have been in a position to bring a claim against the offending party before a court of law for adjudication. One also must consider the importance of preliminary hearings where courts made the determination as to whether or not to hear particular cases, because this would also offer an indication of the sociopolitical priorities of the nation whose existence the courts played a frontline role in sustaining. From this perspective, the fact that the *Oberverwaltungsgericht* was hearing cases where the rights and/or sociopolitical arrangements at stake reflected liberal values again offers an indication of the ascendancy of bourgeois power, even in Prussia. At the same time, what courts chose to hear and the limited access of women to avenues of adjudication also will offer invaluable clues about the rights of certain groups within society.

The challenge for historians, thus, is the continuing need for an historical synthesis that explains the political significance of the rapid development of law and legal institutions in nineteenth-century Germany. Historical scholarship on law remains marked by a tendency to examine individual legislation in isolation from the whole body or puzzle of law of which they were a part. As a result, a defining aspect of modern German political and social development hangs about on the margins of mainstream German historiography. Ledford's point that law needs to be recaptured as a social artifact leads scholars in the right direction, but modern law and control of lawmaking bodies and institutions of adjudication have also been an indispensable channel for sociopolitical transformation and consolidation. The scope of study must be broadened even further, beyond lawyers and other practitioners of law, to encompass examination of the interconnections between theorists, legislators and adjudicators of law and the sociopolitical arrangements they aimed to construct. One must look beyond the written words of the law to discover the deeper sociopolitical dimensions of the intent of legislation as a vital constituting instrument of the nation-state. This approach will help us tease out the more subtle and inverted modes of constitutional transformation and better understand how the exclusive bourgeois social arrangements, constructed via civil legislation, were interlinked to the transformation of the political sphere. Finally, despite the much-needed critical reappraisal of the nineteenth century, an answer to the question of bourgeois revolution remains outstanding. Did the Germans have one or did they not? My hope is that this analysis of legal development, which will situate the BGB in the larger legal–constitutional framework, may contribute to an answer to this question.

Just as the notion of constitutional transformation employed in this study is not altogether novel, the idea of expanding scholarly understanding of the term 'revolution' also is not completely new. Blackbourn and Eley some time ago called for an alternative vision that sought to refocus attention away from a big-bang model of revolution toward a successful bourgeois programme. They cautioned that the German example should not be measured against the course of other Western nations, specifically Britain, and they suggested that scholars need to draw distinction between how revolutions were made and how they were eventually assimilated into the political structure.[62] Scholars were encouraged to distinguish between 'revolution as a specific crisis of state, involving widespread popular mobilization and a reconstitution of political relations' and 'the deeper processes of structural change, involving the predominance of the capitalist mode of production, the potential obsolescence of many existing practices and institutions, and the uneven transformation of social relations'.[63] They continued: 'Perhaps the concept of bourgeois revolution should be disassociated from the necessary introduction of specific constitutional and liberal-democratic forms of rule, and instead should be related more generally to the conditions of bourgeois predominance in society.'[64] The concept of revolution should be freed from 'dependence on the notion of forcibly acquired political liberalism' and redefined to mean the 'inauguration of a bourgeois epoch', in which a legal and political framework is installed for the development of industrial capitalism.[65]

This study also hopes to broaden the meaning of the term 'revolution' even further. Toward this end we need to retain more of the traditional meaning of revolution and focus on how revolutions were made. It is suggested here that a significant occurrence, which clearly marks the reconstitution of political relations and the forcible acquisition of political liberalism remain fundamental, historically evolved components of revolution that are inalienable to the term's meaning. However, scholars need to broaden understanding of how revolutions are made to include nonviolent modes of production. The problem may be our own distance from the nineteenth-century German conception of revolution and our failure to recognize that there were diverse conceptions of revolution even then. The National Liberal concept of revolution was very different from that of Social Democrats, and this was still different from the National Socialist view in the 1930s. Perhaps the unprecedented human destruction of the twentieth-century age of extremes has caused us to interlink revolutionary 'force' with violence? At bottom, however, the reconstitution of political relations involved the transfer of sovereignty, however it was defined in a given age, by a given group of would-be revolutionaries. If we could pinpoint a moment in modern German history in which a transfer of sovereignty from the monarch to the bourgeoisie occurred, we could identify a point of bourgeois revolution. 'Force' was not always violent, but came in the more fluid and intangible forms of coercion, legal constraint or even social obligation. The thing that made *Bürgerliche Revolution* in Germany special in comparison to England, France and the United States was that, while there was a forcible acquisition of political liberalism, revolution was made through nonviolent means.

This brings me to discuss the unique way that I stumbled upon this topic of nonviolent revolution in modern Germany. I have been disturbed by the fact that the false political dichotomies set up by of the *Sonderweg* thesis allowed the United States to escape the facts of its own illiberal history by displacing the unattractive elements of modern sociopolitical ideals onto a defeated German other. While I have rehearsed the requisite historiography here, it is not the body of knowledge that inspired my consideration of the possibility of some kind of nonviolent, German revolution. In fact, I wandered upon this subject as I noticed a continuity of interests in the thought of modern African American intellectuals, namely Booker T. Washington, W.E.B. DuBois, Charles Hamilton Houston and Martin Luther King. They looked not away from, but to the German example as a means of sociopolitical transformation in the United States, where the rising tide of legislated segregation increasingly excluded them from full participation. Washington looked to the *Technische Hochschule* as a model for the development of African American institutions of higher learning. DuBois sat at Treitschke's feet at the University of Berlin in the 1890s and showed interest in German legal development. Houston studied civil law in Spain, where he would have been exposed to the German tradition. King held his German–English dictionary dear, and his note cards are full of references to Schleiermacher and other German intellectuals.[66] In this, African Americans were not alone. The German example also was consciously appropriated in Japan, Turkey, Brazil, Mexico and Peru as a means to the modern, sociopolitical transformation of their own cultures.[67]

I want to close this section of the Introduction on a couple of notes. First, this book is an expansion of the findings in my doctoral dissertation, 'The Civil Code and the Transformation of German Society: The Politics of Gender Inequality 1814–1919', which was accepted by Brown University in 2001.[68] As for this book, I completed the manuscript a few years ago but decided to not to publish it immediately for professional reasons. In the meantime, a number of studies have appeared that also examine legal development in nineteenth-century Germany. In the last few months, I have taken considerable time to incorporate these works in the body of this study and hope that I have done these studies appropriate justice by plugging them into this primary study. In my view, social science involves a process of integrating and building on the work of other social scientists, just as in the natural sciences, and I hope I have been successful in this here.

Second, I was fortunate enough to spend considerable time at the *Max-Planck-Institut für europäische Rechtsgeschichte* in 2002–2003 and have benefited from direct conversations with Michael Stolleis. I also want to reemphasize the importance of his recent publications for this study. Although his work has focused on public law, his findings provide an invaluable point of departure for my analysis of private law, specifically the BGB. In particular, Stolleis indicated that there was a caesura of scholarly attention to public law in the aftermath of the *Wiener Schlussakte* of 15 May 1820.[69] It is suggested here that, because discourse on public law was virtually banned under the *Schlussakte,* the venue of private law emerged as an alternative, and here, liberal political ideology continued to grow unabated, encoded in metaphoric discussions of a remote German legal past.[70] Where Stolleis has pointed toward the importance of developments in public law and theory at the state level even in the face of the Restoration, the middle section of the book emphasizes the striking advance of civil laws that were part and parcel of the liberal agenda at the state level and on the heels of the so-called failed revolution of 1848.[71] As mentioned earlier, Stolleis also emphasized that there was a fundamental transition in the original Reich Constitution of 1871, suggesting that the 'distribution of political weight among the imperial government, *Bundesrat,* and Imperial Diet changed' in the 1890s.[72] Again, through an examination of private law, the major thesis of this book is that there was a bourgeois revolution in 1896, which resulted from a slow constitutional transformation produced by the gradual introduction of civil laws that delivered powerful blows to monarchical public arrangements.[73]

Finally, *Bürgerliche Revolution* in Germany was brought about by a clever group of lawyers, schooled in the art of fine print and struggling to effect constitutional transformation under the nose of formidable forces that were prepared to crush opposition in order to maintain the monarchy and the would-be personal rule of the German kaiser. Because of this fact, measures that transformed the constitution were not announced in the first paragraph of new laws, but were often tucked away here and there in seemingly innocuous sections. As a result of this, and the crafty skills of lawyers, the case for *Bürgerliche Revolution* in Germany depends on teasing together circumstantial evidence. Seeing *Bürgerliche Revolution* is like examining a patchwork quilt. One must see the patches but always remember that they are stitched together to make a whole quilt, and one must keep one's eye on the quilt even while examining the old fabric patches that have been stitched together to make something new. Every piece of legislation, some more important than others, must be seen as a patch in the making of a German constitution and a slow revolution. What is more, the German *Bürgerliche Revolution* was carried forward for nearly a century, and because it was bound up with the historical school of law, which researched the 'immemorial precedents' for every desired right, rigorous examination of even one of the many pieces of legislation requires an unusual degree of historical depth. It is exactly because of these challenging obstacles to discovery that the methodology of linking together both one's own primary findings and the secondary findings of other social scientists is vital in making Germany's *Bürgerliche Revolution* visible.

Sources and Structure of the Book

Before discussing the structure of this book, I would like to mention something about the sources. It draws on rich primary sources located in archives in Germany and the United States. In terms of primary legal sources, I am grateful to the extensive collections of the *Max-Planck-Institut für europäische Rechtsgeschichte* in Frankfurt, without which this study would not have been possible. I am also thankful for the robust collections of the Harvard University and Columbia University law faculty libraries. In terms of the social historical aspect of this work, the voluminous correspondence records of the *Reichjustizministerium* housed at the German National Archive in Berlin figure prominently in later chapters. Numerous records from the Prussian State Archive and the Prussian Cultural Archive also have made this study possible. Additional primary sources on marital property relations located in state archives in Potsdam and Darmstadt have also proven important. Finally, the study has also benefited from a review of Gottlieb Planck's records housed at the University of Göttingen archive. The support and warm reception I received in each of these archives assisted in my locating the primary sources that are so critical to this work.

As the title of this Introduction, 'Transforming the Reich', suggests, the politically active agents in German society that sought constitutional transformation were interested in building a particular type of modern nation. That type was a republic, often invoked in German-speaking Europe through the term *Gemeinwesen.* While liberal-minded historians have demonstrated the strength of liberalism in nineteenth-century German-speaking Europe, research has not taken into consideration the question of exactly what type of nation or state German liberals wanted to construct. From the perspective of the Blackbourn-Eley school, the history of nineteenth-century Germany is one of progress: economic growth, urbanization, industrialization, the rise of a capitalist elite and socialist opposition, bourgeois class formation and the hegemonic influence of bourgeois norms on German cultural and national identity. While this new research presents an important re-evaluation, it runs the risk of obscuring the exclusive basis of legal personality and participation in German society and its troublesome consequences. The trend in historical interpretation has shifted from the extreme of the feudalization thesis to a point where German history is shedding its unattractive elements, rapidly.

This book hopes to find a methodological middle ground by developing a constitutional transformation synthesis that will allow scholars to show how both progressive and regressive sociopolitical prescriptions could co-exist as cooperative elements within a constitutional ideology designed to achieve modern bourgeois revolution. While the participation of propertied men was the intended result of slow revolution, the disfranchisement of women was not an accident. It was an inherent part of a constitutional ideology that identified the subordination of women as the requisite social basis of a republic and as vital to its existence as representative institutions. Liberal, or more accurately, *bürgerliche* constitutionalism was *illiberal* insofar as it called for the exclusion of the majority of the population from participation. Nevertheless, because such exclusion was an inherent part of the constitutional ideology and because, as I argue here, Germany underwent a process of inverted constitutional transformation, the new basis of exclusion, particularly of women, must be seen as one of the leading indicators of slow *Bürgerliche Revolution.*

Bürgerliche Revolution

In addition to encompassing regressive sociopolitical elements, the constitutional transformation synthesis will allow scholars not only to broaden our understanding of how sociopolitical change takes place, but to widen the sphere of human participants in slow revolution. The ideology of inverted constitutional transformation was rationalized after the *Freiheitskriege* as an alternative to violent political revision. It is distinguished from the earlier reform orientation of Stein, Hardenberg and others because its strategy for political revision focused on overcoming the new realities and challenges presented by the Restoration. The idea of constitutional transformation developed, first, in what I have called *Privatrechts-Staatslehre* in order to emphasize the political character of German private law scholarship. Nevertheless, the place of the emerging historical profession and romanticism as part and parcel of constitutionalism cannot be emphasized enough. Constitutional transformation most often found expression in the idea of legal gradualism, and the participants in this project, who will be referred to as 'tranformationist', reflected a range of political persuasions within liberalism.

The goal of the first chapter, 'Prelude to Modern Europe: *Iurisdictio* and the German Idea of Sovereignty' is to lay an historical foundation that will shed light on the development of a modern German idea of sovereignty that forms the ideological origins of nonviolent political revision in Central Europe. As this book is focused on German political development, the approach taken here is to put together existing published materials and blend these findings into a new constitutional transformation synthesis for the German context. Specifically, this chapter examines civic humanism and concepts of jurisdiction as they emerged in German legal thought. The German concept of sovereignty developed out of German-speaking Europe's own history and identified the possession of sovereignty with the possession of jurisdiction *(iurisdictio).* Legal thinkers increasingly defined domestic sovereignty as none other than the possession of legislative authority—the highest power in the state. It also shows how jurisdiction was at the heart of demands for political reform and resistance to would-be absolutism by the closing years of the old Empire. The teasing out of early modern German legal thought is taken up here in order to argue that the German idea of sovereignty was articulated in traditional terms that had grown up in German political culture by 1800.

Chapter 2, 'Toward a Modern Republic', offers a critical reevaluation of Friedrich Karl von Savigny, which situates his writings on law within the ideology of inverted constitutional transformation and argues that he was responsible for the growth of modern legal politics in the aftermath of the *Freiheitskriege.* In contrast to the standard historical interpretation of Savigny as a reactionary conservative, I examine new materials to suggest that he not only was bound up with the transformationist project from the start, but indeed defined its course. He should be seen as one of the most important figures of early-nineteenth-century liberalism, and it was his theory of politics and modern legislation that housed the radical political element in German constitutional thought. Here I rely on the recent publication of Savigny's *Politik und neuere Legislationen,* which comprises the list of sources and notes for his famous *Vom Beruf unserer Zeit für Gesetzgebung und Rechtswissenschaft* (1814).[74] I show how the writings of classical thinkers, as well as English and Italian theories of legislation, gave shape to his understanding of the prescriptive place of custom as the legitimate origin of law. Of particular importance here was his reading of Smith, Burke, Hume, Bacon, Hobbes, Blackstone, Aristotle, Cicero, Machiavelli, Schlegel, Möser, Goethe and others. Of additional importance for the development of Savigny's vision of nonviolent revolution was his reading of Giambattista Vico's *Scienza Nuova (New Science: Principles of the New Science Concerning the Common Nature of Nations)* (1725) and Gaetano Filangieri's *La Scienza della Legislazione*

(The Science of Legislation, From the Italian of Gaetano Filangieri) (1782). Indeed, Filangieri articulated clearly that a decline of a legislative system was a political revolution brought into effect slowly, and it was legislated decline that transformationists strove to effect in modern Germany from 1814 forward. Finally, the idea of nonviolent revolution found wide reception and was articulated not only by Savigny but by other key figures.

In Chapter 3, 'Imagining the *Gemeinwesen*', I argue that embracing Savigny's theory of politics and modern legislation, a generation of young liberals devoted themselves to the study of German legal sources. Remembering the maxim that the people's customs and norms constitute second nature and comprise the fountain of all law, they set out in search of what Savigny called the *vaterländisches Recht*. The period witnessed a flowering of legal journals and treatises dedicated to the rediscovery of German customary law. Increasingly, young liberal legal scholars came to regard themselves not only as the guardians and protectors of German customary law, but as the true political representatives of the people's sovereignty. A modern political culture emerged in legal circles by the late 1840s, which continued to focus on legal gradualism. Many early liberals and romantic writers, most notably Jacob Grimm and Karl Eichhorn, formed the vanguard of this new branch of liberal political theory and increasingly came to view folklore, myths, poetry, etc. as remnants of ancient German law from a so-called free epoch.

It was here that liberal transformationists began to offer an image of the sociopolitical structure of their imagined *Gemeinwesen* that was legislated into existence by 1900. A new legal history centred on a mythical ancient German civil society, purported original freedom of the *Volk* and adulation of customary law nourished the growth and expansion of liberalism during the Restoration. *Privatrechts-Staatslehre* appealed to the ancient laws as a means of proving that the rights transformationist-minded liberals desired in their own time were immemorial and therefore beyond the princes' powers to alter or annul. It was a coordinated project that involved nothing short of the building of a German customary law tradition and one that expressed the same political radicalism as in sixteenth-century England. It also should be pointed out that many of Germany's leading *Staatslehre* scholars cut their teeth on private law scholarship during the reactionary years, including Gerber, Gneist, Haenel and others.

In Chapter 4, 'Undermining Absolutism: The Path of Legalism and Constituting the German States, 1847–1879', I knit together ideology and state-level legal reforms, linking the ideals of transformationist-minded legal scholars with new laws on the books. The formal transition from theory to practice can be traced also to the *Germanisten* conferences held in 1846 and 1847. The attendees included Arndt, Uhland, Ranke, Gervinus, Dahlmann, Pertz, Beseler, Mittermaier, Reyscher and both Grimm brothers. In 1846, Reyscher wrote that he found a meeting of Germanists particularly desirable, because he felt it was their task, gradually, to secure Central Europe's liberation from foreign law (i.e. the Roman law of absolutism) through the careful cultivation of native law and through the preparation of a national code of law.[75] During the 1846 *Germanisten* conference, Friedrich Gaupp stated that the study of law should serve as 'a prophet of the future'.[76] Beseler urged that 'now the question arises whether it is necessary for a people, in the further development of economic and political circumstances, to be completely excluded from the participation in the making and exercising of law and... whether such a separation is healthy'.[77] The 1847 conference closed with a resolution to pursue a unified German civil code, which received thunderous applause. Jaup entered the motion, arguing that *'ein deutsch-nationales Heimatrecht'* would end confessional divisions and antagonism between states, therefore creating a better climate for business.[78]

As I argue in the last two-thirds of this chapter, it is important to consider that the most important areas of modern German law, including constitutional law, procedural law, family law, inheritance law, company law, bankruptcy law, negotiable instruments and commercial law were all derived from the work of the Germanists.[79] More importantly, despite the reactionary years following the failure of the Frankfurt Parliament in 1849, constitutional transformation in these areas of law sped up and continued largely unabated during the second half of the nineteenth century. This process of constitutional transformation that first began at the state level involved the introduction of important civil laws including commercial, procedural and civil codes that increasingly limited the ability of monarchs and carved out a sphere of private liberties for the individual. What began first as a process of constitutional transformation in the various states became a national phenomenon with each successive phase of German unification, and it cannot be emphasized enough that these measures reflected the sociopolitical demands that were contained in the draft constitution of 1849. For example, the Hanover *Proceßordnung* of 1850 not only served as a model for other states before 1866, but drove the introduction of the *Reichsjustizgesetze* in 1879. The same can be said of Saxony's civil code of 1865 and its influence on the BGB.

Finally, this chapter emphasizes the practice of constitutional transformation, showing that political revision was not seen as derived exclusively from a basic written constitutional document, but also involved the introduction of supplemental civil laws. My hope in this regard is to show that liberal constitutionalism was broader than a narrow focus on the substance of constitutional documents allows us to see. It was through the introduction of successive measures of civil law that gaps in the Reich Constitution of 1871 were filled, and through this method liberal transformationists were able to secure much of what they had demanded and been denied in the constitutional document of 28 March 1849. These years marked a critical turning point, because constitutional transformation was no longer merely a theory, but became active in political practice and increasingly effected an alteration of German sociopolitical arrangements.

The legal scholar Stephan Buchholz points out that the social and political relevance of the reconfiguration of *eheliches Güterrecht* (marital property law) in the legislative developments of the nineteenth century remains an obscure subject.[80] Chapter 5, 'A Century of Promise', examines the nature of marital property relations in nineteenth-century Germany. As I point out in earlier chapters, the Germanists' project involved the construction of a German customary law and the claiming of title of prescription for the rights that liberal transformationists demanded in their own time. Their political vision of expanded male liberty and private property ownership, however, was made dependent on the necessary subordination and disfranchisement of women. In this chapter, the realities of marital property relations on the ground are examined in order to juxtapose this against the regressive impact of the BGB on the sociopolitical position of German women. Regress here is seen as an important social indicator of the *Bürgerliche Revolution,* and, indeed, the participation of women after 1900 was decidedly more limited than prior to the BGB.

In no other area of law was legal particularism greater than in the area of marital property relations, as contemporary liberals often complained. Before the Reichstag in 1896, Nieberding described Germany's legal condition as a 'colorful muddle'. 'For so long it has been forgotten', he complained, 'citizens and families have determined their own legal relationships for themselves.'[81] My examination of local court decisions in Hanover, Thuringia and Anhalt suggest that, prior to 1900, women not only retained independent property rights, but had made considerable gains in terms of other independent rights. Women also enjoyed unrestricted access to the courts and relatively independent legal rights. This environment also precipitated the growth of women's wealth and rights, which was accompanied by rising economic and professional expectations. All of this, however, was playing out against the rising tide of the slow bourgeois revolution. While in the late eighteenth century, absolutist states had, one after another, abolished the old sex guardianship and lower courts had issued decisions extending women's rights, as the nineteenth century wore on these decisions were increasingly overturned in upper courts dominated by liberal judges. It was not until the introduction of the BGB, however, that this century of promise and the hopes of women for full participation were dashed.

The 'Last Bastion', chapter six, has a key position in this book and explores the final phase of constitutional transformation at the national level. It takes up the story after the founding of the North German Confederation in 1866 and the Deutsche Reich in 1871. The chapter is divided into three major parts. First, I introduce the major architects of political revision in unified Germany, including 'the Father of the Code', Gottlieb Planck. I link the new generation of crafty lawyers and politicians to the theorists of the first half of the nineteenth century. It is clear from their writings that they remained committed to obtaining nonviolent revolution through constitutional transformation, and one of the remarkable features of the *Bürgerliche Revolution* is that transformationists were able to continue this programme across generations. In his early twenties, Planck wrote to his parents in 1848 that 'the best hope of the German people' was to achieve political revision by undermining the Confederation from within.[82]

Second, I argue that scholars must draw a distinction between Bismarck's geographical unification and the structural unification, which remained a pressing concern long after 1866 and 1871. Long-range victory in domestic politics depended upon winning the battle for structural unification. As the liberal Rudolf Gneist stated before the Lawyer's Congress in 1871: 'Famous victories and dazzling external successes will not turn us away from the unchanging demands for a secure legal system and for political participation in the reconstruction of the law.'[83] Paradoxically, Bismarck's dazzling successes only further mobilized public opinion in favor of legal unity and furthered the process of constitutional transformation. By 1872, even the Bavarian minister of justice reported that he 'could see no end to the clamor for legal unity'.[84] Prussia, which under Bismarck's leadership had resisted German legal unification before 1866, moved 180 degrees on the question by 1871. In 1873, National Liberals were able to push through the important *Lex Miquel-Lasker,* which extended the legislative competency of the Reich to the whole of civil law. From here, a host of measures, including the BGB, effected a constitutional transformation in Germany that transferred sovereignty from the Prussian monarchy to the institutions of the bourgeois state. Although it is often overlooked, the Constitution of 1871 did not firmly install a monarchy for the whole of Germany. Indeed, if one understood the fine language, it specifically stated that the King of Prussia would hold only the *Präsidium* (presidency) of the *Bund.* He was further bound by the constitution to uphold the laws of the land. Between 1871 and 1900, an array of civil laws chipped away at the traditional domestic realm of monarchical authority to such a degree that the kaiser's position became more of a constitutional executive than that of a king.

The main focus of the chapter, however, is dedicated to the contents of the BGB—the code which liberal transformationists believed would bring 'the Crown'. Although I examine other key sections of the Code, I pay particular attention to its largest section, Family Law, for several reasons. First, I link the gender relations that were regulated under the Code to those the Germanists argued existed under the ancient German constitution. Second, it demonstrates that the revolution reached beyond the surface of German society, reconfiguring social relations in everyday life and conforming private relations to the political and economic demands of bourgeois civil society. The reconfiguration of marriage, long conceived in constitutional thought as the beginning of the family, which, in turn, was seen as the core of civil society, offers one of the clearest social indicators of *Bürgerliche Revolution* in late-nineteenth-century Germany.

In Chapter 7, 'Discontent in the *Bürgerliche* Society', I try to show that the rise of oppositional theories of law also offers an indication of successful *Bürgerliche Revolution.* I also explore the growth of an essentially social democratic brand of legal theory. By the last quarter of the nineteenth century, a strong reaction emerged against the exclusive *bürgerliche* model of citizenship and participation. The introduction of codified law gave rise to a theoretical legal redevelopment on the political Left, which rejected exclusive constitutionalism and demanded extensive participation.

Legal theorists on the political Left, including Marx and Bachofen, precipitated a split in the German legal world, which marked the rise of legal anthropology. Following Bachofen's publication of *Das Mutterrecht* in 1861, socialists developed a conception of citizenship and national identity that opposed the masculine model. Scholars elevated a metaphor of the feminine body by discovering a primordial period before the ancient free epoch identified by the Germanists and argued that the origins of society were matriarchal rather than patriarchal. These arguments were not reflective of any emerging feminism, however, but in fact were metaphoric political discussions that were designed to create title of prescription for the rights demanded by marginalized men in German society. This scholarship ultimately gave rise to radical revisionist schools of legal scholarship on the Left such as the *Freirechtsbewegung* in Germany.

In addition to the reaction that was reflected in legal scholarship, popular dissatisfaction with the exclusive *bürgerliche* arrangements installed by the BGB was widespread. The BGB became the symbol of the bourgeoisie's consolidation of authority, and it should come as no surprise that the rise of alternative constitutional theories and conceptions of the nation intensified after 1896. The BGB etched in black and white the supremacy of capitalist interests over all others, and promoted exclusive notions of political participation by denying full citizenship to large sectors of the population. More than any other element, this reality was revealed to ordinary Germans in the BGB, as reflected in the flood of protest letters that inundated the *Reichjustizministerium.* Dissatisfaction found expression in the writings of ordinary Germans and the women's movement, reflecting widespread resentment against the Family Law in particular, and across class and gender lines. It was this resentment against the BGB that later shaped the sociopolitical reform agenda of the Weimar Constitution.

Notes

1. Rudolf Nieberding, 'Erste Berathung des BGB im Plenum des Reichstags' (1896), in Benno Mugdan (ed.), *Die gesammten Materialien zum Bürgerlichen Gesetzbuch für das Deutsche Reich,* vol. 1 (1899).
2. Gerhard von Buchka, 'Erste Berathung des BGB im Plenum des Reichstags' (1896), in Benno Mugdan (ed.), *Die gesammten Materialien zum Bürgerlichen Gesetzbuch für das Deutsche Reich,* vol. 1 (1899).
3. Georg Jellinek, *Allgemeine Staatslehre: Das Recht des modernen Staates,* vol. 1 (1900), p. 651: 'Auch eine Mehrheit von Monarchen kann sich vereinigen, um eine Republik zu bilden. Daher fällt auch das Deutsche Reich, in dem die zur Einheit verbundene Gesammtheit der verbündeten Regierungen herrscht, unter den Typus Republik. Über die Staatsform des Deutschen Reiches schweigen die meisten Schriftsteller des Reichsstaatsrechts. Von einigen wurde

sie als Pleonokratie bezeichnet; dass ist aber nichts Anderes als ein neues Wort für eine alte Sache. Den Republik ist eben Mehrherrschaft im Gegensatz zur Einherrschaft. Dass das Reich Republik sei, hat aber kein Geringerer als Bismarck ausgesprochen'.

4. Buchka, 'Erste Berathung'.
5. Jellinek, *Allgemeine Staatslehre,* pp. 649–73.
6. Georg Jellinek, *Verfassungsänderung und Verfassungswandlung* (1906).
7. Paul Laband, 'Die geschichtliche Entwicklung der Reichsverfassung seit der Reichsgründung', *Jahrbuch des öffentlichen Rechts,* 1 (1907).
8. Heinrich Triepel, *Unitarismus und Föderalismus im Deutschen Reich: Eine staatsrechtliche und politische Studie* (1907), and *Die Reichsaufsicht: Untersuchungen zum Staatsrecht des Deutschen Reichs* (1917).
9. Michael Stolleis, *Public Law in Germany, 1800–1914* (2001), p. 351.
10. Ibid; and Wilfred Fiedler, *Sozialer Wandel, Verfassungswandel, Rechtsprechung* (1972), cited in ibid.
11. Joseph Weiler, *The Constitution of Europe: Do the New Clothes Have an Emperor? And Other Essays on European Integration* (1999), p. 5.
12. Ibid., p. 91.
13. Ibid., p. 16.
14. Michael Stolleis, *A History of Public Law in Germany 1914–1945* (2004), p. 28.
15. Cited in Frank Eyck, *The Prince Consort: A Political Biography* (1975), p. 248, cited in Patricia Kollander, *Frederick III: Germany's Liberal Emperor* (1995), p. 15.
16. Ibid.
17. Stolleis, *History of Public Law,* pp. 20–1.
18. C. Schudnagies, *Der Kriegs- oder Belagerungszustand im Deutschen Reich während des Ersten Weltkrieges: Eine Studie zur Entwicklung und Handhabung des deutschen Ausnahmezustandsrechts bis 1919* (1994), cited in Stolleis, *History of Public Law,* p. 25.
19. August Bebel, 'Das Bürgerliche Gesetzbuch und die Sozialdemokratie', *Neue Zeit,* 2 (1895/96).
20. See Achim Kurz, *Demokratische Diktatur? Auslegung und Handhabung des Artikels 48 der Weimarer Verfassung 1919–1925* (1992).
21. Eckart Kehr, 'The Dictatorship of the Bureaucracy', in Eckart Kehr, *Economic Interest, Militarism, and Foreign Policy,* Gordon Craig (ed.), Grete Heinz (trans.) (1977).
22. Friedrich Meinecke, *Die deutsche Katastrophe* (1946).
23. Hans Rosenberg, *Bureaucracy, Aristocracy, and Autocracy: The Prussian Experience 1660–1815* (1958).
24. A.J.P. Taylor, *Course of German History: A Study in the Development of Germany since 1815* (1945); and Frank Eyck, *Frankfurt Parliament 1848–1849* (1968).

25. Lothar Gall, *Bismarck: Der weisse Revolutionär* (1980).
26. Ralf Dahrendorf, *Society and Democracy in Germany* (1965).
27. Leonard Krieger, *The German Idea of Freedom: A History of a Political Tradition* (1957); and Hans Kohn, *The Mind of Germany: The Education of a Nation* (1960).
28. Hans-Ulrich Wehler, *Deutsche Gesellschaftsgeschichte,* vol. 1 (1987), p. 35.
29. David Blackbourn and Geoff Eley, *The Peculiarities of German History: Bourgeois Society and Politics in Nineteenth-Century Germany* (1984), p. 7.
30. Krieger, *German Idea of Freedom.* For a similar views of German legal development see also Otto Pflanze, 'Juridical and Political Responsibility in Nineteenth-Century Germany', in Leonard Krieger and Fritz Stern (eds), *The Responsibility of Power: Historical Essays in Honor of Hajo Holborn* (1968), pp. 162–82; Reinhart Koselleck, *Preussen zwischen Reform und Revolution: Allgemeines Landrecht, Verwaltung und soziale Bewegung von 1791 bis 1848* (1989); and Mack Walker, *German Home Towns: Community, State, and General Estate, 1648–1871* (1971).
31. Krieger, *German Idea of Freedom* (1972 edition), pp. 458–60.
32. Blackbourn and Eley, *Peculiarities of German History.*
33. For example, Jürgen Kocka (ed.), *Bürgertum im 19. Jahrhundert: Deutschland im europäischen Vergleich* (1988); David Blackbourn and Richard Evans (eds), *The German Bourgeoisie: Essays on the Social History of the German Middle Class from the Late Eighteenth to the Early Twentieth Century* (1991); Hans Puhle (ed.), *Bürger in der Gesellschaft der Neuzeit: Wirtschaft, Politik, Kultur* (1991); and Jürgen Kocka, *Industrial Culture and Bourgeois Society: Business, Labor and Bureaucracy in Modern Germany* (1999).
34. For example, Dieter Langewiesche (ed.), *Liberalismus im 19. Jahrhundert: Deutschland im europäischen Vergleich* (1988); E. Fehrenbach, *Verfassungsstaat und Nationsbildung 1815–1871* (1992); and Lothar Gall (ed.), *Bürgertum, liberale Bewegung und Nation: Ausgewählte Aufsätze.* For earlier studies see, especially, James Sheehan, *German Liberalism in the Nineteenth Century* (1978). For local liberalism see Jan Palmowski, *Urban Liberalism in Imperial Germany: Frankfurt am Main 1866–1914* (1999). For distinctions between liberal factions see Alastair Thompson, *Left Liberals, the State, and Popular Politics in Wilhelmine Germany* (2000).
35. Margaret Anderson, *Practicing Democracy: Elections and Political Culture in Imperial Germany* (2000); and Marcus Kreuzer, 'Parliamentarization and the Question of German Exceptionalism: 1867–1918', *Central European History,* 36/3 (2003), pp. 327–57.
36. There is a notable exception to this absence and promising signs for future growth in this area, most notably the outcome of the AHRB-funded research group 'Constituting the German Nation: The Construction of National Identity through Legal Theory and Practice, 1898–1998'. I was a post-doc in this group during its

three years of existence at King's College-London. The final conference, Citizenship and National Identity in Twentieth-Century Germany, held at Oxford in 2004, drew quite a few scholars, and I am sure the upcoming publication will add considerably to our understanding of the place of law and national identity in twentieth-century Germany. See Geoff Eley and Jan Palmowski (eds), *Citizenship and National Identity in Twentieth-Century Germany* (2007).

37. Dieter Grimm, 'Die Grundrechte im Entstehungszusammenhang der bürgerlichen Gesellschaft', in Kocka (ed.), *Bürgertum im 19. Jahrhundert,* pp. 340–71; Regina Ogorek, 'Individueller Rechtsschutz gegenüber der Staatsgewalt: Zur Entwicklung der Verwaltungsgerichtsbarkeit im 19. Jahrhundert', in Kocka (ed.), *Bürgertum im 19. Jahrhundert,* pp. 372–405; Ursula Vogel, 'Patriarchale Herrschaft, bürgerliches Recht, bürgerliche Utopie: Eigentumsrechte der Frauen in Deutschland und England', in Kocka (ed.), *Bürgertum im 19. Jahrhundert,* pp. 406–38; and Ute Gerhard, 'Die Rechtsstellung der Frau in der bürgerlichen Gesellschaft des 19. Jahrhunderts: Frankreich und Deutschland im Vergleich', in Kocka (ed.), *Bürgertum im 19. Jahrhundert,* pp. 439–68.
38. Franz Wieacker, *Privatrechtsgeschichte der Neuzeit* (1967), and Ernst Huber, *Deutsche Verfassungsgeschichte seit 1789: Bismarck und das Reich,* vol. 3 (1963).
39. Thomas Nipperdey, *Deutsche Geschichte 1866–1918,* vol. 1 (1990), pp. 655–65.
40. Blackbourn and Eley, *Peculiarities of German History,* pp. 190–205.
41. Michael John, *Politics and the Law in Late Nineteenth Century Germany: The Origins of the Civil Code* (1989).
42. Joachim Rückert, *Idealismus, Jurisprudenz und Politik bei Friedrich Carl von Savigny* (1984), and John, *Politics and the Law,* p. 20.
43. John, *Politics and the Law,* p. 89.
44. Michael John, 'Between Estate and Profession: Lawyers and the Development of the Legal Profession in Nineteenth-Century Germany', in Blackbourn and Evans (eds), *German Bourgeoisie* , p. 190.
45. Kenneth Ledford, *From General Estate to Special Interest: German Lawyers 1878–1933* (1996), p. xxviii.
46. Ibid.
47. Kenneth Ledford, 'Lawyers, Liberalism and Procedure: The German Imperial Justice Laws of 1877–79', *Central European History,* 26 (1993), pp. 165–94.
48. Ledford, *General Estate to Special Interest,* p. xix.
49. Ibid., pp. 291–307.
50. Kenneth Ledford, 'Formalizing the Rule of Law in Prussia: The Supreme Administrative Law Court, 1876–1914', *Central European History,* 37/2 (2004), pp. 203–24.
51. Ibid., p. 212.
52. Ibid.
53. Ibid., pp. 216–17.

54. Ibid., pp. 217–18.
55. Ibid., pp. 218–20.
56. Ibid., p. 220.
57. Ibid.
58. Ibid., p. 221.
59. Ibid., p. 222.
60. Ibid.
61. Hermann Kantorowicz, *Rechtswissenschaft und Soziologie* (1911), and Hermann Kantorowicz, *Volksgeist und historische Rechtsschule* (1912).
62. Blackbourn and Eley, *Peculiarities of German History,* p. 82.
63. Ibid., pp. 82–3.
64. Ibid.
65. Ibid., p. 83.
66. This has become even clearer as a result of my research on a second project. In particular, I was able to review King's papers when they were housed at Sotheby's in New York.
67. A great deal of legal history has been written on German influence for Japan, but for a work of history that discusses this see Janny de Jong, '"The Principles of Steam": Political Transfer and Transformation in Japan 1868–1889', *European Review of History,* 12/2 (2005), pp. 269–90. For a brief account on China see Yin-Ching Chen, 'Civil Law Development: China and Taiwan', *Stanford Journal of East Asian Affairs,* 2 (Spring 2002), pp. 8–14. For Latin America see Jacob Dolinger and Keith Rosenn (eds), *A Panorama of Brazilian Law* (1992).
68. Margaret Crosby, 'The Civil Code and the Transformation of German Society: The Politics of Gender Inequality 1814–1919', PhD thesis, Brown University, Providence (2001).
69. Stolleis, *Public Law in Germany,* p. 45.
70. See also Crosby, *Civil Code,* pp. 1–69.
71. Stolleis, *Public Law in Germany,* pp. 25–30; and Crosby, *Civil Code,* pp. 70–134.
72. Stolleis, *Public Law in Germany,* pp. 351–2.
73. See also Crosby, *Civil Code,* pp. 186–333.
74. F. Savigny, *Politik und neuere Legislationen: Materialien zum 'Geist der Gesetzgebung',* Hidetake Akamatsu and Joachim Rückert (eds) (2000).
75. Quoted from Reyscher's journal, cited in R. Hinton Thomas, *Liberalism, Nationalism and the German Intellectuals: An Analysis of the Academic and Scientific Conferences of the Period* (1951), p. 98.
76. Friedrich Gaupp, in *Verhandlungen der Germanisten zu Frankfurt am Main* (1846).
77. Georg Beseler, in ibid.
78. Heinrich Jaup, cited in ibid.
79. As pointed out in Franz Wieacker, *A History of Private Law in Europe (with Particular Reference to Germany),* Tony Weir (trans.) (1995).

80. Stephan Buchholz, 'Ehe- und Familienrecht', in Helmut Coing (ed.), *Handbuch der Quellen und Literatur der neueren europäischen Privatrechtsgeschichte,* vol. 3, *Das 19. Jahrhundert,* vol. 2 (1982), p. 1663.
81. Nieberding, 'Erste Berathung'.
82. Cited in Ferdinand Frensdorff, *Gottlieb Planck: Deutscher Jurist und Politiker* (1914), p. 81.
83. Rudolf Gneist, in *Verhandlungen des Neuesten Deutschen Juristentages* (1871), cited in John, *Politics and the Law,* p. 43.
84. Cited in John, *Politics and the Law,* p. 58.

–1–

Prelude to Modern Germany
Iurisdictio and the German Idea of Sovereignty

> In Germany alone do we see that probity and religion still exist largely amongst the people, in consequence of which many republics exist there in the full enjoyment of liberty, observing their laws in such a manner that no one from within or without could venture upon an attempt to master them.[1]
>
> —Niccolò Machiavelli, *Discourses,* 1513–1517

The belief that law is an essential feature of individual civic identity was apparent in Machiavellian sociopolitical thought. Machiavelli wrote his *Discourses* as a commentary against what he viewed as the corruption of his own Venetian government, and, the fact that he looked to German practices and civic virtues as the example of liberty offers scholars a significant indication of the vitality of indigenous, premodern, self-governing practices in German-speaking Europe. 'The ancient virtue still prevails there in great part,' and their 'honesty is the more to be admired as it is so very rare that it is found only in that country'. 'Their political existence uncorrupted' by French, Spanish or Italian customs, Machiavelli believed that 'a perfect equality' was maintained amongst German citizens.[2] In his *Oration on Factions* (1525), he also espoused a dual conception of law that is very important for this analysis of modern constitutional transformation. Here, Machiavelli warned against the ill-effects of violent means to political transformation, preferring legal methods instead. 'This republic of ours,' he wrote, 'is especially adapted not merely to union but to reformation by means of good procedures and lawful methods.' A 'better Fortune' may be attained 'as a result of better laws', and 'Fortune's malice' may be overcome by prudence, checking unhealthy ambition, the annulment of 'laws that breed factions' and the adoption 'of those suitable to a truly free and law-abiding government'. The 'help of laws' rather than deferment to 'force [of] weapons', he suggested in the sage years of his life, was a better method of political transformation.[3]

The creation of national republics was the modern Western world's great political experiment. Century after century, following the seventeenth-century English experiment, would-be nations embarked on their paths to sociopolitical modernity. Almost without exception the imagined national community was conceptualized as a republic, where the supreme power would be held by a body of citizens, who would participate in the self-governance of the nation, through elected representatives accountable to them. Beyond this basic universal precept, however, the formation of a republic was a largely individual national project. In fact, the defining sociopolitical tenet that was inherent in the basic universal precept of Western constitutionalism was the requirement of individual national development and self-determination. While scholars have discounted the importance of individualism and the process of rationalizing individualistic forces, individualism should be seen as at least *pari passu* with universalism. Individualism was seen, universally, as an intrinsic element of modern constitutionalism and, as a result, scholars might think in terms of distinctive ideologies of republics within Western constitutionalism and consider the fact that ideas varied, not only from nation to nation, but from group to group within nations. The creation of a modern republic was above all else an individual national endeavor, and one shaped by international competition. At the same time, the imagining of community elements, such as representative institutions, how they came into being and the composition of citizenship, was contested within the nation itself.

In contrast to older scholarship that emphasized the development of an ideology of republicanism, it is suggested here that the creation of republics was based on decidedly more individualistic precepts and not universal principles alone.[4] In his analysis of Machiavelli's *Discourses* and the prehumanist origins of constitutional ideas, Quentin Skinner offers some indication of a shift in historiographical direction, suggesting that, while the growth of humanism represented a vital development, 'it is misleading to suggest that it was only with the emergence of these intellectual movements' that an ideology of self-governance began to be formulated.[5] As he points out, Machiavelli not only presented a wholehearted defence of traditional sociopolitical values, but presented that defence 'in a wholeheartedly traditional way'.[6] For Germany, Heinz Schilling argues that 'political thought was pragmatic in character', and 'expressed in the form of statutory law, rather than philosophically and theoretically organized'. Based upon commonly held fundamental principles, 'it can rightly be called an implicit political theory'.[7] More recently, David Bachrach has pleaded for more research on the significant growth of city-state culture in the thirteenth century, particularly in the areas of the Rhenish League.[8]

It is important to recognize and delineate the character of premodern civic identity and self-governing practices, because, in the German context, it was exactly these traditions that modern *Privatrechts-Staatslehre* aimed to recover and rationalize for the purpose of effecting sociopolitical reorganization in the nineteenth century. Accordingly, this chapter explores the indigenous sources of the German civic values that liberals would later appeal to as that basis of their own sociopolitical principles. I argue here that the German idea of sovereignty grew out of an age-old political tradition of local jurisdiction. For this reason, law and legalism occupied more pivotal places in German conceptions of the modern nation, because the principle of jurisdiction had deep roots in the individual legal history of German-speaking Europe and had played a central role in the formation of German civic consciousness.

Here, the strength of the dual conception of law cannot be emphasized enough. Law was not seen as only derivative from political transformation, but as a means to such transformation. It is exactly this recognition of the duality of law and emphasis on the use of law as a means to political transformation that allowed nineteenth-century German transformationists to develop a unique conception of nonviolent revolution and in the hopes of avoiding the force of weapons, which for Germans was the most salient spoiled fruit of the French example.

It is also the goal of this chapter to show that, while German civic humanism also appealed to Greco-Roman sources, that appeal was highly selective. After the language of classical humanism established itself as the mode of high cultural discourse, in late-fifteenth century Germany, Greco-Roman classical thought was appropriated to the degree that it could be used to confirm the efficacy of German sociopolitical traditions. The revival of interests in classical learning must also be seen as one of the major results of the Papal Revolution, which revived Roman law in Europe. In the face of the Church's appropriation of Roman law techniques to achieve the expansion of papal jurisdiction into secular affairs, emperors, princes and townspeople alike began to appropriate Roman law and develop oppositional legal interpretations to counter external interference in secular affairs. It was in this environment that classical learning was counter-appropriated to lend legitimacy to preexisting self-governing practices in local communities. In Germany, preexisting local self-governing practices were lent legitimacy through the development of the new language of classical humanism. As a result, it was not so much that the premodern revival of Greco-Roman thought transformed German sociopolitical values as much as German sociopolitical values shaped the appropriation and interpretation of classical Greco-Roman thought.

Conflict of the Laws

While the principle of legal duality was rationalized for modern purposes, in fact it had deep roots in German-speaking Europe's history of conflict with the Church. Arguably, the Papal Revolution of the twelfth century set the precedent for the use of law as a means to political reorganization in Europe. By the first half of the thirteenth century, the centralizing ambition of the Church was a major source of conflict, not only with German emperors and princes, but also local communities given towards self-governance. Local communities experienced the Papal Revolution as a legal event, when the Church extended its jurisdiction into secular affairs through new ecclesiastical courts, which adjudicated disputes according to classical canon law *(corpus iuris canonici)*. The German idea of sovereignty and the identification of sovereignty with jurisdiction grew out the conflicts of law that erupted around the Papal Revolution.

The making of Latin Christendom was a lengthy, contested and probably never quite complete process. With the exception of the tacit Frankish reception, the

Germanic tribes clung as vociferously to pagan cults as they would to their customary laws. Although the Latin Church was able to form an administrative structure from the old Roman imperial divisions, the process of conversion was slow and, in reality, interest in saving the Germanic flock came only after the swift Muslim conquest of much of Mediterranean Christendom. If either the Latin or Eastern Churches had any hope of continuing the business of Christianity, they faced the challenge of securing viable new markets of souls. The Barbarians, as the Romans had referred to the Germanic tribes, looked more and more capable of Christianity after every Muslim conquest. Nevertheless, Christianizing the new inhabitants of Europe would be a long process. Monks, who were critical in the Christianization process, had their hands full even in the Carolingian regions well into the eighth century.[9] The course of Christianization across the Rhine into Central and Eastern Europe was mud-sluggish. The Scandinavians and Slavs did not convert until the late eleventh century. Deeper into Central Europe, market conditions remained poor into the thirteenth century as Prussians and Lithuanians remained stubbornly pagan for some time.[10]

Despite the growing spiritual authority of the Latin Church, power continued to rest on Germanic customs and political arrangements. In the early period, governance rested on the political idea of tribal sovereignty rather than territoriality. Legal arrangements derived from the principle of personality of law. Law, in effect, was the customary law of the tribal group and was personal to the members of the tribe. Accordingly, Salic law followed a Salic Frank across territorial lines. Although written chronicles of Germanic customary laws appeared in some areas during the sixth century, these were expressions of customary arrangements rather than given law. Germanic custom placed significant limits on the ability of rulers to hand down law and from the time of the migration to the twelfth century, this principle remained firmly entrenched. By the late nineteenth century, legal historians such as Edward Jenks urged that Germanic customary practices had held that law was 'a truth to be discovered' and not 'a command to be imposed'.[11]

The customary conception of law, however, was soon challenged by the changing character of European society. Between the twelfth and thirteen centuries, urbanization and *Verdorfung* resulted in the growth of towns and rural communities. In the German lands, this also led to competition for influence in these communities between the Church and other ruling interests. At the same time, the ambitions of popes and princes alike often came into sharp conflict with townspeople who insisted on maintaining local autonomy. Cities in the Rhineland and elsewhere were able 'to establish themselves as *de facto* city-states within the *de jure* boundaries of the German Empire', relegating bishops to the status of mere 'employee' of the city.[12] In rural areas, *Verdorfung* was characterized by 'the emergence of village autonomy, village jurisdiction, and village legislation as autogeneous rights of the inhabitants'.[13] In a time when the customary conception of law was still strong, the inhabitants of towns and villages were prepared to resist the encroachment of prince and pope alike in municipal affairs.

This was also the era when the Church encouraged religious wars, between 1095 and 1291. Save for the *Reconquista,* as Jacques Le Goff put it in wry terms, the Crusades were an utter failure, and 'the apricot' was the only advantage the West gained. While the linked identity of Europe and Christendom emerged from this failure, the Crusades did little to unite Christendom and resulted in sharpened European rivalries.[14] Paradoxically, the Church now faced the challenge of checking the growing power of the new princely houses its religious wars created, and it was in this environment that the Church turned to law as a means of asserting its influence in European affairs. Even before secular rulers appropriated Roman law to buffer their own powers, the pope was the first to leverage the rediscovery of Roman law to consolidate his authority in Western Christendom.

Roman law, in the form of the *corpus iuris civilis,* which was compiled in the sixth century at the behest of the Emperor Justinian, was rediscovered in the eleventh century. The centre of its recovery was the University of Bologna's newly founded law faculty. It is made up of four parts: *Codex, Novels, Digest* and *Institutes.* The *Codex* contains the collection of imperial decrees from the second century through the time of the Emperor Justinian. The *Novels* are the collection of post-Justinian imperial decrees. The *Digest,* also called *Pandects,* is a compilation of the writings of Roman jurists from the late republic and early principate and would be of particular interest to nineteenth-century scholars of Roman law within the historical school. Finally, the *Institutes,* a series of instructions for lawyers, were compiled largely by Justinian's jurist, Tribonian. When Roman law became the subject of attention at the University of Bologna, focus was on the *Digest.* In the first instance, recovered Roman law was used to lend legal sanction to papal demands for supremacy in European Christendom. Soon thereafter, however, German emperors, princes and townspeople also began to develop competing Roman law-based measures to support their desired political arrangements.

Roman law was a vital element in the making of the Papal Revolution, which began in the twelfth century and was consolidated slowly over a century. Ancient canon law, which was based solely on biblical sources, underwent a process of technical Romanization, at the behest of the papacy, and emerged from this rationalization as classical canon law.[15] This legal project was undertaken for the purpose of advancing papal supremacy, not only in spiritual affairs, but also into the secular realm. It should be emphasized that classical canon law was not the result of the Papal Revolution, but was the means to a revolution that was designed to make the Bishop of Rome the absolute sovereign of European Christendom. Where ancient canon law and papal authority had rested largely on spiritual biblical interpretation, from the time of technical Romanization, the Church no longer appealed to God alone for authority, but thenceforth rested the legitimacy of its actions and new claims to temporal supremacy on a body of law.[16]

Classical canon law, which was the instrument of the Papal Revolution, threatened a fundamental reordering of the power relationships between the Church and lay princes. Pope Gelasius's earlier interpretation of the theory of two swords was meant to prevent emperors from usurping authority that belonged to the 'sacredotal power' alone.[17] In contrast, Gregorian reformers built a new view of the two swords, in which the spiritual sword was deemed inherently superior to the earthly in all matters.[18] This was evident in the major impulse behind the Papal Revolution, which was to put an end to the practice of lay investiture, the practice by which bishops received symbols of episcopal office from emperors and princes. Lay investiture replicated the feudal ceremony of a lord's investiture of his vassals with fiefs, and the vassal's acceptance of same expressed primary loyalty to the lord. Ancient canon law had objected neither to the popular election of bishops nor to the practice of lay investiture. Indeed, for all intents and purposes 'the right to choose bishops had fallen into the hands of emperors, kings, dukes and counts' by the eleventh century.[19] The role of local citizens in determining who would hold bishoprics also had been substantial prior to the Papal Revolution. With the introduction of classical canon law, however, the Church set out to exclude the whole laity from the election of bishops. Election, itself, was suppressed in favor of direct papal appointment, a change that was legitimated by a specious interpretation of the pope's right to confirmation under the new law.[20] By the late twelfth century, the *Decretal* of Pope Celestine III stated boldly: 'No one is to be elected through the clamor of the people.'[21]

The Church, moreover, claimed sole spiritual authority at the same time that classical canon law exempted clerics from secular jurisdiction and threatened to undermine and eclipse local and territorial temporal arrangements altogether. Classical canon law etched in stone the popes' absolutist intentions and backed those ambitions up with a new bureaucracy of legally trained professional bishops. Bishops in the time of the ancient canon law frequently were elected from the laity, but the *Liber sextus* set down strict new eligibility requirements limiting the office to men already within the Holy See. A male candidate had to be of legitimate birth, at least thirty years of age and of 'sufficient learning'.[22] In a transalpine Europe where universities were almost nonexistent, this left popes, who increasingly were trained in law, with significant intellectual power. One might also consider that the exclusive precepts of classical canon law also may have been a tool to limit the ecclesiastical mobility of the Germanic flock. It is rather curious that the Church's heightened determination to consolidate control over the clergy emerged alongside a demographic shift in its makeup. Until the eleventh century, the principle of personality of the law remained dominant. Into the ninth century, as Simeon Guterman shows, most clergy insisted on the right to live according to the ordinary vestiges of Roman law that had survived on the ground. As more persons of Germanic descent entered the clergy in the tenth century, however, they increasing laid claim to the Germanic laws of their birth.[23]

It wasn't just that the Church rested its monopolistic claim over interpretation of the Gospels and temporal authority on the new law, but that ordinary Germans may well have experienced the encroachment of classical canon law in sometimes brutal ways. As the number of towns and villages increased with urbanization and

Verdorfung, so did the proliferation of ecclesiastical courts, and this meant that the Church also possessed the judicial infrastructure to enforce its rule. In cases of concurrent jurisdiction involving the laity, the Church claimed superiority.[24] The remanding and appealing of even civil cases to the papal *Rota* would remain a source of friction between secular rulers and the papacy. Whereas primitive excommunication had been little more than an inconsequential curse, under classical canon law it became a legal sanction and punishable criminal offence.[25] Draconian measures, for the cause of doing God's Will, were meted out under new heresy laws, and classical canon law threatened excommunication or even interdiction of regions where individuals or rulers might refuse compliance. Pope Lucius's (1181–1185) *Ad abolendem Decretal* defined heresy as any belief contrary to that professed by the Church, and it commanded secular judges to execute ecclesiastical judgements by imposing 'condign punishment' upon heretics. Appropriating and exploiting Germanic oath traditions for its own purposes, the Church required all persons in secular authority to swear 'to do all in their power' to administer ecclesiastical justice and imposed the obligation to carry out the dirty business of burning wayward flock at the stake on the secular courts.[26] Anti-heretical oaths were coerced or imposed upon Christian princes after 1215, and, for this reason, classical canon law has been called an 'oath-dominated' system of justice.[27]

At the top of German society, the Papal Revolution severely restricted the imperial sphere of authority by reducing the German emperor's role within the Church to a member of the laity. The investiture controversy was settled at the Concordat at Worms in 1122. However, the emperor had to rely on the support of princes, who now appeared as the 'guarantors of imperial rights', and this also had a deteriorating effect on imperial authority. By the close of the civil wars that marked the Papal Revolution, the emperor emerged dependent on not only old, but many new noble houses, including those of Wittelsbach, Wettin and Hohenstaufen. From the Diet of princes held at Forchheim in 1077 came a resolution, which insisted on the future election of German emperors. The rule was applied at the Diet of Mainz in 1125, when Henry V's heir was rejected and Lothar of Saxony was elected instead. Upon Lothar's death in 1138, the electoral college of princes again passed over an hereditary heir in favor of Conrad of Schwaben, and when he died in 1152, his son also was passed over and Frederick Barbarossa was elected to the imperial office. In matters involving important decisions, the emperor was required further to summon the princes of the realm. Financially, he was left in a state of nearly perpetual weakness vis-à-vis the kings of France or England. The feudal law of *Leihezwang* made the enfeaoffment of any lands escheated to the emperor from his vassals compulsory.[28] In addition, these years also saw the significant development of grounds and methods of impeachment, as Ernst Schubert's study points out, and several rulers were subject to trial and impeachment between the eleventh and fourteenth centuries.[29]

By the late medieval period, royal powers in Germany were deeply concerned about their legitimacy, which was increasingly contested by popes, rival princes and people alike.[30] The power to rule rested on the postulate that the authority to rule 'was grounded in control of adjudication'.[31] German emperors faced severe checks on their authority, and, from the time of the Papal Revolution, theirs was a role limited to the maintenance of peace and justice in the secular sphere. As clashes over jurisdiction continued to be the source of ongoing power struggles, emperors and princes faced the challenge of developing effective legal measures to expand the parameters of peace and justice within their realms.

Emperor Frederick Barbarossa recognized that law could be used as an effective tool for maintaining his authority against not only the papacy, but territorial rulers and the ever-increasing number of autonomous cities, particularly in Lombardy. He responded to the new realities that resulted from the Papal Revolution by employing the technical skills of Roman law jurists to develop legal rules for his own purposes. During his inauguration trip to Rome in 1155, Barbarossa made a point of meeting with members of Bologna's law faculty and recruited Martinus, Bulgarus, Jacobus and Hugo. He requested that they formulate a list of 'all rights to be accorded to the emperor under the ancient laws of Lombardy as they had existed prior to the rise of independent cities'. Three years later, he relied on Bolognese jurists to draft legislation to be put before the Diet of Roncaglia in 1158. The Peace Statute of Roncaglia that resulted was marked by its attempt to secure the emperor's secular jurisdiction. A 1152 statute had introduced Latin legal language such as *lege* and *jus,* but it remained addressed 'to the bishops, dukes, counts, margraves and officials who receive this document'. Conversely, the Roncaglia statute addressed 'all the subjects of [the] Empire' and stated 'by this decreed law, which is to prevail in perpetuity, we order ... '. As new territorial principalities were recognized within the Empire, they received 'all jurisdiction and full power of doing justice' within their territories.[32]

At the same time, technical Romanization, whether for papal or imperial purposes, threatened to overlay new rules of law on a medieval Europe where both urbanization and *Verdorfung* were marked by a trend toward local self-governance. Amongst the new urban centres were episcopal towns, and the presence of a papal or imperial bishop became the distinguishing sign of a town.[33] The expansion of towns thus increased the number of bishops, who, as a result of the reforms, stood increasingly not only at the head of spiritual life, but also laid claim to judicial power in secular life. It also was not long before ecclesiastical courts became an important source of revenue for the Church. Papal absolutism hit home as the Church attempted to superimpose its jurisdiction on towns given toward self-government. To say the least, this created an explosive situation in a society, particularly in the German lands, where people were not yet weaned off Germanic unwritten customary law and practice.

By the twelfth century, the resistance of local communities to threats against their self-governance was reflected in the demand for local jurisdiction. In 1074, merchants and artisans in Cologne revolted against *Erzbischof* Anno II after he attempted to confiscate a merchant ship. Although the revolt was suppressed, it resulted in the expulsion of the archbishop from the city. A second revolt in 1106 secured local jurisdiction in Cologne, and an independent municipal government and system of urban law, referred to as the *jus coloniensis* (law of Cologne), were established.[34] Insistence on municipal autonomy as well as the rights and liberties of the citizens of Cologne remained a key feature of legal discourse through the eighteenth century, as Gerd Schwerhoff shows. By the fourteenth and fifteenth centuries, the citizens of Cologne made clear that their relationship with bishops was conditioned on their upholding and adhering to their 'good old customs' *(gude alde gewoynde)*.[35] Legal process filed by the citizens in the thirteenth century also revealed a conception of basic law or *ius de non evocando*, and appeals to the city's ancient autonomy reflected the existence of an implicit self-governing ideology.[36] In cases before Cologne's *Hofgericht,* lay judges *(Schöffen)* from the body of citizens heard cases and made findings of law that the professional judge was bound to execute. In addition, these findings of law were believed 'to represent the accumulated knowledge of customary law'.[37]

Local jurisdiction also resulted from emperors and princes granting charters of liberty, which guaranteed the right to self-governance. Charters of liberty were granted to quell popular discontent and also in exchange for the acceptance by local communities of peace and protection as mentioned. The contractual nature of these arrangements should be emphasized, because community acceptance of peace and protection was conditioned on the guarantor's agreement to respect local autonomy and uphold the good old laws. Revolts against bishops in Worms (1073), Mainz (1077) and Magdeburg (1129) resulted in such charters of liberty. By the twelfth century, there was a proliferation of grants of local autonomy in exchange for peace and protection. Examples here include Freiburg's Charter of 1120 and Lübeck's Charter of 1181.[38] There is some indication that the granting of charters of liberty also formed the basis of a premodern alliance system during the years of conflict between the papacy and German emperors. In northern Italy, the popular movement in Milan (1057) was led by advocates of the papal reforms, who attacked and drove out the aristocratic clergy and imperial bishop. The formation of the fourteen self-governing communities that formed the Lombard League came into existence under the sanction and protection of the Church, which was interested in limiting the influence of German emperors in the region.[39] By the same token, Emperor Henry IV granted self-governing charters to cities in Tuscany at the height of his struggles with Pope Gregory VII in the late eleventh century.[40]

The importance of the development of what may be seen as constitutional alignment among urban communities in German-speaking Europe cannot be emphasized enough. The 'most dramatic illustration of the birth and growth of a system of urban law', as Harold Berman writes, 'is the process by which the laws of more than a dozen major German cities were formally received in new cities founded between the twelfth and fourteenth centuries.'[41] Lübeck law was received in forty-three cities, the laws of Frankfurt in forty-nine cities, those of Hamburg in four, of Freiburg in nineteen cities, of Munich in thirteen, and of Bremen and Braunschweig in two and three cities, respectively. The most widespread dissemination, however, was of the

Magdeburger Recht, which was received in eighty new cities. As a result, scholars are able to identify the formation of *Rechtskreise,* and here legal disputes were often remanded to *Schöffen* in the mother cities.[42] In his book on the constitutional history of the Hansa cities, Ernst Pitz offers an in-depth analysis of the pattern of development between the fourteenth and fifteenth centuries. Following the growth of trading relationships, legal reception formed a constitutional political union of sorts between the free cities of the Hanseatic League.[43] It is this pattern of reception and expansion of urban law amongst autonomous German cities that would offer the prescriptive model for modern German constitutional transformation when legal scholars rediscovered it in the early nineteenth century.

To sum up this section, it is important for readers to keep in mind a couple of significant points. First, a defining precedent for the dual use and conception of law was set by the Church's use of classical canon law to effect Papal Revolution. Classical canon law was not the result of political transformation, but the means to securing papal supremacy in European Christendom. The Church relied on the new law and ecclesiastical courts, not only to reverse the dominance of lay princes and flock in Church and spiritual affairs, but to impose its supremacy, even in secular affairs, on a Europe experiencing urbanization and *Verdorfung.* Not surprisingly, conflicts of law erupted in the very German-speaking sections of Europe that had been most resistant to Christianization to begin with. It was in this environment of bitter conflict over concurrent jurisdiction that a German identification of sovereignty with jurisdiction developed, which was pragmatic and found expression in the form of imperial, princely and municipal statutory law alike. In each instance, technical Romanization was employed to develop legal measures that would not only counterbalance the legal basis of papal claims to supremacy, but in the case of local communities any claims by external forces to suzerainty over their municipal affairs. Finally, the rationalization of municipal law and the process of constitutional alignment, which resulted in the development of *Rechtskreise,* is vitally important to this study, because it was this historic pattern of constitutionalization that served as the model for the nineteenth-century German constitutional transformation, which I argue effected a slow bourgeois revolution.

Romanization of Local *Iurisdictio* and the Idea of Sovereignty

Equally as important as the growth of systems of urban law was the development of a Roman law-based theory that lent rationalized legal sanction to local *iurisdictio* (jurisdiction), something that would become increasingly important in Central Europe as the *corpus iuris civilis* saw slow reception in transalpine Europe from the fourteenth century onward. Many of the northern Italian *communes* adopted elective systems of government centred on the *podestá.*[44] As emperors in the later medieval period strove to impose their authority on local communities, cities responded by building up an arsenal of ideological weapons of resistance 'designed to combat imperial claims to suzerainty over them'.[45] In so doing, they also invoked a suitable interpretation of Roman law, the chief source of which were the writings of the Bolognese Glossator, Azo (1190–1230).

Azo was the first to offer an interpretation of Roman law that vindicated the sovereignty of independent *communes.* His argument rested on a new understanding of the central concept in the Roman law of corporations, *universitas* and an interpretation of the *Lex regia,* derived from a reading of the *corpus iuris civilis.* The term *universitas* originally referred to lesser organizations such as guilds and monasteries within cities. Azo reinterpreted it to apply to entire groups of citizens 'as bodies politic capable of speaking with a single voice and acting with a unified will in the disposition of their affairs'.[46] Thus, he concluded that 'the consent of the whole people considered as a *universitas* is always needed if the highest powers of *iurisdictio* are to be lawfully instituted'.[47]

From here, Azo arrived at the idea that rulers only possess secondary or given authority, which, for just cause, could be reclaimed by the body of citizens who own the given authority. For this Azo relied on a reference to the *Lex regia.* This was the law referred to in the *Institutes,* whereby the Roman people were said to have made an original grant of *iurisdictio* to the Roman emperor at the beginning of the principate. Azo argued that ' "the power of the Emperor to make law" arose lawfully because "it was assigned to him by the people" in whose hands it must originally have reposed'.[48] From this developed the idea of the consent of the governed and the notion that the authority of representatives is only secondary, given authority. Even after the establishment of a ruler, even if with full *iurisdictio,* Azo argued that 'the power to make laws, if it was a power the people possessed before that time, is one they will continue to possess afterwards'.[49] Thus, the people never transferred the highest power of *iurisdictio* 'except in such a way that they were able at the same time to retain it', and 'from this it follows that, although the emperor is of greater power than any individual member of the populace, he is not of greater authority than the populace on the whole'.[50] For Azo, thus, *iurisdictio* was defined as the 'power to publicly introduce with the necessity of stating the law and establishing equity'.[51]

At the level of high culture, the Azoian doctrine of *iurisdictio* found expression in the writings of Marsilius of Padua, John of Jandun and Bartolus de Sassoferato, amongst others. Marsilius and John's *Defensor pacis* (1324) offered the sharpest attack on what they saw as the papal usurpation of authority, which had resulted from the introduction of classical canon law. In this way, *Defensor pacis* anticipated the road to the Lutheran Reformation to come. 'The whole body of citizens or its majority alone is the human "legislator" ', and 'the "legislator" alone or the one who rules by its authority has the power to dispense with human laws.'[52] The attack levied in the *Defensor pacis* was echoed in the writings of later critics of the Church's claims to secular jurisdiction and papal supremacy. John Hus and Nicholas of Cusa, both of whom had spent significant time in Germany, were two such writers. Cusa laid the foundation for Lorenzo Valla's *De falso credita et ementita Constantini donatione declamatione* (1439). The myth of the Donation of Constantine was relied on by the Church to support papal claims to secular supremacy and was a key document used to justify the Papal Revolution and the technical Romanization of ancient canon law.[53] *De falso* showed that the Donation of Constantine was a fraud, and this not only undermined the basis of papal supremacy, but the legitimacy of the Church's claim to secular jurisdiction. Indeed, the appearance of *De falso* contributed to the slow unraveling of papal supremacy and lit the road that led to the Protestant Reformation.

In addition, the Azoian rationalization of *iurisdictio* also shaped Bartolus de Sassoferrato's understanding of sovereignty as it found expression in *Tractatus de regimine civitatum* (1330).[54] In Bartolus's writing, however, the dual conception of law was more prominent. Developing the concept of *iurisdictio* further, Bartolus identified *ius civile* (civil law) 'as a formative element in the creation of the *civitas* (city-state)'.[55] Through Bartolus both the Azoian doctrine of *iurisdictio* and the dual conception of law were bequeathed to Hugo Grotius and Johannes Althusius, both of whom developed similar ideas in their respective repudiations of Bodin's theory of indivisible sovereignty.

Finally, there are two main points that readers should keep in mind from this section. First, the pragmatic political thought, which had found expression in municipal legal arrangements, was given doctrinal sanction in Azoian theory and in the contemporary linguistic mode of Roman law. Local jurisdiction and self-governing practices became philosophically and theoretically organized. Second, by the early years of the fourteenth century, a premodern identification of popular sovereignty with *iurisdictio* (jurisdiction) also emerged in a theoretically organized form. This is important, because later legal and political thought built on this early identification of sovereignty with jurisdiction, and German political ideology continued to be juridical in orientation.

Classical Humanism and Evangelical Jurisprudence

It was the Swiss historian, Jacob Burckhardt, who first coined the phrase 'Italian Renaissance', in his seminal study *Die Cultur der Renaissance in Italien* (1860). Burckhardt, who was a Germanist, was himself more interested in the rebirth of his contemporary German culture, as Charles Homer Haskins pointed out many years ago. After the publication of Haskin's *The Renaissance of the Twelfth Century* (1927), scholars began to question, altogether, the historiographical constructions of 'humanism' and an 'Italian Renaissance'. Haskins's work pointed to enthusiasm for the classics and emphasis on cultural renewal in twelfth-century France.[56] In recent years, scholars such as Skinner and Charles Nauert have relied on a prehumanism synthesis to explain interests in classical learning prior to the Renaissance, but from here, the story of Renaissance classical humanism continues on its usual historiographical course.[57] As Nauert put it, the concepts of 'Renaissance' and of 'humanism' have rebounded, but with the major caveat that 'the high civilization of the Renaissance developed out of the high civilization of the Middle Ages.'[58] However, the technical Romanization of canon law, its introduction in the twelfth century and the fact that emperors, princes and townspeople alike responded to the Papal Revolution by appropriating Roman law to develop legal countermeasures, raises new questions, not only about a 'Renaissance', but about its Italianate origins. As mentioned at the beginning of this chapter, Machiavelli looked to the many republics of Germany for a contemporary example of liberty and not to Venetian practice.

This study takes the position that individualism was the primary factor in the formation of German sociopolitical and constitutional ideas. The approach taken here, however, is not designed to obscure the place of early modern classical humanism as an important phase in the evolution of indigenous German political concepts and values. While it is significant that the introduction of classical canon law and the conflict it created produced considerable interest in classical legal learning well before the late fifteenth century, it is vitally important to recognize that the new learning was appropriated to demonstrate the efficacy of the traditional view of sovereignty and self-governance. Frederick Barbarossa, as Heinrich Appelet writes, 'showed himself to be a man of his own time and his own culture in using some of the language of Roman law in order to legitimize his assertion of imperial powers'.[59] A similar appropriation by local magistrates adjusted to support the good old law was evident in Cologne: *'Diese Statt nit deß Ertz = Stiffts Cöln/sondern deß Heyligen Reichs uhralte ungemittelte frye Statt seye/die vor Christi Geburt/und lange Zeit/ ehe der christilicher Glaub/Geist = und Ertz = Bischofflicher Stand bekannt ware/ Colonia Romanorum gewesen/von den Freyen Römern erbawet/in gleiche Freyheit angenohmen/post continuam seculorum seriem, an seine Freye Statt/von Kayser Justiniano dem Corpori juris communis in L finali ff. de Censibus einverleibt'.*[60] As research shows for the Hanseatic *Rechtskreise,* there was also a marked turn toward the use of Latin in official language by the mid-fourteenth century.[61] Finally, the growing importance of competitive civil law was reflected in the fact that the Church had to maintain a staff of civil lawyers by the fourteenth century.[62]

German legal responses to the Papal Revolution and the responses of local communities to threats against municipal self-governance demonstrate the practice of selective appropriation. This should not be surprising, because it was often in the context of judicial disputes that claims to jurisdiction were articulated. In addition, there were plenty of references in classical thought that could be used to support the German identification of sovereignty with jurisdiction. 'Justice,' Aristotle wrote in his *Politics,* 'is the bond of men in states for the administration of justice, which is the determination of what is just, and is the principle order of political society'.[63]

Inasmuch as German-speaking Europe was an important bearer of classical ideals and political values, these ideas were appropriated when they met preexisting sociopolitical demands. There was interest in the Aristotelian *polis,* because it was conceptualized as an ancient version of a *Freistadt* and offered historical confirmation of the efficacy of existing local jurisdiction and self-governing practice. Representations of the classics and the ideals of Aristotle, Cicero, Polybius and others were appropriated to the degree that they spoke to and supported the desired traditional sociopolitical values. Already in the twelfth and thirteenth centuries, the life-size, equestrian statue of Otto II in Magdeburg's old market square symbolized the autonomous judicial powers of the *Schöffen,* and the Roland statues depicting raised swords in many towns represented the judicial powers and authority of urban law against external encroachment.[64] As early as 1441, Johannes von Sergovia of Nuremburg distinguished different modes of representation in the body politic.[65] Conrad Celtis made comparisons with the city-states of ancient Greece in describing Nuremburg's patricians as *senators* and *praetors* while he praised the city's laws and history.[66] The iconography of municipal council rooms throughout Germany reminded representatives to put the common good above their private sentiments.[67] In Regensburg, Johann Bocksberger the Younger's woodcut on good government depicted a female personification of *Res publica* guarding *Iustitia,* with sword and scales.[68] Although clearly evolved by the appropriation of classical representations, these examples show a remarkable continuing identification of sovereignty and self-governance with jurisdiction.

On the eve of the Reformation there were no fewer than 364 registered polities in the Empire and just less than half were ecclesiastical polities.[69] Already in the early fifteenth century, even before the appearance of *De falso,* German jurists began calling for a 'thoroughgoing "*reformatio*" (reformation) of private and criminal law'. The process of *reformatio* started in Cologne in 1437 and, by the closing years of the century, several German municipalities had passed 'legal reformations', including Nürnberg (1497), Tübingen (1497), Worms (1498) and Frankfurt (1502). Legal reformations were also passed in the duchies of Baden (1511), Franken (1512), Bavaria (1518) and elsewhere. These legal reformations aimed to reduce local customary laws to writing, and to update and integrate them to some extent. In some areas, local courts and methods of adjudication were also reformed, which was of particular interest to the merchant classes. 'This gradual rationalization, systematization, professionalization, and "scientization", of German law, born of the legal reformation movement', as John Witte writes, 'are now regarded as the most salient features of what traditionally had been called "the reception of Roman law" in Germany.'[70]

In political perspective, however, legal *reformatio* was aimed at breaking the secular jurisdiction of the Church in local affairs. Citing the corruption of ecclesiastical courts and overly complex classical canon law procedures, the 1498 City Reformation of Worms developed independent court procedural measures. In a number of areas, city councils also gained control over the operation of schools, charities, guilds, poor relief and family life from the Church. The 1438 Reformation of Sigismund ordered that 'temporal and spiritual justice must be kept distinct'. City reformations in Nürnberg (1479) and Frankfurt (1502) 'included stern restrictions on the use of prorogation clauses in private contracts and treaties and strict prohibitions against judicial removal of cases from civil to Church courts'. What is more, as Witte writes, 'preambles' to these legal reformations 'castigated the Church for its greed and opulence—its excessive court fees, high tithes and taxes, indulgence trafficking, self-interested laws of testate and intestate succession, vast holdings of tax-exempt realty and ... luxurious clerical and monastic living'. These legal reformations, as he shows, 'were important storm signals of the Lutheran Reformation to come'.[71]

In the heat of the Reformation, Witte argues, that urban civic humanism and republicanism provided the rationale for political action by urban patricians, noblemen and lower territorial magistrates, including the lower nobility and town estates. It was in this environment, Robert von Freiburg suggests, that civic humanism began to inform a new brand of patriotism at the territorial level.[72] The Swiss theologian Heinrich Bullinger's play *Lucretia,* which was staged in Aarau, Basel and Straßburg in the 1530s, extolled the virtues of Brutus in the struggle against tyranny and the establishment of the Roman Republic.[73] The Lutheran jurist Johann von Schartzenberg dedicated his *Memorial der Tugend* (1535) to Lucretia and emphasized that the Tarquin kings were expelled because of their viciousness.[74] In Johannes Ferrarius's (also known as Johannes Eisermann) nine volumes of *De republica* (1556), citations of Cicero's *De officiis* are rivaled only by citations of Aristotle's *Politics. De republica* linked the desired civic virtues of Cicero's *vita activa* with those of lower citizen-magistrates in German towns and territories. It also warned princes against the evil influences of courtiers, personal ambition and despotism by highlighting the plight of the ancient corruptors Catiline and Tarquinius.[75] The citizen-magistrates formed the backbone of the commonwealth, and the prince whom he deemed to be only a supreme magistrate was 'subject to law like any other member of the commonwealth'.[76]

At the same time, classical humanism also must be seen as another linguistic turn, and one that allowed Germans to reassert traditional political values in a new language. In addition to what Freiburg discerns in the writings of Bullinger, Eisermann and others, it also seems clear that the appropriation of classical thought offered a more sophisticated way of articulating the customary pragmatic political thought that was organized around jurisdiction. This is evident, not only in the celebration of lower citizen-magistrates, but in the focus on judicial structures. One must also factor in the impact of the Great Schism (1378–1417), when the Church fell into chaos and scandal as three popes laid claim to papal authority. On the one hand, in this environment, the operations, judicial and otherwise, of the Church slid into decline. On the other, this also would have produced a *de facto* greater autonomy on the ground and local customs were revived. When the Church tried to reconsolidate its authority after 1417, particularly in secular affairs, it was not long after this when municipal *reformatio* was undertaken in many German cities and towns.

For many years, historians interpreted the Protestant Reformation as a religious event. In recent years, however, a few scholars have underscored the importance of understanding the Reformation as, predominantly, a legal rupture. The jurisdiction of ecclesiastical courts, as Berman writes, was one the of the principle objects of attack during the Reformation.[77] Witte argues effectively that the Reformation was a 'watershed in the flow of the Western legal tradition'.[78] Its radicalism was not in Luther's posting of the Ninety-Five Theses in 1517, but the Wittenberg bonfire of 10 December 1520. Organized by Philipp Melanchthon and others, Luther, along with a group of students and faculty, consigned to flames the papal bull threatening him with excommunication, Pope Gratian's *Decretum* and, most importantly, the four books that made up the classical canon law.[79] In an environment in which the Church already faced local rejection of its secular jurisdiction, it was this that distinguished Luther from earlier agitators, and it was this that formed the source of his swift excommunication on 3 January 1521.

A constitutional ideology developed around the battle over canon law, giving rise to an evangelical jurisprudence. This was evident in the Wittenberg School of Philipp Melanchthon, which became influential in seventeenth-century Denmark, and the Marburg School of Johannes Eisermann and Johann Oldendorp, more influential in England.[80] Although erudite knowledge of the classics was apparent in their writings, both Eisermann and Oldendorp had practical experience with local municipal legal structures. Eisermann served as a *Schöffe* on the Marburg *Hofgericht* and his *On the Common Good of Ordering a Commonwealth* (1533) was translated and printed in London in 1559. It emphasized building on the lessons of the classical commonwealths, and that history taught that 'there is not a single foreordained or natural system of society, politics, and law'. Rather 'every people chooses its own social form, its own political structure, and its own system of law' based on a 'combination of nature, custom and reason'.[81] Originally from Hamburg, Oldendorp had helped draft the Rostock legal *reformatio* of 1530 and published some sixty works on law, including *What is Equitable and Right* (1529), *A Statesman's Mirror of Good Policy* (1530) and *A Methodology of Natural, Common and Civil Law* (1539). In his writings, Oldendorp emphasized the preference for the nonviolent resolution of disputes. 'War is justified only for defense against an unjust attack,' and a civil polity should seek to settle conflicts peaceably.[82] Since peace was so linked to law in the German tradition, this also offers additional evidence of the continuing strength of the dual conception of law in German political thought.

By the late sixteenth century, a power vacuum had resulted from the Reformation. This produced, in Dutch and German political thought, a preoccupation with the location of the *suprema potestas* (sovereignty) and the rights and duties of political offices. Debate was provoked by Jean Bodin's conceptualization of sovereignty offered in his *Les six livres de la république* (1576). While there was little dispute with Bodin's view that legislative authority was the first mark of sovereignty, his insistence that sovereignty was indivisible and that this indivisibility rendered impossible the existence of a *respublica mixta* (mixed constitution) was met with strident objection. The mixed constitution referred to a mixture of the three pure forms of government—monarchy, aristocracy and democracy—that were identified in Aristotle's *Politics.* Monarchy, according to Polybius's *Histories,* would inevitably degenerate into its corrupt form of tyranny, aristocracy into oligarchy and, lastly, democracy into anarchy, and in *Politics* the key distinction between the healthy and sick forms hinged on the rule of law. Accordingly the notion developed in humanist political thought that the only way to avoid such degeneration was by combining all three healthy forms in a single polity to form a mixed constitution.

In *De iure praedae commentarius* (1604), Hugo Grotius's *respublica* referred to the multitude of private persons coming together, of their own free will, for protection and acquiring life's necessities through mutual aid.[83] Echoing the Azoian doctrine of *iurisdictio,* for Grotius law emanated from the consent of this unified body, producing a civil contract. 'Civil power', thus, 'manifesting itself in laws and judgments, resides primarily and essentially in the bosom of the commonwealth itself'.[84] Since all of the people in a commonwealth did not concern themselves with the administration of civil affairs, the exercise of lawful power was entrusted to a number of magistrates. Acting for the common good, these magistrates had authority to make laws for the *respublica.* In Grotius, the important theory of civil power articulated by the radical Spanish jurist Fernando Vázquez was merged with the language of the Dutch Revolt. The concept of *magistratus* in Grotius emphasized the idea that those who exercise civil power, whether kings, princes, counts, assemblies or town councils, are administrators, and, therefore, 'public power is constituted by collective consent' derived in the first instance from the freely united body of private persons.[85] His *respublica mixta* thus combined 'the majesty of a prince with the authority of a senate and the liberty of the people'.[86]

In Central Europe, Johannes Althusius, Clemens Timpler and Johann Heinrich Alsted were the main developers of German monarchomach theory, which also rejected Bodin's conception of indivisible sovereignty.[87] *Politica* in Alsted's *Encyclopaedia* (1630) emphasized the principle that voluntary association is the foundation of politics and society.[88] According to Timpler 'every civil society depends on the will and the legitimate consent of those who join together to create civil life'.[89] Appealing also to Vázquez and Bartolus, Althusius asserted that 'the people, or the associated members of the realm, have the power of establishing the right of the realm and of binding themselves to it'.[90] The *populus* came to constitute 'the *respublica,* which, following Cicero's classic definition is therefore literally a *res populi*'.[91] 'Sovereignty', as Alsted would write, 'is the highest power, which the magistrate has amongst the people by consent of the people.'[92]

Political Aristotelianism also was marked by long assessments of the mixed constitutions of ancient Sparta and Rome as well as England, Sweden, Venice and the German Empire.[93] Bartholomeus Keckermann's *Systema disciplinae politicae* (1608) analyzed a range of political bodies, and his *respublica temperata* emerged as a mixture of two or three of the pure forms.[94] The University of Tübingen professor of law, Christoph Besold (1577–1638), expressed a preference for the *respublica mixta* in his *De consilio politico axiomata aliquam multa* (1622), in which senates and popular assemblies were the sources of prudence, stability and virtue.[95] In a mixed constitution, as he later extolled in *Principium et finis politicae* (1626), 'the rights of majesty' are divided between the prince and assemblies of the estates and 'this mixture seems to be the most finely balanced harmony, for some powers are best exercised by one person, such as the power of judging and imposing punishments, there are others in which the participation of the orders or estates could hardly be denied without inequity'.[96]

To close this section, the goal here has been to show, first, that the identification of sovereignty with jurisdiction was informed and strengthened by the political thought of the Reformation. The doctrine of jurisdiction emerged philosophically and was theoretically organized on the basis of German practices and rationalized by German legal scholars. In addition, the continuity in the juridical organization of German political thought should also be kept in mind by readers. Finally, while references to classical learning abounded, this again was appropriated to support the evolving traditional arrangements of self-governance. Both Eisermann and Oldendorp had practical experience in municipal judicial systems and had participated in the *reformatio* of urban laws.

Hermann Conring and Early Modern Legal Radicalism

In the German case, the legal radicalism of the modern era was shaped by the legal radicalism of the premodern period. While, in recent years, scholars have identified the scientization of urban law as the most salient feature of the Reception of Roman Law, typically, the Reception refers to the year 1495, when the *corpus iuris civilis* was accepted in the Holy Roman Empire as the common law of last resort and imperial appellate jurisdiction was introduced with the establishment of the *Reichskammergericht* (Imperial Supreme Court). On the other hand, the tradition of local jurisdiction had produced immeasurable legal variety in the secular laws of the Empire. On the other hand, as classical canon law was invalidated by municipal legal reformations, the Empire would have been left without a law held in common across communities, and this also explains why Roman law became the source of the *ius commune* (law held in common).

The Reception of Roman Law accompanied the *Landfriede* settlement of the 1495 Concordat at Worms, which was supposed to put an end to the violent resolution of territorial disputes within the Empire and demanded that future disputes be adjudicated in imperial courts of law. Obviously, the peace of the land was disrupted by the religious wars associated with the Reformation, and, while Luther and Melanchthon initially criticized the reception of a foreign law code, in the face of the violence associated with the peasant revolts of the 1520s, they soon conceded that it was a necessary expedient in the absence of a rationalized German common law.

Nevertheless, it was Roman law's famous *Princeps legibus solutus est,* which stated that the sovereign was not bound by laws, that appealed to would-be absolutist territorial princes. From the middle of the seventeenth century, the Reception of Roman Law, therefore, was associated with the rise of absolutism in continental Europe. Accordingly, political thought continued to be organized around juridical theory, and the early modern legal radicalism that would precipitate the national scientization and rationalization of German law in the nineteenth century emerged from the rejection of the use of Roman law to support secular absolutism.[97]

Though the historiography on Hermann Conring has been limited, he was perhaps the most important political thinker of the seventeenth century in this regard.[98] Conring's scholarship focused, specifically, on questions of reasons of state. In 1632 he was appointed Professor of Natural Philosophy at the University of Helmstedt, and his inaugural lecture was titled *In Praise of Aristotle* (1632). Conring also edited volumes of Tacitus' *Germania* (1632), Aristotle's *Politics* (1637), Cicero's *De Legibus* (1643) and Machiavelli's *De Principatibus* (1660). His *Theses viriae de morali prudential* (1629) and *Disputatio de natura ac optimis auctoribus civilis prudentia* (1639) show concern for the place of virtue in shaping civic personality. Finally, Conring's political treatises are marked by an attempt to delineate the sources of corruption and degeneration in the body politic and to distinguish between true and corrupt forms of government, as seen in *Disputatio politica de regno et tyrannide* (1640). In *Dissertatio politica de democratia* and *Disputatio politica de oligarchia,* both of which appeared in 1643 with *De legibus,* he emphasized the inherently degenerating nature of the three pure forms of state: monarchy, aristocracy and democracy.[99]

For German-speaking Europe, *Discursus novus de imperatore Romano-Germanico* (1642) was Conring's most important political and legal treatise. It is not an overstatement to emphasize that not since Lorenzo Valla's *De falso,* which exploded the Donation of Constantine myth, had so important a treatise appeared in the German legal world. *Discursus novus* exploded the political myth that the Holy Roman Empire and German emperor were the living manifestations of the Roman Empire and Roman emperor, respectively. This was of fundamental political significance, because just as the myth of the Donation of Constantine had served to buffer papal claims to supremacy and lend legitimacy to the authority of classical canon law, the myth of Roman imperium shored up would-be absolutist imperial and princely claims to indivisible sovereignty, claims which were anchored in Roman law. Conring reasserted the view that the papacy had 'no right to interfere in the affairs of Germany', but, after a lengthy analysis delineating the history of the German and northern Italian regions, he destroyed the Roman law basis of imperial legitimacy as well.[100]

> The German and Italian kingdoms are distinct states from the Roman Empire properly so called, and the Emperor, in so far as he is Emperor, rules neither Germany nor the Lombard Kingdom. It follows that those who maintain that Germany is bound by

> the laws of Justinian, and who claim that the Emperor exercises the same power over Germany as the ancient emperors exercised over the Roman Empire or that the Emperor rules Germany in his capacity as Emperor, suffer from serious delusions.[101]

'Our Emperor,' Conring concluded in *Discursus novus,* 'has no power whatsoever over any independent state, and by virtue of its autonomy even a small independent state as, for example the Republic of Ragusa, enjoys exactly the same rights of sovereignty as a large one.' Since German 'dignity and right of precedence stemmed not from the imperial title,' he wrote, 'the right of the German Kingdom will clearly remain intact even if you abolish the imperial title totally'.[102] The legal and political fallout from this doctrinal explosion fell slowly as it had after Valla's *De falso.* Nevertheless, the foundational myth of the Holy Roman Empire and the Imperial Majesty were undone. It was this that opened the door and formed the prelude to the important rationalization of native German law, which, although interrupted by Napoleon's imposition of French law on German soil, was revived by the historical school in the nineteenth century.

After *Discursus novus,* Conring's political writings were explicitly focused on defining and delineating the political values of the *respublica.* He directed several dissertations on the subject, including G. Pooch's *Disputatio politica de rebus publicis in genere* (1639), E. Nissen's *Disputatio politica de rebus publicis in genere* (1651), J. E. Busch's *De politia sive republica in specie sic dicta* (1652) and O. J. von Osten's *Disputatio politica de republica in communi* (1653).[103] His own *Dissertatio de ratione status* (1651) also opposed Bodin's theory of indivisible sovereignty and could not have been more opposed to Hobbes's *Leviathan,* which appeared in the same year.[104]

It is in *Dissertatio de boni consiliarii in republica munere* (1652), however, where one may detect an evolution of the traditional German identification of sovereignty with jurisdiction. Here, Conring examined how laws *(Gesetze),* government *(Obrigkeit)* and citizenship *(Bürgerschaft)* should function in a polity, in which the aim above all else should be to secure the common good. The form of law, he argued, should agree with the needs of states, and law should hold a mediating position within states. Sovereign authorities *(Herrschende),* he wrote, were not to rule as demigods, but also should be limited by law. Finally, he emphasized the need for citizens to be knowledgeable about the impartial laws of the state, the aim of which was to create harmony between the groups in society. This, he believed, was the basis of a stable and rational state. Citing Florus, Seneca and Aristotle, Conring also emphasized the importance of a virtuous citizenry as the guard against corruption and the need of these citizens to vigilantly guard against intimidation of their social body and usurpation of government authority.[105]

The radical politics of Conring's writings cannot be emphasized enough. Horst Dreitzel, who views Conring as *'ein deutscher Machiavelli',* has emphasized his preference for a mixed constitutional monarchy.[106] Closer to the age, Samuel Pufendorf (1632–1694) regarded Conring as more radical, theoretical and better informed about politics than most in his generation.[107] The ideas of key political thinkers, including Baruch Spinoza, Pufendorf, Gottlieb Samuel Treuer and Ulrich Huber, were in some way indebted to Conring's work.[108] Certainly, through at least Pufendorf, Conring's political thought was bequeathed to the nineteenth-century generation of German legal scholars. Finally, the most important point of this section has been to identify the critical political rupture that resulted from the appearance of *Discursus novus.* There was no longer a legitimate legal basis for imperial absolutism in German-speaking Europe after Conring showed the myth of Roman imperium to be little more than a 'delusion' in his words. *Discursus novus* proved to be the important finding that allowed for the development of the enlightened legal reforms that were already underway, in the German lands, just prior to the French Revolution.

Prelude to Modern Constitutional Transformation

The constitutional crisis of the 1760s formed the immediate prelude to modern German constitutional transformation, and it was in this context that the German identification of sovereignty with jurisdiction began to take on modern form. By the middle of the eighteenth century, a collection of documents was recognized by contemporaries as compromising the constitutional basis of the Empire. The Golden Bull of 1356 was seen as the founding constitutional document. It confirmed and amplified the arrangements set forth in the Declaration of Rehnse of 1338, which firmly established the office of the emperor as an elective one and designated the electors. The second major document was the *Landfriede* of 1495, which, as Johann Jakob Moser wrote, had replaced *Faustrecht* (right of private warfare) and was 'an agreement and law *(Vertrag und Gesetz)* between the emperor and the imperial Estates that nobody in the German Empire shall use force against the other, but rather the course of law'.[109] The year 1495 also witnessed the Reception of Roman Law in the form of the *corpus iuris civilis* and the establishment of the imperial appellate jurisdiction of the *Reichskammergericht* mentioned earlier. In addition to these measures, the Peace of Augsburg of 1555 allowed princes to select Lutheranism or Catholicism for their realms and reaffirmed their autonomy in the states. It was accompanied by the Execution Ordinance, which also formed a part of the basic law of the Empire. Procedural ordinances, electoral capitulations and finally, the Peace of Westphalia of 1648, from which derived the *Landeshoheit* (state autonomy), were seen as the final measures of imperial basic law.[110] It is important to keep in mind that no one single document was understood to stand alone as a basic law. Rather the imperial constitutional outlook subscribed to the idea that the constitution had come into being through successive agreements over time and was comprised of many legal measures.

The event that tested the constitutional basis of the Empire was the Württemberg tax revolt of the 1760s. It was this revolt that produced the two German iconic defenders of constitutionalism, Johann Jakob Moser and Johann Ludwig Huber. Moser's writings on public law were the most influential of the period, and Huber's poetry continued to capture the liberal imagination well into the nineteenth century. The Württemberg tax revolt inaugurated in German-speaking Europe the modern legal orientation of political ideology and demands for political reformation.

The indivisibility of Württemberg under the protection of the emperor was reaffirmed in 1495. So long as they were not in violation of the basic laws of the Empire, legal arrangements were left to the duchies. For purposes of maintaining the peace, contracts between dukes and their estates also found protection under the imperial basic laws. The estates in Württemberg were represented by an assembly called the *Landtag,* and in the absence of a local nobility was dominated by an elite group of families known as the *Ehrbarkeit* or worthies. Duchy constitutions also were not derived from a single document, but were contracts that had developed over time. The strength of the worthies had resulted from the emergence of the money economy and the increasing inability of dukes to live off their own private resources *(Kammergut).* In return for granting taxes and taking over ducal debt, the estates were able to secure important powers in the governance of the duchy, which were guaranteed by charters and actionable in imperial appellate courts. The most important of these for Württemberg was the *Tübinger Vertrag* of 8 July 1514. In the nineteenth century, the liberal poet Ludwig Uhland praised it as Württemberg's *Magna Charta.* In exchange for taking over princely debt, the estates had extracted it from Duke Ulrich in 1514. In each instance of a takeover of princely debt thereafter, the estates consistently extracted concessions in the form of written contracts. The power of the purse and *Landtag* approval of all taxes were the most important powers secured to the estates.

Thus, from the sixteenth century, unless the dukes of Württemberg were able to maintain economic independence, they found their powers significantly restrained by what was called the 'gold old law'. No such independence was forthcoming. Additional agreements also limited ducal access to independent income and, accordingly, limited his unchecked authority in the realm. While Church lands were confiscated under the legal reformation of 1534, the *Landtag* was able to extract a series of church ordinances from the duke in the 1550s. Accordingly, after the deduction of any running costs, all other profits from these lands had to be placed in a *Kirchenkasten* (fund for churches) and could only be used for designated pious purposes. What is more, under the 'gold old law' the estates possessed the sole right to levy taxes against the subjects of the realm. This occurred through the levying of a direct tax. In the emergency climate of the Thirty Years War (1618–1648), a new indirect tax called the *Accise* was introduced. This, however, also remained under the strict authority of the estates and was deposited into their own treasury, the *Landschaftliche Einnehmerei.* From this they made only a voluntary contribution *(Kammerbeitrag)* to the duke. In order the meet the defence demands during the French Wars of Religion, in 1681 the estates introduced an additional direct tax called the *Extraordinari,* but again this was paid only through the *Einnehmerei* into the ducal war treasury *(Kriegskasse).* Obviously, this system worked to the significant advantage of the power of the estates vis-à-vis the duke by serving to keep him financially dependent. The 'gold old law' in Württemberg, as Peter Wilson writes, was a miniature version of a system of checks and balances. Indeed, the living example of Christoph Besold's mixed constitution was Württemberg.[111]

Duke Carl Eugen was only nine when his would-be absolutist father, Carl Alexander, died. There were some immediate struggles for power in 1737, but ultimately the worthies were able to obtain controlling interest. Under the regency that ensued from 1737–1744, the power of the Estates' Committee increased significantly vis-à-vis ducal authority. Prelates sat in the *Landtag* along with delegates elected by local assemblies from the towns and counties. In place of regular *Landtag* assemblies, a committee system emerged composed of two bodies, the *großer Ausschuß* (large committee) and the *engerer Ausschuß* (standing committee). In 1739 a full meeting of the *Landtag* was summoned for the express purpose of crushing the remnants of Alexander's reign, and it resulted in the Compromise of 1739.[112] By the first years of Carl Eugen's adult reign, the War of Austrian Succession (1740–1748) raged around Württemberg and, from the beginning, he tried to circumvent the binding legal proscriptions on conscription and tried to increase the size of the army.

In 1756, when the Seven Years' War erupted, which proved the ruin of French coffers, Moser was already urging that action be taken against the growing authoritarianism of the Duke. For his resistance to ducal authoritarianism, Carl Eugen had the 58-year-old Moser arrested. Without benefit of a trial, he was locked away in severe isolation and confined to one room, in the remote mountaintop castle of Hohentwiel. Even the windows of the neighbouring building, facing his room, were boarded up.[113] He was kept there for four years and denied any items that might allow him to communicate with the outside world. The Duke took brutal measures to meet his contractual infantry and dragoon headcount for the French cause. 'Able bodied men', as Helen Liebel-Weckowicz writes, 'were seized in their beds at night and at church on Sundays.' It was not long before mutinies became a feature of the war, and hostility to the draft was a source of unrest and discontent.[114] There was also the matter of his illegal imposition of direct taxes and seizure of the *Einnehmerei,* which went more to fill the pockets of court performers than to military expenditures.[115]

Although Carl Eugen attempted to secure independent income through foreign subsidies, his options dried up quickly, in 1763, when the French lost the Seven Years' War. After a number of schemes failed to alleviate his worsening financial crisis, Eugen imposed a new system of military taxation. His new military plan of 1763 set taxes at 3.5 times the 1739 level, and, in political perspective, threatened to nullify the need for the estates' committees to meet biannually. The estates responded by demanding that the Duke convoke the Württemberg *Landtag* to have the new measures approved. When the *Landtag* met in September 1763, members declined to support the new taxes. Eugen appealed his position to the *Amtsversammlungen* directly, but only to be rebuffed again. In an effort to shore up popular support for its resistance to the new tax scheme, the Estates' Committee began championing the causes of popular complaints and publishing its own correspondence to prove that it had resisted ducal authoritarian policies during the war. Popular tax strikes broke out and imprisoned figures like Moser and Johann Huber were celebrated for their resistance. When Carl Eugen tried to crush the strike by stationing troops in Tübingen, the Estates' Committee filed a formal complaint with the Imperial *Reichshofrat* in 1764. It was at this point that the Württemberg tax revolt became the subject of international attention, as ambassadors from England, Prussia and Denmark arrived in Stuttgart.[116]

The first blow to Duke Eugen came in September 1764. The *Reichshofrat* handed down its first decision, not only ordering Moser's release from Hohentwiel, but an immediate end to the illegal military taxes. In the face of international pressure exerted on behalf of the estates, a second crippling verdict of 15 May 1765 ordered that the estates were obliged to pay taxes only as set forth under the Compromise of 1739. From these, they were also permitted to deduct a significant portion of the illegal direct taxes that had been levied during the Seven Years' War. In addition, the *Reichshofrat* ordered the Duke to cease all unconstitutional activity. By 1770 when the emperor appeared as the guarantor of the estates' liberties, Carl Eugen had little choice but to sign the *Erbvergleich* (Hereditary Settlement) on 1 January 1770.[117]

The Württemberg tax revolt left an important paradigmatic legacy that influenced the transformationist-minded liberals of the nineteenth century. Liebel-Weckowicz draws the important conclusion that it 'was a first breakthrough to the modern right of parliament not only to control the appropriations of taxes but to oversee the management of the state budget'. 'The first steps towards a modern viable form of parliamentary government,' as she writes, 'had already been taken by 1780' and well before the French Revolution.[118] 'The *Erbvergleich*', as Wilson points out, 'was the classic example of the system of checks and balances' that had become anchored in the Reich constitution. For this reason, Carl Eugen and the dukes that followed 'showed signs of losing interest in maintaining the Reich' after 1770.[119] The securing of guaranteed rights through a series of gradually obtained legal measures, which were actionable in the courts of the Empire, would offer a strong example to nineteenth-century transformationists that successful political and constitutional transformation could be obtained through legal means.

Adding to this, Wolfgang Burgdorf's lengthy study points out that contrary to most opinions that there was no constitutional reform impulse in Central Europe prior to the French Revolution, in fact, 'from 1640 to the end of the Reich in 1806 a constant public debate about reforming the Empire took place'.[120] He offers a thorough analysis of the key writings of reform-oriented political thinkers from the period.

The most important treatise to appear between 1796 and 1798 was the anonymously published three volumes of *Kritik der Deutschen Reichsverfassung* (1796–1798). It was explicitly national and called for the formation of a 'republican constitution' for Germany, with the repertoire of modern rights and liberties. It also argued that the Reich had already undergone some process of transformation. '*Deutschland* is not a monarchical state', the anonymous author wrote, but 'a representative *Pantokratie* of the individual united German states'. The work also reflected the emerging view that both German unification and constitutional reformation could be obtained through *'gesetzliche Verbindung'*.[121] For Burgdorf, these years represent a *'Vorweg'*, and he concludes that the beginning of the 'liberal democratic constitutional tradition in Germany is not in the constitutional document of 1849', but rather 'the state reform discussions of the last third of the eighteenth century'.[122]

Although clearly it was evolved over time, German political thought continued to be organized around law, and the identification of sovereignty with jurisdiction continued to serve as the basis of German conceptions of self-governance. We have also seen that, while German communities were open to the use of more advanced technical elements from external legal sources, such as Roman law, they were extremely resistant to any introduction of actual legal rules and provisions from foreign sources. Loyalty to popes, bishops, emperors and princes, alike, was conditioned on their respect for local legal customs and practices. This characteristic of German political identity also emphasized both the need for all members of society to adhere to the rules of law so long as they had been established on a legitimate basis. In addition, the strength of the dual conception of law as the best means to political reformation and repeated emphasis on the preference for the legal resolution of conflicts would distinguish German sociopolitical individualism from other European cultures. There was considerable truth in Machiavelli's observation that Germans observed 'their laws in such a manner that no one from within or without could venture upon an attempt to master them', as we have seen.[123] This was a lesson that Napoleon would learn the hard way when he ventured to impose his codes on German soil in the early nineteenth century. Nothing, as we will see in the next chapter, did more to foment resistance to French rule and the bitter feelings of Germans for a century than this fatal mistake. It was also the bitter memory of this legal humiliation that fed the determined drive to rationalize German law in the nineteenth century and which served as the backdrop to Friedrich Karl von Savigny's theory of politics and legislation, discussed in the next chapter.

Notes

1. N. Machiavelli, *Discourses*, in *The Prince and The Discourses,* Max Lerner (ed.) (1950), p. 253.
2. Machiavelli, *Discourses,* pp. 253–4.

3. N. Machiavelli, *The History of Florence* (1525), in *Machiavelli: The Chief Works and Others,* Allan Gilbert (trans.) (1989), vol. 3, p. 1148.
4. For a traditional synthesis of republicanism see John Pocock, *The Machiavellian Moment: Florentine Political Thought and the Atlantic Republican Tradition* (1975); B. Worden, 'English Republicanism', in J. H. Burns (ed.), *The Cambridge History of Political Thought 1450–1700* (1991); and Markku Peltonen, *Classical Humanism and Republicanism in English Political Thought 1570–1640* (1995). For recent works calling for greater consideration of republicanism in continental Europe, see Martin van Gelderen and Quentin Skinner (eds), *Republicanism: A Shared European Heritage* (2002).
5. Quentin Skinner, 'Machiavelli's *Discorsi* and the Pre-humanist Origins of Republican Ideas', in Gisela Bock, Quentin Skinner and Maurizio Viroli (eds), *Machiavelli and Republicanism* (1990), pp. 121–41.
6. Ibid., p. 122.
7. Heinz Schilling, *Religion, Political Culture and the Emergence of Early Modern Society: Essays in German and Dutch History* (1992), p. 50.
8. David Bachrach, 'Making Peace and War in the "City-state" of Worms, 1235–1273', *German History,* 24/4 (2006), pp. 505–25.
9. Jacques Le Goff, *The Birth of Europe* (2005), pp. 21–3.
10. Ibid., pp. 33–4.
11. Edward Jenks, *Law and Politics of the Middle Ages* (1897), p. 9.
12. Bachrach, 'Making Peace and War', p. 520.
13. Peter Blickle, *From the Communal Reformation to the Revolution of the Common Man,* Beat Kümin (trans.) (1998), p. 3.
14. Le Goff, *Birth of Europe,* p. 97
15. B. J. McManus, 'The Ecclesiology of Laurentium Hispanus (c. 1180–1248) and His Contribution to the Romanization of Canon Law Jurisprudence', PhD thesis, Syracuse University, Syracuse (1991), pp. 50–74, cited in Peter Clarke, 'The Interdict and Popular Resistance', in Frances Andrews, Christoph Egger and C. Rousseau (eds), *Pope, Church and City* (2004), p. 90.
16. R. H. Hemholz, *The Spirit of Classical Canon Law* (1996).
17. Ibid., p. 342.
18. Ibid., p. 341.
19. Ibid., p. 36.
20. Ibid., pp. 37–46.
21. Ibid., p. 48.
22. Ibid.
23. Simeon Guterman, *The Principle of Personality of the Law in the Germanic Kingdoms of Western Europe from the Fifth to the Eleventh Century* (1988), p. 137.
24. Hemholz, *Spirit of Classical Canon Law,* pp. 194–8.
25. Ibid., p. 370.

26. Ibid., p. 361.
27. Ibid., p. 145.
28. Harold J. Berman, *Law and Revolution: The Formation of the Western Legal Tradition* (1983), pp. 484–5.
29. Ernst Schubert, *Königsabsetzung im deutschen Mittelalter: Eine Studie zum Werden der Reichsverfassung* (2005).
30. See generally Isabel Alfonso, Hugh Kennedy and Julio Escalona (eds), *Building Legitimacy: Political Discourse and Forms of Legitimacy in Medieval Societies* (2004).
31. Berman, *Law and Revolution,* p. 492.
32. Ibid., pp. 489–92.
33. Le Goff, *Birth of Europe,* p. 102.
34. Berman, *Law and Revolution,* p. 382.
35. Gerd Schwerhoff, 'Die goldene Freiheit der Bürger in Köln', in Klaus Schreiner and Ulrich Meier (eds), *Stadtregiment und Bürgerfreiheit: Handlungsspielräume in deutschen und italienischen Städten des späten Mittelalters und in der frühen Neuzeit*, vol. 7 (1999), p. 91.
36. Ibid., pp. 84–119.
37. Berman, *Law and Revolution,* p. 373.
38. Ibid., pp. 375–6.
39. Ibid., p. 387.
40. Ibid., p. 388.
41. Ibid., p. 376.
42. Ibid., pp. 376–80.
43. Ernst Pitz, *Bürgereinung und Städteeinung: Studien zur Verfassungsgeschichte der Hansestädte und der deutschen Hanse* (2001).
44. Quentin Skinner, 'The Medieval Inheritance', in Charles Schmitt, Quentin Skinner, Eckhard Kessler and Jill Kraye (eds), *The Cambridge History of Renaissance Philosophy* (1988), p. 389.
45. Ibid., p. 391.
46. Ibid., p. 392.
47. Ibid., p. 393.
48. Azo, *Lectura super codicem,* cited in ibid.
49. Ibid.
50. Ibid., p. 394.
51. D. Johnston, 'The General Influence of Roman Institutions of State and Public Law', in D. Miller and R. Zimmerman (eds), *The Civilian Tradition and Scots Law: Aberdeen Quincentenary Essays* (1997), p. 95.
52. Marsilius of Padua, *Defensor pacis,* part 3, chapter 2, in O. Thatcher and E. McNeal (eds), *Source Book for Medieval History* (1905), pp. 317–24.
53. John Witte, *Law and Protestantism: The Legal Teachings of the Lutheran Reformation* (2002), pp. 40–1.

54. Skinner, 'Medieval Inheritance', p. 395.
55. Julius Kirshner, 'Civitas Sibi Faciat Civem: Bartolus of Sassoferrato's Doctrine on the Making of a Citizen', *Speculum,* 48/4 (1973), pp. 696, 699–700.
56. Charles Homer Haskins, *The Renaissance of the Twelfth Century* (1927).
57. Skinner, 'Machiavelli's *Discorsi*'; and Charles Nauert, *Humanism and the Culture of Renaissance Europe* (1995). Nauert argues that the earliest reception of classical humanism in transalpine Europe was in Nürnberg.
58. Ibid.
59. See Heinrich Applet, 'Frederick Barbarossa und das römische Recht', *Römische historische Mitteilungen,* 5 (1961/62), pp. 18–34, cited in Berman, *Law and Revolution,* p. 491.
60. Schwerhoff, 'Die goldene Freiheit', p. 96.
61. Compare Phillippe Dollinger, *The German Hansa* (1999), pp. 260–2; and Pitz, *Bürgereinung.*
62. Yves Renouard, *The Avignon Papacy 1305–1403* (1970), pp. 90–1 and 114.
63. Aristotle, *Politics,* bk. I, 2.3.
64. Dollinger, *German Hansa,* p. 272.
65. Robert von Freiburg, 'Civic Humanism and Republican Citizenship in Early Modern Germany', in van Gelderen and Skinner (eds), *Republicanism,* vol. 1 (2002), p. 132.
66. Ibid., pp. 131–2.
67. Ibid., p. 133.
68. Ibid., p. 135.
69. Witte, *Law and Protestantism,* p. 33.
70. Ibid., pp. 43–6.
71. Ibid., pp. 47–9.
72. Freiburg, 'Civic Humanism and Republican Citizenship', pp. 136–7.
73. Ibid., p. 137.
74. Ibid.
75. Ibid., pp. 138–40.
76. Ibid., p. 139.
77. Berman, *Law and Revolution,* p. 267.
78. Witte, *Law and Protestantism,* p. 23.
79. Ibid., p. 54.
80. Ibid., pp. 140 and 142.
81. Ibid., pp. 142–6.
82. Ibid., pp. 154–68.
83. Martin van Gelderen, 'Aristotelians, Monarchomachs and Republicans: Sovereignty and *respublica mixta* in Dutch and German Political Thought, 1580–1650', in van Gelderen and Skinner (eds), *Republicanism,* vol. 1 (2002), p. 203.
84. Ibid.

85. Ibid.
86. Ibid., p. 204.
87. Ibid., p. 205.
88. Ibid.
89. Cited in ibid., p. 206
90. Cited in ibid., pp. 206–7.
91. Ibid., p. 207.
92. Cited in ibid.
93. Ibid., p. 211.
94. Ibid.
95. Cited in ibid., p. 212.
96. Cited in ibid.
97. For more on Roman law see Peter Stern, *Roman Law in European History* (1999).
98. Michael Stolleis (ed.), *Hermann Conring: Beiträge zu Leben und Werk* (1983), and Albrecht von Arnswaldt, *De Vicariatus controversia: Beiträge Hermann Conrings in der Diskussion um die Reichsverfassung des 17. Jahrhunderts* (2004). For a recent English translation see *Hermann Conring's New Discourse of the Roman-German Emperor,* Constantin Fasolt (trans.) (2005).
99. Michael Stolleis, 'Die Einheit der Wissenschaft', in Stolleis (ed.), *Hermann Conring,* p. 17.
100. *Hermann Conring's New Discourse,* p. 63.
101. Ibid.
102. Ibid., p. 81.
103. Constantin Fasolt, 'Introduction', in ibid., p. xxv, fn. 20.
104. Michael Stolleis, 'Machiavellismus und Staatsräson', in Stolleis (ed.), *Hermann Conring,* pp. 177, 180 and 194–5.
105. Ibid., p. 177.
106. Horst Dreitzel, 'Hermann Conring und die politische Wissenschaft seiner Zeit', in Stolleis (ed.), *Hermann Conring,* pp. 135–72.
107. Fasolt, 'Introduction', p. ix.
108. Hans Bödeker, 'Debating the *respublica mixta*: German and Dutch Political Discourses around 1700', in van Gelderen and Skinner (eds), *Republicanism,* pp. 219–46.
109. Johann Jakob Moser, *Teutsches Staats-Recht* (1737–1757), vol. 1, p. 105, cited in Mack Walker, *Johann Jakob Moser and the Holy Roman Empire of the German Nation* (1981), p. 146.
110. Walker, *Johann Jakob Moser,* pp. 145–9.
111. Peter Wilson, *War, State and Society in Württemberg, 1677–1793* (1995), p. 54 and, for the last two paragraphs, pp. 46–54.
112. Ibid., pp. 184–98.
113. Walker, *Johann Jakob Moser,* pp. 237–45.

114. Helen Liebel-Weckowicz, 'The Revolt of the Württemberg Estates, 1764–1770', in Canadian Society for Eighteenth-Century Studies, *Man and Nature: Proceedings of the Canadian Society for Eighteenth-Century Studies,* vol. 2 (1982), p. 111.
115. Ibid., pp. 113–14.
116. Wilson, *War, State and Society,* pp. 228–31.
117. Ibid., pp. 231–4.
118. Liebel-Weckowitz, 'Revolt', pp. 117–18.
119. Wilson, *War, State and Society,* p. 239.
120. Wolfgang Burgdorf, *Reichskonstitution und Nation: Verfassungsreformprojekte für das Heilige Römische Reich Deutscher Nation im politischen Schrifttum von 1648 bis 1806,* (1998), p. 1.
121. Ibid., pp. 478–98.
122. Ibid., p. 512.
123. Machiavelli, *Discourses,* p. 253.

–2–

Toward a German Nation

Friedrich Karl von Savigny and the Growth of Legal Politics

> Now at a time when the old forms are threatened with general destruction, it is more necessary than ever for us to search, independently from the current positive norms and conventional views, for a standpoint that comes from within us. Look at Paris, from whence the rule of philosophy was supposed to emerge! Take notice of the most flagrant acts of injustice and see for yourself that the Revolution created only the opportunity for reform. Reform itself must proceed from the inner sanctuary of the spirit of the people. The people of Paris have remained caught up in the events and we must all struggle to rise above these. And when the spirit of these violent revolutions die down, as I hope and I pray, this higher standpoint will be no less necessary as we ourselves nurture and refine our own customs and bring about tranquil reformation without the high costs of blood, which is slower but safer and more certain.[1]
>
> —Friedrich Karl von Savigny, 1798

As a method of political revision, the French experiment looked like a dodgy proposition to many by 1798, when the 19-year-old Friedrich Karl von Savigny (1779–1861) wrote to his guardian Constantin von Neurath. While the Tennis Court Oath of 1789 had led to the creation of a constitutional monarchy, the Constitution of October 1791 ranks as one of the shortest-lived in history. During the eleven months of its existence, the Legislative Assembly's most notable act was to issue a declaration of war against Austria on 20 April 1792. When the war turned sour, a Jacobin-dominated rump session of the assembly abolished the monarchy altogether and installed the government of the National Convention. While we must credit the Convention for ending the enslavement of Africans in France and its territories and for instituting racial equality, this was also an era of violent political factionalism. On 21 January 1793, the guillotine's blade fell on the former king's neck and, with the fresh blood still dripping, Louis's head was held up for public viewing. His queen, Marie Antoinette, who was also the Austrian emperor's sister, met the same fate in October. Some forty thousand people were executed during the Reign of Terror that continued to 1794, only to be followed by the White Terror. By 1795, there was yet another new constitution and new government of the National Directory. While it enjoyed a comparatively long life of four years, Napoleon Bonaparte's coup of 1799 established the Consulate and soon led to his dictatorship in 1804. In a span of fifteen years, France had undergone five significant political ruptures, and, if we count the slave revolution in Saint Domingue, six. It is no wonder that many contemporaries spoke not of a revolution, but revolutions.

If the goal of the original revolution was to establish a durable, representative republic, from the vantage point of 1798, the French attempt at liberty was an utter failure. Many Frenchmen were worthy of the consternation Montesquieu had once issued against English revolutionaries. God resting his soul by then, it was now his countrymen who offered up to Europe 'a very droll spectacle' and who would soon be obliged to take 'recourse to the very government they had so wantonly proscribed'.[2] Even radicals like Georg Friedrich Rebmann felt that 'no rational German will wish for a revolution in Germany, for its aim—the restoration of the suppressed rights of man—can be achieved by less violent means'.[3] True revolutions should evolve as 'the consequences of the operation of moral laws'.[4]

Observing events anxiously from the University of Marburg in 1798, it is not surprising that Savigny also echoed a few words of reservation about the French path to liberty. Of course there were exceptions, but many Germans who supported political revision, including Savigny, turned away from the French experiment as it grew more and more violent. Like many others who knew of the Terror and who experienced the revolutionary wars, Savigny rejected any reliance on violent means, because he feared that people would remain caught up in events even as human blood spilled into the streets. He expressed this sentiment clearly in his private letter to Neurath, which opens this chapter. Savigny believed that a nonviolent path to political revision was not only possible, but plausible. A nonviolent course was slower, as he wrote, but more certain to secure a durable representative system of government based on limited participation.

The original title for Savingy's famous *Vom Beruf unserer Zeit für Gesetzgebung und Rechtswissenschaft* (1814) was *Politik und neuere Legislationen,* and it offers an important indication of the continuing organization of political thought around juridical precepts. As I argue here, Savigny's theory of politics and modern legislation expressed a pragmatic approach to German political revision, and it is in his writings that we begin to discern the development of an ideology of constitutional transformation. His approach to political revision was shaped by the traditional German identification of sovereignty with jurisdiction and the duality of law tradition in German-speaking Europe. In his letter to Neurath, Savigny early began to identify a path for constitutional transformation in a wholeheartedly traditional way, which emphasized that Germans should nurture and refine their own customs to bring about tranquil reformation.[5] This idea also reflected growing recognition of national self-determination as a vital part in the development of a representative polity, a view that was strengthened by the experience of the imposition of *les cinq codes* on German societies. It also housed a radical reaction against the modern despotism, which had denied Germans the right to self-determination. His theory of politics and modern legislation called for the rationalization and scientization of German laws to meet the needs of what, in his time, would be a national rather than municipal project. It was an ambitious programme designed to achieve, not only political revision, but national unification. In this way, he began to formulate one of the first political theories of nonviolent constitutional transformation.

Historiography on Savigny

When Savigny died at the age of eighty-three on 25 October 1861, Adolfus Rudorff wrote a lengthy memorial article in the second edition of the newly founded *Zeitschrift für Rechtswissenschaft.* In it he described Savigny as a patriotic nationalist, whose work laid the critical foundation for the next phase of Germany's future.[6] In no small measure, however, the idea of German misdevelopment had its origins in Germany's pre-First World War domestic conflicts between traditional liberals and political forces on the Left—a conflict that was internationalized in the 1930s. In this environment, Savigny's legacy was politicized and attacked by legal professors who supported the political aims of socialism. Despite earlier opinion, members of the *Freirechtsbewegung* (Free Law Movement) in Germany set out to discredit Savigny's legacy and to undermine the position of the historical school of law altogether.

Hermann Kantorowicz's essay, *Der Kampf um die Rechtswissenschaft* (1906), published under the politically charged pen-name Gnaeus Flavius, was the movement's founding manifesto, and it reacted against the bourgeois consolidation of law in the late years of the nineteenth century.[7] The original title, *Der Befreiungskampf der Rechtswissenschaft (The Battle of Liberation for Legal Science)* captures more of the movement's political radicalism. Stimulated by an idealized appreciation of the ability of English courts to consider social conditions in the administration of justice, the *Freirechtsbewegung* reacted against textual positivism and the conceptual jurisprudence that they believed restricted the judge's ability to create law. Against this it maintained that 'the judge was entitled, indeed bound, to disapply a statute in any case where to apply it seemed to him unjust or inappropriate'.[8] Arguably, it marked the rise of a conceptual thinking that led to a serious destabilization of the rule of law in Germany after the First World War.[9] 'The idea of departing from the strict language of statute and looking instead to values (which were likely to be subjectively and unpredictably appraised)' was exploited for 'sinister extremes' by those sympathetic to Nazism.[10]

The *Freirechtsbewegung* was part of an effort to build a sustainable legal foundation capable of meeting the political demands of socialism. Kantorowicz joined the Social Democratic Party when he was a student at the University of Berlin. Although he resigned his affiliation in 1904, he wrote to his closest friend, Gustav Radbruch (1878–1949), that he 'retained a platonic love of Socialism'.[11] There was a consistent critique of the Savigny on the German Left, which could be traced from Hegel, through Gans, Marx and Heine down to Kantorowicz and Radbruch. On the fiftieth anniversary of Savigny's death in 1911, Kantorowicz published his *Was ist uns Savigny?,* a rhetorical question which he consistently answered with negative interpretations. It was here that Savigny's legacy was first scrapped up. In an additional pamphlet published the same year, Kantorowicz sought to undermine the place of the historical school altogether, charging that it was bound up with capitalist materialism and *Germanistik.*[12] Kantorowicz was also a founding member of the German Sociological Association with Max Weber in 1909. Marked by a polemical literature of scepticism, the *Rechtssoziologie* (legal sociology) Kantorowicz subscribed to pointed toward English institutions as examples that should be studied and imitated.[13]

In an effort to relieve Germany of the burdens of war guilt, in 1923 the Weimar government commissioned him to research the causes of the First World War in the hopes that he would exculpate Germany. The plan collapsed, however, when Social Democrats abandoned the ruling coalition to protest Gustav Stresemann's failure to deal firmly with the culprits of the Beer Hall Putsch of 9 November 1923. As soon as it became clear that Kantorowicz's findings would, now, only confirm the victor's view of German war guilt, the government suppressed the findings. Nevertheless, his *Der Geist der Englischen Politik und das Gespenst der Einkreisung Deutschlands* (1929) made his position clear. Guilt for the war, Kantorowicz charged, rested squarely with 'those scourges', the ex-Kaiser, Bülow and Tirpitz.[14] 'It is against Germany's greatest sons, therefore, and against her deepest convictions, that we must now do unequal battle,' he wrote before launching into what may be described as a trashing of the Germans and the whole of their history.[15] The Germans had failed, from time immemorial, to measure up to their English cousins in chivalry, objectivity, humanitarianism and a host of virtues.[16]

It should come as no surprise that the cover to his *Dictatorships: A Sociological Study,* published in 1935, read: 'Formerly Professor of Law at the University of Kiel'. Like Hannah Arendt's *The Origins of Totalitarianism* (1951), the term 'dictatorship' emerged as a pseudonym for 'Hitlerism' and the *'Führerprinzip'.*[17] Writing from Cambridge University by 1937, his work was marked by bitter indignation: 'As to Germany—and I wish to make it clear from the outset, that in referring to Germany, I am referring to the period before 1933.'[18] Although justifiably gnashing his teeth and angry about the rise of Nazism and the appropriation of the free law concept for unintended political ends, Kantorowicz wrote with venom, specifically, to machete what was left of Savigny's legacy.[19] From this point onward, a parallel historiography began to grow that located the centre of German misdevelopment in the nation's legal history. An important foundation was laid by Kantorowicz for the historical profession's reception of Krieger's *The German Idea of Freedom* (1957). In his 1967 study on the legal history of German private law, Franz Wieacker described Savigny as a conservative member of the 'social elite of the Old Empire'.[20] Hans Hattenhauer condemned him as an ally of conservative forces and remained suspicious of

Savigny's political views.[21] According to Hans Wrobel, Savigny's ideals were the 'legal expression of those feudal forces working for the preservation and restoration of the old system'.[22]

The 1980s saw some thawing of this sharply negative interpretation of Savigny and the historical school of law. The legal historian, Joachim Rückert, brought Savigny's ties to German romanticism into focus, and, the historian James Whitman suggested that his scholarship marked a revival of Melanchthonian humanism.[23] Michael John acknowledged the closeness of Savigny's views to those of the reforming minister, Freiherr vom Stein, and suggested that he could not be 'termed a reactionary' however much 'his ideas may have been partially appropriated by reactionary interest'.[24] Yet, John still placed Savigny in the camp with those who, like Stein and Karl August von Hardenberg, sought bureaucratic revolution from above. Thus, despite the thaw, it continues to be argued that Prussian officials 'were increasingly influenced by the conservative ideas of Savigny's historical school of law in the decade after 1807'.[25] Even David Blackbourn suggested that aristocratic hostility to reform received support 'from a growing body of conservative intellectuals like Friedrich Julius Stahl and Friedrich Karl von Savigny'.[26] Most recently, Roger Berkowitz has charged Savigny with having separated law from justice, which led unintentionally to the 'amoral social-scientific positivism of the BGB'.[27] Accordingly, he concludes that 'it was no accident that while the Nazi jurists of the 1930s criticized the BGB for its abstraction and value neutrality, they nevertheless found the Code malleable to their own purposes'.[28]

In reality, the historical school was bound up with bourgeois interests from its inception, as Kantorowicz charged. Savigny's influence on the direction of German legal and constitutional development cannot be emphasized enough, and Kantorowicz's preoccupation with destroying his legacy offers a clear indication of this. At the same time, because Savigny's legacy was politicized and shredded during the hyperpolitical conflicts following the First World War, in particular, his place in German history requires significant reconsideration. As a result, this chapter is the longest of the book and makes an effort to condense Savigny's politics and his influence into a chapter setting.

It is suggested here that Savigny borrowed from the larger European constitutional tradition and contributed to its progress. From the publication of his *Politik und neuere Legislationen,* which forms the material sources for *Vom Beruf,* we are offered a sense of breadth of thinking that influenced the growth of his own theory of politics and modern legislation. Some forty names appear on his *Notanda Liste:* 'Christian [Brentano], Thibaut, Rehberg, Machiavelli, Ernst, Filangieri, Montesquieu, Leibniz, Jacobi, Lessing, Möser, Hugo, Hobbes, Herder, Sismondi, Müller, Klein, Wendt, Blackstone, Gazert, Schlosser, Hagemeister, Haller, Bacon, Aristotle (Schlosser), Leonhardi, Vico, Friedrich Schlegel, Linguet, Hume, Home, A. Smith, Garve, Cicero, Schleiermacher, Goethe, Hofakker, Burke and Meuer'.[29] As we reevaluate Savigny's place in German political history here, it will be useful to broaden our scope and consider not only his life and times, but the medley of legal thought and its politics that influenced him.

Finally, this chapter challenges the received interpretation of Savigny's place in German legal and political historiography, which, despite some revision, continues to be tainted by notions of German misdevelopment. As discussed in the last chapter, political thought for as far back as the Papal Revolution had been organized around juridical concepts and reflected a dual conception of law, which expressed the idea that law could also be used as a means to political revision. Savigny's theory of politics and modern legislation was an expression of traditional German values. His insistence on nonviolent means was drawn from the individual German tradition of peaceful political transformation through legal *reformatio,* which had been passed down since at least the Reformation. The German tradition emphasized the peaceful resolution of domestic disputes through judicial means. This was a pillar of German constitutionalism in the eighteenth century, as discussed in the last chapter. In the aftermath of twenty-two years of violent revolutionary wars, nonviolent political transformation was far more appealing than violent revision. Particular attention should be paid to the fact that this was not only the longest conflict since the Thirty Years War, but the standard of violent political revision also produced revolutionary bloodshed beyond Europe in both the French and Spanish colonies in the Americas. The goal of this chapter, thus, is to reposition Savigny as one the early leading minds of an individual German tradition of inverted constitutionalism and situate him as a nonviolent constitutional transformationist.

Biography

It would be impossible to discern or appreciate Savigny's constitutionalism without first understanding his personal history. This biographical information is important because it is the first indicator that he could not have been a reactionary conservative. Savigny was a member of the nobility in name only, and was not 'an aristocrat [who] brought honor to the teaching of Roman law' as Whitman suggests.[30] The de Savignys were early Calvinists in the Lorraine region of Catholic France, and Savigny was acutely aware of the persecution that his forebears experienced during the bloody Wars of Religion.[31] The Edict of Nantes (1598) offered only temporary and tenuous security for Huguenots, guaranteeing limited civil liberties to Protestant minorities. These included towns of safety, the right to hold public office, trial in courts before Protestant judges, and liberty of educational and professional pursuits. With the coronation of Louis XIV, however, anti-Protestantism again became an official policy in France. The Edict of Nantes was reduced to a scrap of paper and, then, completely revoked by the Edict of Fontainbleu in 1685. It went so far as to ruthlessly block off emigration for Protestants wishing to leave France. In 1677 the home of Savigny's paternal forebears, who had lived in relative prosperity, was burned to the ground. His great grandfather, Ludwig Johann de Savigny (1652–1701), witnessed the fiery razing of Grünstadt in 1689, where he had attended school. The family's holdings were destroyed by the *dragonnades* the same year. Targets of state-sponsored violent persecution and having lost everything, the de Savignys fled across the Rhine.

Whatever their lineage, as religious refugees, the family was making a new start, and a legal career offered one of a few paths of professional and social mobility in Central Europe. Savigny's grandfather, Ludwig (1684–1740), who was only four when the family fled France, did not attend a prestigious university, but made do with an education from *Justus Liebig Universität* in the poor principality of Gießen.[32] By the third generation, the family's fortunes began to turn around. Savigny's father, Christian Karl Ludwig von Savigny (1726–1792), studied law at the prestigious universities of Marburg, Halle and Jena and became a member of the diplomatic corps. At the relatively late age of forty, Christian married Phillipine Henriette Groos, who was an orphan with a sizeable inheritance and only seventeen at the time of the marriage. This was a mixed-faith marriage and, by all accounts, Savigny enjoyed a close relationship with his devoutly Lutheran mother. It was Phillipine who schooled him in the family's legacy of religious struggle from an early age.[33]

By the late eighteenth century, the Rhineland that Savigny was born into was a region enjoying economic acceleration and substantial prosperity. The area had experienced an agricultural revolution, and qualitative changes in farming techniques, such as *Besömmerung* (the growing of crops which reinvigorated the soil on fallow land) raised agricultural output. Increased production along with the opening of new export markets for luxury items, such as tobacco, wine, honey and raw silk, supported an expansion of wealth and population in urban centres, and, in turn, this enlarged the market for peasant farmers.[34] Returning home up the Rhine in 1799, Ernst Moritz Arndt (1769–1860) noted the 'immense fields of corn and the extremely assiduous cultivation of clover and potatoes'.[35] Traveling along the banks of the Main River at mid-century, David Hume commented that he 'never saw such rich Soil, nor better cultivated'.[36] 'Germany', he believed, was 'undoubtedly a very fine Country, full of industrious, honest People, & were it united it would be the greatest power that ever was in the World'.[37]

The regions around the Rhineland were also home to Central Europe's burgeoning manufacturing and residential cities. By 1781, the cotton manufactory in Kaiserslautern employed more than 2,000 spinners, and the woolens manufacturer in Monshau more than 4,000. Krefeld's silk manufactory exported all over the world and employed some 3,400 workers. Behind these market leaders were a host of lesser entrepreneurs.[38] Noble patronage in new residential capitals like Bonn, Koblenz and Mainz created dynamic growth and prosperity with a web of interlocking luxury trades and service industries.[39] There was also a considerable growth in the numbers of merchants and businessman, who contributed to burgeoning towns and made up the urban middle class *(Stadtbürger)*.[40] The city of Frankfurt am Main, where

Savigny was born, was an expanding economic centre and home to a wealthy class of international merchants.

Whereas educational, cultural and social demands in Prussia and Austria continued to be eclipsed by the drive for *Machtstaat,* conditions on the ground were very different in the small Rhenish principalities.[41] Here, I would argue, traditions of municipal jurisdiction continued, and the intimate scale of government demanded attention to local needs. On the eve of revolution in France, as Tim Blanning writes, it was already a region with princes promoting economic advancement as well as social reforms.[42] Policies of secularization decreased ecclesiastical influence even in the Catholic regions. Ecclesiastical property was diverted to endow new universities, and the progressive educational climate was evident in the scientific curricula. Reform extended to primary and secondary schools as well.[43] Social reforms produced orphanages, geriatric homes, asylums and a more humane criminal system.[44] A growing civic consciousness sustained a sense of progressive activism, leading to the rise of reading clubs, Masonic lodges and other private associations promoting reform.[45]

Rhinelanders continued to be active in the local law *(Gemeinde- und Stadtrecht)* of their communities in this period. Territorial law *(Landrecht)* and the Roman law-based *ius commune (gemeines Recht)* had effect only on a subsidiary basis. These were laws of last resort in cases where there were no provisions in the urban or town laws. The tradition of municipal jurisdiction, therefore, remained intact. As Blanning also points out, the resolution of disputes hinged on the interpretation of autonomous municipal charters and customs.[46] As changing economic and social conditions raised new legal questions, particularly relative to inheritance, marital property and private property rights, lower magistrates were able to make adjustments. As farm women in Neckarhausen increasingly produced cash crops and contributed greater wealth to the family purse, David Sabean shows that local courts 'shifted the way they related to the family', increasingly, 'allying with whichever spouse seemed to be the most effective commodity producer'.[47] While some aspects of the societal stresses that produced the French Revolution in 1789 were also present in Central Europe, a crucial difference between France and the German lands, as David Blackbourn writes, was the fact that German peasants had greater access to legal remedies.[48] In a manner that was tangible to ordinary Germans, local measures and judicial practice may have offered a greater feeling of participation than existed in France. This, along with the duality of law tradition, meant that there were viable alternatives to violence in the German states, and this may offer a better explanation as to why Germany didn't erupt in violent revolution rather than any notion of bourgeois failure.

In addition to the tradition of municipal jurisdiction, with the Rhenish provinces to the west and Hanau to its east, Frankfurt was in the centre of a Huguenot community rich in the monarchomach constitutional and resistance theory that grew up during the religious wars. Johannes Althusius, Clemens Timpler and Johann Heinrich Alsted, as discussed in the last chapter, developed a strong German monarchomach theory in the seventeenth century that emphasized the legitimate consent of the governed.[49] These forebears in the Huguenot legal world also shaped Savigny's legal worldview and his emphasis on self-determination. The third generation of Savignys was known in Frankfurt's elite legal and social circles, which included the Goethes. Amongst Christian's closest friends were Johann Jakob Moser, and the judge of the Reichskammergericht in Wetzlar, Constantin von Neurath (1739–1816), who would become Savigny's guardian.[50] Moser, who was discussed in the last chapter, was well respected in German reform circles for his resistance to the attempted personal rule of Duke Carl Eugen of Württemberg. During his confinement, Moser began to consider that there were significant deficiencies in the natural law systems of Christian Thomasius (1655–1728) and Gottfried Wilhelm Leibniz's disciple, Christian Wolff (1679–1754). Moser, ultimately, rejected the natural law school altogether. His twelve volumes of *Neues Teutsches Staatsrecht* (1766–82) enshrined him in the German legal world as the celebrated father of German public law and also shaped Savigny's legal and political views.

Despite a relatively comfortable early childhood, where he enjoyed a close relationship with his mother, Savigny's life was haunted by personal tragedies. Of Christian and Phillipine's twelve children, nine died in their first year of life, a daughter lived only to age twelve, and their eldest son made it just to age thirteen. Only Savigny survived to adulthood. This alone must have had a devastating impact on the young boy, but what is more, he lost both his parents by the age of thirteen. He was left, as Rudorff wrote, 'wealthy, but totally orphaned'.[51] Without even a relative to take him in, Savigny grew up with his father's old friend, Constantin von Neurath, as his guardian. While he developed a warm and familial relationship with the Neuraths, he still experienced moments of great melancholy throughout his adult life. Writing to Neurath from the University of Marburg in the winter of 1798, he despaired: 'My heart has suffered from a sad fate, and now I live in cold commonness and indignation, without a friend in life, trying to hold myself together through diversions and work—Oh this is as vexing as my grief.'[52]

Taken together, Savigny's Calvinist roots, his parents' mixed-faith marriage, his family's long association with the German legal world, and the fact that he was born into the cradle of reformist Central Europe, suggests something other than a predisposition toward reactionary conservatism. He was perhaps more a descendant of tolerant Protestant refugees than he was an aristocrat and a man who brought reserve to a euphoric German world that was heady with a host of hasty causes by 1814. The tragedy of having lost his entire family, by the age of thirteen, left him with no option but to make his own name, and in this he was scarcely better off than the sons of middling sorts, as he was aware. Johann Dietrich Gries wrote that he admired Savigny's character and 'determination to define his own life', during their university years.[53] In reality, he had little choice; the need to define himself was a fact of his condition as an orphan. As the prospect of war with France loomed over the horizon in 1792, Savigny's family was dying around him, and he faced the specter of surviving one of the greatest calamities in German history alone. Despite the considerable support he received from the Neuraths, this still must have been an emotionally challenging time for him.

War in the Rhineland

Revolution came to France, violently, in 1789, and despite the initial renunciation of international wars, for a number of reasons, France and the German states were bound to wind up in conflict. Austrophobia fed the revolutionaries' fears of the Foreign Plot. Lavicomterie de Saint-Samon's *Les crimes des empereurs d'Allemagne depuis Lothar I jusqu'à Léopold II* (1793) reflected the fever level of Austrophobia in France. As Thomas Kaiser writes, the Hapsburgs were accused of using 'oblique methods of conquests that traditional misogyny characterized as "feminine", as opposed to the more honest, manly pursuit of war'.[54] According to Lavicomterie, it had taken centuries for the Hapsburg to perfect their contrived system of despotism. 'The breakthrough', as Kaiser points out, was alleged to have 'occurred as a result of the Pragmatic Sanction under Charles VI, which allowed women, in particular Maria Theresa, to come to the throne and thereby to deploy to maximum effect the peculiar feminine methods devised by the Hapsburg's for their aggrandizement.'[55] Having usurped authority from her husband, Maria Theresa amongst other schemes had allegedly groomed her children to carry forward her programme of European domination.[56] Her daughter, the hated Queen Marie Antoinette, who was charged with trying to rule France according to the wishes of her family, had become the symbol of this Foreign Plot and was the embodiment of oblique conquest. In Vienna, Emperors Joseph II (r. 1765–1790) and Leopold II (r. 1790–1792) were the siblings of the ill-fated Marie Antoinette. After Leopold's death, her nephew Francis II (r. 1792–1832) inherited the throne of the Holy Roman Empire.

In the Rhineland, regardless of reform impulses, the Rhenish princes with their pompous titles and tiny territories symbolized the decadence of ancient regime Europe in the minds of French revolutionaries. Elector Clemens Wenzeslaus von Sachsen was not only Louis XVI's uncle, but, worse, allowed his court in Koblenz to become a centre for counter-revolutionary ferment. The elector of Mainz as well as Cardinal Rohan of Straßburg also opened their territories to thousands of royalist *émigrés,* who readily formed themselves into militias. Although some electors would later order the disarming and dispersal of such units, the damage could not be undone. Matters were complicated further by the question of what to do about noble privileges and territorial rights granted to German princes resident in Alsace, by the deposed French monarchy. A report of the Constituent Assembly soon proclaimed that, since the French people had not consented to such privileges, they were invalid and the people were not obliged to compensate for any losses.[57]

These various matters along with the intrigues of a group of multinational exiles in Paris combined to lend support to the war hawks in the *Girondists*-dominated

Legislative Assembly. A declaration of war against Austria was issued on 20 April 1792, and, it should not be underestimated that, in no small measure, French revolutionaries envisioned themselves as liberating the German lands from effiminate rule. Within weeks, Prussia joined the First Coalition against France. Under the banner of *'guerre aux châteaux, paix aux chamières'* French forces swept Belgium and much of the west bank of the Rhineland in the summer of 1792.[58] There were those who embraced the arrival of French troops as a liberating force, to be sure. The French Revolution replaced the American Revolution in Klopstock's odes to liberty. He was joined by other German poets, including Wieland, Tieck, Hölderlin and Wackenroder, amongst other intellectuals. Nonetheless, however many pilgrims of the French Revolution existed initially and however much grub-street writers blithely billed it as the dawn or sunrise, the September Massacres of 1792 and the beginning of the Reign of Terror a year later left many rethinking violent revolution. Caroline Schlegel felt that the Jacobins 'betrayed our ideals and dragged them in the mud, these evil, stupid and base people who no longer know what they are doing'.[59]

The west bank of the Rhine fell to the French in 1797, and it was the character of the French occupation that sparked resentment and stamped an image of despotism in German minds for a century. The war decree of 1792 'announced that the rest of Europe would be forced to be free and then would pay for this compulsory liberation by supporting the French armies'.[60] The French simply wrung the cost of war out of Central Europe. As Carl von Clausewitz wrote, the leaders of the Revolution 'sent their soldiers into the field and drove their generals into battle—feeding, reinforcing and stimulating their armies by having them procure, steal and loot everything they needed'.[61] The French armies were to supply the war 'on their own'.[62] Outrageously high levies were imposed on German towns, not to mention the requisitioning of everything from bread and boots to livestock. Many Germans also faced the deeply resented obligation to meet the gluttonous appetites of French generals, and there was also the humiliation of conscription and forced labor.[63]

Despite the original *paix aux chamières,* in reality even German cottagers fell victim to French soldiers. No historian has described this history better than Blanning. The citizens of Zweibrucker reported that: 'They grabbed people on the street and forced their way into houses, demanding wine, beer, bread, shirts, handkerchiefs, clocks, etc. etc.'[64] French soldiers were billeted almost immediately in German homes, at the homeowners' expense, and on the streets, 'hard-pressed householders' faced the lifting of their portable valuables.[65] Resistance could lead to brutality, as in the case of Konrad Koch, who was 'drilled with a bullet' and killed, after he refused to turn over his cash to French soldiers.[66] Every army had its collection of criminals, but French military exploitation, replete with large raiding parties to strip whole districts clean, took this to new heights. Although smuggling prospered, it is not hard to imagine that the war and occupation had a devastating effect on commerce in the once prosperous Rhineland.[67] Germans must have also questioned when the French maintained old regimes against peasants in the countryside through 1798.[68] All of this was sure to enshrine hatred of all things French at the grassroots of German society, a sentiment that was echoed, in raw terms, by Arndt: 'I hate all the French without exception in the name of God and my people.'[69] While Savigny's letter to Neurath in 1798 did not match Arndt in passion, his comments captured the sense of urgency and fear of the impending destruction of Germany. His growing reservation about violent means was a reaction, not only to the events in Paris, but the shocking brutality that was meted out against ordinary Germans in the occupied areas and in the name of *liberté, égalité, fraternité.*

The Glory of the Emperor?

After Napoleon Bonaparte (1769–1821) established himself as emperor of France in 1804, defeat of continental Europe was swift. The final blow for Central Europe was the crushing of Austrian and Russian forces in 1805. The humiliation was captured on canvas in Gérard's *Napoleon at the Battle of Austerlitz.* When Prussia tried to mount a defence, Napoleon quickly crushed its army at Jena and Auerstädt in 1806. He was in her capital within two weeks, where he issued the infamous Berlin Decrees, banning the importation of British goods. By June Prussian territory was reduced by half, and those areas directly under French rule faced the forced reception of French law. In the aftermath of this catastrophe, it is not difficult to understand the appearance of pamphlets such as *Germany in Its Period of Deep Humiliation* (1806).[70]

The Holy Roman Empire, which Savigny referred to as little more than a 'gussied-up grave', collapsed with spectacular speed.[71] The old Germany, between the Rhine and Elbe rivers, was reorganized by Napoleon into the *Confédération du Rhin,* which included Savigny's *Heimat,* Frankfurt and his university town of Marburg. New satellite states sprang into existence from Napoleon's cannons and old ones were gobbled up. When one considers the long and rich tradition of local jurisdiction and self-governance in German-speaking Europe, the legal consequences of the occupation are far more significant than historians have considered. The imposition of French law codes on German soil not only destroyed local autonomy, but inspired the bitter resentment of Germans for more than a century.

Following close on the heels of Napoleon's troops into the heart of Germany were *les cinq codes,* namely the *Code civil des Français* (1804), *Code de Procédure civile* (1806), *Code de Commerce* (1807), *Code pénal* (1810) and *Code d'Instruction Criminelle* (1811). The most famous of these was the *Code civil,* also known as the *Code Napoléon.* Codification was high on the new political agenda following the revolution, but it was only after Napoleon appropriated it for his own purposes that codification began in France. The *Code civil* came into force in the annexed Rhineland as soon as it was promulgated in 1804. By 1810, French codes were imposed on the citizens of north-west Germany, including the free cities of Hamburg and

Lübeck, with their old and celebrated municipal constitutions and traditions of local jurisdiction. Although there were important modifications, the Civil Code of Baden (1809) was a copy of the *Code civil.* Interned on St. Helena, Napoleon commented: *'Ma gloire n'est pas d'avoir gagné quarante batailles ... ce que rien n'effacera, ce que vivra éternellement, c'est mon Code civil.'*[72]

While the *Code civil* was received willingly in Louisiana and the satellite nation of Poland, it was perhaps overly optimistic for Napoleon to presume that his code would find open reception in German-speaking Europe, where both classical canon law and *corpus iuris civilis* faced hostile resistance. As discussed in the last chapter, the Church's attempt to impose its jurisdiction on the secular affairs of German towns had led to open revolts and was a source of violent conflict between popes and German emperors in Medieval Europe. A leading cause of the Peasants' Revolt of 1525 was the fact that the legal sanction for pushing free peasants into serfdom came from the newly received *corpus iuris civilis—'fremde'* law, and the demand for customary law and jurisdiction figured prominently in the Black Forest Articles.[73] Although he opposed the violence of the Peasants' Revolt, Melanchthon refined an evangelical legal argument to support the territorial princes' rights of resistance against the emperor. According to Melanchthon, it was not only a right, but an ancient canonical obligation for princes to resist the religious tyranny of Emperor Charles V.[74]

Given this history, the imposition of the French law codes served to discredit France as a nation of liberators. The idea of sovereignty was organized around jurisdiction in German-speaking Europe. For this reason, the imposition of foreign law was experienced as a denial of jurisdiction and the sovereign right to self-determination. This, by definition, constituted tyranny in German-speaking Europe, and, according to the evangelical legal thought, which had been handed down from the Reformation, Christians not only had the right to resist, but had the obligation to resist according to Lutheran scriptural interpretation. Memory of the Reformation, even if this was an artificial memory created by writers, offered a powerful historical framework for resistance to jurisdictional tyranny. The imposition of *les cinq codes* was seen as an act of usurpation, and it awakened exactly that element in the German sociopolitical consciousness that had caused Germans to turn from peaceful resolution to armed resistance, time and again. More than any other single act, Napoleon's attempt to oblige ordinary Germans to live according to an *Alltagsleben* reorganized by French private law, in the form of the *Code civil,* probably did as much as anything else to encourage the determination of Germans to take up arms and push the French back across the Rhine.

Indeed, nothing spurred resentment across social lines and symbolized the corruption of the French attempt at liberty for many Germans more than the imposition of French law on German soil. This more than any other single factor produced widespread discontent that was expressed by many liberals in the German legal world. The reformer, Harscher von Almendingen, who co-authored the *Bibliothek für peinliche*

Rechtswissenschaft (1800) with Paul Johann Anselm Feuerbach (1775–1833), was the earliest critic of the imposition of *Code civil.*[75] Echoing a familiar charge by 1809, Feuerbach simmered in a letter to Savigny: 'If we consider the example of the ancient world unfolding before our very eyes, a legislation like the French [Code], which has been forced on Germany, can only lead to literary barbarism and instead of allowing them to seek perfection, will sink into *geistloser Mechanismus.*'[76] Jacob Grimm (1785–1863) 'hated' the French law, which threatened to destroy German jurisprudence.[77] Resentment simply boiled over in the comments of Stein's mentor, August Rehberg (1752–1836): '*Geld und Gut,* which are the booty of foreign armies, one can get over', but the French civil law posed too high a cost by threatening to 'deprive the German nation of what people have in the heart and sentiment'.[78] This feeling resonated on the ground as well. 'What should our lesson be' read an 1815 article in Joseph Görres's *Rheinischer Merkur: 'Ein Reich, Ein Recht!* That should become the aim and bond of all German societies against the *Undeutsch* which threatened us from outside.'[79] The *Freiheitskriege* (1813–1814), as Savigny's biographer Rudorff wrote, also were 'the struggle of the whole nation' against the 'foreign Code'.[80]

Katherine Aaslestad's research on Hamburg, where the *Freiheitskriege* began, also offers some indication of how the imposition of the French law codes set off resistance. While she focuses on the severe economic consequences of Napoleon's ban on trade with England, the loss of local autonomy was also a significant factor. The French replaced Hamburg's constitution and governing bodies, as she points out, and the removal of Hamburg's coat of arms from all public buildings, newspapers, and public notices; and replacement with the imperial eagle 'symbolically underscored the republic's lost independence'.[81] Hamburg's patriots, as Aaslestad writes, sought, first and foremost, 'to preserve and liberate their *Vaterstadt* from oppressive French rule' and 'to recover the city's republican constitution, independence, and autonomy'.[82] As soon as Napoleon was defeated in 1814, Hamburg's traditional governing bodies and constitution were restored immediately.[83]

The visceral reaction against the imposition of French law also was a reflection of the continuing identification of sovereignty with jurisdiction, which had thrived for centuries, and of the strength of local self-governing principles that remained organized around law. Savigny wrote scornfully, after the wars, that the 'pernicious and ruinous' *Code civil* was meant for German 'destruction'.[84] Echoing Burkean sentiments, he also underscored that it had carried France 'backwards' rather than forward in the revolutionary path.[85] It was the product of despotism, and the fruit of a failed experiment in political revision. 'The Revolution', Savigny charged, had 'annihilated, together with the old constitution, a great part of law; both, rather from a blind ire impulse against everything established, and with extravagant senseless expectations of an undefined future, than in the hope of any definite improvement.'[86] The French experiment, above all else, was a failure, which did not result in a stable and durable constitutional polity. 'As soon as Napoleon had subjected everything to a military despotism', Savigny wrote, 'he greedily held fast that part of the Revolution which answered his purpose and prevented a return of the ancient constitution.'[87] The *Code civil,* framed in conditions wholly unfavorable to legislation, was, thus, the spoiled fruit of corruption, and 'in all reality, inclined to the recently developed despotism'.[88]

Even where French civil law saw some open reception, it was largely in the southern states, who were gorging on the once autonomous remnants of the Empire and who needed it to consolidate their own authority, even if of a satellite order.[89] There may have been a few supporters, but for the most part, it did not offer, as Wieacker once suggested, a 'satisfying legacy of Napoleon's rule on German territory'.[90] The continuing effect in Alsace-Lorraine of what was forever not only viewed as a symbol of French rule but high legal and constitutional despotism inspired liberal resentment until the enactment of the BGB in 1896. Indeed, copies of the *Code civil* were set ablaze at the *Wartburgfest* in 1817, an act which probably replicated the Wittenberg bonfire where Luther, Melanchthon and others burned the books of classical canon law.

The war against French despotism was over in 1815, but rooting out home-grown tyranny would also have to be dealt with. Many of modern Germany's most influential legal scholars were decorated veterans of the *Freiheitskriege.* Savigny, Karl Friedrich Eichhorn (1781–1854) and Karl Joseph Anton Mittermaier (1787–1867) all held the Iron Cross for their wartime service. These oracles of law and others emerged from the war determined no longer to live under laws that were not derived from the people's customs and norms. For this reason, not only French law, but Roman law and the other natural law codes which had been introduced in German-speaking Europe became unacceptable as sources for rules of law. Codes were increasingly seen as forms of imposed law, because the lawmaking process occurred without the participation of the people. Of the codes that were sources of legal rules in the German states, all had been produced by personal-rule bureaucracies and commissions. This was true, not only of *les cinq codes,* but also of Prussia's *Allgemeines Landrecht* (1794) and Austria's *Allgemeines Bürgerliches Gesetzbuch* (1811) not to mention Justinian's extant *corpus iuris civilis.* Regardless of how enlightened some of these codes may have been, they were unacceptable to liberals because princely codification denied the people their right to participation in governance through elected representatives, and the conception of participation, at bottom, involved exactly law-making. The experience of the occupation and the imposition of *les cinq codes* sharpened this sentiment. As a result, legal argumentation against laws that were not derived from German traditions was battle-hardened during the conflict with France, and it emerged from the *Freiheitkriege* as one of the key weapons in the liberal political arsenal.

While Savigny closed his *Vom Beruf* with a passage from Melanchthon, he, in fact, disagreed with him on the question of the reception of the *corpus iuris civilis* as a source of legal rules in German-speaking Europe. In the face of the Peasants' Revolt, Melanchthon developed an humanist justification for Roman law as the law of civilization and peace.[91] Although Enlightenment legal scholars later developed a conception of natural law from Roman law, this did not make it more acceptable.[92] Savigny rejected both justifications: 'The advocates of the Roman law have not, infrequently, placed its principle value in its containing the eternal rules of Justice in peculiar purity, and thus being entitled to be itself considered a law of nature sanctioned as a positive law.'[93] 'On looking closer', however, Savigny argued, 'the larger part will appear to be little better than narrowness and subtlety ... almost entirely confined to its theory of contracts', and this 'remainder of the Roma, so cited for its real excellence, is of so general a nature, that it might have been discovered by plain good sense, without any juridical cultivation'.[94] 'For so slight a gain', he stated, 'it is not worth while to invoke the laws and lawyers of two thousand years to help us.'[95] With regard to the *corpus iuris civilis,* Savigny articulated the complaint against Roman law that would find expression in liberal legal thought until the enactment of the BGB. 'If, in the first place', he wrote, 'we consider the juridical works of Justinian, consequently, that form in which Roman law has come down to modern Europe, we cannot but remark a season of decline in them.'[96]

The study of Roman law was freed from the *ius commune* by Hugo and Savigny's own teacher, Philipp Friedrich Weiss (1755–1808), at the University of Marburg amongst others. In the opening article for the *Civilistisches Magazin* Hugo founded in 1791, he wrote that the magazine was dedicated to the 'reformation of legal studies'.[97] After Hugo and the development of classical common law theory, Roman law was increasingly seen as an historical artifact that belonged only to the particular society and customs from which it was derived. This new conceptualization of Roman law already threatened the legal pillar upon which the monarchic principle and personal rule had stood since the Reception. The study of Roman law remained strong in German law faculties, but increasingly as a subject of history. German legal scholars were interested in recovering the technical (scientific) expertise of Roman jurists, in hopes that it would offer a model for the modern rationalization and scientization of German law. As Hugo emphasized, the *Civilistisches Magazin* was dedicated to the scientific rediscovery of ancient Roman law and not the *ius commune.*[98]

The politics of the new approach to Roman law was evident in the fact that there was a keen interest to recover the law and legal order of the Roman Republic rather than the Roman Empire. A frequent contributor to Hugo's magazine, Johann Schlosser emphasized the need for the study of pure Roman law as a source of renewal.[99] Feuerbach wrote in his 1809 letter to Savigny: 'Aside from the academic and literary concerns, we badly need a work of pure Roman law that we can introduce ourselves.'[100] Although it was humanist-like, the new approach to Roman law was distinguished from humanism by the appeal to science. It was an appeal that was also deeply political insofar as it housed a claim to a sphere of academic liberty and autonomy free from the manipulation of the monarchical state. On the eve of the founding of the University of Berlin, Friedrich Schleiermacher's 'Gelegentliche Gedanken über Universitäten in deutschem Sinn' (1808) drew clear distinctions between an earlier era of humanism and his own scientific time, while emphasizing the demand for academic liberty.[101] In his later 'Wesen und Werth der deutschen Universitäten' (1832), Savigny wrote that he stood in *'innere Verbindung'* with Schleiermacher's earlier views.[102] Roman law's continuing value was in the science of Roman jurists and the history of its development rather than as a source of legal rules. 'As to the value of the substance of the Roman law', Savigny wrote, 'there may be many different opinions, but as to its superiority in juridical method, all are undoubtedly unanimous who have a voice in the matter.'[103] The search and recovery of Roman law specifically focused on how the constitution was transformed over time and how Justinian's codification represented its decline. It was this that provided the powerful historical example of the duality of law in the working progress of the state of Rome and as the pillar of a stable and secure representative polity.

Legal codification in Prussia was associated with enlightened absolutism and was also seen, by liberals, as the legal glory of personal rule. Work on the *Allgemeines Landrecht für die Preußischen Staaten* of 1794 (ALR) was precipitated by the need to integrate and consolidate authority over Friederich II's territorial acquisitions. It was envisioned as a replacement for the outdated Roman law system, which had been received in 1495 to serve the interests of emperors and princes. Despite this, the Prussian crown, first encountered resistance to the *Allgemeines Gesetzbuch* (the original name of the ALR) from the Junker elite, already made edgy by the French Revolution of 1789. The Brandenburg noblemen, Ludwig von der Marwitz, called it a *Gleichheitskodex,* while Carl August Struensee feared that it represented 'revolution from above'.[104] Led by Leopold von Danckelmann of Silesia, many objected to expressions of *Recht* in the *Allgemeines Gesetzbuch,* arguing that it should convey only *Gesetze* limited to 'short expressions of command, prohibition or determination of the consequences'.[105] As Berkowitz writes, this amounted to 'an expression of a positivism of nobility in its truest form', which asserted that *Gesetze* 'once posited by a nobleman ... require no justification'.[106]

While the original, planned introduction of the *Allgemeines Gesetzbuch* was suspended when the French Assembly issued the declaration of war against Austria in 1792, it was later introduced as the ALR in 1794. Despite any expressions of legal security for ordinary Germans, in reality the liberal provisions were removed in the final version. It confirmed the *Standesstaat* on a new basis, as Günter Birtsch confirms, proclaiming that the 'rights of man arise from his birth, from his estate, and from actions and arrangements with which the laws have associated a certain determinate effect'.[107] It banned individuals from engaging in certain professions on the basis of birth.[108] Although inspired by enlightened natural law, the ALR was shaped by backward-looking values of 'unconditional loyalty' to an absolute monarchy, a view of law based on social orders and paternalistic thinking.[109] This also underscores the unique challenges that German liberals faced. Whereas in France an old regime was still in place, in Central Europe personal rule had been resanctioned and placed on a modernized legal footing. German liberals had to develop effective discourse against the new legal basis of personal rule and means to undo what were, essentially, modernized monarchies.

After the war, liberal opposition to the ALR was consolidated, and the legal arguments against it reflected the opposition legal thought that had been mobilized against the imposition of French law on German society. For liberals, the ALR offered another example of how the philosophical school of enlightened lawmaking failed to offer participatory security and proved that the law of reason could be easily co-opted to serve the needs of the monarchic principle, a principle which excluded the people from participation. It was, therefore, also unacceptable as a source of law. It was guaranteed only by the good will of a prince and, therefore, could not provide the legal security liberals demanded, because it left sociopolitical institutions vulnerable to arbitrary personal rule.

In contrast to the reactionary critics of the *Allgemeines Gesetzbuch,* Savigny's comments in 1814 offered an expression of growing liberal criticism of the ALR. He wrote, cynically, that the framers had hoped to 'accomplish something excellent'.[110] Its only merit, as far as Savigny was concerned, was that since it had been introduced as only a subsidiary law, at least, it had not destroyed local sources of law, especially Saxon customary law.[111] Composed of nearly twenty thousand paragraphs in an attempt to encompass all aspects of law, the ALR aimed to exclude even the interpretation of law by jurists. For Savigny, this represented not only a flaw in legal ideology, but political ideology. 'Every government is to blame which is ignorant of or disregards the intelligence of its age', and 'in this respect, the Prussian legislation is certainly open to reproach'.[112] It was a powerful denunciation of not only bureaucratic lawmaking, but the legal rules and institutions that were introduced to sustain the monarchic principle on a new legal basis in Prussia. In this way, Savigny's comments underscore the emerging strength of the liberal political idea, which emphasized the participation of the people in the lawmaking process.

In a larger perspective, Savigny argued that comprehensive codes could not meet the needs of an organic society, and, again, this was because the extant codes in the German states had not emerged from living legislative institutions. Austria's *Allgemeines Bürgerliches Gesetzbuch* of 1811 (ABGB) also met with Savigny's disapproval. Specifically, he complained that its notion of *Recht* was 'too general', and the code resembled a compendium of *Institutes* of the *corpus iuris civilis* rather than legislation.[113] On the whole, Savigny concluded that 'an excellence of the purely mechanical character must be ascribed to codes, and it would be impossible to regard them as anything grand or desirable'.[114] All encompassing codification of this sort was viewed as a symptom of the sociopolitical degeneration of a state. Savigny's example was ancient Rome, where 'so long as the law was in active progression' with the growth of the nation, 'no code was discovered to be necessary, not even at the time when circumstances were most favorable'.[115] Codification had occurred after the collapse of the Western empire and the *corpus iuris civilis* was a product of decline.

Refining the Old Common Law of Europe

While the imposition of French law was the straw that broke the camel's back, additional factors also fueled the burgeoning legal consciousness in the German states. From the perspective of intellectual history, the Prussian, Austrian and French codifications represented the apex of the law of reason. Legal scholarship was never less vital than in this period when absolutist lawmakers rejected commentary. In Prussia, judicial interpretation was subjected to ministerial commissions, and, after the Revolution, to the legislature itself in France. The original vitality of the law of reason was in its constant interplay with scholarship, but 'when these tenets hardened into recipes for legislators determined to lay down rules of eternal validity, they became something of a straightjacket'.[116] 'The downfall of the law of reason in Germany', as Wieacker wrote, 'was due to the feeling of oppression and disenfranchisement which led people with a burgeoning civic consciousness and a culture reinvigorated by humanism to attack the mechanical lawmaking of the authoritarian state.'[117] This was the essence of Feuerbach's criticism of the French codification, a criticism Savigny would later apply to all the natural law codes.

A profound intellectual shift occurred across Europe in the eighteenth century. 'The concept of natural law accessible through reason' was abandoned, as Wieacker wrote, 'an abandonment which was to become so complete that in the nineteenth century scarcely any idea was less fashionable'.[118] The anti-philosophical approach to law observed that 'laws in fact differ from one country to the next, that there are objective and discoverable factors which cause this to be so, and that laws ought to be suited to the particular conditions of the people for whom they are intended'.[119] The theory of monads, as developed by Leibniz, began the recognition of history's creative function, but, more importantly, Giambattista Vico (1668–1744), sometimes seen as the father of social science, advanced the idea that 'far from there being a natural law setting the same standards for men at all times and places, each society grew organically in its own peculiar environment, and its institutions, including its laws, reflected its own peculiar history'.[120] David Hume (1711–1776), in his *Treatise on Human Nature* (1740), suggested that human behavior 'is not dictated by an unvarying antecedent standard of natural law, but is the product of human motives and inclinations'.[121] The most well-known writer here was, of course, Montesquieu (1689–1755). In his *Spirit of the Laws* (1748), he wrote, laws 'should be adapted in such a manner to the people for whom they are framed [and] it will be a mere accident if those of one nation should suit another'.[122] Finally, Gaetano Filangieri's *La Scienza della Legislazione* (1782) was also instructive on this point: 'Nations do not resemble nations, one government is not like another, and it appears that nature, desirous of showing her grandeur in a rich variety of rich physical productions, is no less anxious to display her prodigies in the diversity of moral bodies.'[123] 'We may therefore lay it down as an axiom', he continued 'that the laws ought to follow this tremulous vibration in political bodies, and correspond with their variations.'[124] Law, in effect, should be peculiarly adapted to the individual polity. This is important also because Leibniz, Vico, Hume, Montesquieu, Filangieri and others that subscribed to these views, including Schleiermacher and Linguet, appear on Savigny's *Notanda Liste.*

In the German world, these ideas emerged clearly in the writings of Immanuel Kant (1724–1804), Johann Gottfried Herder (1744–1803) and Justus Möser (1720–1794). The intellectual nail in the coffin for the law of reason was when Kant disproved the philosophic basis of both the older natural law and the law of reason, by showing that ethical decisions are conditioned by the context in which they must be determined.[125] For Herder, 'people figure as the torchbearers in the divine plan, determining history; he heard the "voice of the people" in poetry which, being tied to language, was the product of the people who spoke it'.[126] At the same time, it is important to keep in mind that Kant's and Herder's critical views were also an evolution and product of the critique of natural law that was already well underway in Europe. Kant's views invalidated, in particular, 'the objectionable way in which absolutist legislators had treated the traditional law of [European] peoples'.[127] Herder's views fueled German demands for the interest of the peoples' sovereignty and demand for self-determination after the tyranny of the French occupation. Henceforth, the justice of law would turn not only on the Kantian view that 'law must respect the moral autonomy and moral will of the individual', and 'permit him the maximum of freedom compatible with the equal freedom of others in society', as Wieacker suggested, but also on the notion derived from Herder that the customs of the German people were the origin of and only legitimate source of law.[128] Law was no longer seen as a product of rational state legislation, but as a 'branch of culture "quietly" blossoming in the collective unconscious of the peoples'.[129]

Savigny was undoubtedly familiar with Kant's views, but Kant is not on his *Notanda Liste.* This may have been because Kant continued to support the French Revolution or perhaps Savigny rejected Kant's pushing of the 'race' concept and sided with Herder in this dispute. Herder does appear on the list. However, in *Vom Beruf,* Savigny mentioned only Hugo and Möser, in this regard. 'Amongst the German jurists', Savigny wrote, 'Hugo has the great merit of having, in most of his works, systematically striven against the prevailing theories.'[130] He reserved special merit for Möser, whose example, he felt, had been regrettably 'to a great degree neglected by jurists ... since he was not of their craft, and has neither delivered lectures nor composed books.'[131] 'High honor' was 'due to the memory of Möser, who generally aimed as interpreting history in the most comprehensive sense, and often with particular reference to law'.[132] Möser's *Osnabrückische Geschichte* had imagined the original freedom of Osnabruck peasants. Influenced by Montesquieu, Möser's *Patriotische Phantasien* (1775–1786) implied a preference for the organic development of a constitution in opposition to the arbitrary imposition of law according to the personal rule of a sovereign.

While the theoretical shift away from natural law was of significant importance, the consolidation of classical common law theory and its practice in England shaped transformationist legal and political thought in Central Europe. This, perhaps more than any other factor, offered German liberals a viable, alternative constitutional doctrine. Although the first scientific consolidation of classical common law theory was effected by English legal scholars, it was a reflection of the broader shift taking place across Europe, which appealed to cultural manifestations of the old common law of Europe as the proper basis for national development. Well before Rudolf Gneist's important work, by the second half of the eighteenth century, as Wolfgang Pöggeler has shown, there was a flowering of interest in classical common law theory in German-speaking Europe.[133] Leading English classical common law theorists appear on Savigny's *Notanda Liste,* including Henry Home, Hume and, most importantly, William Blackstone and Edmund Burke.[134]

Common law thought began to take shape in opposition to the absolutist ambitions and attempted personal rule of the Stuart monarchs, who had ruled Scotland. It refined a potent historical doctrine of English national sovereignty and a belief that the deeper reality of law, manifested in public statutes and judicial decisions, could not be based on universal rational principles, but were 'historically evidenced national custom'.[135] Time was understood as 'a rich tapestry of acts, words, thoughts, and sentiments of a people with whom one identifies as members of a "partnership" across time'.[136] All law in England, it was believed, either is or is grounded upon common law and, according to Sir John Davies (1569–1626), 'the Common Law of England is nothing else but the Common Custom of the Realm', which 'cannot be made or created either by Charter, or by Parliament' as 'consisting of use and practice, it can be recorded and registered no-where but in the memory of the people'.[137] The very legitimacy and just authority of the law, for Sir Matthew Hale (1609–1676), turned on this point of public recognition: 'They are grown into use, and have acquired their binding Power and Force of Laws by a long and immemorial Usage, and by the strength of Custom and Reception in this Kingdom. The Matters, indeed, and the Substance of those Laws, are in Writing, but the formal and obliging Force and Power of them grows by long Custom and Use.'[138] As Edmund Burke (1729–1797) later confirmed, the partnership was 'between those who are living, those who are dead, and those who are to be born'.[139]

This potent historical doctrine of law was rationalized by William Blackstone (1723–1780), whose chief contribution was to formulate it on a scientific basis. In his *Commentaries on the Laws of England* (1765–1769), Blackstone also recognized Roman technical expertise as a valuable science for the formation of national laws, but this was to lend legitimacy to the efficacy of rationalizing traditional English common law conceptions. Common law was derived from common and immemorial custom, Blackstone instructed, an 'ancient collection of unwritten maxims and customs', a body of practices, attitudes, conceptions and patterns of thought recorded in the memory of the people and 'handed down by tradition, use [and] experience'.[140] 'The goodness of custom', he explained, 'depends upon having been used time out of mind; or, in the solemnity of our legal phrase, time whereof the memory of man runneth not to the contrary.'[141] In effect, recognition through use by the people is what gave law its validity: 'This it is that gives it its weight and authority.'[142] 'Goodness' referred not only to the 'validity, the legality, the authoritative status, of the rule of custom', but also to the 'wisdom, justice, or reasonableness of the custom'.[143] Three notions—authority/validity, reasonableness, and historical appropriateness are intimately linked, and the continued practice both manifests and reinforces the reasonableness and historical appropriateness of the rules and concepts of common law. Law exists and is only known through practice and 'a rule becomes law or a decision marks a new departure in the law only if it is taken up into the practice of the community'.[144] It is only the public demonstration of the suitability of the rules over time that qualifies them for status as law. 'Our constitution', Burke confirmed in 1782, 'is a prescriptive constitution ... whose sole authority is, that it has existed time out of mind,' and 'prescription', he urged 'is the most solid of all titles, not only to property, but, which is to secure that property, to government.'[145]

In the aftermath of the French catastrophe that left no hovel untouched from the bloody streets of Paris to burning Moscow, the appeal to classical common law theory reacted against the philosophical approach to lawmaking, which was increasingly seen as the French example. In opposition to this, classical common law theory offered an historical approach. There was no louder critic of the French attempt at liberty than Burke, and he located French failure, exactly, in their reliance on philosophical abstractions. 'By following those false lights', he wrote scathingly, 'France has bought undisguised calamities at a higher price than any nation has purchased the most unequivocal blessings', bought 'poverty by crime', and 'abandoned her interest, that she might prostitute her virtue'.[146]

Central to Burke's argument in *Reflections on the French Revolution* (1790) was an appeal to classical common law as a superior source of political transformation. 'The (English) Revolution', as he wrote, 'was made to preserve our *ancient,* indisputable laws and liberties, and that *ancient* constitution of government which is our only security for law and liberty.'[147] 'You will observe', he suggested 'that from the Magna Charta to the Declaration of Right, it has been the uniform policy of our constitution to claim and assert our liberties, as an *entailed inheritance* derived to us from our forefathers, and to be transmitted to our posterity, as an estate specially belonging to the people of this kingdom, without reference whatever to any other more general or prior right.'[148] It was the guiding purpose of the great oracles of law from Coke to Blackstone 'to prove the pedigree of our liberties'.[149] The English constitution, he suggested, was only one national expression of what could be derived from what he viewed as a general European common law tradition, and his core criticism of the French was that they had failed to follow this sure course. Instead of representing the French as a bunch of recently freed 'Maroon slaves':

> Had you made it understood ... that you were resolved to resume your ancient privileges, whilst you preserved the spirit of your ancient and your recent loyalty and honor; or if,

diffident of yourselves, and not clearly discerning the almost obliterated constitution of your ancestors, you had looked to your neighbor in this land, who has kept alive the ancient principles and models of the old common law of Europe meliorated and adapted to its present state by following wise examples, you would have given new examples of wisdom to the world.[150]

The Thibaut-Savigny Controversy Revisited

The mood in the German legal world was jubilant when victory seemed final in 1814. News of German troops marching towards Paris inspired the University of Heidelberg professor, Anton Thibaut, to publish his *Über die Notwendigkeit eines allgemeinen bürgerlichen Rechts für Deutschland,* in June of 1814, calling for a common civil code for the German lands. 'Deutschland', he opened his famous treatise, 'has restored its honor through the liberation of its ground and won for itself the hope for a happy future.'[151] 'I am of the opinion', he urged, 'that our civil law (under which falls private law, criminal law and procedure) needs a complete and rapid alteration.'[152] Savigny was also jubilant. He wrote to Leonard Creuzer in February of 1814: 'I am so lucky that I live in this great time and to have been amongst the people who started Germany's new rising—a time that one can look back on only with admiration.'[153] However, Savigny's *Vom Beruf* raised the critical objections to Thibaut's call for the immediate introduction of a German-wide code, calling instead for a period of progressive jurisprudence.

At this juncture, it is important to recall how the constitutional debate of 1814 was interpreted in post-Second World War legal historiography. Following Kantorowicz, an argument was put together, which repeatedly cited Savigny's objection to Thibaut's programme as evidence of his reactionary-conservatism. According to Wieacker, Thibaut's treatise was 'the declaration of an alert and liberal citizen'.[154] Hattenhauer charged Savigny with being 'little more than a political dilettante or a totally apolitical mind'.[155] In the meantime, Wrobel celebrated Thibaut's views as the 'legal expression of the progressive ideals of the bourgeoisie', while censuring Savigny's ideals as the 'legal expression of those forces working for the preservation and restoration of the old system'.[156] However, we should return to Wieacker, because his prose on the controversy was almost poetic:

The duel between Savigny and Thibaut was fundamentally one of personal attitudes: aristocratic culture *versus* the politics of democracy; European tradition against nascent national feeling; scholarship on the one hand and active practice on the other. One can compare the positions of Goethe and the young Schiller as regards the French Revolution and the modern nation: on the one hand the observer concerned with stability, on the other the revolutionary moralist; here the pupil of Plotinus and Spinoza, there the follower of Rousseau and Kant. Like Goethe, Savigny was rooted in the Europe of the eighteenth century, and the great movements since 1789 made them feel the earth trembling

> underfoot, a reaction incomprehensible to those who found these events stimulating and full of promise.[157]

Paradoxically, neither Plotinus nor Spinoza appeared on the *Notanda Liste.* In terms of classical thought, it appears from the *Liste* that Savigny relied on Schlosser's translation of Aristotle's *Politics* and Garve's work on Cicero. Goethe was shaped neatly by Wieacker to fit into his puzzle, but one is still left with the names of Christian Bretano, Lessing and Friedrich Schlegel, not to mention Möser, all of which are on the *Notanda Liste.*[158]

Analytical approaches to understanding the constitutional debate of 1814, which focus on intellectual history alone, do not allow scholars to appreciate the social environment in which decisions were made. As indicated earlier in this chapter, any feeling of the earth trembling underfoot was more likely produced by the experience of French cannons and the movement of troops across the Rhine. As Blanning and others have shown, the human suffering of many ordinary Germans was considerable under the French occupation.[159] Germans were probably also made wary when Napoleon reinstituted slavery after it had been abolished, and, in this light, their fear of enslavement was real. In addition to these factors, the imposition of French law on German soil cut a wound in the souls of Germans so deep that it became a unifying factor across all social divides. This factor caused ordinary Germans, who identified sovereignty with local jurisdiction, to put an end to French aggression and was a source acrid resentment into the twentieth century. Arguably, rejection of the French path to liberty by Savigny and others was democratic insofar as it was merely the resonance of widespread popular antipathy. Nevertheless, the historiographical myths that were created in the postwar era continue to serve as a leitmotif in major constitutional debates, including those concerning the European Union. On the question of contract law, Ole Lando has described those who wish for codification in Europe as the Thibauts and the antagonists as the Savignys, who prefer 'creeping' harmonization.[160]

In reality, Thibaut's call for immediate codification was compromised by a number of factors, not the least of which was the fact that he was a rather passionate personality and far too often failed to exercise restraint in his public writings. In 1802, he published a sharply worded criticism of Feuerbach's theory of criminal law, and he was also at odds with Gustav Hugo, the chief spokesman for the reform of Roman law studies. After jumping to Görres's defence in his political dispute with Goethe, Thibaut had to retract his comments, and Goethe chastised him, suggesting that he needed to 'learn the way of the world'.[161] Thibaut also wrote *Notwendigkeit* in only fourteen days and here, again, embarked on a bare-knuckle attack against Savigny and others in the German legal world.

In contrast, Savigny's reserved response and the strength of his argument went a long way toward gaining support amongst German liberals. Niebuhr wrote to Dora Hensler in November of 1814 that, under the circumstances, he felt that Savigny's response to Thibaut was 'mild', and marked by a sharpness of intellect never before seen.[162] Jacob Grimm wrote to his brother Wilhelm that he was pleased with Savigny's response and was in total agreement with his opinion.[163] Savigny also was not alone in his opposition to Thibaut's proposal. Hugo, Wilhelm Pfeiffer, and G.F.W. Hegel (1770–1831) amongst others published alternative views. Pfeiffer complained with some justification that the debate was dominated by scholars to the exclusion of practicing lawyers and that they 'would also like to have word on the need for a new civil code for Germany'.[164]

These various conflicts also offer an indication that Thibaut was out of step with both the general direction of legal scholarship and the politics of the lawmaking by 1814. First, he explicitly opposed German unification, arguing that 'large state systems' suffered constantly from 'unnatural tension', and stifled 'fraternal feeling between sovereigns and subjects *(Regenten und Untertanen)!*'[165] He believed that the system of small German states *(ein Bund kleiner Staaten)* should be maintained and that the only form of unification necessary was his proposed code. This position, in particular, stood at odds with the growing nationalist movement in the German states. In addition, while he called for a code *'ganz nach den Bedürfnissen der Untertanen',* his programme did not offer a path for the participation of the people in the lawmaking process.[166] His plan called for a code commission to be made up of legal scholars from the various German lands, and it was they who would draft a code. This was a view of lawmaking that ran counter to the hope for a constitution that would lead to a representative assembly, where law would be derived from a legislative process. Thibaut's proposed plan of codification smacked, in practice, of the very bureaucratic lawmaking which excluded the participation of the people and was discredited by Kant, Herder and Hugo, not to mention the French legal imposition. As early as his 1809 letter to Savigny, Feuerbach expressed the view: 'If we are to have a national legislation, we must first be a nation, and, in order for us to produce a good national legislation, the public life must no longer be found only in the *Geheimenrathscollegien und Büreau's* (bureaucracies), but in the nation itself.'[167]

What was emerging by 1800 was a split within liberal constitutionalism with rationalist codifiers of the philosophical school on one side and, on the other side, scholars of the historical school of law, who looked to find a prescriptive basis for civil rights in German legal traditions and history. Thibaut remained committed to the philosophical approach to law and the law of reason.[168] 'Above all else', as Rudorff suggested, he 'was a man of the eighteenth century'—the 'philosophical century', where 'notions of abstract *Weltbürgerthum* and the Enlightenment' also encouraged the introduction of arbitrarily conceived law—the '*Universalcodex* for all times and all people'.[169] Published in 1798, Thibaut's *Über den Einfluss der Philosophie auf die Auslegung der positiven Gesetze* was a monument to the philosophical approach to law. He argued that history without philosophy could not adequately interpret the meaning of law. A year later, he refined this view in his treatise *Theorie der logischen Auslegung des römischen Rechts* (1799). The work that would make Thibaut famous, *System des Pandektenrechts* (1803), was an attempt to use philosophical insight to develop a new code on the basis of the *Digests* of the *corpus iuris civilis* and was the first major attempt to do so since Leibniz. The *System* emphasized the ideals of rational law *(Vernunftsrecht),* and, here, *Recht* was both preceded and bound by obligation *(Verbindlichkeit). Recht,* accordingly, exists as coercive right *(Zwangsrecht).*[170] Thibaut tried to rescue the law of reason and the eighteenth-century approach to enlightened lawmaking, an effort that was doomed by events.

Within a few years after the publication of the *System,* the philosophical approach to lawmaking, which was already in decline following Kant and Herder, was completely discredited, in Central Europe, by the experience of the revolutionary wars. More than any other factor, the French legal imposition of *les cinq codes* contributed to the sharp decline of enlightened lawmaking or, in effect, philosophical codification. Its ill repute in the German states was sealed, because since Napoleon was able to employ it for his despotic political ends, it could not be seen as a reliable source of legal security. The imposition of the *Code civil* had undermined the basis of German private rights, in large measure, by destroying German sovereignty itself. The French legal imposition left no German untouched and was deeply resented by ordinary Germans and intellectuals alike. As Isabel Hull has shown for Baden, a major source of discontent had to do with the way the code's family laws contradicted its basic principles by energetically installing heinous discrimination against women and young persons.[171] Thibaut's call for the speedy introduction of a philosophical law code, after the considerable legal upheaval that was the most salient feature of the French occupation and just as Germans were, finally, ridding themselves of Napoleon, legal imposition and all, probably failed because it was out of tune with the mood in Central Europe.

Politics and Modern Legislation

In the aftermath of the French occupation, the sociopolitical challenges faced by German liberals were far more complicated than the task of doing away with unreformed absolutism had been for French revolutionaries. On the one hand, reformers faced the challenge not of undermining age-old absolutism, but of justifying the revision of the legal systems that sustained personal rule on a new and, purportedly, enlightened basis. On the other, the fact that ordinary Germans were in no mood for any more mucking up of their treasured local autonomy and municipal laws was also a formidable obstacle. The French legal disruption was resented across Central Europe, in Baden, Hamburg and the other Hansa cities and in Württemberg as well. When Hamburg's constitution was restored, the Senate rejected even limited reforms and remained highly suspicious of even moderate reformers.[172] In 1813, when Hanseatic envoys met in Frankfurt, they were also wary of 'Prussian attempts to expand in a "French manner" across northern Germany'.[173] Indeed, as James Brophy shows, the imposition of its enlightened law on communities in the Rhineland was one of the many factors that led to violent revolts.[174]

Writing in 1814, Savigny, in fact, agreed with Thibaut's political ends as he stated in his closing to *Vom Beruf.* 'We desire a sound system of law, secure against the encroachments of caprice and dishonesty, as also, the unity of the nation, and the concentration of its scientific efforts upon the same object,' but Savigny believed that a code 'would only produce the desired unity for one half of Germany, and separate the rest by a line of demarcation, more strongly marked than before'. 'I see the proper means', he wrote, 'in an organically progressive jurisprudence, which may be common to the whole nation.'[175] He also had a greater appreciation for the attachment of the German people to their local laws. Whereas Thibaut was the son of a Hanover military officer, Savigny had grown up in the presence of judicial officials and lawyers. For this reason, he may have had an instinctive understanding that political revision, which was fundamentally a question of jurisdiction, was a highly volatile matter in the German lands, particularly since the memory of the French legal imposition was still fresh. Savigny recognized the need for political revision and worked actively in the Stein-Hardenberg reform circle prior to the liberation. After the war, however, he also had the prudence to recognize the very real potential for disaster if reformers pushed too hard, particularly in the northern German regions where people were very bitter about the French abrogation of their local autonomy. For anyone hoping to achieve unification and political revision, the *Freiheitskriege,* which may, in part, be seen as a response to the French legal imposition, offered a powerful lesson and warning. Savigny understood that ordinary Germans might well have revolted if anyone had tried to impose, of all things, a new code just as they were getting rid of the French ones.

With an eye toward these considerations and perhaps more wisely than historians have considered, Savigny recognized the need to find an alternative course for political revision. It was in this environment that he began to develop an idea of constitutional transformation, grounded in the traditional German identification of sovereignty with jurisdiction. By the early years of the nineteenth century when he wrote, he could also draw on classical common law theory, which had been consolidated on a scientific basis by Blackstone and which also confirmed the efficacy of building a German system from German customs. His theory of politics and modern legislation reflected exactly the belief that a German constitution must be fashioned from the ancient principles and models of the old common law of Europe, as Burke called it. Only this would offer the desired security for German liberties and, more importantly, it was the only way Germans would accept and use any national legislation. History rather than philosophy emerged as the critical social science, and the major work of the historical school involved proving the pedigree of prescriptive German liberties so that they could be rationalized into a system capable of meeting the needs of an envisioned German nation. In the process, a northern German customary law constitutionalism was created, which was distinct from southern written constitutionalism and ultimately had the greatest impact on the course of German constitutional development.

In 1800, Savigny completed his legal studies under Anton Bauer and Philip Friedrich Weiss at the University of Marburg. Bauer was a pioneer of criminal law reform, and Weiss was known for his work on medieval legal history. Savigny stayed at Marburg as a *Privatdozent,* where Jacob Grimm was amongst his star students. It was Savigny who introduced the Grimm brothers to German romantic circles and who read the initial drafts of their fairy tales. Jacob and Savigny, in particular, remained very close friends for the rest of their lives. It is also from Jacob Grimm's notes that we have Savigny's *Juristische Methodenlehre* (1803). Here, Savigny began to link a philological study of law to scientific inquiry and the historical development of a given people. He argued that the source for the rules of law for the development of any system of law must be derived from the specific cultural context in which they would be introduced. 'The individual data grasped as a result of philological treatment', as Savigny instructed his students, 'must at the same time be thought into the system as a whole'.[176] 'The content of the system', he explained, 'is the law as laid down, that is, the rules themselves.'[177] The same year, Savigny published his first major work, *Das Recht des Besitzes: Eine civilistische Abhandlung* (1803). As much as it was a monument to the historical approach to Roman law studies, it is also important for its discussion of the right to private property *(Sachenrecht).*[178]

In 1804, Savigny married Kundigunde Brentano (1780–1863), whose siblings were Bettina (von Arnim), Clemens and Christian Brentano. He married into the German romantic world, and his was a mixed-faith marriage between a Protestant and Catholic, which was uncommon in the nineteenth century. Savigny's beloved Gunda did not convert, and the Savigny children were allowed to choose their own faiths. The pair also spent considerable time educating their only daughter, Bettina (1805–1835), who was named after her progressive and liberal aunt. In 1834, she married one of Savigny's Greek students, Constantinos Dimitrios Schinas, who was a supporter of Greek independence from the Ottoman Empire. The pair moved to Greece after independence was secure. Schinas, who was active in the founding of the University of Athens, was appointed professor of history and the institution's first rector. Savigny was devastated by news of Bettina's premature death within a few months of her arrival in Athens. The Savignys' eldest son, Karl Friedrich von Savigny (1814–1875), represented Prussia in the important diplomatic discussions between 1849 and 1866 and, after 1871, became a founding member of the Catholic Center Party. This private dimension of Savigny's life, again, was not characteristic of man predisposed to reactionary conservatism.

Under the strong influence of the reforming minister Montgelis, Bavaria took a step, albeit imperfect, toward modern political organization with the introduction of the first German constitution in 1808. By then Savigny was a professor of law at the University of Landshut in Bavaria. In an 1808 letter to Jacob Grimm, Savigny wrote optimistically that 'looking to the examples of Lessing, Herder, Johann Müller and many others in the universities, especially Schleiermacher, I feel with conviction and understanding that we live primarily in a time of rebirth'.[179] As he set his sights on a representative constitution in 1810, Wilhelm von Humboldt recruited Savigny to help found the new University of Berlin's law faculty. Amongst his closest friends and allies at the university was the liberal professor of history, Barthold Niebuhr.

In addition to his professorship, Savigny was actively engaged in effecting the Stein-Hardenberg reforms. Along with his Roman law professorship, he was also third rector of the university and responsible for organizing the law faculty's *Spruch-collegium* (tribunal competent to remit legal opinions in cases submitted by the ordinary courts). At the same time, his political activities extended well beyond the halls of the University of Berlin. On 22 May 1815, Hardenberg was finally able to secure a decree from King Wilhelm III promising a written constitution for Prussia and a representative assembly, which would include the new provinces on an equal basis. In 1817, Savigny was appointed to the commission to organize the *Provinzialständen* (provincial diets) that were to be built from the bottom upwards and to the *Justizministerium* (Ministry of Justice) in the Prussian *Staatsrat* (Privy Council). He also served on the Supreme Court of Appeals for the Rhine Provinces in 1819 and, in 1820, on a commission called to revise the unsatisfactory *Allgemeines Landrecht.* Savigny was very close to the constitutional movement in these years, and when hope collapsed with Hardenberg's death in November 1822, Savigny sank into depression and went on extended travel leave. It is noteworthy as well that it was Savigny who secured positions for the Grimm brothers after the Göttingen Seven dismissal in 1837. Finally, out of sympathy for the times, he resigned his official positions with the Prussian crown in 1848.

By 1815, it was clear to those in government circles that liberal hopes for German unification and political revision would not be realized by the Congress of Vienna. Savigny was especially guarded about expressing his political views in public writings. His letters from the period, however, offered a much stronger statement of his sentiments. In the summer of 1814, after the publication of Thibaut's *Notwendigkeit,* but prior to his own contribution to the legal debate, Savigny wrote to Jacob and William that 'we must not delude ourselves about the conditions that led to the final disaster, where the old states existed only for appearance—a terrible fraud'.[180] 'We want', he continued, 'to be sure that we are able to obtain what people, in fact and truthfully, have in their hearts, and this cannot be achieved in commissions and conventions.'[181] In April of 1815, he expressed in a letter to Jacob that he was concerned about Metternich's growing influence and that of the Austrian system of administration, which he referred to as *'undeutsch'.*[182] 'One must keep in mind', he wrote, 'that we can never realize an enduring satisfactory condition for Germany without a legitimate Kaiser of our own.'[183] These points are important also, because they shed new light on Savigny's political sentiments around 1814 and indicate that he was a supporter of the *klein Deutschland* idea, excluding Austria, that was emerging amongst liberal nationalists in these years. Savigny viewed law, as Rudorff wrote well before Kantorowicz's revision, as a critical element in the 'struggle for national existence', and his call for an organic and progressive jurisprudence *(fortschreitende Rechtswissenschaft)* was designed to serve this political end.[184]

Savigny developed his own understanding of progressive constitutional transformation and a programmatic approach to achieve it from his readings of Vico's *Scienza Nuova* (1725) and his disciple Filangieri's *La Scienza della Legislazione* (1782), mentioned earlier. In terms of the approach to political revision in Germany, they are perhaps the most important thinkers on the *Notanda Liste.* Vico's thought was overshadowed in his own time by the dominance of philosophical natural law in the eighteenth century. However, in the closing years of the century, *Scienza Nuova* was revived in the German world and transmitted to nineteenth-century transformationist-minded intellectuals through Herder, Goethe, Friedrich Jacobi and Schleiermacher.

A critical part of Vico's analysis was his delineation of basic principles or *axioms.* Here, he set forth his new science. He elevated the ability of philology to explain human events and shape civil society against that of philosophy alone. 'If philosophy is to benefit humankind,' according to *Axiom* 5, 'it must raise and support us as frail and fallen beings, rather than strip us of our nature or abandon us in our corruption.'[185] Philologists included all the grammarians, historians and critics who contributed to the awareness of 'people's languages and deeds, including both their domestic customs and laws, and their foreign wars, peaces, pacts, travels and trade'.[186] He drew distinction between political philosophers and philological legislators. 'Philosophy considers people as they should be, and hence', Vico suggested, 'is useful only to the very few who want to live in the republic of Plato, rather than to sink into the dregs of Romulus.'[187] 'Legislation', in contrast, 'considers people as they really are, in order to direct them to good purposes in society.'[188] Legislation was the creator of 'civil happiness', and, from the three vices of ferocity, avarice and ambition that plague the human race, legislation created 'armies, trade and the courts, which formed the might, affluence, and wisdom of commonwealths'.[189] Vico made the ordinary *conscienza* or common sense of the people a proper source of scientific inquiry and elevated the role of the people's wisdom to that of the original creative source of human institutions. 'Popular traditions', he argued 'always have a public basis in truth', and, as he set forth in *Axiom* 69, 'governments must conform to the nature of the people governed'.[190]

As important as his basic principles, Vico's interpretation of the history of the classical world was of vital importance to the nineteenth-century mindset. *Scienza Nuova* offered philological treatments of the constitutional histories of various polities, which showed legislation acting as the creator of civil happiness. While he examined the ancient world, generally, his main laboratory was ancient Rome. Romulus founded Rome by means of clientships, and it was based on the protection Roman fathers offered those who sought asylum in Rome. These 'day laborers' or 'refugees had none of the privileges of citizenship and hence no share in the civil liberty'.[191]

The good Tarquin King, Servius Tullius, later instituted the census by granting the laborers bonitary ownership of the patricians' lands, and this, according to Vico, was the first agrarian law in the world. When Brutus drove out the tyrannical Tarquins and restored the Roman Republic to its original principles, the plebeians suffered a political setback, when he established the two consuls as aristocratic kings. 'In this way,' Vico wrote, 'Brutus re-established the partricians' liberty from tyrannical rulers, but not the plebeians liberty from the patricians.'[192] When the patricians began to ignore the agrarian law in practice, the plebeians created the two tribunes of the people, to defend their bonitary ownership of the fields and set out to acquire the right of civil ownership from the patricians.

The patricians, however, continued to reclaim the fields despite the fact that the plebeians had cultivated them. Lacking any civil process for pressing their own claims, the tribunes of the people demanded passage of the Twelve Tables, which Vico emphasized 'only resolved this issue and no other'.[193] It only granted the plebeians *quiritary* (citizen rights of ownership over their fields). They soon realized that, despite this limited right, 'they still could not bequeath the fields to their relations', a vital right which hinged on marriage. The plebeians 'could neither make intestate bequests, since without celebrating solemn marriages, they had none of the relations through which legitimate succession could pass,' and 'nor could they dispose of fields by testament,' because this meant that 'they lacked the rights of citizenship'.[194] As a result, they asserted 'their claim to share in patricians' *concubium* (right to solemnized marriages)', the greatest of which was the auspices, 'the great source of all Roman law, both public and private'.[195] In obtaining the *concubium,* the plebeians effectively secured rights of citizenship. More legal concessions followed: 'The plebeians secured from the patricians all those rights of private law which depended on the auspices: paternal authority, direct heirs, paternal kinsmen, and clan kinships.'[196] By virtue of these rights, they secured the rights to legitimate successions, testaments and guardianships. It was only after securing their private rights that 'they claimed those rights of public law dependent on the auspices, first securing access to the consulship, with its attendant right to *imperium* or military command, and then to priesthoods and pontificates, with their attendant knowledge of the laws'.[197] With the Publian and Poetelian laws, the plebeian laws became universally binding on all Romans, securing their superior position over the patriciate. As Vico wrote, 'in this way, the Roman Republic had naturally become a government of popular liberty'.[198]

Several elements of Vico's philological treatment of Roman constitutional development were of immeasurable importance to the growth of constitutional transformation thought in nineteenth-century German political theory. First, he offered a history that revealed to Germans that plebeians had gradually obtained their right to full citizenship. It was 'with steady steps,' he emphasized, that 'the tribunes advanced their power to make laws'.[199] Second, the identification of civil marriage as the basis for obtaining full citizenship and private property rights exercised a formative influence in shaping the inverted direction of German constitutional development. It also led to the unprecedented politicization of civil marriage, in Germany, as the very fountain from which full citizenship and male liberty sprang and the pillar upon which government on the basis of popular liberty rested. In addition, the example of plebeian political revision was one that had focused on the rights of private law first, and it was only after these were secure that they claimed the rights of public law. Finally, as Vico's history emphasized, it was not through violent conflict that a government based on popular liberty was obtained, but rather, gradually, through steady steps and legislation, a point that cannot be emphasized enough.

It was Filangieri, however, who took Vico's philological treatment of Roman constitutional history and developed it into a programmatic theory of legislative revolution.

> The first step to be taken is to create in the public a wish for the proposed reformation. A chance in the constitution of a country is not the work of a moment, and to prepare the way for it, the inclinations of the people should be gradually led towards it. They should be made fully sensible of the inefficacy of their established laws, and be convinced their hardships and oppression are owing to them. The ablest writers should be employed to state the errors and inconveniences of the old system, and the propriety as well as the necessity of abolishing it, and adopting a more advantageous one.[200]

The existing order could easily be undermined, Filangieri suggested: 'Composed of the laws of a people at first free, but afterwards slaves; compiled by an opinionated civilian, in the reign of a feeble emperor; confounded with an immense number of local and contradictory edicts, with the decisions of courts frequently eluding those very edicts, and with a variety of barbarous customs originating in the ignorance or caprice of feudal anarchy, and incompatible with the revolutions to which the world has been subject; this heterogeneous system requires little trouble to bring it into disrepute.'[201] 'After prejudicing the public opinion against existing conditions', he pointed out that 'a necessary predilection' for the new order would exist.[202]

As far as mobilization for such an effort, Filangieri emphasized that it 'might be dangerous to entrust this important task to a single person'; rather 'the united labors of a numerous body of men of the first talents and characters, and possessed of the popular esteem, would greatly facilitate the work; and whilst it silenced any individuous suggestions, would create a respect for their joint productions'.[203] 'Expedients of this kind', he encouraged, 'have been resorted to in all nations, under all governments, and in all ages, and it appears from experience that they have seldom failed.'[204] Most importantly, Filangieri proclaimed his expedient to be a form of revolution. 'A decline of the legislative system is a political revolution,' as he clearly instructed, 'but a revolution affected slowly, which advances by sensible steps, and takes up ages to reach its termination.'[205] Legislative revolution was not 'instantaneous in its nature', but rather, he wrote, the 'process of a revolution in a legislative system is slow, and consequently there is opportunity for its reformation'.[206]

The variety of political thought that appears on his *Notanda Liste,* especially the programmatic ideas of Vico and Filangieri, reveals an element of political radicalism in Savigny's theory of politics and modern legislation that has not been explored by scholars. It is important to keep in mind that political thought continued to be pragmatic and implied in character. On the one hand, this was the fruit of tradition, and, on the other, it provided a kind of encoded mode of political communication that offered some measure of security against the reactionary forces that were consolidating authority in Vienna. Programmatic political thought, therefore, was often expressed by appropriating classical references, by reliance on common scholarly knowledge, and by pointing towards writings where the relevant programmatic thought had already been articulated.

In his *Vom Beruf,* Savigny divided law into two interlocutory elements. The political element he identified as the 'connection of the law with the general existence of the people', and the technical element was the 'distinct scientific existence of the law'.[207] The customs of the people, as Savigny explained, were the source of the political element.

> Under a republican constitution, the political principle will be able to preserve an immediate influence longer than in monarchical states; and under the Roman Republic in particular, many causes cooperated to keep this influence alive, even during the progress of civilization. But in all times, and under all constitutions, this influence continues to show itself in particular applications, as where the same constantly recurring necessity makes a general consciousness of the people at large possible ... The sum, therefore, of this theory is, that all law is originally formed in the manner, in which, in ordinary but not quite correct language, customary law is said to have been formed; i.e. that it is first developed by custom and popular faith, next by jurisprudence—everywhere, therefore, by internal silently operating powers, not by the arbitrary will of a lawgiver.[208]

This political element, which could be derived from no other place than the customs of the people, Savigny believed was a vital dimension of participation.

> The well-being of every organic being, (consequently the states) depends on the maintenance of equipoise between the whole and its parts—on each having its due. For a citizen, a town, a province to forget the state to which they belong, is a very common phenomenon, and every one will regard this as an unnatural and morbid state of things. But for this very reason a lively affection for the whole can only proceed from the thorough participation in all particular relations; and he only who takes good care of his own family, will be a truly good citizen. It is, therefore, an error to suppose that the common weal would gain new life by the annihilation of all individual relations ... When, therefore, the influence of law on the love of country is the question, the particular laws of particular provinces and states are not to be regarded as obstacles. In this point of view, the law merits praise, in so far as it falls in, or is adapted to fall in, with the feelings and

> consciousness of the people; blame, if, like an uncongenial and arbitrary thing, it leaves people without participation.[209]

On the surface, Savigny's technical element may appear as purely scientific. However, once one takes into consideration Vico's emphasis on the gradual development of popular liberty through legislation in ancient Rome and Filangieri's programmatic conception of legislative revolution, the technical element emerges as a species of civic activity and mobilization. Jurists were Savigny's body of men of the first talents and characters.

> With the progress of civilization, as national tendencies become more and more distinct, and what otherwise would have remained common, becomes appropriated to particular classes; the jurist now become more and more a distinct class ... law perfects its language, takes a scientific direction, and, as formerly it existed in the consciousness of the community, it now devolves upon the jurists, who thus, in this department, represent the community. Law is henceforth more artificial and complex, since it has a twofold life; first, as part of the aggregate existence of the community, which it does not cease to be; and, secondly, as a distinct branch of knowledge in the hands of the jurists.[210]

In 1815, Savigny founded the *Zeitschrift für geschichtliche Rechtswissenschaft* with Karl Eichhorn and Johann Göschen. The politics of the technical element were more clearly expressed in his 'Ueber den Zweck dieser Zeitschrift' (1815), which opened the first edition. The editors wished 'to give new stimulation to the *vaterländisches Recht*' and provide like-minded friends a point for unification. 'It is necessary for every individual to think as a member of a family, a people, a State,' he insisted, 'the continuation and evolution of all previous times.'[211] Every age came into being 'in unbroken synergy with the whole past'. Law 'comes out of the Nation's innermost essence and history'—the past and present spirit of the German people.[212] The mission of the historical school of law, as defined by Savigny, was to 'take up the subject of the laws seeing it through the whole past of the Nation'.[213] Savigny closed his opening article calling for a philological approach to the rationalization and scientization of German legal customs, by issuing a summons, not only to jurists, but those working in other areas of philology. Henceforth, the work of the historical school focused on discovering and proving the pedigree of German liberties. It is no accident that both of Eichhorn's articles, 'Ueber das geschichtliche Studium des Deutschen Rechts' (1815) and 'Ueber den Ursprung der städtischen Verfassung in Deutschland' (1815), appeared in the first edition of the journal. Eichhorn argued that a scientific approach and study of German laws *(Deutsches Recht)* was a critical element of national character *(Volkseigentümlichkeit)*.[214]

The customary law constitutionalism that emerged from Savigny's theory of politics and modern legislation was never separated from liberal political demands. In 1815, the first volume of Savigny's *Geschichte des römischen Rechts im Mittelalter* was also published. 'The peculiar practice and application of [the] old law depended, for the most part on a series of symbolical acts of accurately determined form,' and, he instructed, 'these were the principle studies and employments of the most celebrated Jurists, and the subjects of juridical works. Indeed, the Jurists may be considered the true guardians and protectors of the strictness and distinguishing features of the old law.'[215] 'In the law', after the rise of the Roman Empire, 'more of old Rome had been preserved than in any other branch of public affairs', and, 'consequently, he who still possessed the feelings of a Roman must in the Law have found the most congenial subject; and the noblest intellects must thus have been devoted to the study of Jurisprudence'.[216] These comments may be read as an attempt to mobilize like-minded Germans for what was now going to be a long-term programme of constitutional transformation. Since reactionary forces were gathering steam in Vienna and it was increasingly clear that the treasured goal of German unification could not be achieved in the immediate term, this approach provided an important alternative path for political revision.

Notes

1. Friedrich Karl von Savigny to Constantin von Neurath (end 1798), in Adolf Stoll (ed.), *Savigny: Ein Bild seines Lebens mit einer Sammlung seiner Briefe*, vol. 1, *Der junge Savigny* (1927), p. 70.
2. Montesquieu, *The Spirit of the Laws,* Thomas Nugent (trans.) (1949), p. 20.
3. See Timothy Blanning, *The French Revolution in Germany: Occupation and Resistance in the Rhineland 1792–1802* (1983), p. 265.
4. Ibid.
5. Savigny to Neurath (end 1798), p. 70.
6. Adolphus Rudorff, 'Friedrich Karl von Savigny: Erinnerungen an sein Wesen und Wirken', *Zeitschrift für Rechtswissenschaft,* 2 (1863), pp. 1–68.
7. Franz Wieacker, *A History of Private Law in Europe (with Particular Reference to Germany),* Tony Weir (trans.) (1995), p. 457; and J. Kelley, *A Short History of Western Legal Theory* (1992), p. 359. For a recent study on Kantorowicz see Sebastian Silberg, *Hermann Kantorowicz und die Freirechtsbewegung* (2004).
8. Wieacker, *History of Private Law,* p. 457.
9. For a defense of Kantorowicz against these charges see Vivian Curren, 'The Critique of Classicism', in Annelise Riles (ed.), *Rethinking the Masters of Comparative Law* (2001).
10. Kelley, *Short History,* p. 360.
11. Frank Kantorowicz Carter, 'Gustav Radbruch and Hermann Kantorowicz: Two Friends and a Book—Reflections on Gnaeus Flavius' *Der Kampf um die Rechtswissenschaft* (1906)', *German Law Journal,* 7/7 (2006), p. 661.

12. Hermann Kantorowicz, *Was ist uns Savigny?* (1911); and Hermann Kantorowicz, *Rechtswissenschaft und Soziologie* (1911), pp. 32–3.
13. Wieacker, *History of Private Law,* p. 305.
14. Hermann Kantorowicz, *The Spirit of British Policy and the Myth of the Encirclement of Germany,* W. H. Johnston (trans.) (1932), pp. 20–3.
15. Ibid., p. 51.
16. See generally Kantorowicz, *Spirit of British Policy.*
17. Hermann Kantorowicz, *Dictatorships: A Sociological Study* (1935).
18. Hermann Kantorowicz, 'Savigny and the History School', *Law Quarterly Review,* 53 (1937), p. 326.
19. Ibid., pp. 326–43.
20. Wieacker, *History of Private Law,* p. 304.
21. Hans Hattenhauer, 'Einführung', in Jacques Stern (ed.), *Thibaut und Savigny: Ihre programmatischen Schriften* (1973), p. 46.
22. Hans Wrobel, 'Rechtsgeschichte, Wirtschaftsgeschichte, Sozialgeschichte: Die Thibaut-Savigny-Kontroverse', *Kritische Justiz,* 6 (1973), cited in Hans Keither, *Ideal wird was Natur war: Abhandlungen zur Privatrechtsgeschichte des späten 18. und des 19. Jahrhunderts* (1997), p. 189.
23. Joachim Rückert, *Idealismus, Jurisprudenz und Politik bei Friedrich Carl von Savigny* (1984); and James Q. Whitman, *Legacy of Roman Law in the German Romantic Era: Historical Vision and Legal Change* (1990), pp. 112–15.
24. John, *Politics and the Law,* p. 20.
25. H. Beck, *Origins of the Authoritarian Welfare State in Prussia: Conservatives, Bureaucracy and the Social Question 1815–70* (1995), p. 238.
26. David Blackbourn, *The Long Nineteenth Century: A History of Germany 1780–1918* (1997), p. 102.
27. Roger Berkowitz, *Gift of Science: Leibniz and the Modern Legal Tradition* (2005), p. 108.
28. Ibid.
29. F. Savigny, *Politik und neuere Legislationen: Materialien zum 'Geist der Gesetzgebung'*, Hidetake Akamatsu and Joachim Rückert (eds) (2000), p. xxiii.
30. Whitman, *Legacy of Roman Law,* p. 107.
31. This point is emphasized in biographies about Savigny.
32. Stoll, *Savigny,* vol. 1, pp. 4–9.
33. Rudorff, 'Friedrich Karl von Savigny', pp. 10–11.
34. Blanning, *French Revolution in Germany,* pp. 24–5.
35. Ernst Moritz Arndt, *Reisen durch einen Theil Teutschlands, Italiens und Frankreichs in den Jahren 1798 und 1799* (1803), cited in Blanning, *French Revolution in Germany,* p. 24.
36. J.Y.T. Greig (ed.), *The Letters of David Hume* (1932), pp. 121–2, cited in Blanning, *French Revolution in Germany,* p. 28.
37. Ibid.

38. Blanning, *French Revolution in Germany,* p. 31.
39. Ibid., pp. 31–2.
40. David Blackbourn, 'The German Bourgeoisie: An Introduction', in David Blackbourn and Richard Evans (eds), *The German Bourgeoisie: Essays on the Social History of the German Middle Class from the Late Eighteenth to the Early Twentieth Century* (1991), p. 2.
41. Blanning, *French Revolution in Germany,* p. 41.
42. Ibid., p. 37.
43. Ibid., pp. 38–9.
44. Ibid., p. 41.
45. Ibid., p. 44.
46. Ibid., p. 47.
47. David Sabean, *Property, Production and Family in Neckarhausen, 1700–1870* (1990), p. 174.
48. Blackbourn, *Long Nineteenth Century,* p. 53.
49. Martin van Gelderen, 'Aristotelians, Monarchomachs and Republicans: Sovereignty and *respublica mixta* in Dutch and German Political Thought, 1580–1650', in Martin van Gelderen and Quentin Skinner (eds), *Republicanism: A Shared European Heritage* (2002), pp. 205–7.
50. Stoll, *Savigny,* vol. 1, pp. 12–13.
51. Rudorff, 'Friedrich Karl von Savigny', p. 11.
52. Savigny to C. von Neurath (14 January 1798), in Stoll, *Savigny,* vol. 1, p. 16.
53. Stoll, *Savigny,* vol. 1, p. 15.
54. Thomas Kaiser, 'From Austrian Committee to Foreign Plot: Marie-Antoinette, Austrophobia and the Terror', *French Historical Studies,* 26/4 (2003), p. 590.
55. Ibid., pp. 590–1.
56. Ibid., p. 591.
57. Blanning, *French Revolution in Germany,* pp. 59–63.
58. Ibid., pp. 63–4.
59. Blackbourn, *Long Nineteenth Century,* p. 55.
60. Blanning, *French Revolution in Germany,* p. 66.
61. Ibid., p. 83.
62. Ibid., p. 86.
63. Ibid., pp. 98–134.
64. Ibid., p. 88.
65. Ibid., p. 91.
66. Ibid., pp. 89–90.
67. Ibid., p. 141.
68. Ibid., pp. 186–7.
69. Cited in Blackbourn, *Long Nineteenth Century,* p. 89.
70. Cited in Thomas Nipperdey, *Germany from Napoleon to Bismarck 1800–1866* (1996), p. 13.

71. Savigny to Wilhelm Grimm (29 April 1814), in A. Stoll, *Savigny: Ein Bild seines Lebens mit einer Sammlung seiner Briefe*, vol. 2, *Professorenjahre,* p. 104.
72. Wieacker, *History of Private Law,* p. 271, note 20.
73. Isabelle Deflers, 'Melanchthon und die Rezeption des römischen Rechts in Sachsen und im Alten Reich', in Adrian Schmidt-Recla, Eva Schumann and Frank Theisen (eds), *Sachsen im Spiegel des Rechts* (2001), p. 192.
74. Ibid., pp. 190–2.
75. August Wilhelm Rehberg, *Ueber den Code Napoleon und dessen Einführung in Deutschland* (1814).
76. Feuerbach to Savigny (13 January 1809), in Herbert Kadel (ed.), *Paul Johann Anselm Feuerbach and Friedrich Carl von Savigny: Zwölf Stücke aus dem Briefwechsel* (1990), p. 34.
77. Jacob Grimm, *Jacob Grimm: Selbstbiographie* (1984), p. 30.
78. Rehberg, *Ueber den Code Napoleon,* p. ix.
79. *Rheinischer Merkur,* no. 219 (1815), cited in Wilhelm Burkhard Pfeiffer, *Ideen zu einer neuen Civil-Gesetzgebung für Teutsche Staaten* (1815).
80. Rudorff, 'Friedrich Karl von Savigny', pp. 30–1.
81. Katherine Aaslestad, 'Remembering and Forgetting: The Local and the Nation in Hamburg's Commemorations of the Wars of Liberation', *Central European History,* 38/3 (2005), p. 389.
82. Ibid., p. 390.
83. Ibid., p. 394.
84. F. Savigny, *Of the Vocation of Our Age in Legislation and Jurisprudence,* Abraham Hayward (trans.) (1999), p. 43.
85. Ibid.
86. Ibid., p. 41.
87. Ibid.
88. Ibid., p. 42.
89. Blackbourn, *Long Nineteenth Century,* pp. 74–6.
90. Wieacker, *History of Private Law,* p. 275.
91. Savigny, *Of the Vocation,* p. 29.
92. Ibid.
93. Ibid.
94. Ibid.
95. Ibid.
96. Ibid.
97. Gustav Hugo, 'Ueber den Plan, die Absicht und die Grenzen dieses Journals', *Civilistisches Magazin,* 1 (1790), pp. 1–22.
98. Ibid.
99. Johann Schlosser, 'Ueber das Studium der reinen Römischen Jurisprudenz', *Civilistisches Magazine,* 1 (1791), pp. 72–108.
100. Feuerbach to Savigny (13 January 1809), p. 36.

101. F. Schleiermacher, 'Gelegentliche Gedanken über Universitäten in deutschem Sinn', *Heidelberger Jahrbücher für Philologie, Historie, Literatur und Kunst,* 3 (1808), pp. 296–305.
102. F. Savigny, 'Wesen und Werth der deutschen Universitäten', *Historisch-politische Zeitschrift,* 1/4 (1832), pp. 569–92, reprinted in F. von Savigny, *Vermischte Schriften,* vol. 4 (1850), pp. 255–69 and 270–308.
103. Savigny, *Of the Vocation,* p. 31.
104. Cited in Berkowitz, *Gift of Science,* p. 78.
105. Cited in ibid., p. 80.
106. Berkowitz, *Gift of Science,* p. 80.
107. Günter Birtsch, 'Reform Absolutism and the Codification of Law: The Genesis and Nature of the Prussian General Code', in John Brewer and Eckhart Hellmuth (eds), *Rethinking Leviathan: The Eighteenth Century State in Britain and Germany* (1999), p. 347.
108. Ibid.
109. Ibid., p. 356.
110. Savigny, *Of the Vocation,* p. 57.
111. Ibid., pp. 53–4.
112. Ibid.
113. Ibid., pp. 59–60.
114. Ibid., p. 65.
115. Ibid., p. 30.
116. Wieacker, *History of Private Law*, p. 280.
117. Ibid., p. 279.
118. Ibid., p. 271.
119. Ibid.
120. Ibid., p. 272.
121. Ibid., p. 271.
122. Montesquieu, *Spirit of the Laws,* cited in ibid., p. 273.
123. Gaetano Filangieri, *The Science of Legislation, from the Italian of Gaetano Filangieri,* Richard Clayton (trans.), vol. 1 (1806), pp. 45–9.
124. Ibid.
125. Wieacker, *History of Private Law,* p. 282.
126. Ibid., p. 285.
127. Ibid, p. 282.
128. Ibid.
129. Ibid., pp. 282–5.
130. Savigny, *Of the Vocation,* p. 20.
131. Ibid.
132. Ibid.
133. Wolfgang Pöggeler, *Die deutsche Wissenschaft vom englischen Staatsrecht: Ein Beitrag zur Rezeptions- und Wissenschaftsgeschichte 1748–1914* (1995).

134. Savigny, *Politik,* p. xxxiii.
135. Gerald Postema, *Bentham: Moral, Political and Legal Philosophy* (2002), p. 4.
136. Ibid., pp. 5–8.
137. Sir John Davies, *Irish Reports* (1612), cited in Postema, *Bentham,* p. 4.
138. Sir Matthew Hale, *A History of the Common Law of England* (1713), C. Gray (ed.) (1971), p. 17, cited in Postema, *Bentham,* p. 5.
139. Edmund Burke, *Reflections on the Revolution in France* (1790), cited in Postema, *Bentham,* p. 23.
140. William Blackstone, *Commentaries on the Laws of England* (1767), cited in Postema, *Bentham,* p. 4.
141. Blackstone, *Commentaries*, cited in Postema, *Bentham,* p. 5.
142. Ibid.
143. Postema, *Bentham,* pp. 5–8.
144. Ibid.
145. Edmund Burke, *Speech on the Reform of Representation of the Commons in Parliament* (1782), cited in Postema, *Bentham,* p. 29.
146. Burke, *Reflections on the Revolution in France,* paragraph 60, in *The Harvard Classics* (1909–14).
147. Ibid., paragraph 51.
148. Ibid., paragraph 55.
149. Ibid., paragraph 52.
150. Ibid., paragraph 59.
151. Anton Thibaut, *Über die Notwendigkeit eines allgemeinen bürgerlichen Rechts für Deutschland* (1814).
152. Ibid.
153. Savigny to Creuzer (18 February 1814), in Stoll, *Savigny,* vol. 1, p. 19.
154. Wieacker, *History of Private Law,* p. 310.
155. Hattenhauer, 'Einführung', p. 46.
156. Wrobel, 'Rechtsgeschichte', cited in Keither, *Ideal wird was Natur war,* p. 189.
157. Wieacker, *History of Private Law,* p. 314.
158. Savigny, *Politik,* p. xxiii.
159. Blanning, *French Revolution in Germany*; Blackbourn, *Long Nineteenth Century*; and Aaslestad, 'Remembering and Forgetting', have been cited here.
160. Ole Lando and H. Beale, *Principles of European Contract Law* (2000).
161. Wieacker, *History of Private Law,* pp. 310fn.
162. Barthold Niebuhr to Dora Hensler (1 November 1814), cited in Stern (ed.), *Thibaut und Savigny,* p. 14.
163. Jacob Grimm to Wilhelm Grimm (1814), cited in ibid.
164. Pfeiffer, *Ideen,* p. 5.
165. Thibaut, *Notwendigkeit,* pp. 7–8.
166. Ibid.

167. Feuerbach to Savigny (13 January 1809), pp. 34–5.
168. Wieacker, *History of Private Law,* p. 310.
169. Rudorff, 'Friedrich Karl von Savigny', p. 30.
170. Anton Thibaut, *System des Pandektenrechts,* vol. 1 (1803), pp. 23–6.
171. Isabel Hull, *Sexuality, State and Civil Society in Germany 1700–1815* (1995), pp. 371–406.
172. Aaslestad, 'Remember and Forgetting', p. 394.
173. Ibid.
174. James Brophy, 'Violence between Civilians and State Authorities in the Prussian Rhineland 1830–1846', *German History,* 22/1 (2004), pp. 1–35.
175. Savigny, *Of the Vocation.*
176. F. Savigny, *Juristische Methodenlehre nach der Ausarbeitung des Jacob Grimm* (1803), cited in Wieacker, *History of Private Law,* pp. 281–2.
177. Ibid.
178. F. Savigny, *Das Recht des Besitzes: Eine civilistische Abhandlung* (1803), pp. 21–32.
179. F. Savigny to Jacob Grimm (1808), cited in Savigny, *Politik,* p. 147.
180. F. Savigny to Jacob and Wilhelm Grimm (18 June 1814), in Stoll, *Savigny,* vol. 1, p. 109.
181. Ibid.
182. F. Savigny to Jacob Grimm (1 April 1815), in Stoll, *Savigny,* vol. 1, pp. 131–2.
183. Ibid.
184. Rudorff, 'Friedrich Karl von Savigny', pp. 31–2.
185. Giambattista Vico, *New Science: Principles of the New Science Concerning the Common Nature of Nations,* David Marsh (trans.) (1999), p. 77.
186. Ibid., p. 79.
187. Ibid., p. 78.
188. Ibid.
189. Ibid.
190. Ibid., p. 99.
191. Ibid., pp. 67–8.
192. Ibid., p. 68.
193. Ibid., p. 69.
194. Ibid.
195. Ibid.
196. Ibid.
197. Ibid., pp. 69–70.
198. Ibid., p. 71.
199. Ibid., p. 70.
200. Filangieri, *Science of Legislation,* p. 57.
201. Ibid., p. 58.
202. Ibid., pp. 58–9.

203. Ibid., p. 59.
204. Ibid.
205. Ibid., pp. 66–7.
206. Ibid., p. 67.
207. Savigny, *Of the Vocation,* p. 19.
208. Ibid., pp. 19–20.
209. Ibid., pp. 34–5.
210. Ibid., pp. 19–20.
211. F. Savigny, 'Ueber den Zweck dieser Zeitschrift', *Zeitschrift für geschichtliche Rechtswissenschaft,* 1/1 (1815), pp. 1–17.
212. Ibid.
213. Ibid.
214. Karl Eichhorn, 'Ueber das geschichtliche Studium des deutschen Rechts', *Zeitschrift für geschichtliche Rechtswissenschaft,* 1 (1815), p. 124.
215. F. Savigny, *History of the Roman Law in the Middle Ages,* E. Cathcart (trans.) (1829), pp. 2–3.
216. Ibid.

–3–

Images of the *Gemeinwesen*
The Germanists and the Growth of Customary Law Constitutionalism

> My purpose is in equal measure a practical one, for what could be more practical than awakening a feeling for the Fatherland in so far as I succeed in capturing your attention and putting into your hands old or misplaced keys ... which can disclose the basis of German law. In doing so, much material must be adduced which concerns the language, poetry, and religion of former times.[1]
>
> —Jacob Grimm, University of Berlin, 1841

> The oldest law of Rome, as among all nations, was founded on the common understanding and consent of the people ... and this we are accustomed to call the *consuetudinary* law. The changed political relations of the different orders of society, and not discontent with this condition of law, occasioned, at a very early period, a grand fundamental ordinance, which besides the constitution of the state, contained a great part of the old customs. In this sense, the Twelve Tables preserved the original principles of the civil law, and such continued to be their character until the time of Justinian.[2]
>
> —Friedrich Karl von Savigny, 1815

The theory of legislative revolution emerged from the debates of 1814 and 1815 as a programme for constitutional transformation. While this programmatic approach to political revision had broad support in liberal circles, it nevertheless still had to be effected, and, in the technical language of law, the data for the system had to be discovered. In the first phase, which spanned the years between 1815 through 1846, the progressive jurisprudence Savigny had called for focused on recovering the data for a system, namely, the *vaterländisches Recht.* This was, of course, the political element, and what Grimm, in his lecture at the University of Berlin, referred to as 'old or misplaced keys'.[3] As noted above, Savigny also did not fail to point out to the readers of his *Geschichte des römischen Rechts im Mittelalter* (1815) the political importance of customary law. Relying, again, on classical references to communicate contemporary political mobilization, he reminded his readers that during 'the existence of the free Republic, eloquence and jurisprudence were, besides war, the only paths to favor and renown'.[4] This effort to recover the *vaterländisches Recht* gave birth to customary law constitutionalism in Central Europe. It subscribed to a potent historical doctrine, which held that German customs and traditions were the prescriptive source of German liberties, a belief that was bound up with liberal demands for political revision.

The effort to recover the *vaterländisches Recht* also was marked by the widespread mobilization of not only German jurists, but the ablest writers generally, and most notably, historians. A critical indication of this mobilization was the rapid proliferation of new legal journals. This trend began in the 1820s and accelerated after 1850 and with each phase of constitutional transformation. In these journals, German constitutionalism continued to flourish even during the reactionary years following 1819, and, in them, scholars are offered not only a rich source of German sociopolitical thought, but also sociopolitical images of the national *Gemeinwesen* or commonwealth that liberals intended to bring about through constitutional transformation. At the same time, legal antiquarianism extended the mobilization into the realm of popular culture. It allowed for the reliance on sources well beyond the realm of formal law and expanded the producers of the data for a system of law to include poets, folklorist, musicians and the like. The moral of every fairy tale came to be seen as an expression of prescriptive German liberties. If ordinary Germans could not grasp the highly technical legal writing, they could know their prescriptive constitution through alternative expressions of German customs. As a result of this mobilization, a national legal culture developed in German-speaking Europe well prior to formal unification in 1871.

The Politics of Roman Legal History

Perhaps more than a deep political dissension, the division between Romanist and Germanist in the historical school after 1815 reflected an apportionment between the technical and political elements of German jurisprudence. The study of Roman law continued to flourish, but on the alternative historical and technical basis discussed the in last chapter. 'Roman law' was seen 'as a great teacher that would permit modern lawyers and legislators to aid the development of their own uniquely nationalist legal systems'.[5] The purpose of the new Roman legal history was to lend support to the efficacy of rationalizing German customary laws and a programme of constitutional transformation. Savigny's comments mentioned in the closing paragraph of the last chapter are worth repeating here. After the collapse of the Roman Republic, 'more of old Rome had been preserved [in the law] than in any other branch of public affairs'.[6] 'Consequently,' he urged, 'he who still possessed the feelings of a Roman must have found in the law the most congenial subject; and, thus, the noblest intellects must have been devoted to the study of jurisprudence.'[7] Savigny made these comments with an eye towards German conditions in his own time, and it was a call to arms for transformationist-minded intellectuals.

The growing primacy of politics in legal scholarship was also evident in the precipitous decline of interest in the study of the *ius commune,* which was still in effect as a source of law in many regions. Karl Marx praised the 'instinctive legal sensibility' of German customs, which, he believed, safeguarded the well-being of the poor.[8] In 1853, Rudolf von Jhering wrote that he 'thirsted, as a student, for an exciting work on Roman law'.[9] 'Roman law has always struck me as a branch of classical and, particularly, Latin philology, hence as part of a vast field encompassing the whole of antiquity,' Johann Bachofen wrote to Savigny.[10] What interested Bachofen, who was also one of Savigny's students, 'was the ancient world itself and not the applicability of its lessons to present day needs; it was ancient and not modern Roman law that I really wanted to study'.[11] Behind the widespread decline of interest in the *ius commune* was also a questioning of the usefulness of its rules to modern conditions. 'In modern commercial life', as J. Kuntze wrote in 1856, 'we do not have the good fortune to be able to wander shepherded by the Roman jurists.'[12]

Scholars of the *ius commune* had failed to address modern concerns, particularly economic needs. The *ius commune* did not offer provisions for negotiable instruments, a matter of pressing concern in the face of growing industry and trade interests. By the mid century, Jhering complained that 'commerce manages to satisfy its needs without bothering itself about the question of whether its institutions and legal principles, which enrich our law, fit the ideas of the jurists or confuse them'.[13] German courts simply enforced the rights of the bill holders as a matter of customary commercial law and ignored Roman law as thoroughly irrelevant to this sort of transaction. In the meantime, scholars of the *ius commune* clung to old patterns of legal thought. They continued to assume that obligations were created personally, by direct relations between two individuals, and that property rights were created by direct relations between an individual and a thing. Needless to say, this was useless in a modernizing nineteenth century, where commercial relations and international trade were indirect, and the transfer of goods increasingly occurred by shipping.[14]

The mobilization of legal scholars for the cause of constitutional transformation was evident in the articles that appeared in the *Zeitschrift für geschichtliche Rechtswissenschaft* (ZGR), which was founded by Savigny, Eichhorn and Göschen in 1815. While Savigny and Göschen were representatives of Roman legal history, Eichhorn focused on German legal sources. In addition, Jacob Grimm, who became the leading representative of German legal antiquarianism, was also a frequent contributor to the ZGR. The journal was, above all else, an organ for constitutional transformationists.

The primacy of politics was reflected in the articles that appeared in the ZGR on Roman legal history. They focused primarily on recovering the constitutional arrangements from the era of the Republic. In the first edition, Karl Unterholzner, who was a professor of law at the University of Breslau, published an article on

Cicero's legal defence of the actor, Q. Roscius, in a case with C. Fannius Charea involving money claims. The article represented an attempt to recover legal procedure from the era of the Roman Republic. Unterholzner was interested, specifically, to understand in what type of civil matters the *'Collegium von Geschworenen'* (collegium of jurors) served.[15] Savigny's 'Beytrag zur Geschichte der Römischen Testamente' was marked by his concern to recover the laws governing last wills and testaments from the Republic, which had been changed by the *corpus iuris civilis.* During the 'time of the Republic', there had been 'two different forms of written private wills, both fully valid, so that one had a choice *(Wahl)* between both'.[16] This liberty of choice between a 'civil will with *Mancipation*' and 'the praetorian will with seven witnesses and seven seals,' was no longer possible under the 'Justinian law,' and choice was lost when only the form of *Manicipation* was recognized.[17] In the second volume, Unterholzner offered an article on the Twelve Tables.[18] Göschen's 'Einige Bemerkungen in Beziehung auf das ältere Recht der Freylassungen bey den Römern' (1817) was interested to delineate the ancient law covering release from custody on bail.[19]

In 1817, Savigny reported Barthold Niebuhr's discovery of the *Institutes of Gaius* in Verona, and published a fragment of the letter from Niebuhr regarding his find.[20] He offered thankful praise to the man, who had done 'brilliant service for the historical basis of our science'.[21] In the same volume, Niebuhr also offered an article about his discovery.[22] In, yet, another article in 1817, he published the full text of his original letter to Savigny.[23] The importance of the discovery of the *Institutes of Gaius* cannot be emphasized enough. It came close to doubling what was then known about Roman law. In contrast to the sources of Roman law prior to this discovery, what the *Institutes of Gaius* offered was history. For the first time, it was actually possible for scholars to research the constitutional and legal history from the era of the Republic. In addition, it was a source of knowledge on key areas of Roman public and private law, including the legal status of persons, property rights and contracts. Finally, it was an invaluable source of information about Roman legal procedures, and there was very little information on this subject prior to Niebuhr's find.[24] The discovery of the *Institutes of Gaius* ensured that the historical approach to Roman law, on a social scientific basis, would continue to flourish in German universities.

In fact, it was the historian, Niebuhr, who offered the suitable, social scientific interpretation of Roman political and constitutional history that would support constitutional transformation. As he wrote in the *Preface* to the 1826 edition of his *Römische Geschichte* (1811), he had been languishing in Rome and suffering from writer's block, until 'the point on which an inquiry hinged would come forward into clear light while I was conversing with Savigny'.[25] The *Preface* also offers an important window into the social and political world that Niebuhr's *Römische Geschichte* spoke to. 'The history of Rome', he opened, 'was treated, during the first two centuries after the revival of letters, with the same prostration of understanding and judgement to the written letter that had been handed down, and with the same fearfulness of going beyond it, which prevailed in all other branches of knowledge.'[26] If anyone had thought to question 'the credibility of the ancient writers and the value of their testimony, an outcry would have been raised against such atrocious presumption'.[27] While every now and then an 'independent mind' broke 'through this fence', soon thereafter 'a sentence of condemnation was forthwith pronounced against him'.[28] It is this questioning of the historical accounts of the classical writers that distinguished *Römische Geschichte* from earlier writings. The interpretation, Niebuhr offered, was marked by lengthy comparative analysis of classical accounts. This critical questioning is what defined Niebuhr's account of Roman history as social science and separated it from previous classical humanism and the Enlightenment approach to classical learning. As he wrote, history, 'strictly so called' had produced little other than 'dry compilations' and 'detached observations which led to nothing beyond'.[29]

Philology, according to Niebuhr, began to change these conditions in the late seventeenth century, and Roman history was touched by the 'youthful spirit of freedom'.[30] The era was a new one in Germany, where 'men were no longer satisfied with a superficial view in any field of knowledge'.[31] Yet, he also rejected the pure rationalism of the eighteenth century and emphasized that 'the work of destruction, which had given pleasure to the preceding age, in its anger against the continuance of authority founded only on usurpation', was no longer accepted.[32] His 'countrymen', Niebuhr wrote, 'strove after definite and positive knowledge', and a literature 'worthy of our nation and our language' resulted from this commitment.[33] Philology in Germany recognized 'its calling, to be the mediator between the remotest ages, to afford us the enjoyment of preserving through thousands of years an unbroken identity with the noblest and greatest nations of the ancient world by familiarizing us, through the medium of grammar and history, with the works of their minds and the course of their destinies, as if there were no gulf that divided them from us'.[34]

Here, we begin to get an understanding of how the study of Roman legal history and history, even on a social scientific basis, was, nevertheless, an expression of emerging liberal nationalism and constitutionalism in nineteenth-century Germany. The 'critical treatment of Roman history, the discovery of the forms of the constitution which had till then been misunderstood, was a fruit that time had been maturing', until 'a multitude of fortunate circumstances combined to foster its growth'.[35] In 1810, when the University of Berlin opened, it was a 'time full of hope', and Niebuhr wrote that 'to have enjoyed this, and to have lived in 1813—this is enough to make a man's life, notwithstanding much sad experience, a happy one'.[36] The 'revival of Roman history was in accord with the spirit of the age', and 'nay our age may discern itself to be immediately called by Providence to this inquiry, inasmuch as, within the eleven years since it commenced, three new and rich sources have been opened to us by the publication of Lydus, Gaius, and Cicero's *Republic*; whereas centuries had previously elapsed without adding to our means of knowledge'.[37] Niebuhr closed the *Preface* by thanking Savigny and others for their support and by making the primacy of contemporary politics explicitly clear: 'Of the principles on which the political opinions in my work are formed, there is not one that may not be found in Montesquieu or Burke.'[38]

While Savigny had articulated a theory of constitutional transformation, in his lectures and *Römische Geschichte* Niebuhr offered a classical example of it in practice. His Roman history focused on the history of laws and institutions. Influenced by Vician theory, perhaps through Savigny, it told a history of a progressive struggle for equality in sociopolitical relationships. Ancient Rome's history, in this regard, was one marked by temporary constitutional setbacks for disfranchised groups struggling for civil rights and equality, but the struggle was successful in the long term. More than anything else, at every possible point in his lectures and books, Niebuhr showed that violent means only produced short-term and fleeting gains. Rather, the security of full civil equality and rights was obtained through a gradual but conscious pursuit of the introduction of legislation—*rogations*—by those demanding full civil rights.

Niebuhr's emphasis on gradualism was the embodiment of constitutional transformation, and, in reality, it was focused on fostering such development in the German lands. This was evident, first, in his account of *The Beginning of Rome and Its Earliest Tribes*. 'In every nation of antiquity', Niebuhr wrote, 'there was a peculiar immemorial mode of division into a stated number of tribes,' and, where 'the citizens of a state, whether the whole body of them, or a portion of that body, enjoyed an equality of civil rights, and at the same time did not live united together in a central capital ... these were subjected to the same principle arrangement.'[39] In the case of the union of the original Romans, who had emerged from two distinct tribes, it had become 'firmer', and, 'in the course of time, when the feeling that citizens of the two towns were one people had been fostered by intermarriages and a common religious worship, they came to an agreement to have but one senate, one popular assembly, and one king, who was to be chosen alternately by the one people out of the other.'[40] Although the union remained, the establishment of this equality, in the immediate term, was thwarted 'by a usurpation on the part of the Romans'.[41] Even after the distinctions between the Romans and the ancient Quirites ceased, according to Niebuhr, the term *Quirites* was synonymous with plebeians, although the plebeians were later composed of different tribes.[42] The first two original tribes became known as the patricians, while a third tribe, the Luceres, were kept 'below them', distinguished by their 'difference in civil rights'.[43]

In Niebuhr's account, the story of the expulsion of the Tarquins was, predominately, that of the patricians struggling for rights against the tyranny of the Tarquin kings, with the exception of the reformer, Servius Tullius. It should also be emphasized, at this juncture, that Niebuhr's political argument continued to reflect the traditional organization of political thought around juridical concerns. 'Among the measures of Servius for promoting freedom,' he wrote, 'he established judges for private actions [civil cases].'[44] However, a later 'counter-revolution' of Tarquinius and the patricians drove back 'the commonality so far from the fair right it had reached that centuries were needed before it could again make its way against wind and tide into the harbour where after that royal legislation it was lying'.[45] Even after the expulsion of the Tarquins, the patricians contrived to prevent a restoration of the plebeians' civil rights for centuries.[46]

The classic struggle for constitutional transformation in his account, thus, emerges as that of the plebeians striving for civil equality with the patricians that began after the establishment, by Brutus, of what was an exclusive republic. This story, which emphasized multiple legal rogations in the transformation of the Roman constitution, was told and retold in his lectures at both the universities of Berlin and Bonn. In this way, it left a paradigmatic imprint on the minds of those who would effect political revision, in the second half of the century.

The violent opposition of the patricians notwithstanding, constitutional transformation began with the establishment of the *tribune plebes.*[47] Although the powers of the Tribunes were in the beginning 'very slender and modest; they were partly of a negative character, and partly administrative in a limited way, but not at all legislative', and, Niebuhr wrote, 'their power was a seed from which a tree was destined to grow up one day to overshadow the others'.[48] This overshadowing began with the Publilian law. 'The great importance of the Publilian law,' Niebuhr told his students at the University of Berlin, 'is that the Tribunes now obtained the initiative; until then it had been quite in the power of the Senate and the patricians either to allow a legislative proposal to be discussed or to prevent it.'[49] 'There were points which urgently required a change', he continued, 'and, without the Publilian rogation would never have been discussed in a constitutional way.'[50] It was a law, however, that 'could not remain without consequences destructive of internal quiet'.[51] Nevertheless, the violence plebeians experienced at the hands of patricians, which prevented them from voting, resulted in the *lex Junia,* which declared such activity treasonous against the commonality.[52] The agrarian laws also led to the redistribution of public lands to the plebeians.

The capstone in the process of constitutional transformation was the *lex Terentilian* or Terentilian rogation. As Niebuhr first broached the significance of this rogation, he stated that the 'legislations of antiquity embraced not only civil and criminal laws and the mode of procedure, but also the political laws and regulations of a temporary nature'.[53] 'It was the avowed object of the legislation', as he emphasized to his students, 'to abolish the differences between the two estates, to modify the constitution so as to make them as much as possible one united whole, and lastly to effect a limitation on the consular *imperium.*'[54] The result of the rogation was, ultimately, a civil code commission composed of both patricians and plebeians to draft the new law, and, as Niebuhr pointed out, 'besides the task of establishing a general law, the commissioners had to settle the constitution on the principle that the two estates were to be put on a footing of equality'.[55]

This is of vital significance to this account of modern constitutional transformation in Germany and the development of transformationist political thought. While

Savigny had drawn on the writings of Vico and Filangieri to suggest the idea of constitutional transformation, it was Niebuhr who offered a version of Roman history that showed it in working practice. The rights, specifically civil rights, of the plebeians were obtained over time and through a series of legislations or rogations. What is more, the capstone of this process of constitutional transformation was the Terentilian rogation. Here, it cannot be emphasized enough that the aim of this rogation was a body of written civil law, and wrapped up in it were all of the remaining political demands of the plebeians for equal civil rights and the leveling of all sociopolitical distinctions. All in all, the full revolution spanned more than two centuries, from the time of the establishment of the Tribunes (494 B.C.) through the Terentilian rogation (461) and on through the Canuleian law (445), which gave plebeians the rights of intermarriage with patricians, and the *lex Hortensius* (286), when the laws of the Tribunes became binding on all citizens. Niebuhr continued to emphasize these themes in his lectures at the University of Bonn for groups who obtained rights later in Roman history. 'It is a very common but erroneous opinion', he explained to his students, 'that the *lex Julia* conferred the privileges of Roman citizenship upon the Italians, who, in fact, never acquired those privileges by one law, but gained them successively one by one.'[56]

Finally, to close this section, it should be emphasized again that the technical element of law was never removed from the political element. The one was the means to obtaining the ends of the other. Niebuhr's proving of the efficacy of constitutional transformation, by scientifically locating an historical example of it and showing that it was the means by which constitutional equality was obtained in the ancient Roman Republic, consolidated the approach liberals would take to political revision in their own time. There was to be no sudden revolution, but a slow one, obtained in the honorable way of the ancient Roman plebeians, through successive measures and legislative rogations. The capstone would come with a *lex Terentilian,* civil code commission and civil code of their own, at some point in the future.

The Germanists and the *Vaterländisches Recht*

The effort to both recover and rationalize German law into a system was supported by the dominance of the historical school in Germany for the rest of the century. It was also nurtured by the numerous new legal journals that were founded in the 1820s, and by the rapid publication of scholarship on every area of German private law. The *Zeitschrift für geschichtliche Rechtswissenschaft* continued to be an important legal journal until its final edition in 1850. In 1829, Karl Mittermaier and Heinrich Zachariä published the first edition of their *Kritische Zeitschrift für Rechtswissenschaft und Gesetzgebung des Auslandes,* which circulated until 1856. The *Kritische Jahrbücher für deutsche Rechtswissenschaft* was founded, in 1839, by Amelius Ludwig Richter and circulated until 1848. Also in 1839, Wilda and Reyscher founded the *Zeitschrift für deutsches Recht und deutsche Rechtswissenschaft.* In addition to these German-wide journals, this trend was preceded by the founding of a number of state-level legal periodicals in Saxony, Prussia, Mecklenburg, Bavaria, and elsewhere. These may have been the result of modern legal reforms in these states. Perhaps the longest circulating state journal was the *Archiv für Zivil- und Kriminalrecht der Königlich-Preussischen Rheinprovinzen,* which continued publication from 1820 to 1906.

The coordinated effort to develop what Savigny had referred to as the data for a system, in this case the data for a legal system based on German sociopolitical values, was evident in the first edition of the ZGR. Here, Eichhorn offered two lengthy treatises. His 'Ueber das geschichtliche Studium des deutschen Rechts' (1815) emphasized the need for 'scientific instruction' in and recovery of German private law *(deutsches Privatrecht),* which continued to exist as 'unwritten particular law' and whose existence had been threatened by the French occupation.[57] This project, he believed, was of vital importance to the German people and should be the highest priority of 'scientific interest'.[58] He went on to identify for legal historians the primary sources where German private law could be located. In a second article, 'Ueber den Ursprung der städtischen Verfassung in Deutschland' (1815), Eichhorn focused on municipal legal arrangements as a vital source of German constitutional history. The *'ius civitatus, Weichbildrecht, Stadtrecht'* had developed in Germany in the twelfth century and marked the existence of the first civic privileges *(Gerechtsamen).*[59] The constitutions that predated this period had resulted from charters of liberty granted to the old Roman towns.[60] Eichhorn, then, went on to offer a detailed philological analysis of the development of urban constitutionalism, which was organized around juridical precepts.

Eichhorn's *Einleitung in das deutsche Privatrecht mit Einschluß des Lehenrechts,* which was published in 1823, was a reflection of the changing political climate. Whereas he focused on constitutional law prior to 1819, he had transferred his political writing to scholarship on private law by 1823. Like so many other writers in the period, Eichhorn claimed that his interest was only in law and not politics, but, in reality, this claim was only a disclaimer to avert the attention of the censors. *Einleitung in das deutsche Privatrecht* was part and parcel of liberal constitutionalism and political through and through. In the first section, he discussed the important sources of German private law, identifying customary laws *(Gewohnheitsrecht)* in particular.[61] Most importantly, however, in the second section, Eichhorn developed a detailed system of German private laws *(System des deutschen Privatrechts),* which took up the remaining 800 pages of the book.[62] It was in the various systematic treatments of the data, produced in the first half of the nineteenth century, that legal historians, essentially, offered images of a German *Gemeinwesen.* It is also for this reason that the whole of the study of the history of German private law must be seen as *Privatrechts-Staatslehre,* as I suggested in the Introduction.

In Book 1, the law of Persons *(Personenrecht)*, Eichhorn underscored the private law basis of public liberties *(privatrechtliche Bedeutung der Freiheit).*[63] Here, he identified three types of personality: full personality or liberty *(vollkommene Freiheit),* limited personality or liberty *(unvollkommen Freie),* and incapacity *(Unfreie).*[64] It is at this point that the exclusive basis of the state that German liberals wished to bring into existence, through constitutional transformation, became clear. There were five qualifications for full liberty: ownership of real property *(Eigenthum an Grundstücken),* full legal and business capacity *(Fähigkeit zu allen Rechtsgeschäften und Handlungen),* right of the wergild *(Recht des Wehrgeldes),* right to private feuds *(Fehderecht)* and right to bear arms *(Waffenrecht).*[65] Only members of the community who were in full possession of these rights enjoyed full liberty and participation in the state. This was confirmed in the last pages of his treatise, when he returned to the importance of the municipal constitutions. 'Political liberty *(Bürgerrecht)*' hinged, in all German municipal constitutions, on the possession of private property and concurrent full management and usufruct rights relative to that property.[66]

In addition, Eichhorn's system offers an indication of the continuity of political thought between the early theoretical period of German liberalism and the practice of constitutional transformation after 1850. It mirrors the structure of the BGB that was enacted in 1896. Book 1, as I have mentioned, covered the law of persons. Book 2, *Recht der Forderung,* systematized juristic personality. In Book 3, property law *(Rechte an Sachen)* was delineated. In Book 4, Eichhorn turned his attention to family law. Here, he delineated not only the German basis of marital property relations, but the necessity of sex guardianship over women. Inheritance law was taken up in Book 5. Finally, the broad constitutional and political significance of Eichhorn's system of private law is evident in Book 6, *Recht der Gemeinheiten und Gewerbe.* Here, he returned to the importance of municipal constitutions, but added an analysis of village constitutions *(Verfassung der Dorfgemeinden).* In addition to this, a liberal political focus on developing a constitution that would meet the needs of capital was important, and, indeed, Eichhorn closed his *Einleitung in das deutsche Privatrecht* with four chapters on business associations: guild law, business law, shipping rights and the regulation of trade.[67]

The structure of Eichhorn's system is important also because scholars have suggested that the structure of the BGB was derived from Roman law. As I argue here, and as Eichhorn's system shows, German law underwent a scientific process of technical Romanization, but the norms were based on a rationalization of German customary law. Eichhorn's system did not stand alone. There were many others produced in these years. In the third volume of the ZGR, Mittermaier's 'Beiträge zur Geschichte der ehelichen Gütergemeinschaft, des Erbrechts und der Freiheit zu testiren im Mittelalter' (1815) appeared, and it was here that he began to identify *deutsches Mundium* as the proper basis of marital property relations.[68] He wrote his *Der gemeine deutsche bürgerliche Prozeß in Vergleichung mit dem preußischen und französischen Civilverfahren und mit den neuesten Fortschritten der Prozeßgesetzgebung* on common German civil procedure in 1820. He wrote his *Lehrbuch des deutschen Privatrechts* in 1821, but it was in his *Grundsätze des gemeinen deutschen Privatrechts* (1823) that he offered a systematic treatment. It was republished in the 1840s.

It should also be emphasized that the various legal journals covered different aspects of German legal development. While the ZGR published articles on legal history, Mittermaier and Zachariä's *Kritische Zeitschrift für Rechtswissenschaft und Gesetzgebung des Auslandes* published articles on the development of European law generally. It was a vital organ for the dissemination of other European legal traditions, especially English constitutional developments. In the 'Ueber den Zweck dieser Zeitschrift', Zachariä opened with the statement that 'there will come a time, when all people of Germanic origin will become one people with regard to knowledge and science—our philosophers and scholars only have to create this great union.'[69] The magazine emphasized the need to build the 'the unity of European people and of European culture'.[70]

In addition to these major German-wide journals, the rise of customary law constitutionalism was apparent in the numerous articles written by legal collectors in local legal journals. An 1826 article written by a collector of legal documents, Dr. Kleinschmidt, is a good example of this genre of political writing. The article was designed to emphasize the role of the people in court decisions and to show them in the exercise of their jurisdiction. In the matter of *Amelunke et al. v. Spengler,* Kleinschmidt reported that 'the royal ministry in Bilderlahe took cognizance of the customary measures'. Apparently in 1646, the local prince decreed that the standard for weights and measures in Hildesheim should follow Braunschweig customs. The precedent for the court's decision on the law was set by the people's customs. The ministry at Bilderlahe made its decision only after 'several field witnesses and old people *(Feldsgeschworene und alte Leute)* from Bockenem' testified to the same effect. For Kleinschmidt, this confirmed the participatory liberties of the people and that their customs were alive as the legitimate source of law.[71]

Kleinschmidt's article reflected emerging customary law constitutionalism, which clearly articulated the demand for modern rights in a traditional way. It added data for the system of court procedure imagined by liberal jurists. The court's decision was based on customs and made only after hearing the testimony of old people. Thus, it could be argued that the people's customs were the legitimate source of law, and the testimony of old people confirmed that they were of time out of memory and there was no written record to the contrary. Here, the court did not give law, but only made a finding of law in accordance with customary legal arrangements. Finally, because the Bilderlahe court in Kleinschmidt's own time based its decision on the 1646 decree, it could be established that usage of the custom was long and continued, without interruption. Thus, the customary usage was established by the consent of the people, and the rights and liberties involved were allowed under German customary law. These were not rights and liberties granted by a prince, but rather the people were the creator of law. It also is significant that Kleinschmidt emphasized the fact that the weights and measures of Hildesheim were based on Braunschweig customs.

This pointed toward the historical existence of *Rechtskreise*; Braunschweig was one of the celebrated cities within the Hanseatic League. This kind of customary law politics—custom breedeth right—posed a fundamental challenge to the theoretical basis of the monarchical state by threatening to overturn the very basis of its indivisible sovereignty with the people's jurisdiction.

It is clear that customary law acquired increasing political imperative in German-speaking Europe after the *Freiheitskriege* and that it was absorbed into the liberal programme, which called for the rationalization, scientization, systemization and professionalization of highly particular German customary laws. At the same time, it is important to consider legal conditions prior to the consolidation of law in the late nineteenth century. The practicing lawyer, Pfeiffer, offered an informative description of conditions in 1815 Hesse.

> Roman law is the main source of *gemeines Recht,* although various territorial laws have changed a great deal of it. The greatest multiplication of laws, however, is based on customs, which can be viewed in part as common German customs, in part as customs of all Hesse, in part as customs of single provinces, and in part merely as customs of the kind ... often nothing more than a large village has preserved them in an old tale and in a grimy community chest. This great heterogeneity of legal sources has had, as its inevitable consequence, the most remarkable lack of uniformity in the civil law of the individual parts of this state.[72]

The collection of the data for the *vaterländisches Recht,* even if it was confined to the existing customary laws of Hesse alone, was a formidable task and indeed probably impossible. It was exactly the great heterogeneity of the customary laws, however, that supported liberal interests. Transformationist-minded jurists could simply pick and choose those customs that fit their political demands, give them social scientific sanction and use them to develop a system of what was, in effect, classical German customary law.

Legal Antiquarianism and Images of the *Gemeinwesen*

In the aftermath of postwar historiography that viewed the Thibaut–Savigny controversy as a sharp political divide between the forces of reactionary conservatism and democracy, later debates in the German legal world were also seen as indications of major political divides. However, the disagreements in the German legal world may also be seen as an indication of the steady growth of the primacy of politics and customary law constitutionalism. The controversy between the Romanist and Germanist, namely Georg Friedrich Puchta (1798–1846) and Jacob Grimm, may be seen in this light. Puchta was also one of Savigny's students and took his chair in Roman legal history at the University of Berlin when Savigny retired in 1842. Although the publication of Puchta's *Das Gewohnheitsrecht* (1828) was said to have created a split within the German legal world, in reality, he expanded Savigny's argument on gradualism into a three-stage theory of national legal development. The first stage Puchta described as a period of innocence and the second as a period of particularism or variety. It was in the final stage that professionally trained legal scholars would carry legal particularism to the 'higher unity' of 'science', a stage that he felt characterized his contemporary age.[73] The problem, however, emerged when Puchta suggested that science itself was a source of law. 'Science finds a productive use in the recognition of customary law,' he wrote, 'and here science itself enters the list of sources of law.'[74] While Putcha still viewed the *Volksgeist* as the ultimate source of the laws, von Mehren and Gordley suggest that doctrinal thinking dominated his work to such a degree that it had no practical significance.[75] Nevertheless, the publication of *Das Gewohnheitsrecht* underscored how important customary law constitutionalism had become in German sociopolitical thought.

As Savigny's most celebrated student from his Marburg years, it was Jacob Grimm, more than anyone else, who championed the development of a popular discourse on the political element and the *vaterländisches Recht.* Savigny and Jacob remained close friends throughout their lives. When Savigny traveled with his new wife to Paris in 1804, the two were buggy-jacked by thugs just outside the city, and this was an incident that did little to raise Savigny's opinions of the French experiment. The thugs stole and made waste of, amongst other things, his considerable research notes. It was in the aftermath of this buggy-jacking that he wrote to Jacob, requesting that he come and assist him in Paris. In fact, both Grimm brothers corresponded frequently with him, and it was Savigny who introduced them into German romantic circles. The brothers sent him the first copies of their *Kinder und Hausmärchen* (1812) for his review and for him to test read with young Bettina. In his *Selbstbiographie,* Jacob faced a loss of words for the man who had 'such a decisive influence on my whole life and education'.[76] Not long after his dismissal from Göttingen, in an 1838 letter, he wrote to his '*Lieber* Savigny, you are the oldest and truest friend of my life.'[77] The relationship, like the close ties between Niebuhr and Savigny, also underscores Savigny's tremendous influence in the German intellectual world, generally. Both William and Jacob corresponded frequently with him as they were preparing the folk tales, and, as I mentioned earlier, it was Savigny who secured posts for both brothers, at the University of Berlin, after the notorious Göttingen Seven dismissal.

Jacob is better known for his work with William on the *Hausmärchen,* their other folklore compilations, and, of course, *Das Deutsche Wörterbuch,* which they began to work on in 1838. However, he was also a lawyer and one of the leading figures in the German legal world. In the same years that the major works of Savigny, Eichhorn and Puchta appeared, Jacob Grimm published his first long work on German legal history, *Deutsche Rechtsalterthümer* (1828). He was the founder of German legal antiquarianism, and its influence cannot be emphasized enough. In addition to his *Rechtsalterthümer,* which was one of the most influential legal works of the early period, Jacob published several articles in German legal journals, and his *Weisthümer* (1840–1842) supplied a history of legal precedents and findings of law by the *Schöffengerichte,* which liberals held up as paragons of German liberty. Increasingly, following Jacob's legal writings, precedents, maxims and principles from what became known as an ancient free epoch were linked to contemporary folk customs and also deemed a prescriptive basis of German liberties. Liberals respected and looked to Jacob, not only for his work on German folklore and the history of German language, but for his contribution to German legal history. Indeed, he was elected president of both Germanisten conferences that were held in Lübeck and Frankfurt in 1846 and 1847, respectively.

In the first edition of the ZGR, along with articles by Eichhorn and others, Grimm published an article which introduced the idea of a *Lebendigkeit* (organic relationship) between the common folklore alive amongst the people in the German countryside and ancient German liberties.[78] In 'Ueber eine eigene altgermanische Weise der Mordsühne' (1815), Jacob's discussion of ancient German customs *(altgermanische Weisen)* was his first attempt to offer a statement on prescriptive German rights. Using common folklore and language as his sources, he argued for the prescriptive right of persons to tort claims in instances of loss or damage to private property. A good example of this is his *Tale of Otr.*

> According to an old wise tale, the farmer Hreidmar lived with his three sons, Fahnir, Otr, Regin and his two daughters, Lyngheid and Lohnheid. As his name already implied, Otr transformed himself into an Otter and dashed into a stream to catch fish. One day while Otr sat on the bank of the stream, eating a salmon in just a blink of an eye, from up the road along came three hunters *(Asen)* named Loki, Odin and Hönir. Spying the content Otter, Loki took and cast a stone, killing the resting Otter. Very pleased with his kill, he skinned the animal and carried on. Oh! But much to their surprise the next morning, they found it necessary to make an urgent trip to Hreidmar's house and without knowing anything about Otr's close relatives. Soon after they arrived, Hreidmar and his sons recognized the skin and laid hands on the young hunter, desiring an answer for the murder of their loved one, Otr.[79]

According to Jacob's account, Hreidmar and his sons detained Loki, while his fellow hunters secured gold to cover the loss of Otr. And so it followed 'in the poetic language', he wrote, the terms *Ottersgeltung* and *Asennothgeld.* Accordingly, Jacob argued that *lutra* and *lytra* could be translated as Otter and when joined to the term *lytrum,* one found the root of the legal concept of *Lösegeld* (money damages for tort claims).

As Murray Peppard writes, the Grimm brothers' interest in German folklore was driven by the belief that they contained remnants of ancient German law and liberties.[80] These notions had been given social scientific legitimacy by Vico's *Scienza*

Nuova, which had reacted against Cartesian metaphysics and demanded greater consideration of spiritual and intangible elements. The *Tale of Otr,* a folk tale from time out of mind, was a testament to ancient custom and was used to argue the right to money damages for loss of private property. The moral of the story was that the ancient Germans possessed private property rights and that these rights were part of an entailed estate, a prescriptive and inborn constitution. In his 'Von der Poesie im Recht' (1816), published in the second edition of the ZGR, Jacob invested German poetry with the same legal authority. Here, he emphasized the spiritual and symbolic origins of law. He suggested that folk poetry and that which could be derived from 'the mouth and customs of our common man' was a living witness to an ancient constitution.[81]

Jacob's legal scholarship, and arguably the *Hausmärchen* and *Wörterbuch,* involved nothing less than the formation of a kind of *völkische lex regia,* and the underlying claim was that although it may not have existed in theory, it had thrived in ordinary practice. In point of fact, disclosing the political element and discovering the data for a system was a rather dubious project. However much legal historians may have believed themselves to be engaged in a scientific endeavor, the appeal to custom, as a source of data, disclosed that the political element was more a product of liberal political imagination than objective science. Time and again the historical data seemed, peculiarly, to bear witness to the sociopolitical system that liberals wished to bring into existence. Nowhere is this questionable aspect of German jurisprudence more apparent than in Jacob's major work, *Rechtsalterthümer.* He 'held his *Deutsche Rechtsalterthümer* in higher regard than any of his other works' and considered it to be 'a draft foundation' for future legislation, as Andreas Heusler and Rudolf Hübner wrote a generation later.[82]

While Eichhorn and Mittermaier had relied on written legal sources, Jacob expanded the pool of customary law sources to include mythology, folklore, poetry and the like. 'On every corner', Jacob wrote in *Rechtsalterthümer,* 'I find sprouts for growth.'[83] Celebrating Möser's *Patriotische Phantasien,* where he had called for the organic development of the state and its institutions, Jacob argued for the revival of *'deutsche Rechtsantiquare'*.[84] The progress of legal antiquarianism, however, led German jurisprudence down a somewhat precarious path. Legal antiquarians vested the rights of the people in remoter and still remoter periods in the German past, while at the same time asserting that the evidence of the continuous usage and expression of ancient liberties could be found in the living and inarticulate *Volk* culture of their own time. The data collected for the *vaterländiches Recht* was purported to have deep roots in a free epoch of German antiquity, an era well before the rise of absolutist monarchs. The *vaterländisches Recht,* accordingly, was prescriptive, beyond the power of personal rulers to abolish or annul, and, therefore was available to be reclaimed by the German people at any time. Jacob had loosened the bands on legal history and freed liberals from written legal sources. As Wieacker once wrote, following the publication of *Rechtsalterthümer,* Germanists dedicated themselves to rediscovering 'the law of the Germany of yore'.[85]

Jacob praised Eichhorn for his contribution to German legal history and for inaugurating a new era in the study of German legal sources. He explained that legal antiquarians and traditional Germanists, like Eichhorn, were in agreement relative to the recovery of German legal sources as a critical phase in the development of a German system.[86] 'In antiquity', however, Grimm argued, 'everything was expressed spiritually *(sinnlich)*', whereas 'in modern times, everything had gathered itself together intellectually *(geistig)*'.[87] The key distinction between traditional Germanists and the new 'school of German legal antiquity *(schule deutscher rechtsantiquare)*' was that antiquarian research would also focus on the 'materials of the spiritual element *(sinnliche element)* in German legal history'.[88] 'In particular', Jacob argued, 'the legal precedents of the lay judges *(Weisthümer)* on German rights, in their high wisdom and content' were, in fact, 'totally comparable with the common folk language and folksongs' of the people.[89] 'In addition', he added, this school would engage, not only jurists, but 'antiquarians' working on 'language, poetry and the history of our ancestors', generally.[90] 'The experiment of a primary work in this sense', he explained, is to offer 'more oil than salt', and his *Rechtsalterthümer* offered 'a work full of materials'.[91]

A critical dimension of the nineteenth-century project of recovering the *vaterländisches Recht* involved not only the discovery of the data for a system, but the thinking of that data into a system, as we have seen. While historians have tended to focus exclusively on Roman law, in reality, there were many systematic treatments of German legal sources in the period, all of which, remarkably, seemed to confirm the efficacy of liberal political ideals. This was evident in Mittermaier's work, Eichhorn's *System des deutschen Privatrechts* and, to a lesser degree, in Savigny's *System des heutigen römischen Rechts* (1840). Jacob's *Rechtsalterthümer* was no exception to this direction in German jurisprudence. It also offered a similar image of a German *Gemeinwesen,* but one confirmed by a systematization of the *sinnliche element* of German legal history. It must be emphasized, however, that, while it drew data from this element, it nevertheless sustained the political elements found in Mittermaier and Eichhorn's systems and elsewhere in German legal thought. What made it unique was its attempt to appeal to popular culture and popular language style. In this way, *Rechtsalterthümer* laid the critical foundation for building a popular constitutionalism accessible to ordinary Germans and also set the stage for the broader mobilization of intellectuals working in other areas of German cultural expression.

As I mentioned earlier, the rise of the historical school marked the growth of a specifically north German customary law constitutionalism, and nowhere was this stated more clearly than in *Rechtsalterthümer.* It was marked by the solemnization of the *Sachsenspiegel,* which German liberals brandished as the source of ancient liberties. Grimm's usage of the term *'Recht',* rather than *'Gesetz',* pointed toward the primacy of politics and, as he stated, the term *'deutsch'* specifically referred to 'northern and Anglo-Saxon sources'.[92] Jacob also expressed the widespread political objections against the *ius commune* as a source of legal rules in German-speaking

Europe: 'It is not *vaterländisch* to us, was not produced and grown on our ground and stands, in its essence, in fundamental conflict to our way of thinking, and, for that very reason, can never satisfy us.'[93] Rather, as he stated poignantly, the legal precedents spoken 'from the mouth of the country people *(landvolks)*' formed a 'highly peculiar phenomenon in our ancient constitution, that is not found amongst any other people and is a glorious witness to the free and noble nature of our native laws'.[94]

The north German constitutional politics of the Grimm brothers' folklore research and work on the *Deutsches Wörterbuch* was evident in *Rechtsalterthümer.* In the lengthy, 300-page *Einleitung,* Jacob developed what was essentially legal philology. The symbolism of common folk language was treated as an organic storehouse of the ancient constitution. This brand of legal philology was a central feature of *Rechtsalterthümer,* and it marked the beginning of a kind of hyper-politicization of every ordinary element of German culture. *Arm und Hals* 'appeared as the symbols of subjection', he argued, and 'to lay ones throat or neck under an arm or to have an arm laid over ones throat', implied that person was unfree and owned by another person.[95] He also offered a lengthy discussion on the legal symbolism of *Hand und Finger,* reasoning that 'considered symbolically, the hand was like a scepter in the importance of power'.[96] *Haar und Bart* 'were the symbols and dress of the emancipated, free class'.[97] *Der Hut* was a symbol of freedom and 'for the delegation of goods and fee or feudal tenure'.[98] *Der Hammer,* originally a weapon, became a symbol of court authority: 'A judge slammed down his hammer after the legal transaction of goods.'[99]

It cannot be emphasized enough that liberal political goals were at the heart of burgeoning research on the history of German private law and what I have called *Privatrechts-Staatslehre.* The ultimate right that liberals claimed was *bürgerliche* sovereignty, at the heart of which was the right to make the laws. Conferring title of prescription on the people's right to sovereignty was critical, and the research of legal antiquarians was designed to prove the pedigree of German liberties. This encouraged a belief in an ancient German constitution, which was nourished by the myth of original freedom. At the same time, this led to preoccupation with the original sociopolitical constitution of all German relationships, and, increasingly, this purported original character became the justification for constitutional form. On the one hand, there was original liberty, but, on the other, as was already evident in Jacob's philological treatment, there were also a host of original unfreedoms.

By the 1820s, political writers were preoccupied with the law and increasingly identified with the *Gemeinwesen* (commonwealth) as the normative form of a free state. According to *Conversations-Lexikon* (1820), 'republic in the sense of ancient times' referred to a 'commonwealth of the citizens.'[100] In his frequently cited *Die Staatswissenschaft im Lichte unserer Zeit* (1827), Karl Pölitz wrote: 'The basic character of a republican form of government, in contrast to a monarchy, is that the ruler *(Regent)* in a republic is only the highest civil servant *(Beamte)* of the State.'[101] Written for scholarly and popular audiences, Johann von Aretin's *Staatsrecht der constitutionellen Monarchie: Ein Handbuch für Geschäftsmänner, studierende Jünglinge, und gebildete Bürger* (1824) declared: 'All rights of governance have the origin in the whole body of the people *(Gesamtkörper des Volkes)* and the government [has power] only through and for the people.'[102] Karl Rotteck's *Lehrbuch des Vernunftrechts* (1840) instructed that the difference between despotism and a republic was the 'private will of the ruler, in contrast to the rule of the collective will of the community of the members of the state'.[103] He also urged that: 'The aim of a republic is the rule of the true totality of wills,' and, 'in so far as a constitution is crafted for the realization of this basic idea, it is republican and the State a true free State.'[104]

In legal discourse, the making of this constitution involved not only a theoretical reconstitution of the monarch into a civil servant, but the leveling of relationships by awarding rights to the bourgeois commonality. Jacob's system, which followed his lengthy legal philology, was divided into six books. Book 1, *Stand,* identified and treated the five social groupings. In Book 2, *Haushalt,* Jacob examined family law and all familial relationships. Books 3 and 4, *Eigenthum* and *Gedinge,* focused on rights of private property. In Book 5, *Verbrechen,* Jacob explored customary criminal law amongst the ancient Germans, and, finally, in Book 6, *Gericht,* he offered a treatment of the customary basis of the courts and court procedures.

Rechtsalterthümer began by identifying five social groupings amongst the ancient Germans: rulers *(Herrschende),* the nobility *(Der Edle)*, the free *(Der Freie),* slaves *(Knechte)* and foreigners *(Der Fremde).* The usage of the term *Herrschende,* rather than *Könige,* reflected his attempt to reconstitute monarchs as civil servants, and this posed a fundamental challenge to the legitimacy of personal rule in Central Europe. In Jacob's account, the spirit and constitution of the ancestors seemed to boldly object to the existing political conditions: 'Kings could choose dukes not only come from the nobility, but also from amongst the free people.'[105] Moreover, 'the king could be hereditary or elected'.[106] Citing Wilken's *Handbuch der deutschen historie* (1810), Grimm proclaimed: 'After the time of the Frankish kings, *Deutschland* became a *Wahlreich* and was no longer ruled by [Frankish] sons.'[107] 'The vote [for the ruler] took place in a common people's assembly *(allgemeiner volksversammlung)*', and 'since the time of Otto III, the German kaiser was elected on German soil in Frankfurt am Main'.[108] 'Elections', Grimm suggested, 'were held only in the instances where the line became extinct or if the ruler was incompetent.'[109] Here, Jacob cited amongst other sketchy sources, Beowulf on the Anglo-Saxons: 'The *Saegeâtas* voted, after the fall of the young king, Beowulf to the throne.'[110] The 'incompetence *(Untüchtigkeit)* of kings', he wrote, meant 'not only criminal conduct or absence from his administrative duties', but could also result from 'losing wars *(kriegsunglück)* or starvation [amongst the people]'.[111] To support his finding, in a footnote, he offered an excerpt from Paulus's seventeenth-century piece, *Diaconus historia gentis Langobardorum bei Muratori scriptores I: 'sed cum Adaloaldus eversa mente insaniret* (insanity), *de regno ejectus est* (ejected from rule).'[112] In this way, he created a prescriptive right to impeachment, which clearly objected to existing conditions.

Whether or not a ruler was hereditary or elected, he was still bound by law and certain obligations to the people. The chief obligation, naturally, was to uphold the sovereignty and free liberties of the people, the allegiance to which he demonstrated in symbolic acts. At the beginning of a ruler's government, the people had to recognize him and vowed their loyalty, but this loyalty was conditioned on his adhering to and upholding their laws. Citing *Heliand poema saxonicum,* Giesebrecht's *Gregorius von Tours zehn bücher fränkischer geschichte* and Tacitus' *Germania,* Jacob explained in symbolic terms: 'The new king, whether elected or hereditary, was elevated on a shield so that everyone could behold him as he was carried three times around the assembled people, who acknowledged him and gave their approval though handshakes.'[113] 'The first business of new kings was to ride around the empire', and on this trip, Grimm continued, he would 'state the rights and peaces of the people'.[114] He cited a poem from his own *Weisthümer* as evidence of this tradition: 'The Lord shall confirm to everyone the liberty of the people.'[115] 'In every community', he wrote, 'a special court was held', and 'the king confirmed the liberty of the people.'[116]

Significant political suggestions were contained in the *Herrschende,* which involved the decentring authority away from the bureaucratic state by reinforcing the regional and customary rights, indeed, the prescriptive rights of the people. The reconstitution of the monarch as a ruler was part and parcel of liberal efforts to reconstitute the state as a mythical, juristic person, the *Gesammtkörper* of its members. According to Pölitz, the 'ruler is not a physical person like in a monarchy, but a moral (mythical) person, whose sovereignty is not personal, but given authority to administer the State'.[117] The head of state, thus, was limited in the exercise of authority, first and foremost, by the sworn duty to uphold the rights of people. In his system, Jacob emphasized that the ruler was required to address the 'people's assemblies *(volksversammlungen)*', and, citing Pertz, he detailed that these regularly held assemblies met two or three times a year, in spring and autumn.[118]

As seen in *Rechtsaltherthümer, Privatrechts-Staatslehre* was focused on dismantling the *Ständestaat* by leveling distinctions and awarding noble status and privileges to the *bürgerliche* commonalty, and here Niebuhr's account of the plebeian's path to civil equality must have offered a powerful example. Jacob collapsed social distinctions between the three groups at the top of ancient German society. In his chapters on *'Der Edele'* and *'Der Freie',* Grimm redeveloped the concept of nobility, first, by emphasizing immediate parentage rather than age-old lineage. He opened his chapter on the nobility with a philological treatment of the two terms, and, here, he chose to use the term *Edel* rather than *Adel.* The term *Adel* was weighted with traditional conceptions of an hereditary aristocracy, but *Edel,* by contrast, referred to personal nobility and nobility based on virtue. 'Ennoblement', he added in a footnote, 'was synonymous with liberty.'[119] Amongst other authors, he cited the French writer Méon's *Fabliaux et Contes* (1808), whose definition revolved around '*gentix et bien enparentés*'.[120] Jacob chose the word *'wohlgeboren',* which merely translates in today's English into well-born. Nevertheless, there was more political symbolism attached to this term than may be immediately apparent. *'Wohl'* was weighted with liberal conceptions of the state; the *Gemeinwohl* referred to the public good or common good of the *Gemeinwesen. Wohlgeboren,* therefore, did not impart a traditional conception of the nobility, but a rethinking that associated status with good citizenship or worthiness. Although the nobility possessed privileges, Jacob argued that 'the free and the nobility have all essential rights in common and in this way are equal'.[121]

There can be no doubt that the free were, in fact, a metaphor for the nineteenth-century *Bürgerthum,* and, once Jacob had leveled distinctions between the nobility and the bourgeoisie, he leveled all further hierarchies. 'The King', accordingly, 'was elected from the nobility ... and therefore, the nobles were of equal birth *(ebenbürtig)* with him.'[122] It was in the chapter on *Der Freie* where Jacob drew down any further distinctions and where a theoretical ascendance of the bourgeoisie was most evident. He opened the chapter with the bold assertions that: 'The free are the main part and power of the whole people; they themselves emerged as the source of the nobility.'[123] From here, he deconstructed the distinction between king and people. The title *Karl,* accordingly, had originally referred to the *Stammherr* of the free families. Hence, he argued that the words for king, namely *Kral, Krol* and *Karolus,* in the Slavic languages, *Charlemagne* in French and *Karl der Große* in German, referred to the leader of freemen rather than to a king in the traditional sense.[124] The ruler's social station had been reconfigured, and he suddenly appeared as no higher or lower on the social scale than the people whose interests he was elected to look after.

The rest of his chapter on *Der Freie* offered nothing less than a declaration of prescriptive bourgeois liberties, which found both symbolic and real expression. 'The outward symbol of freemen is long, curly hair,' while criminals and slaves 'must wear their hair short' and are prohibited from washing it. This was a right reserved for freemen.[125] High on the list of liberties was freedom of movement: 'Every freeman had the right to go, unhindered, where ever he wanted.'[126] 'Every freeman', as Jacob wrote, 'carried a weapon.'[127] The right to bear arms, however, was contingent on the ability and willingness to defend the nation.[128] In times of peace, the freeman's primary public obligation was to serve as jurors and lay judges.[129] The right to private property, as it had in Eichhorn's system, also emerged as the most critical right of all. 'Every free property owner', and only property owners, as Jacob emphasized, 'had his part in the public power and the capacity for all rights.'[130]

Despite the theoretical leveling of sociopolitical distinctions at the top of society, the imagined *Gemeinwesen* was based on exclusive participation. Indeed, Grimm had already instructed in his section on rulers that 'strict voting law *(strenges wahlrecht)*' limited participation in public elections.[131] German civic participation was conceived, not only as masculine, but was developed around the principal of legal personality, as I have mentioned. The standard for majority was not age, 'but the outer powerful appearance of the body's mass'.[132] A boy became a man when he could 'swing a spear'.[133] Only 'the *Hausherr* was free and unrestricted' and 'the wife, his sisters and children fell under his guardianship *(Schutz* or *Mund)*'.[134] He cited Tacitus' *Germania* when he described the position of the *Hausherr* as 'like a king on the throne, the judge on the highest chair, so is the *Hausvater* in his pride of place *(Ehrensitz)*'.[135] The organization of the family, thus, was seen as a vital cornerstone of civil political arrangements, because as Eichhorn pointed out, marital property relations housed significant ramifications for legal personality. Savigny also identified civic rights with marital property relations.[136]

Power relations in the family were a metaphor for power relations in the broader society. On the one hand, male liberties seemed to extend from their rights in the home. The rights of men, in times of peace, were contingent on the fulfillment of family obligations and originated in their role as 'husband and father of a wife and children, that were under his authority'.[137] On the other, the denial of rights to women stemmed from their subjugation in the home. This division of power started from the moment of birth and was apparent in the way that Jacob contrasted the meaning of *Der Speer* and *Die Spindel.* 'At the birth of a *Mädchen*', he wrote, 'a spindle was laid at the door.'[138] 'The spindle', accordingly, was 'the symbol of the woman and housewife'.[139] In the ancient legal language, however, 'the spear' was the symbol of manhood and the male line. It could be used to legitimate children, whereas, as he specifically mentioned, the spindle could not.

In the primary instance, the feminine emerged as the living symbol of incapacity. Married women 'could no longer let their hair fly freely, but had to bind it in a knot, tightly'.[140] Women, Jacob wrote, were assigned 'other symbols and punishments'.[141] 'In many ways women were worth less than men,' he added.[142] 'A newborn child was more respected if it was a boy than if it was a girl.'[143] 'Girls,' he did not fail to emphasize, 'were often given away into slavery.'[144] Women, in Jacob's system, were not private property right holders, but were themselves private property. Similar legal meaning was defined for *Schuh* (shoe), ring and *Schlüßel* (key). Fathers could adopt or legitimate sons by placing a shoe on their right foot. Where women were concerned, the shoe served a similar purpose: 'The groom brings it (shoe) to the bride; as soon as it has been placed on the foot she becomes considered as under his power.'[145] This certainly gives new meaning to the legal symbolism that was attached to the glass slipper in the fairy tale of Cinderella. Similar legal symbolism was attached to the ring: *'Ist der finger beringt, so ist die jungfer (virgin) bedingt.'*[146] Although *Schlüßel* (key) symbolized 'the power of the housewife', women in reality were only the *Schlüßelträgerin* (carrier of the keys) of their husbands.[147] *Der Gürtel,* the 'innermost clothing', was something given by a freeman to someone who was a subject to his authority. 'Women who were cut out from inheriting, from their deceased husbands', Jacob explained, 'either had to remove their girdle during the burial at the grave or appear before a judge and witnesses to remove their girdle.'[148]

This imagining of the place of women in the home was the direct corollary to the basis of their exclusion from full citizenship and participation. An indication of this comes in Jacob's analysis of *Wehrgeld* (wergild), which readers will recall Eichhorn had identified as one of the five requirements for *vollkommene Freiheit.* Deemed incapable of bearing arms, women would be shut out of participating in the new arenas of commerce and politics by limiting their access to, and control of, property. 'Women under the oldest law', Jacob argued 'were either denied or limited in terms of inheritance.'[149] When women did inherit, they always received significantly less than 'the father's son'.[150] Women received only half as much inheritance as the man, and this extended from their lower value in wergild. For example, in the case where a father had a son and a daughter, the son received two-thirds, the daughter one-third; if he had a son and two daughters, the son received one-half and both daughters one-half together.[151] If a woman did inherit, the effects of her marriage would still deny her full capacity. Jacob wrote that 'what property the wife contributed as well as what her father had given her, became the property of the man.'[152] Her property was no longer her property but fell under the management and usufruct of her husband. This left the wife's property under the guardianship of her husband, and this guardianship translated into her personal position as a ward of her husband. As a result, a wife's *Fähigkeit* was limited, reflecting her position in the home, and the basis of national order.

Jacob painted a vivid and colourful picture of the imagined *Gemeinwesen* to come. The union of freemen, in his system, composed the mythical, juristic person, which was the free state. It was nothing more than the *Gesammtbürgerschaft* and *Rechtsgenoßenschaft:*

> Outside of the family union, freemen stood amongst each other in a firm communal fraternity, in joint assurance and legal association. Only in the community, to which they belonged as members, could freemen possess rights and peace. His neighbor was his equal and his neighbor had common liberties.[153]

Citing Savigny and Eichhorn's *Einleitung in das deutsche Privatrecht,* Jacob explained that: 'Freedom is in truth the capacity to own private property *(eigenthumsfähig).*'[154] 'On this property', he continued, 'hung the wider rights to take part in court proceedings and people's assemblies, participation in which the unfree were denied.'[155] Women, who were in every way *eigenthumsunfähig* in Jacob's system, 'were totally shut out of government over the nation and people', and were not allowed to take oaths.[156]

The Age of Recovery

Below the surface of the Restoration that beset Central Europe after the Congress of Vienna, there was, quietly, going on a recovery of the *vaterländisches Recht.* Transformationist-minded liberals were no less committed to obtaining political revision than the French revolutionaries had been. By the time they embarked on this course, however, reactionary regimes were well aware that the failure of French authorities to check the growth of short political treatises and stump speeches had contributed to the old regime's demise. For this reason, the Carlsbad Decrees were designed to stamp out the old styles of discursive, opposition thought, which was associated with the French revolutionary era. The only loophole was that the Decrees did not address areas of discourse which had not yet been developed, and both legal history or private law scholarship fell into this category. While the focus on the legal history of German private law had already emerged prior to 20 September 1819, this loophole left an opening for the continuing growth of liberal political thought and activism in German-speaking Europe. Liberals could discuss politics while publicly claiming only interest in private law or legal history.

Journals that attempted to overtly discuss public law and constitutional matters were decidedly short-lived during the entire period of liberal political vulnerability and before the consolidation of law in the late years of the nineteenth century. The *Kritische Zeitschrift für Staatsregierung und Gesetzgebung* survived only through the publication of two editions in 1817. Local journals suffered a similar fate. The *Jahrbücher für die bayerische Gesetzgebung, Rechtswissenschaft und Staatsverwaltung* died after only one publication in 1838. Also snuffed out soon after they began were the *Zeitschrift für Gesetzgebungs- und Verwaltungsreform* (1858/59) and the *Zeitschrift für deutsches Staatsrecht und deutsche Verfassungsgeschichte,* which was killed after only one publication in 1867. The *Zeitschrift für Gesetzgebung und Praxis auf dem Gebiete des Deutschen öffentlichen Rechtes* was comparatively long-lived, but it circulated later in the century, between 1875 and 1880.

As I have tried to show here, the Restoration, replete with the Carlsbad Decrees, in fact had little impact on the new brand of north German constitutionalism that was developed in the interim years between 1814 and 1819. Liberal political thought continued to find expression in the many journals that focused, at least publicly, on legal history and private law. Adding to the major organs I have mentioned here, numerous other law journals were founded in the nineteenth century. The archives of the *Max-Planck-Institut für europäische Rechtsgeschichte* house more than four thousand books produced on every area of German private law. In this way, *Privatrechts-Staatslehre* emerged as the dominant mode of political theory and discourse in German-speaking Europe, and it is in this body of scholarship that we can see constitutional transformation at work and where we are offered an image of the nation liberals planned to legislate into existence.

The *Privatrechts-Staatslehre* that was produced in the years following the publication of the first major systems echoed and supported the sociopolitical arrangements which had been identified by Mittermaier, Eichhorn and Jacob Grimm. Above all else, the massive production of legal history on German customary law involved the recovery of the data for a system. The system, in reality, was none other than a German nation. While the earlier generation set constitutional transformation in motion and developed the early systematic treatments, the great bulk of the data for the envisioned system was produced by that generation of German liberals who were born after the French Revolution and who were too young to bear arms during the *Freiheitskriege.* They, nevertheless, carried out the work of recovering the critical data and continued the course of constitutional transformation.

In his 1836 speech, *Ueber die Stellung des römischen Rechts zu dem nationalen Recht der germanischen Völker,* given in Basel, Georg Beseler delivered a familiar condemnation of Roman law as a source of legal rules in German-speaking Europe.[157] Roman law, he urged, was the product of the eastern 'Roman world monarchy'.[158] It was adopted by European princes to build their power and enslave originally free Germans: 'Only a few peasants were able to keep their freedom and dignity, most were forced into slavery.'[159] 'I do not speak here of the state of [Roman law] in the early time of the Republic', he emphasized, where 'the Prätur [was] an organ of people's opinion for legislative needs'.[160] On the contrary, 'the Roman law ... when it took over the national law of the German people, was solely Justinian's compilation, which bore the name of the *corpus iuris civilis.*'[161] 'Just think', he urged his listeners 'of the time when this collection was born.'[162] 'We see an empire without freedom', one with only 'power and unnatural living ... military rule and despotism', and a 'people without nationality mixed with aliens [and] torn apart by religious parties.'[163] In contrast to this system of despotism, German law stood only for the interests of liberty and common good of the people. German law was not the fruit of despotic lawmaking, but had evolved naturally through the active involvement of the people in government and the courts. Equal, individual, free Germans, 'as members of an association *(Genossenschaft),* a family' had built the system through the 'complete public nature of the assemblies and courts'.[164] 'The people were the sole source of their laws', and 'judges and lay judges *(Schöffen)* ... constituted living control of the justice system'.[165] 'The German law was the law of the people *(Volksrecht)* in the fullest sense of the word', applied through the 'natural organ of the public people's courts', whereas 'Roman law was derived from a monarchy in the hands of the Emperor and his jurists'.[166] As Beseler urged his audience, a 'revolution of all German relationships that must be brought into existence'.[167]

These political views were reiterated in his longer study, *Volksrecht und Juristenrecht* (1843).[168] Beseler's *Die Lehre von den Erbverträgen* was published in two volumes, in 1837 and 1840 respectively. It, like so many other works, contributed to the data of German inheritance law.[169] His later *System des gemeinen deutschen Privatrechts,* which was published in three volumes between 1847 and 1855, also reflected the sociopolitical values of German liberalism and the imagined *Gemeinwesen.*[170]

In 1839, Wilhelm Wilda and August Ludwig Reyscher started the *Zeitschrift für deutsches Recht und deutsche Rechtswissenschaft.* Reyscher had already won the esteem of Jacob Grimm and was well known for his scholarship on German private law. In 1828, the same year that the early systematic treatments appeared, Reyscher published his *Ueber die Bedürfnisse unserer Zeit in der Gesetzgebung* (1828), which was a follow-up on Savigny's earlier treatise.[171] Echoing Jacob's call for consideration of the *sinnliche* element, Reyscher published *Symbolism in Germanic Law* (1833).[172] In the introductory article to the *Zeitschrift für deutsches Recht*, Reyscher explained that 'the aim of the journal' was not 'merely to provide a meeting point for investigations into the field of native German law, but also to contribute towards the encouragement of a national study of law and thereby to the creation of a *vaterländisch* science of law'.[173] He went on to say that 'the specifically national element' did not consist of 'a failure to recognize the merits' of other nations, and that jurists could 'therefore, without contravening our principles, regard as our own not merely that which has already established itself among us, but we shall also try to incorporate as part of our spiritual possessions all real progress which we perceive in other countries'.[174] Amongst Wilda's important writings was his *Das Strafrecht der Germanen* (1842).[175]

Liberal legal scholars embraced the idea of constitutional transformation, and many kept one foot in academia and the other in local diets. Germanists' legal history and legal antiquarianism were important arteries of liberal constitutionalism, and the political alliance with scholars in other fields, notably history and philology, only strengthened the drive toward constitutional transformation. Jacob Grimm described his *Geschichte der deutschen Sprache* (1848), which he dedicated to the historian Georg Gervinus, as 'political through and through'.[176] He was joined in this genre of Germanist political writing by many others in the German legal world. In addition to his other publications, Mittermaier also tilted toward legal antiquarianism in his *Polemik des germanischen Rechts: Land- und Lehnrecht* (1832). Citing Tacitus, Savigny and Jacob Grimm, he urged that 'there was no nobility in the time of the ancient Germans'.[177]

It should be emphasized also that, as important as it is to understand the deep politics of the Germanists' scholarship, it is equally important to understand that they were successful because they developed principles to redress the deficiencies in the existing laws. Where scholars of the *ius commune* waited until too late to address commercial concerns, this was a core element of Germanist legal scholarship from the outset. The most important areas of modern German law, including constitutional law, procedural law, family law, inheritance law, company law, bankruptcy law, negotiable instruments and commercial law were derived from the work of the Germanists. In addition, they had a strong impact on the development associations' law, land law and property held jointly or in trust.[178] The programme of legislative revolution was successful, precisely because Germanists developed rules of law to meet the demands, real or imagined, of industry. As the *ius commune* grew more and more obsolete, liberals were able to increase their political influence by penetrating the legal structure and offering legal remedies for pressing economic and social concerns.

Notes

1. Jacob Grimm, quoted in Murray Peppard, *Paths through the Forest: A Biography of the Brothers Grimm* (1971), p. 196.

2. F. Savigny, *History of the Roman Law in the Middle Ages,* E. Cathcart (trans.) (1829), p. 2.
3. Grimm, cited in Peppard, *Paths through the Forest,* p. 196.
4. Savigny, *History of Roman Law,* p. 5.
5. Michael Hoeflich, *Roman and Civil Law and the Development of Anglo-American Jurisprudence in the Nineteenth Century* (1997), p. 77.
6. Savigny, *History of Roman Law,* pp. 2–3.
7. Ibid.
8. James Q. Whitman, *Legacy of Roman Law in the German Romantic Era: Historical Vision and Legal Change* (1990), p. 214.
9. Ibid.
10. Johann Bachofen, 'My Life in Retrospect', in *Bachofen: Myth, Religion and Mother Right,* G. Boas (trans.) (1974), pp. 3–4.
11. Ibid.
12. J. Kuntze, *Der Wendepunkt der Rechtswissenschaft* (1857), p. 21, quoted in Whitman, *Legacy of Roman Law,* p. 222.
13. Rudolf Jhering, quoted in Whitman, *Legacy of Roman Law,* pp. 223–4.
14. Whitman, *Legacy of Roman Law,* p. 223.
15. Karl Unterholzner, 'Ueber die Rede des Cicero für den Schauspieler Q. Roscius, und über die litterarum obligatio insbesondere', *Zeitschrift für geschichtliche Rechtswissenschaft,* 1 (1815), pp. 248–69.
16. F. Savigny, 'Beytrag zur Geschichte der Römischen Testamente', *Zeitschrift für geschichtliche Rechtswissenschaft,* 1 (1815), p. 78.
17. Ibid., p. 80.
18. Karl Unterholzner, 'Ueber die Stelle der zwölf Tafeln, Si in jus vocat', *Zeitschrift für geschichtliche Rechtswissenschaft,* 2 (1816), pp. 432–40.
19. J. Göschen, 'Einige Bemerkungen in Beziehung auf das ältere Recht der Freylassungen bey den Römern', *Zeitschrift für geschichtliche Rechtswissenschaft,* 3 (1817), pp. 242–89.
20. F. Savigny, 'Neu entdeckte Quellen des Römischen Rechts', *Zeitschrift für geschichtliche Rechtswissenschaft,* 3 (1817), pp. 129–72.
21. Ibid., p. 130.
22. Barthold Niebuhr, 'Nachricht von einem Breviarum des Justinianischen Codex: (Aus einem Schreiben an Savigny)', *Zeitschrift für geschichtliche Rechtswissenschaft,* 3 (1817), pp. 389–96.
23. Barthold Niebuhr, 'Notizen über Handschriften in der Vaticana: Erster Brief', *Zeitschrift für geschichtliche Rechtswissenschaft,* 3 (1817), pp. 408–20.
24. For this section on the importance of the discovery of the *Institutes of Gaius,* I am indebted to Professor Charles Donahue of Harvard Law School, with whom I discussed this project in 2003. He graciously offered me a private discussion on the historical significance of the *Institutes of Gaius,* and the historiography on Roman legal history in the nineteenth and early twentieth centuries.

25. Barthold Niebuhr, *The History of Rome,* Julius Hare and Connop Thirlwall (trans.), vol. 1 (1835), p. xii.
26. Ibid., p. vii.
27. Ibid.
28. Ibid., p. viii.
29. Ibid.
30. Ibid., p. ix.
31. Ibid.
32. Ibid.
33. Ibid., p. x.
34. Ibid., p. xi.
35. Ibid.
36. Ibid.
37. Ibid., p. xiii.
38. Ibid.
39. Ibid., p. 228.
40. Ibid., pp. 223–4.
41. Ibid., p. 224.
42. Ibid.
43. Ibid., pp. 231–2.
44. Ibid., p. 228.
45. Ibid.
46. Ibid., pp. 228–9.
47. Barthold Niebuhr, 'Lecture XVI', in *Lectures on History of Rome,* Leonard Schmidtz (ed.), vol. 1 (1844), p. 142.
48. Ibid., p. 145.
49. Barthold Niebuhr, 'Lecture XXI', in *Lectures,* p. 171.
50. Ibid.
51. Barthold Niebuhr, 'Lecture XXII', in *Lectures,* p. 177.
52. Ibid., p. 180.
53. Ibid., p. 178.
54. Barthold Niebuhr, 'Lecture XXIV', in *Lectures,* p. 195.
55. Ibid., p. 197.
56. Barthold Niebuhr, 'Lecture XXXIII: The Social or Marsic War, The *Lex Julia*', in *Lectures,* p. 186.
57. Karl Eichhorn, 'Ueber das geschichtliche Studium des deutschen Rechts', *Zeitschrift für geschichtliche Rechtswissenschaft,* 1 (1815), pp. 124–5.
58. Ibid., p. 126.
59. Karl Eichhorn, 'Ueber den Ursprung der städtischen Verfassung in Deutschland', *Zeitschrift für geschichtliche Rechtswissenschaft,* 1 (1815), p. 147.
60. Ibid., p. 148.
61. Karl Eichhorn, *Einleitung in das deutsche Privatrecht mit Einschluß des Lehenrechts* (1829), p. 82.

62. Ibid., pp. 111–920.
63. Ibid., p. 140.
64. Ibid.
65. Ibid., pp. 140–1.
66. Ibid., pp. 887–8.
67. Ibid., pp. 897–920.
68. Karl A. Mittermaier, 'Beiträge zur Geschichte der ehelichen Gütergemeinschaft, des Erbrechts und der Freiheit zu testiren im Mittelalter', *Zeitschrift für geschichtliche Rechtswissenschaft,* 2 (1816), pp. 318–61.
69. Heinrich Albert Zachariä, 'Ueber den Zweck dieser Zeitschrift', *Kritische Zeitschrift für Rechtswissenschaft und Gesetzgebung des Auslandes,* 1 (1829), p. 1.
70. Ibid., p. 4.
71. Kleinschmidt, 'On the Customary Measures of Hildesheim', *Juristische Zeitung für das Königreich Hannover,* 1 (1826).
72. Wilhelm Pfeiffer, cited in Whitman, *Legacy of Roman Law,* p. 102. (I have changed Whitman's translation slightly based my reading of the original text.)
73. G. F. Puchta, *Pandekten* (1844), cited in Arthur von Mehren and James Gordley, *The Civil Law System: An Introduction to the Comparative Study of Law* (1977), p. 67.
74. Ibid.
75. Mehren and Gordley, *Civil Law System,* p. 62.
76. Jacob Grimm, *Jacob Grimm: Selbstbiographie* (1984), p. 27.
77. Jacob Grimm to Savigny (13 February 1838), in Wilhelm Schoof (ed.), *Briefe der Brüder Grimm an Savigny* (1953), p. 396.
78. Jacob Grimm, 'Ueber eine eigene altgermanische Weise der Mordsühne', *Zeitschrift für geschichtliche Rechtswissenschaft,* 1 (1815), pp. 323–37.
79. Ibid.
80. Peppard, *Paths through the Forest.*
81. Jacob Grimm, 'Von der Poesie im Recht', *Zeitschrift für geschichtliche Rechtswissenschaft,* 2 (1816), pp. 25–99.
82. Andreas Heusler and Rudolf Hübner, 'Vorwort zur Vierten Ausgabe' (1899), in Jacob Grimm, *Deutsche Rechtsalterthümer* (1965), p. xxii.
83. Grimm, *Deutsche Rechtsalterthümer,* p. xxii.
84. Ibid.
85. Franz Wieacker, *A History of Private Law in Europe (with Particular Reference to Germany),* Tony Weir (trans.) (1995), p. 319.
86. Grimm, *Deutsche Rechtsalterthümer,* p. vii.
87. Ibid.
88. Ibid.
89. Ibid., p. ix.
90. Ibid., p. viii.

91. Ibid.
92. Ibid., p. viii.
93. Ibid., p. xvii.
94. Ibid., pp. ix–x.
95. Ibid., p. 190.
96. Ibid.
97. Ibid., p. 201.
98. Ibid., pp. 205–8.
99. Ibid., pp. 223–5.
100. Friedrich Brockhaus, *Conversations-Lexikon* (1820), cited in W. Mager, 'Republik', in Otto Brunner, Werner Conze and Reinhart Koselleck (eds.), *Geschichtliche Grundbegriffe: Historisches Lexicon.* p. 619.
101. Karl Pölitz, cited in ibid.
102. Johann von Aretin, cited in ibid., p. 622.
103. Karl Rotteck, cited in ibid., p. 623.
104. Ibid.
105. Grimm, *Deutsche Rechtsalterthümer,* p. 314.
106. Ibid., p. 318.
107. Ibid., p. 321.
108. Ibid.
109. Ibid., pp. 318–19.
110. Ibid., p. 319.
111. Ibid.
112. See footnote, ibid.
113. Ibid., p. 323.
114. Ibid., pp. 329–30.
115. Ibid.
116. Ibid., p. 331.
117. Mager, 'Republik', p. 619.
118. Grimm, *Deutsche Rechtsalterthümer,* pp. 340–1.
119. See footnote, ibid., p. 370.
120. Ibid., pp. 372–3.
121. Ibid., p. 373.
122. Ibid., p. 376.
123. Ibid., p. 391.
124. Ibid., p. 393.
125. Ibid., p. 396.
126. Ibid., p. 399.
127. Ibid., p. 400.
128. Ibid., pp. 404–9.
129. Ibid.
130. Ibid., p. 404.

131. Ibid., p. 321.
132. Ibid., p. 572.
133. Ibid.
134. Ibid., p. 557.
135. See footnote, ibid., p. 557.
136. F. Savigny, *Vom Beruf*, cited in Mehren and Gordley, *Civil Law System*, p. 63.
137. Grimm, *Deutsche Rechtsalterthümer*, p. 455.
138. Ibid., p. 236.
139. Ibid., p. 190.
140. Ibid., p. 612.
141. Ibid., p. 564.
142. Ibid., p. 557.
143. Ibid.
144. Ibid.
145. Ibid.
146. Ibid., p. 244.
147. Ibid.
148. Ibid., pp. 215–17.
149. Ibid.
150. Ibid.
151. Ibid.
152. Ibid., p. 592.
153. Ibid., pp. 404–5.
154. Ibid., p. 403.
155. Ibid.
156. Ibid., p. 563.
157. Georg Beseler, *Ueber die Stellung des römischen Rechts zu dem nationalen Recht der germanischen Völker* (1836).
158. Ibid., pp. 5–10.
159. Ibid.
160. Ibid.
161. Ibid.
162. Ibid.
163. Ibid.
164. Ibid.
165. Ibid.
166. Ibid.
167. Ibid., p. 10.
168. Georg Beseler, *Volksrecht und Juristenrecht* (1843).
169. Georg Beseler, *Die Lehre von den Erbverträgen* (1837–1840).
170. Georg Beseler, *System des gemeinen deutschen Privatrechts* (1847–1855).

171. August Ludwig Reyscher, *Ueber die Bedürfnisse unserer Zeit in der Gesetzgebung* (1828).
172. August Ludwig Reyscher, *Symbolism in Germanic Law* (1833).
173. August Ludwig Reyscher, 'Ueber den Zweck dieser Zeitschrift', *Zeitschrift für deutsches Recht und deutsche Rechtswissenschaft,* 1 (1839), pp. 1–10.
174. Ibid.
175. Wilhelm Wilda, *Das Strafrecht der Germanen* (1842).
176. Grimm, cited in R. Hinton Thomas, *Liberalism, Nationalism,and the German Intellectuals: An Analysis of the Academic and Scientific Conferences of the Period* (1951), p. 92.
177. C. Gründler, *Polemik des germanischen Rechts, Land- und Lehnrecht: Nach den Systemen des Herrn Geheimrat Prof. Dr. Mittermaier und Geheimrat Prof. Dr. G. L. Böhmer* (1832–1839).
178. Wieacker, *History of Private Law.*

–4–

Undermining Absolutism
The Path of Legalism and Constituting the Nation 1846–1879

> We in Germany are a collection of states that can be made into a whole from all the single parts, so that we can become, as they say in North America: *e pluribus unum.*[1]
>
> —Anton Christ, *Germanistentag* in Lübeck, 1847

In this chapter, this study begins to shift its focus from the theoretical developments to the practice of constitutional transformation. In the long term, it proved to be a successful programme for political revision. This was, however, a course filled with peaks and valleys. The censorship measures, which were a main feature of the reactionary Carlsbad Decrees of 1819, delayed data production. Publication for many legal treatises had to be shelved and even the ZGR went out of circulation from time to time. Yet, by the late 1820s when censorship enforcement was relaxed, new legal journals were founded and the major systematic treatments of Eichhorn and Grimm were published. Within three years following the revolutions of 1830, new constitutions in some north German states, including Hanover (1830), provided for legislative assemblies, boosting constitutional transformation. At the same time, this transition also was set back by the reactionary Six Acts and Ten Articles of 1832. Following these measures, a fresh round of even more rigorous censorship enforcement ensued. Some five thousand books were banned in Austria, including the works of Goethe and Schiller. Even inscriptions on gravestones, cuff links and tobacco boxes were censored. A ban was instituted on political gatherings and associations. The wearing of certain political colours, flying political flags and the planting of a liberty tree could land a person in jail or worse. In Bavaria, the growing of moustaches was banned as a badge of radicalism.

Despite these realities, liberal transformationists were able to cope with obstacles to sociopolitical revision and to weather setbacks, in large measure, because the theory of constitutional transformation anticipated periodic obstruction. Niebuhr's *Römische Geschichte* emphasized that true political revision resulted from a long-term class struggle, which was carried forward across generations, and Filangieri's *La Scienza della Legislazione* suggested that a major benefit of a process of legislative revolution was that there was always the opportunity to regroup. Once the genie was let out of the bottle in 1815, there was no lasting way to rebottle it. Henceforth, constitutional transformation, in Hanover and elsewhere, was like a box turtle moving along a course. If it needed to retract its vulnerable limbs into its protective shell from time to time, it did so, and when it was safe again, it continued to move slowly and steadily, but cautiously, along its path.

Constitutional transformation was driven, above all else, by the primacy of the programme and not by unexpected events. Again, the old *Rechtskreise* of the Hanseatic League was a powerful model and, for this reason, the slow and incremental character of the political revision cannot be emphasized enough. Even the celebrated *Zollverein* of 1834 was sixteen years in the making, and it was not until 1871 that it reached its fullest development. On the whole, however, the reactionary censorship enforcements following 1819 and 1832 caused temporary slowdowns in the production of data for a system, and the net result was that the necessary critical mass of legal data did not exist until the mid-1840s. It was at this point that liberal transformationists reached the turning point and turned from theory to practice. After 1848, constitutional transformation made steady and relatively uninterrupted progress in Central Europe. This formal, programmatic shift can be traced to the many legal conferences that were held between 1846 and 1847, and, from the perspective of constitutional transformation, these events were at least as important as Frankfurt. It was from the Reformierte Kirche in Lübeck, where the *Germanistentag* of 1847 was held, and not from Paulskirche in 1848 that Anton Christ issued his call for German *e pluribus unum,* which opens this chapter.

This chapter also challenges the argument that the whole of Germany underwent Prussianization after 1866. While the considerable research that has been produced in the last twenty years has made the other regions of Germany visible, it has not shown how traditions in these regions shaped national development. As a result, the argument persists that Prussia played the formative role in German development and that 'its institutions, political culture, and values molded Imperial Germany, the Weimar Republic, and the Third Reich'.[2] Bureaucratic absolutism, Beck writes, remained a reality after 1848, and disciplinary legislation allowed the old elite to control civil officials.[3] Here, the impact of the Prussian Constitution of 1850 was discounted, because it, apparently, lacked an implementing or regulatory statute for enforcement. This failing crippled the effectiveness of its liberal provisions.[4] The net result was that the Prussian bureaucratic tradition survived into the Kaiserreich, and the ideas and practices of bureaucratic absolutism survived to serve as the model for National Socialism after 1933.[5]

As I argue in this study, it was neither Prussian dominance nor south German constitutionalism which exercised formative influence. Rather, more consideration should be given to the possibility of Hanoverization, particularly with regard to structural unity. The practice of constitutional transformation began at the state level and was nationalized in each successive phase of German unification. With regards to Hanover in particular, state reforms that were underway before 1866 were absorbed into the North German Confederation. In addition, many of the figures who sat on the key legal codification commissions for the North German Confederation after 1866 and the Reich after 1871, including Adolf Leonhardt, Rudolf Bennigsen and Gottlieb Planck, were hardened veteran *politicos* of the Hanover constitutional conflicts of the 1850s. Indeed, liberal constitutionalism, which was in serious trouble in Hanover in 1865, was given a new life after the founding of the North German Confederation in 1866.

The *Germanisten* Conferences

The *Germanisten* conferences of 1846 and 1847 have been mentioned in the literature on German history. The most thorough treatment, however, remains R. Hinton Thomas's study of 1951.[6] His work made these previously obscure conferences visible. However, Thomas wrote prior to the advance of social history, and it did not take into consideration the economic crisis and social upheavals that hit Central Europe in the 1840s. His approach was that of intellectual history, and, for this reason, the Germanisten conferences were considered in isolation from other events. Factoring in the economic and social crisis, however, helps to reveal the considerable political opportunism that was at the heart of these conferences. It was no fluke of history that the Germanists suddenly chose to hold a conference in these years.

Crop failures in 1845 and the economic downturn that followed by 1847 produced widespread hunger in the German lands. Both the 1844 weavers' rising in Silesia and the peasants' revolt in Galacia of 1846 were ominous signs of human suffering, and liberals, including the ranks of the Germanists, interpreted these events as an indicator of the failure of governments to feed their own people. By the time of the potato revolution in Berlin of 1847, hunger mixed with general discontent regarding noble privileges, including judicial privileges, was a strong source of acrid discontent. While liberal transformationists could not have had a hand in the crop failures or economic downturn, the character of the demands expressed by discontented crowds was not altogether spontaneous. In reality, it had been cultivated by the Germanists, who after Jacob Grimm included anyone and any genre so long as they or it offered data to support the liberal sociopolitical agenda.

Through a variety of modes of communication, the Germanists had led the inclinations of the people toward constitutional transformation and encouraged an awareness of the inefficacy of the existing arrangements. At the popular level, the indictments against noble privileges had been spoon-fed to the young generation of 1848. They were born in the 1820s and were the first generation to be sent off to slumber with their little heads filled with folk tales. Ordinary Germans may not have been able to absorb the complexities of Eichhorn, Mittermaier, Grimm or Reyscher's systems, but they could identify with arbitrariness of Mother Gothel in the tale of *Rapunzel* or the jealous cruelty of the Queen in *Snow White.* Indeed, the *Hausmärchen* depicted noble women and others in authority as unnatural villains and the feminine, increasingly, appeared as a metaphor for imbalance and disorder.

It was in the environment of economic downturn and social unrest that the *Germanisten* conferences of 1846 and 1847 were held. Calls for the introduction of a unified civil code reemerged for the first time since the Thibaut–Savigny controversy. This summons, however, differed markedly for Thibaut's programme insofar as any new measure would be derived from German legal sources. Reyscher wrote in his journal that the contemporary task of the Germanists was gradually to secure Central Europe's liberation from foreign law through the careful cultivation of native law and through the preparation of a national code of law.[7] In order to advance this task, a meeting of Germanists was 'particularly desirable'.[8] The signatories to the invitation included poets such as Ernst Moritz Arndt and Ludwig Uhland, historians like Leopold von Ranke and Georg Gervinus, the philologists Karl Lachmann, Wilhelm Grimm, Johann Lappenberg and Georg Pertz, and jurists such as Beseler, Mittermaier, Dahlmann and Reyscher, not to mention the man who presided as president over both conferences, Jacob Grimm.[9] The *Germanisten* conferences offer a visible point in German history where the change from theory to practice of constitutional transformation may be observed.

Although the conferences were composed of scholars from across disciplines, these men were mobilized for a drive toward constitutional transformation, and questions of law dominated the discussions. At the 1846 *Germanistentag,* held in Frankfurt, Friedrich Gaupp urged that the study of law should serve as 'a prophet of the future'.[10] 'It was soon clear', Georg Beseler wrote of the 1846 *Germanistentag* 'that the nationalist tendency in the political movement of the time was bound to find expression.'[11] The conferences were modeled on parliamentary procedure and various commissions were set up to examine specific issues in advance of the conference. At the same time, the commission structure also mirrored the approach to lawmaking that was identified by Niebuhr and was followed, consistently, in the later drafting of national codes.

In legal perspective, the most important debates of the 1846 *Germanistentag* concerned the continuing reliance on Roman law as a source of legal rules in Germany; it was after all the major legal source of noble privileges. The conference president, Jacob Grimm, raised the matter in his opening speech. Roman law had 'flooded' the entire surface of the legal system, leaving German law in a 'peculiar position'.[12] In Jacob's view, however, it should not be 'violently' torn out. Rather, he urged that German customary law should be rescued, as he and others had done, to prepare the way for the revision of the entire legal system through the institution of a unified German code of law.[13] Mittermaier, on the other hand, went straight to the political point in his comments. 'Our law', he stated unequivocally, 'stands in opposition to life, to the national consciousness, to the needs, customs, attitudes and ideas of the people.'[14] 'Nationality', he continued, 'expresses itself in its purest and best form in the law of the people.'[15] His complaint was that Roman law was *Juristenrecht,* and not *Völkerrecht.* It was rigid and did not have the ability to adapt itself to new conditions.[16] 'Now the question arises', Beseler queried the attendees, 'whether it is necessary for a people, in the further development of economic and political circumstances, to be completely excluded from participation in the making and exercising law and ... whether such a separation is healthy.'[17] Although these comments were framed around the inadequacies of the Roman law, in fact, the discussion was far more political and radical than it may have seemed to unsuspecting observers. Liberals had encoded and hidden their political ideals in a science of German private law, and they continued to shield themselves from reactionary authorities by appealing to a mere need for new laws to meet modern needs.

If one looks to the specific areas of discussion, it becomes clear that liberal political demands were the motivation behind the *Germanisten* conferences. What appeared on the surface to be merely a scholarly conference was in reality a political gathering cloaked in an academic robe. The discussion on marital property relations is informative in this regard. Since male participation was contingent on the ownership of private property and the exclusion of women, there was considerable anxiety about property-owning women in Germanist political thought. The specific examples Mittermaier used to illustrate existing legal insecurity were not focused on arbitrary acts and princely personal rule, but on what he viewed as the problem of women and property. At the 1846 *Germanistentag,* he complained: 'I know of a case, in North Germany, in which a man left his estate to his son,' but also had to provide for 'a sickly, weak daughter'.[18] For this reason, the father conditioned the son's inheritance on an obligation to 'maintain the sister during her lifetime and pay her a monthly income'.[19] Apparently, as Mittermaier explained, after the father's death 'it was realized that the daughter, unfortunately, had not signed [the will]'.[20] A lawsuit soon followed, and the court held that 'that contracts are not valid for third parties', and therefore the daughter was shut out of the inheritance.[21] While at first glance, it may seem that Mittermaier was in sympathy with the plight of the daughter, he was more concerned about the fact that the father's last will and testament was not honored by the court. It seemed ridiculous and 'un-German' to Mittermaier that the lack of the daughter's signature would render the father's last wishes invalid. The liberal demand for *unvollkommene Freiheit* of women was couched in protectionist rhetoric, which in reality called for the institution of sex guardianship over women. 'Gentlemen', as he concluded his talk, 'it is time to conjure up the spirit of German law, the spirit of the German nation, in order that it penetrate our law.'[22]

In reality, Mittermaier was concerned to create security and stability for male property rights. Again, the ownership of private property was a prerequisite for full legal personality or *vollkommene Freiheit,* in Eichhorn's words. Female property ownership was increasingly seen as a problem because it destabilized male property rights and threatened to undermine the masculine basis of the civil society that liberals wished to bring into existence through constitutional transformation. This is particularly clear in Mittermaier's talk given to the 1847 *Germanistentag,* again, on the subject of marital property relations. He began his comments, stating that it would be wonderful when every member of the smallest state could say 'I am a German citizen'.[23] Soon after, however, he pointed out that he took up the contemporary legal problems 'in the name of merchants and the great interests of industry'.[24] The German people had given their heart's blood for the throne and the Fatherland, and he rhetorically asked 'what's to come of Germany now and their hopes for a German citizen's law *(Bürgerrecht)*'.[25]

After a brief discussion of how legal particularism inhibited economic growth, he turned to 'the civil laws on the position of married women and marital property relations'.[26] It was impossible to get a handle on the situation, because of the 'unending differences of the law in the various parts of Germany'.[27] He cited a case involving an Austrian woman who owned property in Rhenish Bavaria, emphasizing the fact that she was Austrian. Apparently, the woman, an independent property owner, traveled to the region with the intent of selling her property, all without the authorization of her husband. There was some question as to whether her 'rights' should be construed under Austrian law, where she could freely dispose of her own property, or under the customary law of Rhenish Bavaria.[28] This confusion, Mittermaier complained, hindered trade because there were no provisions as to whether or not a wife could independently dispose of her property. In response, he did not call for legal clarity, but urged that some other understanding had to be reached on the position women, and he demanded the reinstitution of *'Deutsches Mundium',* namely, sex guardianship.[29] For the sake of 'peace in the family', as well as the economic life, he called for draft legislation on the position of married women and marital property.[30]

During the 1847 conference, the important decision was made to pursue the introduction of a unified code. It was here that constitutional transformation began in practice. Jaup made the first suggestion, and, as Karl Hegel later wrote, it was a call that evoked a 'storm of enthusiasm'.[31] Jaup opened his speech saying: 'Our beautiful Germany has so much that uplifts the heart and spirit and we can be proud to possess this Fatherland.'[32] He went on, however, to lament the absence of a unified civil code. *'Ein deutsch-nationales Heimathsrecht,'* as he referred to it, would end confessional divisions in Germany and antagonism between German states and, therefore, create a better climate for business, and 'especially, a common German civil law would finally embody a powerful promotion of the national consciousness'.[33] Following Jaup's remarks, Mittermaier 'demanded this German civil code in the name of industry'.[34] The revolutionary implications were clear in Anton Christ's words that open this chapter. Again, he urged before the entire conference body: 'We in Germany are a collection of states that can be made into a whole from all the single parts, so that we can become, as they say in North America: *e pluribus unum.*'[35]

The second generation of German liberals remained committed to constitutional transformation. In a letter to Friedrich Dahlmann in 1847, Georg Gervinus acknowledged that it was his generation's role to carry the programme forward. It would be their lot to maintain progress, Gervinus wrote, and 'to achieve the advantages of political revision without violent movements, wisely to learn from the sufferings and errors of foreign countries and gradually, following the path of legalism and through the power of the spirit, to gain what other nations have achieved by means of sudden attacks and by violence.'[36] Gervinus's views developed in a more radical direction in 1848. Nevertheless, the approach that those moderate liberals who congregated in the Casino Party at Paulskirche took to securing sociopolitical revision was never focused on a single constitutional reform, but rather on obtaining political revision through successive legislative measures over time. Indeed, one of the remarkable aspects of this slow revolution is that German liberals seemed to have pursued it with the clear knowledge that they might not live to see its completion.

Procedural Reform

Michael Bush argues effectively that 'privilege and nobility were so interconnected that the latter was not possible without the former.'[37] The nobility's 'composition and class-consciousness were essentially determined by privilege since it was the only constant distinction between noble and commoner'.[38] These privileges were either seigniorial or noble and granted both rights and indemnities. Seigniorial rights bestowed upon nobles their authority as rulers, while noble privileges awarded them special rights in society. Seigniorial rights affected the landlord–tenant relationship and gave noble landlords property rights over their tenants and dependents. These rights included the administration of patrimonial justice, taxation and conscription as well as control over whether or not tenants and dependents could marry, migrate, change occupation or possess property. Privileges, conversely, indemnified nobles against taxes, certain service obligations and judicial proceedings, while, at the same time, awarding them preferential promotion, right to titles, property and fiscal concessions, including hunting and fishing rights.[39]

The goal of constitutional transformation, as I have emphasized, was to level these distinctions by awarding privileges to the propertied male commonality. Simple tales like Jacob and Wilhelm Grimm's 'The Fisherman and His Wife' were loaded with political symbolism in this regard. 'Once upon a time a fisherman who lived with his wife in a pigsty ... everyday went out fishing', and the tale went, 'he fished and he fished'.[40] 'Then' one day 'his line suddenly went down, far down below, and when he drew it up again, he brought out a large flounder'.[41] The poor flounder pleaded for his life.

> Hark you fisherman, I pray you let me live. I am no flounder really, but an enchanted prince. What good will it do you to kill me. I should not be good to eat. Put me in the water again, and let me go.[42]

The fisherman agreed and put the flounder back in the water. Empty-handed, he returned to his pigsty home and relayed the story of the flounder to his wife. 'Did you not wish for anything first,' the power-hungry woman inquired.[43] She sent the humble fisherman back to the sea to wish for a little hut. Reluctantly returning to the sea, the fisherman called:

> Flounder, flounder in the sea
> Come, I pray thee, here to me.
> For my wife, good Isabel,
> Wills not as I'd have her will.[44]

'Well what does she want, then,' the flounder said. He listened to the fisherman and graciously granted the woman's wish. Oh, but this wasn't enough for the woman, and she sent the fisherman back to the sea five more times. Each time the fisherman called to the flounder, flounder in the sea and each time the increasingly frustrated flounder asked: 'Well, what does she want, now.'[45] The second time, the woman asked for a 'great stone castle', and her next three wishes were to be king, emperor and then pope.[46] When this was not enough, the power-hungry woman sent the humble fisherman back to wish that she be made 'God'. 'Flounder, flounder in the sea' he called and once more the flounder swam up and asked: 'Well, what does she want, now.'[47] Hearing the woman's most recent wish, the flounder replied: 'Go to her, and you will find her back again in the pigsty.'[48]

'The Fisherman and His Wife' is a simple and colourful fairy tale, but it was at the same time loaded with subliminal, sociopolitical symbolism. In a society where hunting and fishing rights remained in the exclusive hands of noble landowners, the ordinary man fishing and fishing everyday, according to his own desires, undermined exclusive conceptions of fishing and hunting by showing the exercise of that privilege by a pigsty dweller. The fisherman returned again and again to the sea without objection from the enchanted flounder prince. Flounder prince and fisherman were equal in the nobility of their character. The woman was the problem, and the tale encouraged the denigration of women in authority. The greedy woman usurped and gobbled up more and more authority until finally she had to be put back in her original place. Again, in 'The Fisherman' the sociopolitical pairing of male commoner rights with the need for female exclusion was subliminally and symbolically confirmed.

It cannot be emphasized enough that this gender dimension of constitutional transformation, which was already present in the systems of Eichhorn, Mittermaier, Grimm and others was brought into existence with the introduction of every major law code. Even if not in the immediate state-level reforms, procedural reform, which was a major pillar of legislative revolution, was no exception. Germanist legal thought and the demands for the legal consolidation of German law that they represented were important expressions of liberal nationalism. As Karen Hagemann has shown, anxiety over women and the fear of feminization was a strong element in the idea of the nation.[49] The preoccupation with the place of women in society infected every dimension of liberal legal politics. Thus, even as we move forward into a discussion of the progressive advance of constitutional transformation, one must keep in mind that as male participation increased, female participation was pushed into decline.

The drive for procedural reform, nevertheless, was an attack on patrimonial justice and demand for the leveling of distinctions between the hereditary nobility and the bourgeoisie in the German lands. Noble privileges, as Bush notes, 'could be undone without formal abolition, usually when rendered meaningless ... through being awarded to the commonality'.[50] Judicial indemnities safeguarded nobles from normal court procedures, and also awarded them use of procedures that were closed to commoners.[51] German nobles possessed the right to trial by public tribunal. This form of process was designed to protect hereditary nobles from private and arbitrary court decisions, in effect, the very arbitrary and secret decision making that ordinary Germans faced in legal cases. Nobles were further absolved from appearing in lower courts.[52] Seigniorial rights in Saxony, for example, allowed for *Patrimonialgerichte* (patrimonial courts), where landlords personally controlled the administering of justice to tenants. In light of noble judicial privileges, procedural reform was more than a call for the rights of persons. It also housed an attack on the judicial indemnities of the nobility as well as the social and political inequality those privileges represented.

Jacob's system was the only one that addressed the constitution of the courts and, in such a way, that his discussion was also a metaphor for Germany's many princely courts.. Book 6, *Gericht,* closed *Rechtsalterthümer* and was one of the longest sections. Courts, Jacob wrote in his opening paragraph, had their origin in the public forum of the peoples' assemblies: 'The combined *freie männer* formed the core of the courts.'[53] Confirming the original free constitution of the Germans, he drove home the point that any authority a judge exercised was only secondary and given authority. Opening his section on *Gerichtsleute,* he underscored this point, writing: 'All judicial authority was exercised by the association of free men *(genoßenschaft freier männer)* under the presidency of an elected or hereditary leader.'[54] Jacob then moved forward to offer a lengthy treatment of the courts, replete with his usual philological analysis and *sinnliche element.* Just before launching into his ode to ancient German liberty, however, the other shoe fell: '*Frauen* amongst all German peoples are banned from the court.'[55] With the matter of the place of women out of the way, Jacob focused on the free constitution of the courts.

The constitution of the courts is another area in which scholars have drawn a political divide between those who supported the *Geschworenengericht* (jury court) or the *Schöffengericht* (court with lay judges or mixed court). In 1798, the French introduced the jury trial for criminal cases in the occupied Rhineland, and it is true that there were those in the German legal world who initially rejected the jury trial system. Feuerbach's *Betrachtungen über das Geschworenengericht,* which was published in 1813, is an example.[56] However, this should be considered against the visceral hatred of the imposition of French law on German soil, discussed in the second chapter. Feuerbach was a reformer, as I have shown, and it was more likely that he rejected the jury court because it arrived in the form of the French legal imposition.

Although scholars have continued to suggest that the *Schöffengericht* 'was scarcely mentioned in the literature before 1848', it, in fact, figured in the *Privatrechts-Staatslehre* I have identified here.[57] Examinations of the *Schöffengericht* appeared in the studies of the various regional and local legal histories. This trend was begun by Eichhorn's series, 'Ueber den Ursprung der städtischen Verfassung in Deutschland', published in the early ZGR editions.[58] Another example is August Reyscher's *Vollständige, historisch und kritisch bearbeitete Sammlung der württembergischen Gesetze* (1828), and here he also weighed in for the cause of procedural reform.[59] Grimm attached considerable political symbolism to *Schöffen* decisions, as I mentioned in the last chapter. He also discussed the distinctions and similarities between the roles of *Schöffen* (lay judges) and *Geschworene* (jurors). Both systems had their origin in the common source of the public assemblies of German people, although the jury system developed in England and France, where the system of lay judges was common to the German lands. The key distinction was that jurors were only competent to 'decide on truth', facts of the case, while lay judges could also decide questions of law.[60] Here, Jacob cited Rogge's *Das Gerichtswesen der Germanen* (1820), Maurer's *Geschichte des Altgermanischen Gerichtsverfahrens* (1824) and Savigny's discussion in *Geschichte des römischen Rechts.*

In fact, court procedure was amongst the most prominent subjects of Germanist scholarship. Jacob Grimm's three-volume work, *Weisthümer* (1840–1842) took up the question of procedure. In it he examined a collection of decisions handed down by the *Schöffen,* and it stood as one of the seminal studies on the *Schöffengericht.*[61] The point of his analysis was to create prescriptive legitimacy for the judicial arrangements liberals planned to effect through constitutional transformation. At the same time, it embodied the rejection of patrimonial justice and demand for the extension of judicial privileges to the commonality. This included the reinstitution of *Schöffengericht,* which scholars of German law located in the free municipal constitutions. Without a doubt, however, Mittermaier was the most prolific writer on procedure, specifically criminal procedure in the early nineteenth century. As early as 1820, he wrote his comparative study of common German, Prussian and French civil procedure.[62] He wrote countless articles on the jury system for the *Kritische Zeitschrift für Rechtswissenschaft* he founded with Zachariä. Indeed, he was the leading proponent of the institution of the jury court system in German-speaking Europe.[63]

By the time of the 1830 revolutions, procedural reform was amongst the most prominent demands of German liberals, and they continued to press for this in local assemblies even after the revolutions waned. Mittermaier published two political treatises calling for procedural reform. *Ueber die Bestimmungen einer zweckmässigen Gerichtsverfassung und Processordnung* was published in 1831, and his *Die künftige Stellung des Advokatenstandes* in 1832.[64] Heinrich von Gagern called for procedural reform in the Hessian *Landtag.*[65] Georg Beseler, the most vocal proponent of the 'people's law', advocated, consistently, in the 1830s, in favor of trial by jury and lay judges, both of which he argued were in existence amongst the ancient Germans. In his early polemic against Roman law, he argued that German law had evolved naturally through the involvement of the people in government and the courts.[66] Free and equal Germans had built a system where assemblies and court procedures were public.[67] 'The people were the only source of law', and 'judges along with lay judges ... constituted living control of the justice system'.[68]

The history of legal reform in Hanover, where procedural reform made its first breakthrough, offers a classic example of the up and down course of constitutional transformation. As I mentioned earlier, following the 1830 revolutions a constitution was promulgated in 1833. A representative assembly, the Landtag, was the main fruit of the *Staatsgrundgesetze.* It was composed of an upper and a lower house, and, importantly, had legislative competency. In 1837, however, the Duke of Cumberland, Ernst August succeeded to the throne. August was no supporter of constitutionalism, and his first major act was to declare the *Staatsgrundgesetze* of 1833 invalid. Given the concern that liberals expressed about the position of women in society, it is worth noting that August's succession occurred only because Hanover law barred Victoria from ascending to the throne because of her gender. For the first time in 123 years the crowns of Hanover and Great Britain were separated, and, paradoxically, liberals probably would have secured the political reforms they desired if Victoria had become queen.

The Germanist, Dahlmann, well known later for his *Die Politik* (1835), had played a major role in drafting the *Staatsgrundgesetze,* and it was his disciple, Gervinus, who wrote the protest treatise. They were joined in this effort by five other Göttingen professors, Jacob and Wilhelm Grimm, Wilhelm Albrecht, Wilhelm Weber and Heinrich Ewald. All seven were dismissed from the university and banished from the state of Hanover in 1837. This was the infamous Göttingen Seven affair which attracted liberal attention throughout German-speaking Europe. It was in the wake of this incident, as I mentioned earlier, that Savigny secured new appointments for Jacob and Wilhelm Grimm at the University of Berlin.

During the six years of its duration, the Landtag passed three groundbreaking pieces of legislation. These were the *Zivilprozeßordnung,* the *Polizeistrafgesetzbuch* and the *Gewerbe-ordnung.*[69] This early *Zivilprozeßordnung* for Hanover was co-drafted by Wilhelm Planck.[70] Planck was a Germanist and was widely respected for his research on procedural legal history. Planck's role in drafting the first Hanover *Zivilprozeßordnung* is significant, because his only child was Gottlieb Planck, the father of the BGB. In any event and despite these early legislative advances, the appeal to the German Confederation to save the *Staatsgrundgesetze* failed. Ernst August responded by employing the rhetoric of customary law constitutionalism to install a new constitution suited to his illiberal aims. This was the *Landesverfassungsgesetze* of 1840. It forestalled further constitutional transformation by abrogating the legislative power of the Landtag's two chambers and most of the legislation it had passed. This also shows how Central European monarchs were capable of appropriating constitutional transformation and employing lawmaking for their own purposes. The Landtag, in fact, did not regain its critical power to legislate until 1848.

This political demand for procedural reform was not a demand for either the *Geschworenengericht* or the *Schöffengericht*, but both forms, the former for serious criminal cases and the latter in lighter cases. During the Lübeck *Germanistentag* of 1847, members of a procedural reform commission that included Beseler, Dahlmann, Welcker and Mittermaier discussed the merits of the *Geschworenengericht* in comparative perspective to English, French and American models along with the *Schöffengericht*. They emphasized, more than anything, the need for public and oral court proceedings to protect ordinary citizens from arbitrary and private judgements.[71] Wilhelm Planck was also present to make the case for procedural reform. Procedural legislation was, therefore, a fixed element of the liberal political platform well before 1848, and the decision to actively push again for procedural reform had already been made. Lawyers, even at the local level, increasingly demanded *Schöffen,* jury trials, and that court procedures be conducted directly, orally and publicly, instead of in secret. They demanded the right of citizens to legal representation by counsel of their choosing and the right of litigating parties to control the evidence.[72]

Accordingly, while scholars have expressed surprise at the speed with which the committees of the Frankfurt Parliament were able to draft legal measures, in fact, this is explained by the fact that a robust *Privatrechts-Staatslehre* had been produced for nearly half a century and by the earlier procedural reforms in Hanover.[73] The key provisions of the constitutional document of 1849 were, in reality, reflections, not only of the systems produced by Eichhorn, Grimm, Mittermaier, Beseler and others, but the abrogated legal reforms of the 1830s. In addition to these important sources, there was a tremendous body of both book and article literature or more accurately data for a German system that they were able to draw on. What is more, the major goals had already been hammered out at the *Germanisten* conferences of 1846 and 1847. Finally, most of the participants from the various conferences held in these years emerged as leading deputies at Paulskirche in 1848 and major players on the various committees.

The constitutional document of 1849, therefore, should also be seen as a reflection of the momentum that the programmatic approach to sociopolitical revision had gained in Central Europe, since Savigny's call for the *vaterländisches Recht*. The document itself only consolidated the systems and data that had been produced by legal scholars since the 1820s, and there were several constitutions and attempted legal reforms available by 1848 that they could use as models. The constitutional document of 1849 offers an indication that subsequent legislation would be seen as an organic part of a constitution itself. With regard to procedural reform, Article 128 read:

> A special law shall be promulgated to regulate the institution and organization of the Reich Court, its procedures and the implementation of its decisions and rulings. To this law shall also be reserved the regulation of whether and in which cases a verdict of the

> Reich Court shall be based on jurors. The same applies to whether and how far this law is to be regarded as an organic part of the Constitution.[74]

In addition to the call for procedural reform, there were two other important concepts contained in this article. First, it reflected an idea that was inherent in liberal conceptions of legislative revolution, essentially, that it would be necessary to execute additional legal measures to secure full reform. Even more important than this was the suggestion that additional laws would be regarded as organic parts of the constitution. The road toward full sociopolitical revision continued, even at Paulskirche, to be seen as a gradual process rather than as an immediate event. It was this dimension of constitutional transformation that made it possible for private law, which included procedure, to assume the primary function of inverted political revision.

When procedural reform followed almost immediately after 1849, spreading from state to state, it leveled distinctions by awarding judicial privileges to the commonalty and in this way undermined the old judicial arrangements. The courts and procedures were reformed into institutions that reflected liberal political demands. It should not come as a surprise that Hanover, where liberalism flourished in the legal community, was the first state after 1848 to introduce procedural reform in 1850. *Die bürgerliche Proceßordnung für das Königreich Hanover* of 8 November 1850 made effective the reforms favored by *Vormärz* liberals that were contained in the constitutional document of 1849. The legal historian Werner Schubert has pointed out that in the Hanover legislation, the maxim of new liberal procedural principles, particularly orality and uniformity, were made effective.[75] It made trial procedure public and oral, which was a core right included in the constitutional document of 1849. Article 178 read, in part: 'Court proceedings shall be public and oral.'[76] In terms of the basic right of citizens to uniformity in procedure, Article 182 would have ended administrative justice and police justice. Instead, it held that 'courts are to decide all matters of the law'.[77]

Moreover, the Hanover *Proceßordnung* gave the people greater representation in judicial decisions. It introduced the long-celebrated *Schöffengericht.* In addition, it guaranteed the right of citizens to legal representation by the lawyer of their choice. While these provisions guaranteed basic rights, they also had the double impact of expanding an important liberal political constituency. The right to representation strengthened and facilitated the expansion of the legal profession. Under the *Proceßordnung,* the profession was divided into *Advokatanwälte,* admitted in restricted numbers to argue civil cases, and *Advokaten,* admitted in unlimited numbers to counsel clients and prepare civil cases as well as argue criminal cases.[78] The Hanover *Proceßordnung* was held in high regard, as the most progressive measure in the German lands, and it was the model for procedural legislation elsewhere.[79]

Procedural reform in Saxony, the largest German state next to Prussia and where noble privileges were more extensive and deeply entrenched than in other German states, marked a watershed in the history of constitutional transformation at the state level. Under the *Gerichtsverfassung* of 1854, the courts were reorganized, giving the judiciary independence and dividing the courts into regional and local courts.[80] This provision, as well as others, had been expressed in the constitutional document of 1849. Its Article 175 stated: 'The courts shall exercise their judicial powers independently.'[81] At the same time, the *Gerichtsverfassung* dismantled Saxony's judicial bureaucracy by abolishing, altogether, the old *Patrimonialgerichte* (patrimonial courts).[82] In this way, it annulled an important seigniorial privilege and vested citizens with the basic right to a hearing before an impartial judiciary. Again, provisions for the abolition of patrimonial courts were contained in the 1849 constitution document. Article 174 stated: 'All jurisdiction emanates from the State. There shall be no patrimonial courts'.[83]

Following the introduction of the *Gerichtsverfassung,* the *Strafprozeßordnung* (1855) was introduced in Saxony, which secured more basic rights for ordinary citizens. Like Hanover's procedural legislation, it made trial procedure public and oral, and it awarded citizens the right to independent counsel.[84] Courts became the centre of adjudication and, increasingly, safeguarded common men against arbitrary justice in criminal cases. In addition, the institution of the *Kollegialgericht* (panel of judges) offered a safeguard against arbitrary judgement.[85] While I have only discussed the procedural reforms in Hanover and Saxony, procedural legislation was also enacted in Oldenburg (1857), Baden (1862), Württemberg (1868) and Bavaria (1869). From 1850 onward, the number of lay judges, jury courts, commercial courts and trade tribunals increased steadily in Central Europe.[86]

The aim of procedural legislation was to subject the whole society to the same laws and to draw down any legal distinctions between the bourgeoisie and hereditary aristocracy. In addition to delineating court procedures, procedural codes organized the court system, the constitution of which was crucial to the ability of liberals to implement and enforce legislative revolution and liberal rule in their envisioned *Gemeinwesen.* Procedural reform also increased the number of courts. In this manner, it expanded the reach and the authority of a new apparatus of liberal social control. It gave liberals the means to secure that the people's behavior conformed to liberal sociopolitical standards and gave them the means to exert disciplinary control in the case of infraction. This expanding arm of the emerging civil society, increasingly, exerted control over ordinary private matters, such as the registration of births, deaths and marital relations. Every individual increasingly fell within the liberal state's purview and within reach of its disciplinary authority. The courts and laws increasingly replaced the old structures and slowly emerged as the institutional backbone of private and public life.

The New Periodicals

A strong indicator of the advance of constitutional transformation was not only the founding of new law journals, but the changing nature of these journals. Where the journals of the 1820s had been general in subject matter, the journals founded at mid-century focused on specific areas of law. This new trend reflected the consolidation of key political revisions. *Der Gerichtssaal* was founded by the lawyer, Ludwig Jagemann, in 1849. His opening article, *Der Uebergang vom alten zum neuen Rechte* (1849), clearly anticipated a wholesale legal restructuring of German society. He was explicit in explaining that the journal was dedicated to obtaining certain 'pure political institutions, namely, the constitutional state, associations and trade rights'.[87] He emphasized that the formation of civil and criminal procedures were vital elements in any constitutional state, and he wrote specifically that the journal would publish on key areas of the debate at the sitting *Reichsversammlung* in Frankfurt.[88] Indeed, it was a major organ for members of the Parliament who advocated for the jury trial system, including Mittermaier and the lawyers, Leue from Cologne and Drechsler of Rostock.[89] In addition to high profile liberal names, *Der Gerichtssaal* was also an organ for rank and file liberal legal professionals, who were the foot soldiers of constitutional transformation in the courts.

Unlike the earlier journals, which attempted to address constitutional concerns, *Der Gerichtssaal* was not shut down after 1849, and its continuing circulation was sustained by the procedural reforms that began in 1850. It also covered the trials of major liberal figures who faced prosecution after the revolution failed in 1849. The Mannheim lawyer Amman's article, 'Über den Proceß gegen Gustav von Struve und Karl Blind aus Mannheim, wegen Hochverraths: Die erste Verhandlung vor einem Badische Schwurgerichte' (1849), was concerned that the very procedures that liberals had fought to install were now being used to persecute them.[90] The radical Struve had called for the *Vorparlament* to make itself permanent. When this was rejected and the ministry in Baden acted to curb radicalism, Struve along with Friedrich Hecker had proclaimed a republic in southern Baden.[91] In his article, Amman published a long tract of Mittermaier's comments to the Frankfurt Parliament's procedure commission, in which he emphasized that even those charged with political crimes were entitled to a trial by a jury of their peers.[92] His analysis, however, did not stop with an assessment of the plight of Struve and Blind. Rather, he emphasized that behind these high-profile trials, many, many lesser-known figures were be dragged before the courts. Some 4,279 persons were charged with treason, in Baden, between March and September of 1848 and some 1,266 for their involvement in the September coup attempt. Of these, 850 of those charged with treason and 730 charged for their September activities were under arrest. Many, as he also noted, had simply taken flight; 383 persons charged with treason and 196 from the other group.[93]

Der Gerichtssaal and other organs played an important role in the continuing mobilization for constitutional transformation. Johann Seuffert and Christian Glück's *Blätter für Rechtsanwendung,* which was founded earlier in 1836, was renamed in honor of Seuffert in 1859 to *Dr. J. A. Seuffert's Blätter für Rechtsanwendung* and continued to be a major organ for Bavaria until 1913. Seuffert (1794–1857) was typical of the rank and file liberal lawyers who sustained constitutional transformation.

He had served as an army field lieutenant in the *Freiheitskriege* and took his education after the war. In addition to this local legal journal, Seuffert also founded the national organ, *Archiv für Entscheidungen der obersten Gerichte in den Deutschen Staaten* in 1847. It was also renamed after his death and continued in circulation until the 1870s.

Even in Prussia, J. Gruchot was able to get his *Beiträge zur Erläuterung des preußischen Rechts durch Theorie und Praxis* into circulation in 1857. Although it came some years behind the ZGR, it was dedicated to a 'scientific approach to Prussian law', as Gruchot wrote in his brief preface.[94] It was renamed in 1867 to the *Beiträge zur Erläuterung des preußischen Rechts, des Handels- und Wechselrechts durch Theorie und Praxis,* reflecting the tremendous legal and economic transformations that were taking place in Central Europe. The *Jahrbuch der deutschen Rechtswissenschaft und Gesetzgebung* was founded by the law professor and judge H. Schletter in 1855, and it was published, in fourteen volumes, until shortly after German unification in 1873. Founded in 1855 by two law professors, the *Jahrbuch des gemeinen deutschen Rechts* also reflected the changes taking place in German society. E. Bekker's opening article, 'Über das gemeine deutsche Recht der Gegenwart und dessen Behandlung', offers an indication that the concept of *gemeines Recht,* which had earlier referred to the *ius commune,* was increasingly applied also to common German law.[95] The old guard continued to publish in these newer journals. Jacob Grimm's 'Recht von Hiesfeld' appeared in the *Jahrbuch's* first edition.[96] In addition to these old names, leading figures from the new generation also began to publish. Otto Stobbe's 'Die Grundsätze der deutschen Rechtsquellen des Mittelalters über den Gerichtsstand' continued the Germanist tradition.[97] He would become particularly well known for, amongst other studies, his lengthy *Die Juden in Deutschland während des Mittelalters* (1866), which did a great deal to lend legitimacy to the full emancipation of Jews in German society. Although he was a Christian, his work was the first to trace the constitutional history of Jews in German history, and he sat on a committee for the recovery of Jewish history.[98] J. Pötz's *Kritische Vierteljahresschrift für Gesetzgebung und Rechtswissenschaft* was another major national organ. It was founded in 1859 and was published until the collapse of the Reich in 1919.

These journals kept up the pressure for legislative reformations. Rank and file lawyers, like Amman, monitored and reported on legal proceedings in their areas and were the eyes and ears on the ground. Even after the state-level procedural reforms in Hanover, which *Der Gerichtssaal* monitored, Jagemann continued to demand national revision. He opened his 1851 article, 'Zur deutschen Nationalgesetzgebung', pointing toward Christ's additional call for a unified civil code, published in the *Deutsche Vierteljahresschrift* in 1850.[99] The contemporary demands, as he underscored, were the product of more than forty years of labor, which 'the younger generation' would carry forward.[100] He pointed specifically to Savigny, not mentioning Thibaut, as the founder of the movement. While Savigny had emphasized the place of Roman legal science, a German system would come from the 'flesh and blood of German life'.[101] Jagemann also explained the important place of the Lübeck *Germanistentag,* where Christ had issued his original call for a unified code, and emphasized that this was particularly important relative to family law and marital relations.[102] Eduard Pape, who would head the first BGB Commission before his death in 1888 also published an article in the same edition.[103]

These legal infrastructural developments and the constant work of the German legal world kept constitutional transformation moving forward. Indeed, in 1862, well before the founding of the North German Confederation in 1866, a commission was set up to begin work on a procedural code for all the German states and under the leadership of Hanover's liberal justice minister, Adolf Leonhardt, who was the lead editor for the 1850 legislation. In 1867, in an effort to appease Hanover, Bismarck secured Leonhardt's appointment to the position of Minister of Justice for Prussia, and the earlier work was absorbed in the planned code for the Confederation. In the end, Leonhardt would head the national procedure code commission for the Reich after 1871.

Commercial Law

Although commercial law was a critical area of private law, it is not the major focus of this study. However, a few comments are in order. The consolidation of areas of law dealing with business and commercial matters followed a pattern of development similar to that of procedural reform.[104] Whereas legal scholars for a long time suggested that study and research in the field of commercial law was neglected until the 1840s, this view may also now be reconsidered.[105] Mittermaier's system dedicated considerable attention to the legal history of commercial, exchange and maritime law.[106] Following this general history, legal research reflected not only the search for data and the recovery of local customary arrangements, but followed local legal developments in strong commercial centres.

This was first evident regarding exchange law. Friedrich Bodungen published his *Das königlich-hannoverische Wechselrecht in alphabetischer Ordnung* in 1824.[107] Jacob Pestalutz offered a comparative study, *Abhandlung über das Züricherische Wechselrecht, mit Vergleichung der Augsburger, Sct. Galler und Basler Wechselordnung* (1827).[108] The same year, Heinrich Daniels attempted to delineate the basic legal principles of exchange law in his *Grundsätze des Wechselrechts.*[109] Hermann Rothschildt produced the seminal study on the old *Hansestadt* of Braunschweig.[110] His *Die bei dem Verkehre mit Wechseln zu beobachtenden Formen nach gemeinem Rechte und der Braunschweigischen Wechselordnung* appeared in 1841.[111] Eduard Souchay studied Frankfurt in his *Anmerkungen zu den Wechsel-Gesetzen der Freien Stadt Frankfurt, mit besonderer Bezugnahme auf die offizielle Ausgabe der Wechselordnung vom Jahre 1845* (1845).[112] Finally, the same year as the first *Germanistentag,* Gustav Nürmberger, who was the foremost scholar on Nürnberg, published *Sammlung von Beiträgen und Anmerkungen zu praktischer Erläuterung der Nürnberger Wechselordnung* (1846).[113]

These studies are just examples of the literature that was in production for some twenty years prior to 1848. Unlike the other measures that were introduced after 1849, the well-known *Wechselordnung* (General Bills of Exchange Law) was pushed through in 1848. Just as the decision to pursue the introduction of a civil code and procedural reform was decided in 1847, the *Wechselordnung* was, in fact, a product of a Leipzig legal conference of 1847. This was also an area of law in which enough data for a system had been produced, and an experimental phase with the introduction of local measures had occurred earlier. In point of fact, the *Wechselordnung* had been a long time in the making, however much 1848 may have provided the chance for its introduction.

While the *Wechselordnung* has long been celebrated as an advance by legal scholars and historians alike, it should come as no surprise that liberal gender protectionism also made its national appearance here. Under Article 1.3, claims could not be filed against women 'who were not engaged in business or some other trade'.[114] Although implemented under the auspices of protection, this measure, in fact, served to keep women out of the public courts. Liberals jammed through their social agenda anywhere they could. In addition, Article 1 also made clear that exchange law, which had heretofore been the subject of private law scholarship, was considered to be 'public law *(öffentliches Recht)*'.[115] This also underscores the point I have made about *Privatrechts-Staatslehre,* and how many areas of German public law first developed in the realm of private law scholarship.

Following this major legal advance, a new area of legal scholarship focused on practice quickly grew up around the new law. Eduard Siebenhaar and Theodor Tauschnitz started the *Archiv für deutsches Wechselrecht* in 1850. Mittermaier published two articles in the first edition. In 'Das Indossament nach dem Verfalltage: Erläuterung des §16 der Deutschen Wechselordnung', he offered an explanation and commentary on the law itself.[116] This was an early indication of the practice that was followed after the introduction of major legislation in Germany. His 'Ueber den Einfluß höherer Gewalt auf die Regreßklage im Falle der Unterlassung wechselrechtlicher Pflichten nach der deutschen Wechselordnung', by contrast, dealt with how a particular dispute would be interpreted under the new law.[117] In addition to these journals, larger legal textbooks were produced in the aftermath of the *Wechselordnung's* passage and marked the growth of specialized practice in this area of law. These included Franz Haimerl's *Anleitung zum Studium des Wechselrechtes* (1855) and Leopold Bleibtreu's *Die Lehre von den Wechseln mit Hinweisung auf bestehende Gesetze* (1860).[118] Achilles Renaud's three-volume textbook, *Lehrbuch des allgemeinen deutschen Wechselrechts* (1857), was an important work in this area.[119]

In the post-1850 era and after procedural reform, commercial law was the next major target of constitutional transformationists. Again, however, the demand for commercial law reform was heard in years following the *Freiheitskriege.* Johann Ziegler published a treatise on free trade, *Ueber Gewerbefreiheit und deren Folgen* as early as 1819, and the demand for reform was also evident in Johann Leuch's *Vollständiges Handelsrecht* (1822).[120] The treatise, *Durch welche Bedingungen ist das System der Handelsfreiheit ausführbar?* (1834) had to be published anonymously during the censorship crackdown following the Six Acts and Ten Articles of 1832.[121] Johann Hoffmann's *Die Befugniss zum Gewerbbetriebe zur Berichtigung der Urtheile über Gewerbefreiheit und Gewerbezwang* appeared in 1841.[122] *Gewerbefreiheit für Nürnberg* was published anonymously in 1846, the year of the first *Germanistentag.*[123] The pressure was kept on into the 1860s, when Hermann Rentzsch published his *Die Gewerbefreiheit und Freizügigkeit* in 1861.[124]

Behind the demand for commercial law reform was the steady production of legal history and, thus, the recovery of data for a system. The most important figure here, before Levin Goldschmidt, was Heinrich Thöl, who published the first comprehensive study, *Das Handelsrecht,* in three volumes from 1841.[125] Following Thöl many studies were produced on local arrangements and legal developments. Carl Kleinschrod wrote on Bavaria in 1840.[126] Nürmberger published two studies in 1846, *Sammlung einiger nürnbergische Handelsrechts-Gewohnheiten* and *Sammlung von Beiträgen und andern Anmerkungen zur praktischen Erläuterung der Nürnberger Handelsgerichtsordnung.*[127] In 1852, Carl Billich offered a study of Württemberg and, in 1856, Ferdinand Fischer's *Preußens kaufmännisches Recht* was published.[128] Two studies were published on proposed legislation for Saxony in 1857 and 1859.[129] In 1856, the influential Germanist Wilhelm Kraut updated Mittermaier's old findings in his general system and published his *Grundriss zu Vorlesungen über das Deutsche Privatrecht mit Einschluss des Lehns- und Handelsrechts nebst beigefügten Quellen.*[130]

It was, however, ultimately, Thöl's work that influenced the Nürnberg Draft. This draft measure was the source of the *Gemeines Handelsgesetzbuch* of 1861. It was enacted by various states between 1862 and 1863. After unification in 1871, it was reenacted for the whole Reich and remained the basis of commercial law until it was replaced by a new commercial code in 1897. In this regard, the Thöl-Goldschmidt debate was another legendary legal dispute in the German legal world. This will not be examined here, because, again, commercial law reform is not the major focus of this study. Nevertheless, Goldschmidt, who was Jewish, was far more wedded to German nationalism and the Germanists than Thöl had been. Indeed, Goldschmidt founded the *Zeitschrift für das Gesamte Handelsrecht* for this reason in 1858.[131] Goldschmidt, as his writings from the late 1850s show, was a critic of the proposed commercial code of 1861.[132] His major works reflected the demand that any system of law be derived from German customary arrangements. In this regard, his *Das Handbuch des Handelsrechts* (1864) and *System des Handelsrechts*

(1887) are important.[133] In the end, Goldschmidt headed the drafting commission for the national *Handelsgesetzbuch* that was enacted in 1897 and introduced as a part of the new legal regime in 1900.[134] It was in commercial legislation, as Wieacker wrote, that 'the special law of the entrepreneurial class in trade and industry' was instituted in German society.[135] Indeed, special commercial courts were set up for the adjudication of commercial matters. The reason why industrial capitalism proved more dynamic than agriculture, time and again, in the second half of the nineteenth century, was partly because it was helped along by friendly, commercial legislation and judicial arrangements.

The Civil Code of Saxony

The codification of civil law, like procedural and commercial law reform, was bound up with the broader political revision, which rested on a programme of constitutional transformation. Whereas procedural reform secured basic judicial rights and the means to have these rights enforced, civil codes defined specific rights and obligations. The systems and codes that were produced after 1815 reflected the nationalist political and social platform of *Vormärz* liberals, particularly that of the Germanists. The Dresden Draft of Obligations Law, based on Germanist theory, was cause for celebration in liberal circles.[136] Draft civil codes were produced in Württemberg, Hesse and Bavaria between the 1850s and 1860s. These earlier state drafts were important to the history of legal reform after unification, because the national codes were modeled after the earlier state codes. While the Dresden Draft was never introduced, it was the model for the obligations law of the BGB. As a result of this tendency, private law offers a window into the continuity of liberal development in German history.

Saxony is where the drive for unified civil law had its greatest success prior to unification. Christian Ahcin offers an informative study on the liberal politics that stood behind the drafting of Saxony's Civil Code. As he points out, a clear link to the growth and impact of liberalism in Central Europe can be seen in the history of the Code. It had its roots in the early century and represented a culmination of the reformist movement that began after 1815.[137] Primarily, however, work on the Code was a product of Saxony's constitution, which had made it possible.[138] As Ahcin writes, the first draft met with strident conservative criticism, which protested that the proposed draft of private law was the fruit of liberal agitation and a concession to liberalism.[139] Major Germanist figures such as Mittermaier, Arndt and Beseler weighed in favor of the draft and demanded that the content reflect German customary law.[140] No other piece of civil legislation shared the spotlight with Hanover's *Proceßordnung* as much as the *Bürgerliche Gesetzbuch für das Königreich Sachsen* of 1863 (BGBS).[141] Promulgated in 1863, it went into effect in 1865.

The BGBS is worth examining in some detail for several reasons. First, in Saxony, a vibrant industrial economy centred at Leipzig existed alongside the most backward political conditions in Central Europe outside the Mecklenburgs. The combination of forces was a harbinger of what was to come in united Germany as the century wore on. Second, and although the Code still reflected older norms, much of what liberals had only imagined before 1863 became a living reality and there were tremendous social ramifications for private relationships in Saxony. Finally, the popular response of Saxonians to the BGBS foreshadowed what would happen at the national level following the introduction of the BGB.

As I suggested earlier, civil law provided liberals an alternative avenue to install citizenship and to secure the basic rights of citizens. The *Allgemeiner Teil* (General Part), as Ahcin notes, was an expression of German customary law principles.[142] This section secured the right to personality, defined the legal capacity of natural and juristic persons and the rights of associations.[143] The second book on *Sachenrecht* (property rights) offered the nineteenth century's strongest statement on the right to private property and the rights of property owners.[144] Book three defined the right to contract and obligations in commercial and service relationships.[145] Indeed, it even contained a section that provided for bankruptcy law.[146] Amongst the most prominent of basic rights conferred on commoners, however, was the right to marry. The BGBS's marriage law offers an example of how the regulation of seemingly benign private matters was in reality deeply political. The marriage law curbed noble privileges in private matters and made liberal political and social theory a living reality. It struck at the social core of absolutism by redefining and restructuring the family into one that fit liberal rather than monarchical constructions of society.

Saxony's nobles, as was the case in other parts of Central Europe, were not subject to any comprehensive laws. Rather, family law came in the form of private *Familienverträge* (family agreements). At the same time, family law did not exist for commoners, but remained a privilege of the nobility, which reinforced their right to property and power. In Saxony, *Familienverträge* gradually evolved from contracts that were written for all adult members of the noble family into documents that governed the entire family of cousins. 'The competition of noble families with each other and with other social groups', writes Josef Matzerath, 'caused Saxony's nobility to make great efforts to place feudal tenures in joint-property, to conclude inheritance associations, to adopt for themselves family regulations, to establish entailed estates and to close the entailed estates of families.'[147] Although they also regulated education, marriage, conduct and religion, the purpose of these agreements, in the first instance, was to secure that family property remained within the family and within the nobility. This secured the consolidation of property and power.

It was this old order that the Family and Guardianship Law of the BGBS began to undermine in Saxony. Paragraph 1568 read: 'Engagement is the contract through which two persons of different sexes pledge themselves to the contraction of a marriage.'[148] This paragraph was loaded with liberal political demands. The institution of civil marriage extended the right to contract to commoners under private law and therefore annulled noble seigniorial privilege. Moreover, the redefinition of marriage as a contractual relationship undermined the authority of the church in private affairs, an institution conservatives allied themselves with in an attempt to ward off the influence of liberalism. Not only did civil marriage undo the influence of the church, it worked toward the separation of church and state. As Buchholz pointed out, civil marriage represented the secularization of marriage and was part and parcel of liberal demands for the separation of Church and state.[149]

Although vestiges of church influences remained in Saxony after 1865, the liberal model of social organization was given legal legitimacy. Civil marriage redefined the family into a secular institution and leveled disparity between the rights of citizens and nobles, making equality the basis for political organization. Marriage between two individuals became the basis of the family relationship in the place of hereditary ancestry. The nuclear family stood in opposition to that of nobles, which emphasized the extended family. In addition, one of the chief means by which the nobility prevented property from falling into non-noble hands was through the intermarriage of cousins, or those who were only indirectly related. Paragraphs 1608 to 1614 placed restrictions on such patterns of marriage, although it was possible to receive dispensation in some cases.[150]

Contractual marriage was, furthermore, bound up with property rights, and it confirmed the rights of commoners to property. The right to marry confirmed the right to take oaths as well as to contract. It gave men possession of themselves, if nothing else, and increased their power before the state. Accordingly, Paragraph 1570 reads 'no engagement can be closed by persons of the male sex before eighteen and female sex before sixteen'.[151] While this challenged the marriage norms of the nobility, where marriage typically did not occur before the mid-twenties, it also confirmed the basic right to independent legal personality before the state.[152] Moreover, it essentially lowered the age of majority and the point at which one could own property. The right to property was, in turn, bound up with the right to participate in public affairs.

At the same time, a double tendency was already evident in the BGBS. On the one hand, it was politically progressive, while on the other, it was socially regressive. The right to marry was only awarded to Christians.[153] The Code extended basic rights to a broader sector of the male population, but it rigorously denied these rights to women. Here, the egalitarian promises of Vormärz liberal constitutionalism did not apply. This was in part due to the fact that challenging the old order from the bottom of society involved setting up norms that challenged those of the nobility. Therefore, the norms that Germanists set up tended to be the opposite of noble norms. Where court Jews had enjoyed special status under Central European absolutism, this order was leveled in both the writings of the Germanists and under subsequent bourgeois laws.[154] Illegitimate children also were victims to the new civil code. The provisions on *Erbrecht* denied illegitimate children the right to inherit from the paternal line.[155] Whereas noble women inherited property, exercised independent control of that property and bequeathed it to others, liberals disavowed these rights for women in theory and in practice.

It is important not to forget women in our political analysis of the liberal challenge to the old order. As Bush writes, no distinction was made between noble men and women with regard to privileges, and the privileges of noble women were targeted as well.[156] The new provisions of civil law resembled the customary laws that were identified by the Germanists. Instead of conferring the right to property and to contract freely upon women, civil marriage denied most women these rights and gave control of their property to their husbands. Paragraph 1655 of the BGBS read: 'The husband has the right of usufruct and management of the property, which the wife possessed at the time of the closing of the marriage or acquires during the marriage.'[157] Not only did the husband have the right to manage the wife's property, but any earnings that accrued to her property or through her labor belonged to him. Moreover, Paragraph 1656 read: 'All of the tangible things in the house, in case of doubt, belong to the husband' with the exception of the wife's personal effects.[158] The fact that women were denied full independent property rights meant that they were also denied basic public rights. Under Paragraph 1638, women could not execute legal transactions with third parties without the consent of their husbands, denying them the right of freedom to contract.[159] Paragraph 1641 legislated that a business entered into by a woman without the consent of her husband was invalid before the law.[160] Moreover, women were denied the right to possess an independent name and status under Paragraph 1623, which required that they take the name and class of their husbands.[161] Under Paragraph 1645, women were accorded the right to contract without the consent of their husbands only so long as it involved 'the aim of the management of the household'.[162] This was the so-called *Schlüsselgewalt,* but again women were only the *Schlüsselträgerinnen* of their husbands. These measures did not reflect the independent civil rights women had enjoyed before 1865. Moreover, these provisions were not designed to give women power in the home, but rather to confine them to it and deny them basic legal personality and participation rights.

In response to this legislation, voices of opposition were raised in Saxony. Up until 1865, Germanist theory on the place of women in society had only been talk. After the promulgation of the BGBS, however, the unequal separation of the sexes became a living reality in Saxony. The BGBS set a trend in gender legislation toward the denial of women's civil rights, a trend that continued until a new Law of Associations was promulgated in 1908. While the response of women will not be discussed in this chapter, the legislated denial of rights under civil law that Saxony's women faced for the first time in 1865 offers an additional explanation as to why the *Allgemeiner Deutscher Frauenverein* (ADF) was founded in Leipzig that same year. The convention was composed largely of working women, who were the hardest hit by the BGBS's marital property provisions and who made up the majority of Saxony's industrial workers.

Impact of Unification on Constitutional Transformation

The legal reformations that were already taking place at the state level informed the development of the national legal system after German unification. This is important because historians have argued that Otto von Bismarck redirected nationalist and liberal momentum by securing unification under the Prussian flag, and the Reich Constitution of 1871 has long been criticized for the conspicuous absence of basic rights provisions. It is useful, however, to distinguish between geographical unification and structural unification, which was still a pressing question that demanded an answer. Shortly after the founding of the North German Confederation in 1866, a political cartoon under the title 'Something is rotten in the State, etc' appeared. The cartoon depicts the front and back sides of a peacock's feathers. On the front, it shows the various states in the North German Confederation fanned on the peacock's tail. On the back side, however, it shows an array of pressing legal questions. The caption reads: 'It looks magnificent from the front, but when you get to the bottom of it—Oh dear!'[163]

Rather that focusing on Prussianization, in fact, scholars should give much greater consideration to the fact that Prussia not only annexed states where constitutional transformation was making considerable inroads, but populations of veteran legal liberals and constitutional transformationists. This is particularly important with regard to Hanover. Paradoxically, given the complicated structural disunity that resulted from unification, liberal legislation was the only tool available for such a monumental task as structurally unifying the new Reich, and, this reality, as Frensdorff wrote, was not lost on Gottlieb Planck.[164] More biographical information about Gottlieb Planck is offered in Chapter 7, but, for now, it will suffice to emphasize the he emerged as one of the most active Hanover liberals of the mid century.

The Hanover *Prozeßordnung* of 1850 was made possible by the *Verfassungsgesetz* of 1848, which restored the key provisions of the *Staatsgrundgesetze* of 1833. Ernst August, however, hastily gave back the constitution to save his own neck during the upheaval of 1848, and, as soon as the danger cleared, he was again prepared to renege, this time, on the 1848 *Verfassungsgesetz.* However much the *Prozeßordnung* was celebrated in Central Europe and it represented advance, its introduction was followed the same year by the king's dismissal of the liberal ministry. A bitter constitutional struggle erupted just before his death in November of 1851. The new King, George V, shared his father's reactionary political views and, from the start of his reign, he set out to kill the *Verfassungsgesetz.* While he faced strident resistance from the second chamber, he ultimately won his appeal to the German Confederation in the *Bundesbeschlüsse* of 12 and 19 April 1855, which declared the *Verfassungsgesetz* of 1848 invalid. George V then restored the hated *Landesverfassungsgesetze* of

1840.[165] The heated constitutional struggles continued in Hanover right up to 1865, and liberals were in a decidedly weakened position. In his *Die Rechtswidrigkeit des in Hannover bestehenden Verfassungszustandes,* which he published anonymously in 1861, Gottlieb Planck described these events in detail and defended the validity of the 1848 *Verfassungsgesetz.*[166] As Frensdorff wrote, liberals in Hanover were indeed disheartened after 1855 by the weakening of much of the legislation they had introduced after 1848, including the 1850 procedural code.[167]

Paradoxically, constitutional transformation was given a new life by Hanover's defeat at Prussian hands in 1866. It was Planck who wrote the key articles in the *Zeitung für Nord Deutschland* following annexation.[168] Here, he argued that a new epoch had begun and that annexed lands and Prussia must work together. In particular, he emphasized that the 'passive role that Hanover had played in the last months' must be changed, and the annexed lands must as quickly as possible be made into living members of the Prussian State', on an equal basis.[169] 'The aims of the National Liberal Party', he wrote, 'would remain German unity and securing liberty'.[170] As he noted, Prussia had secured only military and financial unity, but it still had to secure the moral and spiritual unity of the annexed lands and this was exactly where he felt that Hanover, specifically Hanover's liberals, could exercise decisive influence.[171] Indeed, as Frensdorff wrote, the triad of Hanoverians, namely Bennigsen, Miquel and Planck, wished to inject 'fresh blood' into the liberal movement in Prussia.[172]

Bismarck essentially reversed his position on legal reformation in these years and probably out of absolute necessity. He initially resisted calls to consolidate the legal system before unification, and Prussia abstained from participation in the drafting and introduction of the *Gemeines Handelsgesetzbuch* of 1861. Bismarck went so far as to begin legal reforms in Prussia in an attempt to make them an attractive alternative for the other German states. Yet, as James Brophy has shown, the Prussian state accommodated the juridical and economic demands of the business elite.[173] This would seem to indicate that Bismarck faced the need to compromise at least as much as German liberals. Indeed, after the Austro-Prussian War of 1866, 'legal reform provided Bismarck with an opportunity both to flatter the Hanoverians and to demonstrate to the suspicious middle states the good faith of Prussia in pursuing a national consolidation of Germany that, while under the auspices and to the advantage of Prussia, did not simply consist of an extension of the Prussian system to all of Germany'.[174]

The problem of how to integrate the newly acquired territories was a pressing structural problem, and we should not underestimate the degree to which Bismarck may have backed himself and conservatives into a corner. Under the threat of the approaching Landtag elections in 1866, Bismarck warned conservative officials not to oppose the election of moderate liberals lest Prussia be turned over to radical liberals and the revolutionary forces of liberal nationalism. His hope, as Otto Pflanze argued, was 'to overthrow parliamentarianism with parliamentarianism'.[175] Clearly, he hoped to compromise liberalism by embracing it, as other scholars have argued, but one has to wonder about the probability of success for such a policy, particularly when legal reformation is factored into the equation. A host of measures were passed or in production by 1871, and most of these were derived from the Hanover legislation of the mid century. The *Strafgesetzbuch* of 1870, which was introduced in the North German Confederation, became the law for the whole Reich in 1871. Work on German-wide civil procedure legislation began in Hanover, in 1861. Leonhardt, Planck and Bennigsen all sat on this strategic planning commission and its work, ultimately, was absorbed into the North German Confederation in 1866 and, again, once procedural reform was approved by the Reichstag in 1871. Under the auspices of the practical needs of the nation, liberals were slowly, but surely in the process of introducing significant legal reforms.

Over the course of the last three decades of the nineteenth century, despite Bismarck's special laws, liberals increasingly obtained basic rights through legislation. The success of conservatism, particularly Bismarck's policy of compromise, must be reconsidered in this regard. Between 1849 and 1874, his position on civil marriage changed by 180 degrees. Compulsory civil marriage had already been adopted in the Rhineland, by Frankfurt in 1850 and by Baden in 1869. It was closely allied with liberalism and seen as a means to secure the separation of church and state. As a consequence of annexation, Prussia found itself in possession of a large Catholic population with suspect loyalties to the pope. Bismarck's change in position was part of his struggle against a perceived threat of ultramontanism, and his suspicion of a Catholic conspiracy sometimes clouded his political judgement.[176] This was apparently what led him to change his position on civil marriage.

Indeed, Bismarck sponsored the *Gesetz über die Beurkundung des Personenstandes und die Eheschließung* that was first introduced in Prussia in 1874 and then for all of Germany in 1875. Bismarck's reversal drew heavy criticism from conservatives, who made the connection between annexation and the increased pressure to promulgate liberal law. They rightfully feared the long-term effect this would have on their position. Indeed, the basic right to marry, reflected in the demand for the institution of civil marriage, was a prominent feature of the constitutional document of 1849. This in turn was tied to liberal demands for the separation of church and state and the earlier Christian faith proviso of the BGBS was abrogated. Article 150 read: 'The validity of marriage in civil law is only dependent on the completion of the civil registration. A church wedding may take place only after the completion of the civil registration [and] adherence to a different religious faith is no obstacle to civil marriage.'[177] 'Marriage registers,' according to Article 151, 'shall be kept by the civil authorities'.[178]

During the revolutionary years of 1848 and 1849, Bismarck originally opposed the introduction of civil marriage, but his position changed radically after unification. In his 'Civil Marriage and the Reich Chancellor', Leopold von Gerlach described the legislation as the 'considerable work of the Reichskanzler' at the height his of 'national and church politics', pointing to Bismarck's recent change of policy.[179] In 1849, the government struggled against the revolutionary tendency and 'in this sense, the Herr Reichskanzler struggled hand in hand with members of the Conservative Party'.[180] Then Bismarck attacked civil marriage on religious, cultural and philosophical grounds, and, with regard to women, accused liberals of 'enslavement in the name of freedom', 'French charlatanism', and the 'swindling of loot'.[181] He argued that people were entitled to 'the right of government under Christian principles,' the right to get married in a Christian manner and to raise their children in a Christian upbringing, in accordance with their views, closing his speech with the strong comment, Gerlach recalled: 'In the course of time, I still hope to witness the ship of [liberal] fools shatter to pieces on the rock of the Christian church.'[182]

In 1874, however, Bismarck changed his position on civil marriage, causing Gerlach to question rhetorically what could cause such a change, and how could words so 'deep and cutting' be forgotten.[183] He laid the blame squarely at the door of Bismarck's expansionist politics, pointing out specifically that Hanover, Hesse-Nassau and Frankfurt, the most liberal states in Germany, were now to be assimilated into Prussia. 'The Herr Reichskanzler is no liberal—at least not totally,' he quipped.[184] Gerlach was clearly questioning the reasoning and possible ramifications of the annexation of liberal territories. 'The liberal ideas for a state without a heavenly king', he stated, 'for the separation of church and state, freedom and equality, people's sovereignty, and a constitutional Kaiser who does not govern, are not his ideas'.[185] Bismarck, Gerlach pointed out, had struggled against these ideas 'until 1866'.[186] His speech is very instructive, because it duly noted Bismarck's reversal and showed that even contemporary conservatives realized that embracing private law was a potentially dangerous course. It was indeed a political product of liberalism, and it was bound to undermine the conservative position.

Obligatory civil marriage was introduced in Prussia in 1874 and, on the initiative of Reichstag liberals, it was introduced for all of Germany in 1875. Bismarck had initially resisted this demand for national promulgation, but capitulated when the liberal Minister of Culture and member of the National Liberal Party, Adalbert Falk, threatened to resign. The *Gesetz über die Beurkundung des Personenstandes und die Eheschließung* of 1875 did not address the character of the marital relationship.[187] It was important to the course of German liberalism for two reasons. First, it established citizenship and citizens' basic right to legal personality before the state. Second, it gave citizens the basic right to marry the person of their choosing. Third, it made the separation of church and state a reality in Germany. Most importantly, however, it set an important precedent for the introduction of additional supplemental laws. By 1875 when the law was passed, work on the BGB had been underway for two years. Bismarck's civil marriage law prepared the population for what was to come, and it also meant that Bismarck, and not the liberals, would have to bear the brunt of public criticism.

The long-term liberalizing effects of legal reformation came into even sharper focus with procedural reform. Leonhardt, who, as I mentioned earlier, was Hanover's justice minister at the time of Austrian defeat and who drafted *Die bürgerliche Prozessordnung für das Königreich Hannover* of 1850, was appointed Minister of Justice by

Bismarck in 1867. Well before the founding of the Deutsche Reich in 1871, Bismarck asked Leonhardt to prepare legislation on the organization of the courts. After the motion passed the *Bundesrat,* a commission was set up to begin work on a code of civil procedure. In reality, however, the commission had been sitting under Leonhardt's leadership since 1861, when a commission was set up to begin work on civil procedure legislation for all of Germany. Under the pretext of organizing the courts, liberals took what was a yard and made it a mile. The *Civilprozeßordnung* of 1879 was promulgated as one of the *Reichsjustizgesetze,* which included three other codes. These were the *Gerichtsverfassungsgesetz* (Law on the Constitution of the Courts), a new *Strafprozeßordnung* (Code of Criminal Procedure) and the *Konkursordnung* (Bankruptcy Code). All became effective on 1 January 1879. The *Reichsjustizgesetze* did away with the courts in the several states and created the court structure of present-day Germany, including the *Reichsgericht* seated at Leipzig. The legislation was an expansion of Hanover's liberal Code of Civil Procedure of 1850.

The *Gerichtsverfassungsgesetz* was particularly important, because it went a long way toward nullifying noble privilege and establishing basic rights that were missing in the Constitution of 1871. It revolutionized the courts in Germany, instituted liberalism in this sphere, and undermined Prussian bureaucratic absolutism. Both the *Schöffengericht* and the *Geschworenengericht* were instituted in the Reich. Again, while the right to trial by jury was not a feature of the 1871 Constitution, it had been a core liberal demand that was incorporated into the constitutional document of 1849. Paragraph 30 of the *Gerichtsverfassungsgesetz* gave lay judges equal voting power with judges.[188] Paragraph 31 specifically stated that 'the office of the *Schöffen* is an office of honor', to which only Germans could be appointed.[189] The institution of *bürgerliche* privileges was evident in not only the law's definition of who could serve as *Schöffen,* but who could not.

Here two categories of persons emerged. In the first instance, the law denied those persons who were likely to be conservative the right to serve as *Schöffen.* Under Paragraph 34, amongst others, persons who were in imperial, state, religious or military service were barred from the *Schöffen.*[190] The same standards applied for the *Geschworenengericht.*[191] The oath of office was not sworn to the Kaiser, but rather the *Schöffen* were read the words: 'Do you swear before Almighty and All Knowing God to faithfully perform the duty as a *Schöffe* and according to the depth of your conscience and knowledge'. Then he had to respond: 'I swear it, so help me God.'[192]

While these provisions transformed the court system in Germany into the system liberals had long imagined and worked to obtain, socially regressive tendencies were evident in procedural reform as well. Under Paragraph 32, persons who had committed even misdemeanors were barred from service as *Schöffen* or jurors, along with those who were 'limited in the power of disposal over their wealth', which hit women especially hard.[193] Under Paragraph 33, a person could not be called if they were under age thirty, 'had sought public relief for themselves or their families', were 'spiritually or bodily defective', or in domestic service.[194] These provisions ensured that society's lower orders would not have equal access to courts.

Compromise on procedural reform was particularly dangerous for anyone who wanted to sustain the monarchical arrangements, because it installed the very infrastructure that liberals needed to make their sociopolitical values stick in society. Even if legislation was not perfect, this could be adjusted in the courts, and, since legal professionals were overwhelmingly liberal, the new courts were stacked in their favor. This was also a danger where bourgeois lay persons sat on courts, either as *Schöffen* or as jurors. Legislation might not pass legislatures in ideal liberal form, but, as a result of liberal procedural reform, it could be appropriately adjusted in the courts. There was also a fresh round of founding new legal journals after the major reforms at the national level. On the whole, however, liberals did not miss a beat in pushing through their social and political programme where constitutional transformation was involved. The later procedural legislation in 1898 even reformed military judicial practices, securing liberal reforms here as well. For certain groups in society, however, these were hardly courts of equal opportunity. If you were a nobleman, a woman or a member of the lower strata you might find it tough to get a fair trial. This was no longer noble patrimonial justice, but arguably it had become a system of exclusive *bürgerliche* justice, which demanded conformity to legislated standards.

The reforms in the area of private law made considerable inroads into the structure of Central European society at the state level before unification. These reforms allowed liberals to secure many of the basic rights they had sought during the 1848 Revolution and that were expressed in the constitutional document of 1849. Moreover, procedural reform suggested a transfer in judicial authority, which undermined the strength of Prussian bureaucratic absolutism. After unification, when Bismarck embarked on his policy of compromise, liberals seem to have had great success in securing these reforms at the national level. While the Constitution of 1871 did not contain provisions on basic rights, liberals essentially achieved these basic rights through the introduction of supplementary measures of private law. As Wieacker wrote, by the late nineteenth century liberals gained 'the upper hand in areas of land law, family property and succession, so crucial for the whole social order'.[195] By the time the national reforms I have discussed here went into effect, work on the BGB was underway. The National Liberals Eduard Lasker, Johannes Miquel and later Gottlieb Planck had procured an amendment to Article 4, Paragraph 13 of the Constitution in 1873, at the height of liberal power in the Reichstag. This gave parliament power to legislate civil law, generally. Key figures in this enterprise were from Hanover and all had been active in other legal forums. They had all sat on the *Reichsjustizgesetze* commission at some point, and they were veterans of the mid-century political conflicts.

Notes

1. Anton Christ, in *Verhandlungen der Germanisten zu Lübeck* (1847), p. 213.
2. H. Beck, *Origins of the Authoritarian Welfare State in Prussia: Conservatives, Bureaucracy and the Social Question 1815–70* (1995), p. vii.

3. Ibid., p. 224.
4. Ibid., p. 225.
5. Ibid., pp. 237–60.
6. R. Hinton Thomas, *Liberalism, Nationalism and the German Intellectuals: An Analysis of the Academic and Scientific Conferences of the Period* (1951).
7. Ibid., p. 98.
8. Ibid.
9. 'Einladung an die Germanisten zu einer Gelehrten-Versammlung in Frankfurt a.M.', reprinted in *Verhandlungen der Germanisten zu Frankfurt am Main* (1846), pp. 5–6.
10. Friedrich Gaupp, in *Verhandlungen der Germanisten zu Frankfurt am Main,* p. 125.
11. Georg Beseler, quoted in Thomas, *Liberalism,* p. 88.
12. Jacob Grimm, in *Verhandlungen der Germanisten zu Frankfurt am Main,* pp. 15–16.
13. Ibid.
14. Karl Mittermaier, in *Verhandlungen der Germanisten zu Frankfurt am Main,* p. 64.
15. Ibid.
16. Ibid., pp. 46–7.
17. Georg Beseler, in *Verhandlungen der Germanisten zu Frankfurt am Main.*
18. Mittermaier, in *Verhandlungen der Germanisten zu Frankfurt am Main,* pp. 69–71.
19. Ibid.
20. Ibid.
21. Ibid.
22. Ibid.
23. Karl Mittermaier, in *Verhandlungen der Germanisten zu Lübeck am 27, 28 und 30 September 1847,* p. 204.
24. Ibid.
25. Ibid.
26. Ibid., p. 206.
27. Ibid.
28. Ibid.
29. Ibid., p. 207.
30. Ibid., p. 208.
31. Jaup, cited in Thomas, *Liberalism,* p. 103.
32. Jaup, in *Verhandlungen der Germanisten zu Lübeck*, p. 201.
33. Ibid., p. 202.
34. Mittermaier, in ibid., p. 205.
35. Anton Christ, in ibid., p. 213.
36. Georg Gervinus to Friedrich Dahlmann, cited in Thomas, *Liberalism,* p. 125.

37. Michael Bush, *Noble Privilege* (1983), p. 18.
38. Ibid.
39. Ibid.
40. Jacob Grimm and Wilhelm Grimm, 'The Fisherman and His Wife', in Margaret Hunt (trans.), *Grimm's Household Tales* (1884).
41. Ibid.
42. Ibid.
43. Ibid.
44. Ibid.
45. Ibid.
46. Ibid.
47. Ibid.
48. Ibid.
49. Karen Hagemann, 'Of "Manly Valor" and "German Honor": Nation, War, and Masculinity in the Age of the Prussian Uprising against Napoleon', *Central European History,* 30/2 (2001), pp. 187–220.
50. Bush, *Noble Privilege,* p. 71.
51. Ibid., p. 66.
52. Ibid., p. 76.
53. Jacob Grimm, *Deutsche Rechtsalterthümer* (1828), p. 351.
54. Ibid., p. 357.
55. Ibid., p. 358.
56. A. Feuerbach, *Betrachtungen über das Geschworenengericht* (1813).
57. Arnd Koch, 'C.J.A. Mittermaier and the 19th Century Debate about Juries and Mixed Courts', *Revue internationale de droit pénal,* 72 (2001), pp. 347–53.
58. See Chapter 3, pp. 170–1.
59. August Ludwig Reyscher, *Vollständige, historisch und kritisch bearbeitete Sammlung der württembergischen Gesetze* (1828).
60. Jacob Grimm, *Weisthümer,* 3 vols (1840–1842).
61. Grimm, *Deutsche Rechtsalterthümer,* vol. 2, p. 401.
62. See Chapter 3, pp. 170–1.
63. Peter Landau, 'Schwurgerichte und Schöffengerichte in Deutschland im 19. Jahrhundert bis 1870', in A. Schioppa (ed.), *The Trial Jury in England, France, Germany 1700–1900,* vol. 4 (1987).
64. Karl Mittermaier, *Ueber die Bestimmungen einer zweckmässigen Gerichtsverfassung und Processordnung* (1831) and *Die künftige Stellung des Advokatenstandes* (1832).
65. Heinrich von Gagern in Hessian *Landtag* (3 October 1833), in Paul Wentzcke and Wolfgang Klötzer (eds), *Deutscher Liberalismus im Vormärz: Heinrich von Gagern, Briefe und Reden 1815–1848* (1959).
66. Georg Beseler, *Ueber die Stellung des römischen Rechts zu dem nationalen Recht der germanischen Völker* (1836), p. 7.

67. Ibid.
68. Ibid.
69. Ferdinand Frensdorff, *Gottlieb Planck: Deutscher Jurist und Politiker* (1914), p. 76.
70. Ibid., pp. 37 and 302.
71. *Verhandlungen der Germanisten zu Lübeck* (1847), pp. 68–91.
72. Franz Wieacker, *A History of Private Law in Europe (with Particular Reference to Germany),* Tony Weir (trans.) (1995), p. 368.
73. David Blackbourn, *The Long Nineteenth Century: A History of Germany 1780–1918* (1997), p. 148.
74. 'The 1849 Constitution', in Elmar Hucko (ed.), *The Democratic Tradition: Four German Constitutions* (1987), p. 104.
75. Werner Schubert, *Entstehung und Quellen der Civilprozessordnung von 1877* (1987), p. 4.
76. 'The 1849 Constitution', p. 113.
77. Ibid.
78. Kenneth Ledford, 'Lawyers, Liberalism and Procedure: The German Imperial Justice Laws of 1877–79', *Central European History,* 26 (1993), p. 176.
79. Schubert, *Entstehung und Quellen,* p. 4.
80. Franz Helmut Richter, 'Gesetzgebung, Rechtsprechung und Verwaltung', in Hermann Heckmann (ed.), *Historische Landeskunde Mitteldeutschlands* (1985), pp. 117–18.
81. 'The 1849 Constitution', p. 112.
82. Richter, 'Gesetzgebung, Rechtsprechung und Verwaltung', pp. 117–18.
83. 'The 1849 Constitution', p. 112.
84. Richter, 'Gesetzgebung, Rechtsprechung und Verwaltung', pp. 117–18.
85. Ibid.
86. Wieacker, *History of Private Law,* p. 368.
87. Ludwig Jagemann, 'Der Uebergang vom alten zum neuen Rechte: Zugleich als Prospect der Zeitschrift', *Der Gerichtssaal,* 1/1 (1849), p. 13.
88. Ibid.
89. See *Der Gerichtssaal* generally.
90. Amman, 'Über den Proceß gegen Gustav von Struve und Karl Blind aus Mannheim, wegen Hochverraths: Die erste Verhandlung vor einem Badischen Schwurgerichte', *Der Gerichtssaal,* 1/2 (1849), pp. 201–13.
91. Blackbourn, *Long Nineteenth Century,* p. 144.
92. Amman, 'Über den Proceß', pp. 205–6.
93. Ibid., p. 209.
94. J. A. Gruchot, 'Vorwort', *Beiträge zur Erläuterung des preußischen Rechts durch Theorie und Praxis,* 1 (1857).
95. E. I. Bekker, 'Über das gemeine deutsche Recht der Gegenwart und dessen Behandlung', *Jahrbuch des gemeinen deutschen Rechts,* 1 (1857), pp. 1–23.

96. Jacob Grimm, 'Recht von Hiesfeld', *Jahrbuch des gemeinen deutschen Rechts,* 1 (1857), pp. 257–65.
97. Otto Stobbe, 'Die Grundsätze der deutschen Rechtsquellen des Mittelalters über den Gerichtsstand', *Jahrbuch des gemeinen deutschen Rechts,* 1 (1857), pp. 427–62.
98. Otto Stobbe, *Die Juden in Deutschland während des Mittelalters* (1866).
99. Ludwig Jagemann, 'Zur deutschen Nationalgesetzgebung', *Der Gerichtssaal,* 3/1 (1851), p. 272.
100. Ibid.
101. Ibid., p. 273.
102. Ibid., p. 274.
103. Eduard Pape, 'Ueber die Organisation und Zuständigkeit der gerichtlichen Behörden', *Der Gerichtssaal,* 3 (1851), pp. 1–12.
104. For more on commercial law in Germany and the Commercial Code of 1861 see Karl Otto Scherner (ed.), *Modernisierung des Handelsrechts im 19. Jahrhundert* (1993).
105. James Wigmore, Edwin Borchard and Frederick Pollock, *The Progress of Continental Law in the Nineteenth Century* (1918), pp. 333–40.
106. Karl Mittermaier, *Grundsätze des gemeinen deutschen Privatrechts: mit Einschluss des Handels-, Wechsel-, und Seerechts* (1824).
107. Friedrich Bodungen, *Das königlich-hannoverische Wechselrecht in alphabetischer Ordnung* (1824).
108. Jacob Pestalutz, *Abhandlung über das Züricherische Wechselrecht, mit Vergleichung der Augsburger, Sct. Galler und Basler Wechselordnung* (1827).
109. Heinrich Daniels, *Grundsätze des Wechselrechts* (1827).
110. Hermann Rothschildt, *Die bei dem Verkehre mit Wechseln zu beobachtenden Formen nach gemeinem Rechte und der Braunschweigschen Wechselordnung* (1841).
111. Ibid.
112. Eduard Souchay, *Anmerkungen zu den Wechsel-Gesetzen der Freien Stadt Frankfurt, mit besonderer Bezugnahme auf die offizielle Ausgabe der Wechselordnung vom Jahre 1845* (1845).
113. Gustav Nürmberger, *Sammlung von Beiträgen und Anmerkungen zu praktischer Erläuterung der Nürnberger Wechselordnung* (1846).
114. Schulze (ed.), *Allgemeine deutsche Wechselordnung nebst Einführungsgesetz für das Königreich Hannover* (1849), p. 3.
115. Ibid.
116. Karl Mittermaier, 'Das Indossament nach dem Verfalltage: Erläuterung des §16 der Deutschen Wechselordnung', *Archiv für deutsches Wechselrecht,* 1 (1850), pp. 10–31.
117. Karl Mittermaier, 'Ueber den Einfluß höherer Gewalt auf die Regreßklage im Falle der Unterlassung wechselrechtlicher Pflichten nach der deutschen Wechselordnung', *Archiv für deutsches Wechselrecht,* 1 (1850), pp. 147–64.

118. Franz Haimerl, *Anleitung zum Studium des Wechselrechtes* (1855); and Leopold C. Bleibtreu, *Die Lehre von den Wechseln mit Hinweisung auf bestehende Gesetze* (1860).
119. Achilles Renaud, *Lehrbuch des allgemeinen deutschen Wechselrechts* (1857).
120. Johann Ziegler, *Ueber Gewerbefreiheit und deren Folgen* (1819); and Johann Leuch, *Vollständiges Handelsrecht* (1822).
121. *Durch welche Bedingungen ist das System der Handelsfreiheit ausführbar?* (1834).
122. Johann Hoffmann, *Die Befugniss zum Gewerbbetriebe zur Berichtigung der Urtheile über Gewerbefreiheit und Gewerbezwang* (1841).
123. *Gewerbefreiheit für Nürnberg* (1846).
124. Hermann Rentzsch, *Die Gewerbefreiheit und Freizügigkeit* (1861).
125. Heinrich Thöl, *Das Handelsrecht: Als gemeines in Deutschland geltendes Privatrecht mit Berücksichtigung des ausserdeutschen Handelsrechts* (1841), *Das Wechselrecht* (1847) and *Das Transportgewerbe* (1880).
126. Carl Kleinschrod, *Beiträge zu einer Deutschen Gewerbeordnung mit Rücksicht auf die bayerische Gewerbsgesetzgebung* (1840).
127. Gustav Nürmberger, *Sammlung einiger nürnbergischen Handelsrechts-Gewohnheiten* (1846); and *Sammlung von Beiträgen und andern Anmerkungen zur praktischen Erläuterung der Nürnberger Handelsgerichtsordnung* (1846).
128. Carl Billich, *Das württembergische Gewerbe-Recht* (1852); and Ferdinand Fischer, *Preußens kaufmännisches Recht* (1856).
129. Wilhelm Meißner, *Beleuchtung des Entwurfs einer Gewerbe-Ordnung für das Königreich Sachsen* (1857); and Heinrich Bodemer, *Zur Beurtheilung des Entwurfs einer Gewerbe-Ordnung für das Königreich Sachsen* (1859).
130. Wilhelm Kraut, *Grundriss zu Vorlesungen über das deutsche Privatrecht mit Einschluss des Lehns- und Handelsrechts nebst beigefügten Quellen* (1859).
131. 'Levin Goldschmidt', *Allgemeine Deutsche Biographie,* pp. 438–48.
132. Levin Goldschmidt, *Kritik des Entwurfs eines Handelsgesetzbuchs für die Preussischen Staaten* (1857); and *Gutachten über den Entwurf eines deutschen Handelsgesetzbuchs nach den Beschlüssen zweiter Lesung* (1860).
133. Levin Goldschmidt, *Das Handbuch des Handelsrechts* (1864); and *System des Handelsrechts* (1887).
134. Karl Otto Scherner, 'Die Modernisierung des Handelsrechts im 19. Jahrhundert', in Scherner (ed.), *Modernisierung des Handelsrechts,* pp. 9–17.
135. Wieacker, *History of Private Law,* p. 366.
136. Ibid., p. 368.
137. Christian Ahcin, *Zur Entstehung des bürgerlichen Gesetzbuchs für das Königreich Sachsen von 1863/65* (1996), pp. 63–103.
138. Ibid.
139. Ibid., p. 208.

140. For full discussion see ibid., pp. 173–206. For example, see Karl Mittermaier, *Die neuesten Gesetzgebungsarbeiten auf dem Gebiete der Civilgesetzgebung mit besonderer Beziehung auf die neueren Civilgesetzbücher oder Entwürfe für das Königreich Sachsen, für das Grossherzogthum Hessen, für das Herzogthum Modena und die Schweizer Gesetzbücher oder Entwürfe für Zürich, Slothurn, Freiburg, Thurgau, Wallis, Aargau, mit Entwicklung der Rücksichten, welche die Prüfung dieser neuen Arbeiten leiten müssen* (1853).
141. Ahcin, *Zur Entstehung des bürgerlichen Gesetzbuchs,* p. 149.
142. Ibid., p. 149, fn. 192.
143. Ibid., p. 150.
144. Ibid.
145. Ibid., pp. 151–5.
146. Ibid., pp. 157–60.
147. Josef Matzerath, 'Die Familienverträge des sächsischen Adels vom 16. bis zum 19. Jahrhundert', in Katrin Keller und Josef Matzerath (eds), *Geschichte des sächsischen Adels* (1997), p. 292.
148. Eduard Siebenhaar (ed.), *Das Bürgerliche Gesetzbuch für das Königreich Sachsen* (1883), p. 282.
149. Stephan Buchholz, 'Ehe- und Familienrecht', in Helmut Coing (ed.), *Handbuch der Quellen und Literatur der neueren europäischen Privatrechtsgeschichte,* vol. 3, *Das 19. Jahrhundert* (1982), pp. 1626–7.
150. Eduard Siebenhaar (ed.), *Das BGBS,* pp. 288–9.
151. Ibid, p. 282.
152. See, for example, the *Geschlechtsordnung* of the von Schönberg family in Matzerath, 'Familienverträge', p. 310.
153. Ahcin, *Zur Entstehung des bürgerlichen Gesetzbuchs,* p. 155, fn. 257.
154. Vivian Mann and Richard Cohen (eds), *From Court Jews to the Rothchilds: Art, Patronage and Power 1600–1800* (1996); and Selma Stern, *The Court Jew: A Contribution to the History of the Period of Absolutism in Central Europe,* Ralph Weiman (trans.) (1950).
155. Ahcin, *Zur Entstehung des bürgerlichen Gesetzbuchs,* p. 156, fn. 263.
156. Bush, *Noble Privilege.*
157. Siebenhaar, *Das BGBS,* p. 295.
158. Ibid.
159. Ibid., p. 292.
160. Ibid., p. 293.
161. Ibid., p. 292.
162. Ibid., p. 293.
163. W. A. Coupe (ed.), *German Political Satires from the Reformation to the Second World War: Part II 1849–1918* (1987), p. 51.
164. Frensdorff, *Gottlieb Planck,* p. 253.

165. Gottlieb Planck, *Die Rechtswidrigkeit des in Hannover bestehenden Verfassungszustandes* (1861).
166. Ibid.
167. Frensdorff, *Gottlieb Planck,* pp. 184–5.
168. Ibid., p. 253.
169. Ibid.
170. Ibid.
171. Ibid.
172. Ibid., p. 277.
173. James M. Brophy, 'Salus publica suprema lex: Prussian Business Men in the New Era and Constitutional Conflict', *Central European History,* 28 (1995), pp. 122–51.
174. Ledford, 'Lawyers, Liberalism and Procedure', p. 179.
175. Otto Pflanze, *Bismarck and the Development of Germany: The Period of Unification 1815–1871,* vol. 1 (1990), p. 353.
176. Ibid., p. 368.
177. 'The 1849 Constitution', p. 108.
178. Ibid.
179. Leopold von Gerlach, *Die Civilehe und der Reichskanzler* (1874), p. 1.
180. Ibid.
181. Bismarck, quoted in ibid., p. 5.
182. Ibid., pp. 5–6.
183. Ibid., p. 6.
184. Ibid., p. 11.
185. Ibid.
186. Ibid.
187. See 'Gesetze über die Beurkundung des Personenstandes und die Eheschließung von 6. Februar 1875', in *Reichs-Gesetzblatt,* 4.
188. 'Gerichtsverfassungsgesetz', in R. Sydow (ed.), *Reichs-Justizgesetze* (1878), p. 22.
189. Ibid.
190. Ibid., p. 24.
191. Ibid., p. 46.
192. Ibid., p. 30.
193. Ibid., pp. 22–3.
194. Ibid., p. 23.
195. Wieacker, *History of Private Law,* p. 371.

–5–

A Century of Promise

Eheliches Güterrecht, Women's Wealth and Independence in Nineteenth-Century Germany

> In many ways women were worth less than men.[1]
>
> —Jacob Grimm, *Deutsche Rechtsalterthümer,* 1828

The legal measures that were introduced across German-speaking Europe in the third quarter of the century marked an important transition stage in the history of constitutional transformation. As I suggested in the last chapter, it is perhaps better to see the big revolutionary event of 1848 to 1849 as merely one event within a much larger series of political meetings that took place in these years. While the unexpected events of 1830 and 1848 were opportunities for advance and, in fact, resulted in important new state constitutions, because constitutional transformation was understood to be a long-range process, these events did not make or break the course of political revision in Central Europe as much as post-Second World War studies argued. Already on the heels of 1849, the Hanover *Prozeßordnung* was made law in 1850, and, by 1865, a uniform civil code was introduced in Saxony. These measures and others in the German states show that the practice of constitutional transformation had begun to advance. However exclusive, liberal conceptions of participation were also advancing alongside the leveling of distinctions between the male bourgeoisie and the hereditary nobility. Nowhere was this more evident than in the family law of the *Bürgerliches Gesetzbuch für das Königreich Sachsen* of 1863. On the one hand, it met liberal demands for separation of church and state; on the other, it also imposed the sex guardianship that was rigorously sanctioned by Grimm, Mittermaier, Beseler and the Germanists generally. As I have shown, Germanist constitutional theory made the expansion of male liberty, based on private property ownership, dependent on the subordination of women.

The question remains, however. Were women worth less, as Jacob Grimm so stridently argued? In this chapter, the realities of nineteenth-century marital property relations are examined in order to juxtapose existing conditions against the regressive impact, not only of the state-level reforms we have already examined, but with an eye toward the BGB. In no other area of law was legal particularism greater than in the area of *eheliches Güterrecht* (marital property law). While the legal historian Stephan Buchholz suggested some time ago that the political relevance of the reconfiguration of *eheliches Güterrecht* in the legislative developments of the nineteenth century remains an obscure subject, historians have not produced research on this subject.[2] It is suggested here that, after liberals were able to successfully legislate sex guardianship in the nineteenth century, these constructed gender relations, which in fact were the product of partisan liberal politics, billed as immemorial prescriptive custom, came to be accepted as historical fact. The idea of original patriarchy became entrenched in the western psyche, and the myth of original patriarchy was born. Over time, it developed into what Joan Scott identifies as an unquestioned 'foundationalist discourse'.[3]

The sex guardianship that liberal legislation imposed introduced gender relations that were in stark contrast to existing relations in German-speaking Europe. In the late eighteenth century, states, one after another, abolished sex guardianship, and lower courts in the nineteenth century issued decisions which extended rights to women. My examination of local court decisions in Hanover, Thuringia and Anhalt suggests that, prior to 1900, women not only retained independent property rights, but had made considerable gains in terms of other independent rights. Women also enjoyed unrestricted access to the courts and relatively independent legal rights. This environment also precipitated the growth of women's wealth and property rights, which was accompanied by rising economic and professional expectations. All of this, however, was playing out against the rising tide of liberal-led constitutional transformation. As liberals gained the upper hand in German appeal courts in the nineteenth century, lower court decisions were overturned. It was not until the introduction of the BGB, however, that this century of promise was completely lost.

Legal Particularism

For nearly three decades after geographical unification, legal particularism remained the norm in Germany, and the nation was still fragmented, legally, if not geographically. While formal unification occurred in 1871, civil law was not unified until the introduction of the BGB on 1 January 1900. In his opening speech to the Reichstag's debates on the BGB, in 1896, the Minister of Justice and long-time National Liberal Rudolf Nieberding described Germany's legal condition as a 'colourful muddle'.[4] He pointed out that there were more than one hundred different legal forms of marital property relations in the 'heart of Germany' alone.[5] 'For so long it has been forgotten,' he complained, 'citizens and families have determined their own legal relationships for themselves.'[6] 'The Code is needed above all other needs of our time,' he urged, 'so that the higher aim of unified law for every inhabitant and, therefore a higher moral order may be reached.'[7] Nieberding's comments captured not only the nature of legal particularism, but the reality of cultural fragmentation and fluidity in Germany prior to the introduction of the BGB in 1900. Moreover, he continued the tradition of Eichhorn, Grimm, Mittermaier, Beseler and other Germanists in his remarks. The code, he stated, was the fruit of the previous generation's work and had been drafted with respect for the 'great interest groups the economic life demands'.[8]

The conditions so vividly described by Nieberding had serious implications for the social reality of gender relations in German society before 1900. In no other area of culture was there more legal fragmentation than in the area of marital property law *(eheliches Güterrecht)*. In *Geschichte des ehelichen Güterrechts in Deutschland* (1863), the leading Germanist legal historian on marital property relations, Richard Schroeder, pointed out that 'no other branch of German law has suffered so much under the particularism of our people'.[9] States one after another had annulled the old *Geschlechtsvormundschaft* regulations in the eighteenth century.[10] This, combined with legal particularism, left women living in a deregulated environment. In this fluid environment, women acquired a relative level of equality and considerably more independence, legal personality and property rights than ever before. Describing German conditions prior to the BGB, in 1919, Rudolf Hübner recalled a popular view on the ALR in legal circles: '*Willkür* breaks city law, city law breaks territorial law, [and] territorial law breaks common law.'[11] Conditions were not much different in the southern regions of German-speaking Europe. As late as 1894, a Munich newspaper reported:

> As the saying goes, other cities—other girls. So it can be said for the greater part of our Kingdom, other cities—other laws. Indeed, the legal regulations are still often very different, particularly in northern Bavaria, from hamlet to hamlet, village to village, from address to address and even from house part to house part![12]

While the *Gesetz über die Beurkundung des Personenstandes und die Eheschließung* (1875) made civil marriage mandatory, it did not regulate marital property relations. In many areas of Germany, therefore, there continued to be a great deal of fluidity in this area. It also was possible for couples to simply contract their own marital property arrangements, whether or not those arrangements were contrary to existing statutes. As a result, the major reforms that the enlightened law codes were designed to produce were foiled by the right to contract. While laws governing marital property relations appeared on the books, German couples could simply ignore the law and make their own marital property arrangements. In the deregulated environment of the nineteenth century, particularism sustained the autonomy of the marital community, and for this reason the laws before 1900 do not offer an accurate guide for understanding the reality of gender relations on the ground. Even where civil codes were produced, with the exception of Saxony, there was little means to enforce them. Legal procedure remained underdeveloped until the time of the state reforms that began in Hanover in the 1850s and until the passage of the *Reichsjustizgesetze* on the national level in 1879. Actual social conditions, therefore, reflected far more variety than historians have considered.

Marital Property Relations

Under the heading 'women', in the indexes of books on German history, the words 'and poverty' are linked to women, but not 'and property'. The underlying assumption has been that women, historically, did not independently own or control property. Women were not viewed as economic actors within the family or society at large. To support this narrative of female poverty, the law was cited often.[13] Before the dawn of the twentieth century in Germany, however, the rationalization of civil law was a project, not a reality. With more pressing concerns about political legitimacy at the state level, the affairs of family property were left to families and individuals, particularly with regard to inheritance and marital property. Here, Central Europe was characterized by the conspicuous absence of uniform regulations. As Nieberding bitterly complained before the Reichstag: 'What are people supposed to think of the authority and the higher aim of the laws, when inheritance in one place is absolutely different in a neighboring place as the case is for us; in one place the wife inherits, while in another she does not, and in one place no distinction is made between full siblings and half siblings—in one place they inherit equally, in another they do not'.[14]

Although legal particularism has not figured prominently, scholars have reconsidered the traditional view of women's economic position in the family and broader society. In *Fertility, Wealth and Politics,* Ernest Benz examined women's property rights in the Baden villages of Grafenhausen bei Lahr, Kappel am Rhein and Rust. His study provides valuable insight on inheritance and how it changed the status of women in German society.[15] In the region he examined, each surviving child, male or female, received an equal share of their parents' estate, and this custom of inheritance contributed to a more egalitarian social structure, because each family member had a 'concrete stake in the community'.[16] Individual inheritance and the wealth of the eligible parties became one of the most significant factors that determined the nature of marriage.[17] In the instance where the wife contributed more resources to a marriage, husbands found their economic and social position determined by her family, and the wife's decision-making power increased accordingly.[18]

From the perspective of the public space, Heide Wunder has shown that women in early modern Germany were by no means excluded from political authority. 'Even though it was clearly expressed in the public and legal status of women', she notes 'scholars failed to realize just how normal the regency of noblewomen was, and that the running of a peasant household, an artisan's workshop, or merchant business was possible only on the basis of the shared responsibility of wife and husband'.[19] From a young age, merchants' daughters were trained for the future field of work, often keeping the books in their fathers' businesses.[20] As a result of this egalitarian distribution of power, wives represented their households in the public space as mistresses of the house and not only as their husbands' representatives.[21] These conditions were a far cry from Jacob Grimm's imagined place of women as the *Schlüsselträgerinnen* of their husbands.

In his study on Neckarhausen, David Sabean has shown that, as farm women increasingly produced cash crops in the early nineteenth century and contributed greater wealth to the family purse, they began to demand a say in the disposal of both the products they produced and their proceeds. Husbands and wives met on a more equal footing and, as Sabean demonstrates, these changing economic conditions were reflected in local court decisions. 'Courts', accordingly, 'shifted in the way they related to the family.'[22] While, in the beginning, 'they sought to effect control by enhancing the authority of the *Hausvater*', over time, 'they came to act more flexibly, allying with whichever spouse seemed to be the most effective commodity producer'.[23]

The daily reality of nineteenth-century gender relations did not reflect liberal sociopolitical demands or their imagined *Gemeinwesen*. At the same time, it is important to understand also that the family was a metaphor for the state in the Germanists' political theory. In the aftermath of the Carlsbad Decrees of 1819, as I have mentioned, the discussion of public law and constitutions was virtually banned. It was in this environment that political science found expression as legal history on German private law. This changing reality was evident in Eichhorn's shifting focus from municipal constitutions to private law. However, Eichhorn inverted the basis of participation and pointed toward the critical importance of private property ownership as the basis of *vollkommene Freiheit*. While participation and everything connected with it underwent a process of masculinization, exclusion underwent a theoretical process of feminization. This was evident in Grimm's analysis of symbols and language, for example. It also served to underscore a point that Dieter Grimm makes, namely, that the codification of private law 'at no time was isolated from the social reality and questions of political organization'.[24]

Accordingly, descriptions of gender relations in the family were the metaphoric alter ego of public relationships of power and conceptions of exclusive legal personality. It was a narrative that did not target wealthy women alone, but also the dangers of working-class women, who were also acquiring property. Kathleen Canning has shown how 'narratives of danger about female factory labor were constituted across a range of statements, texts, signs, and practices: from academic lectures and scientific surveys, state inquiries and parliamentary resolutions, to union brochures and [anti-]feminist tracts, employers' sanctions, and even calls for strikes against the hiring of women workers'.[25] These narratives contributed to the passage of so-called protective legislation, namely, the Labor Code of 1878, which prohibited female labor in the mines at the same time that it required three weeks maternity leave; and the revised Code of 1891, which, amongst other policing measures, prescribed the separation of the sexes wherever possible in the workplace. Paragraph 120 called for separation 'on the shop floor, in cafeterias, courtyards, and washrooms', for example.[26] Indeed as the century wore on, Social Darwinism also came to the aid of liberal demands for sex guardianship. The infusion of Social Darwinism into German legal thought was present in Jhering's *Der Kampf ums Recht* (1872), which reacted against the dominance of the historical school.[27] This element came through clearly in Geyer's summary article, 'Der Kampf ums Recht' (1873), which appeared in *Der Gerichtssaal.*[28] Although new arguments rested on an alternative scientific foundation, the demand for female exclusion remained consistent with the systems developed by Grimm and others.

Despite the infusion of Social Darwinism into legal thought, on the whole, the writings of the Germanists remained the dominant source of political discourse. When later generations of Germanist scholars encountered the unfortunate contradiction of existing conditions, they routinely invoked immemorial customary law to support their views. One of the most important legal histories of early twentieth century was Rudolf Hübner's *Grundzüge des deutschen Privatrechts* (1908). He opened his discussion on civil marriage by freely recognizing and listing a number of secondary sources that acknowledged the fact that the forms of marital unions were recognized as legal in an earlier period. However, he drew distinction between a union and marriage, asserting the legitimacy of the heterosexual model. 'Although different varieties of sexual union were once not only actually practiced but also recognized by law', he wrote, 'nevertheless marriage, as that form of sexual community, which involved the most far-reaching legal consequences, was always distinguished by a special form observed in its creation, on the strength of which it, alone, was conceded its privilege of full legitimacy'.[29]

Hübner's *Grundzüge* goes on to summarize the consensus of nineteenth-century scholarly opinion on the history of *eheliches Güterrecht.* It is worth examining here for several reasons. First, Germanists acknowledged that the long-term evolution of marital property relations had resulted in changes that were favorable to women. Marital property relations had advanced well beyond the administrative community *(Verwaltungsgemeinschaft).* Second, Hübner offered a description of the five basic systems of marital property relations that were identified by the Germanists and that will be useful when I examine the state reports later in this chapter. Finally, Hübner's work serves an additional purpose as a primary source. He acknowledged that this progressive trend was reversed with the reintroduction of the *Verwaltungsgemeinschaft*—the system of marital property relations, which was preferred by liberal Germanists and which they identified as the customary law of the ancient Germans.

By 1908 when Hübner wrote, the BGB had been the law of the land for eight years. It is taken up before our discussion of the BGB, however, to show how history was used to justify innovations that liberals knew were regressive at the time they were introduced. More than anything else, Hübner's *Grundzüge* summarized the scholarly opinion that had been building for a century. As early as the age of the folk laws, he wrote, the idea of an undivided property in the husband was relaxed in favor of the wife.[30] The provisions of the folk laws, 'by no means [showed] ... a subjugation of the wife's entire property to her husband's ownership', as was peculiar to the original customary law.[31] On the contrary, scholars conceded that the law already recognized a wife's ownership of certain portions of the marital property.[32] 'This important advance was a consequence', Hübner wrote, 'of the gradually increasing legal and economic independence of women, especially their capacity to inherit.'[33] Here he cited the work of Huber, who had argued that 'the increasing improvement in woman's position was the real leaven in the entire later development of the law of marital property'.[34] Beginning in the early epoch:

> As soon as daughters became capable of holding and inheriting property within their own families, they were in a position to bring with them in marriage property of considerable value to their husbands ... Again, when the wife came to be regarded as the subject of independent property rights, her husband's gift ... might become her property. With this step the original undivided marital estate necessarily disappeared. It was now possible, for the first time, to speak of an actual marital community of goods in the sense of a regulation of the spouses' legal rights, created by their marriage, in the property constituting the marital estate; for it was only now that property existed in which not merely the husband but also the wife had rights; it was only thenceforth that there existed, during marriage, a wife's in addition to the husband's estate.[35]

Nevertheless, Hübner continued to uphold the Germanist theory of *hausherrliche Gewalt,* although his own analysis seemed to undermine it. While the wife's property was vested in her person, by virtue of the husband's *Mundium,* he held possession of her property—distinct ownership was maintained, but the entire marital estate united in the possession of the husband. 'The result', he wrote 'was that as early as in the folk laws the original undivided property had been replaced, in the main, by a system of community property'.[36] This system, moreover, was variously identified by such figures as Beseler, Johann Bluntschli and Heinrich Brunner as the *Verwaltungsgemeinschaft* (administrative community), wherein the entire property was administered by the husband. Incidentally, it is worth noting that Hübner had in fact studied with Beseler.

The sociopolitical ideals of Germanist thought were evident in Hübner's description of the *Verwaltungsgemeinschaft,* for example, in his emphasis on rights accompanied by obligations. On the one hand, husbands had the right to profit from their wives' estates, but on the other, they were obliged to manage them in a responsible manner.[37] The denial of full property rights to women was, again, justified under the auspices of protection. In other words, the husband was expected to be prudent. While husbands managed and profited from their personal estates as the owners, they profited from their wives' estates as *Mundium* holders (guardians).[38] The argument for sex guardianship continued to rest on the powerful historical doctrine, but it was increasingly also justified by a narrative of virtuous and necessary protection of the weaker sex. The husband's role was a protective one. Regardless of this justification, the net effect on the wives was that they were denied full capacity *(Geschäftsfähigkeit)* and could not transact business without the consent of their husbands, except over paraphernalia.[39] Hübner confirmed that this measure had found its original modern expression in the *Code Napoléon.* Article 213 laid down the law that 'the man owes his wife protection; she owes him obedience.'[40] Hübner's description bore a striking resemblance, not only to the systems of the Germanists, but also to the legal norms that were introduced under the BGB.

According to scholarly opinion at the time of Hübner's work, the evolutionary process in marital property relations continued and a new system emerged alongside the *Verwaltungsgemeinschaft.* By the Frankish period of the fifth century, according to Hübner, in some areas, a community of acquisitions *(Errungenschaftsgemeinschaft)* was recognized instead of an administrative community, which was vested in the husband alone.[41] In contrast to the later system, under the *Errungenschaftsgemeinschaft,* only property acquired by the spouses during the life of the marriage was held jointly and subject to the husband's administration. The property held by the individuals prior to the marriage remained separate from the marital estate.[42] Moreover, the new system granted wives independent rights in the acquired property.[43] In Westphalia, rights in the joint property were split fifty-fifty, with the wife possessing an independent right in half of all the acquisitions.[44]

In the post-Frankish period, marital property relations in the greater portions of Franconia, Westphalia, Thuringia, Schwaben and Bavaria progressed toward the equal distribution of property rights between husbands and wives.[45] Hence, the concept of a *Gütergemeinschaft* or community of goods, as Hübner wrote, 'signified an intimate union into an indivisible whole of the individual pieces of property that were derived from husband and from wife; the whole being subject to their mutual rights of collective ownership'.[46] If this community extended to each partner's entire property, it was called an *allgemeine Gütergemeinschaft,* but limited communities, such as the *Errungenschaftsgemeinschaft* and *Mobiliengemeinschaft* (community of movables) also fell into this category.[47]

Relative to the condition of women, nineteenth-century scholars identified two other progressions in marital property relations. *Dotalrecht* was the fruit of the Reception of Roman law in the fifteenth century. This system was characterized by the absence of a marital community. Wives contributed only a dowry *(Dos)* to the marriage, but managed and distributed their other property independently. This was the system that Beseler complained so bitterly about in his 1836 speech in Basel.[48] *Dotalrecht* stood in stark contrast to Beseler's idealized system of marital property relations, which 'corresponded to the tenderness of the couple's union, and the wife, even though dependent, was, therefore securely positioned'.[49] *Getrenntes Güterrecht* (separate property) was essentially *Dotalrecht* under a German name; in many instances women possessed full disposing capacity and were responsible for their own debts. These two systems, in particular, were the targets of Germanists' demands for reform.

Nevertheless, Hübner's *Grundzüge* made it evident that there was a wide range of marital property relations prior to 1900. No other area on the German legal map offered such a motley of variation.[50] Marital property relations, as he suggested, were marked by such extreme particularism that the area of law was difficult to survey.[51] There was by no means a consensus of legal opinion, which supported the view that marital property relations were, historically, characterized by the subjugation of a wife's property to the management and usufruct of her husband. Indeed, development in this area was altogether inconsistent, and marital property relations and the position of women were considerably varied, as Hübner's historiographical sketch showed.

In the nineteenth century, with the breakdown of ecclesiastical courts and the collapse of old *Geschlechtsvormundschaft* ordinances, women enjoyed considerable independence not only with regard to property rights, but, according to the standards of the time, basic rights in general. Paradoxically, given that the Family Law of the BGB instituted the *Verwaltungsgemeinschaft,* the most compelling records, which show that gender relations between husbands and wives were more egalitarian, are contained in the Family Law Commission's files. In November of 1875, just after the code's various editors were appointed, the chief editor of Family Law, Gottlieb Planck, requested reports from the state-level departments of justice on the existing conditions of marital property relations.[52] The November request letter asked for information on the existing forms of marital property relations, population in the various legal regions, whether or not the nature of marital property relations changed with the birth of a child, whether or not there were any special exemptions on the basis of class and, finally, if marital contracts were permitted, and, if so, the statistics on the nature of the contractual regimes.[53] The state reports began trickling into the Reichkanzler's office in the summer of 1876 and were forwarded to the Family Law Commission, under Planck's authority. More than any other primary source, these reports demonstrate that the character of gender and marital property relations was far more egalitarian than those installed by the BGB and that the editors of Family Law had clear knowledge of this before they drafted its provisions.

The ALR has often been cited by historians to support the narrative of wives' subjugation in every way to their husbands' authority. 'The *Allgemeines Landrecht*', as Richard Evans wrote in his seminal study, *The Feminist Movement in Germany* (1976), 'firmly declared that the husband was the head of the family, and made him the legal guardian of his wife,' and 'without his permission she could not take a job, sign a contract or engage in litigation; she was not a "legal person" in civil law'.[54] For this reason it will be informative to start with Prussia's report. It was prepared by the newly appointed Minister of Justice, Adolf Leonhardt, who was famous for his drafting of the Hanover *Prozessordnung*.[55] It was forwarded to Bismarck's office on 30 August 1876.[56] The Prussian report was divided into two sections. For the years 1871 to 1875, the first section provided demographic information and statistical data on the rate of contractual exclusion of one of the five prevailing systems of marital property relations: *allgemeine Gütergemeinschaft, Errungenschaftsgemeinschaft, Mobiliengemeinschaft* (also known as the *Fährnisgemeinschaft*), *getrenntes Güterrecht* and *Dotalrecht.* I will refer to this section as the Prussian Contract Report (PCR). The second section identified local, largely obsolete statutes on marital property relations, which varied widely from *Bezirk* to *Bezirk, Amt* to *Amt* and *Stadt* to *Stadt.* Indeed, it revealed even greater particularism in marital property relations than the PCR showed. I will refer to it as the Prussian Statute Report (PSR).

In addition to the PSR, which showed that the ALR was not the exclusive source of statutory law in Prussia, Hübner also emphasized that 'complete freedom of contract' had existed all over Central Europe.[57] 'The general rule prevailed', he wrote, 'contract breaks the law of the land.'[58] In the vast majority of Prussia, the effect of the ALR's provision receded, not only behind local and city statutes, but indeed behind mere contracts between individuals. Whole localities adopted, adapted, rejected or adopted and then rejected the ALR at will. Brandenburg, for example, suspended the ALR, as did the southern region of Westphalia. In East and West Prussia, the ALR receded behind provincial laws, and in Silesia, Pomerania, the Province of Saxony, Middle Franconia and other tiny areas it receded behind old local laws. In reality, the ALR was the principal source of law only in Posen, northern Westphalia, Ostfriesland, regions of the Rheinprovinzen (that had not revolted) and the tiny port of Wilhelmshaven.

Over the course of the nineteenth century, an environment in which every individual was his or her own law soon came to reflect the state of legal affairs in Prussia. Despite statute, in reality, as Nieberding complained, people made up their own arrangements. Nowhere was this practice more widespread than in the area of marital property relations. Even where regulations existed on the books, the freedom of contract meant that couples could simply amend or ignore the law and set up alternative arrangements. As a result, the ALR should not be seen as a guide to gender relations. It was essentially only a law of last resort and existed in a sort of intestate fashion.

In this extremely checkered legal landscape, Prussia became even more riddled by particularism when it acquired new territories in 1866. The *Code civil* was still in effect on the west bank of the Rhine. In Schleswig, which liberals laid claim to as properly German, Jutish law was a source of civil law where it existed, and, in Holstein, various county and city laws from the Reformation remained on the books. Despite procedural and court reforms, a tremendous variety of customary practices continued to characterize Hanover and Hesse, lands which Germanists had long brandished as the pure source of immemorial German liberties. The PCR confirmed the reality of particularism and showed that Prussians, both age-old and at sword point, and from East Prussia to Westphalia and from the Province of Saxony to Mecklenburg, attempted to maintain both contractual freedom and the more egalitarian marital property relations of the precodification era. The attempt to introduce the *Verwaltungsgemeinschaft* under the ALR met with considerable popular resistance. Many Prussians simply invoked their freedom to contract and either amended or suspended the ALR's provisions outright.

In Posen and northern Westphalia, where the ALR was the principal source of the statutory regime, propertied couples contracted alternative arrangements. While the overall contract rate in these regions was comparatively low, the highest contract rate was amongst the very middle-class constituency that liberals claimed to represent and, who, therefore, should have welcomed the *Verwaltungsgemeinschaft.* In Posen, for example, in 5.2 percent of all marriages there were registered agreements and these prenuptial contracts suspended or amended the ALR's provisions.[59] Of the 3,704 registered contracts, 2,384 were entered by couples classified in the '*Handel und Gewerbe* (business and trade)' category. This meant that 64 percent of all marital contracts came from Posen's middle class. The PCR showed a high contract rate amongst Jews, as well, some 684 contracts of the total 3,704. Posen had a large Jewish community, where *Dotalrecht* was the preferred form, but, as the numbers show, prenuptial agreements were, in fact, more common amongst the gentile bourgeoisie. Although the marriage statistics for northern Westphalia were less reliable, the report showed some 1,802 marital contracts. Again, the lion's share were filed by middle-class couples.[60] The PCR showed 1,339 small business owners and 69 large business owners, for a combined rate of 78 percent out of the 1,802 total. Following the small business owner, the next highest contract rate came from small landowners. They registered 246 contracts or 13.6 percent of the total. The report showed 27 contracts for large landowners or 1.5 percent. The combined rural rate was 15 percent of the total.

In Prussian regions where the ALR was not the source of the statutory regime, but rather an older form of marital community was the statutory system and where conditions were more favorable to women, the contract rate dropped significantly. In Brandenburg, where the ALR was suspended altogether as well as the Province of Saxony and Silesia, where its marital property law was suspended and replaced with *getrenntes Güterrecht,* the marriage rate was 4 percent (8,859,572 people with about 350,000 marriages), and there were no registered agreements. In contrast to Posen, in Pomerania, where the business class comprised only a small section of the general population, the contract rate fell to from 5.2 percent to 3.7 percent. While the marriage rate was also 5 percent, out of some 66,500 marriages, there were only 2,487 contracts. In areas where *Dotalrecht* was in effect, the number of agreements increased. However, this seems to have involved the fixing of terms and conditions relative to the dowry.[61]

By comparing the PCR's numbers on eastern Koblenz and the Rhineland, an even sharper indication of popular resistance to the reintroduction of the *Code civil's* administrative community is discernable. In Koblenz, where the German form of *Errungenschaftsgemeinschaft* and *Mobiliengemeinschaft* remained the basis of marital property relations, the contract rate was significantly lower than in the Rhineland.

The PCR showed 8,292 marriages in a total population of 160,696 people. There were only 62 contracts, for a 5 percent marriage rate and .72 percent contract rate. In the Rhineland, however, where the *Code civil* introduced the administrative community and rigorously disenfranchised women, the marriage rate dropped and the contract rate was much higher than in Koblenz. The PCR showed a population of 3.2 million with 140,000 marriages and a staggering 9,938 registered prenuptial agreements. The marriage rate was lower, only 4 percent, but the contract rate escalated to 7.1 percent compared to the 5 percent and .72 percent in eastern Koblenz.[62] Of the 9,938 contracts registered in the Rhineland, 5,221 were from couples classified in the *Handel und Gewerbe* category and 779 from the *Grosshandel* category. That was a rate of 52.2 percent and 7.8 percent, respectively, and a combined rate of 60 percent of the total 9,938. Interestingly, the percentage of rural contracts also increased significantly compared to other regions in Prussia. The report showed 3,889 couples from the *ländliche Bevölkerung* category and 204 from the *grosse Besitze* category. The contract rate here was 39 percent and 2 percent, respectively, and a much higher combined rate of 41 percent, in contrast to Westphalia's 15 percent.[63]

In the South, Bavaria's report, *Darstellung des im Königreiche Bayern bestehenden ehelichen Güterrechts* (1877), showed such great variation in the nature of marital property relations that it was impossible to draw a general assessment on the basis of the report. The report indicated that the most common regime was separation of property in the form of Roman *Dotalrecht* and various, unidentified *partikulare Gütergemeinschaften.* For the years 1851 to 1875, the overall contract rate stood at 38 percent (821,027 marriages and 314,301 marital agreements). Yet, in Oberbayern, Niederbayern, Oberpfalz and Schwaben, the rate was much higher, 56 percent, 62.5 percent, 57 percent and 54 percent, respectively. These were regions where there had been some attempt to reintroduce an administrative community. In Oberfranken and Mittelfranken the rate was comparable to Posen, Pomerania and Westphalia. The report showed rates of 13.3 percent in Oberfranken and 12 percent in Mittelfranken, respectively. Unterfranken had the lowest contract rate of 8.5 percent, and, not surprisingly it was a region of varied local and city laws.[64]

Nowhere are historians offered a sharper image of couples' resistance to the reintroduction of the administrative community than in Baden. In 1809, the Civil Code of Baden attempted to void the particular laws and create legal uniformity. The Code's family law mirrored the *Code civil* and tried to introduce a system of *Verwaltungsgemeinschaft.* However, the liberty to contract returned after the *Freiheitskriege.* As a result, Baden's report on marital property relations revealed a staggering rate of marital contracts.[65] For the years 1871 to 1874, only 52 percent of couples in Baden maintained the statutory regime. According to the report, in 48 percent of all marriages, there were written contracts that outright abandoned the statutory regime of Baden's Code. In 32 percent of marriages, the *Errungenschaftsgemeinschaft* was adopted and, in 16 percent, the *allgemeine Gütergemeinschaft* was the basis of marital property relations. An even stronger indication of the unpopularity of the administrative community was evident in the county numbers, where in some areas only 15 percent of couples maintained the statutory regime. Out of the 57 localities, only 27 showed percentages over 50 percent and most of these were concentrated close to the French border, such as Karlsruhe and Mannheim. Thirty of the 57 were under 50 percent, with only 4 towns approaching 50 percent. The rest fell well under this range, with 16 in the 30 percent range, 5 below 30 percent and 3 just at 15 percent.[66]

While I have focused on the statistical information provided in some of the state reports, given the realities of particularism, combined with the freedom of contract, it can also be suggested, from the very high contractual rate, that there was probably a great deal more quiet deviation from the law. In all probability, there were likely many more marriages where the partners followed the pattern of particularism and simply arranged their affairs as they saw fit without regard to the law. At the same time, it cannot be emphasized enough that contracts generally were designed to protect women's property rights. The contract rate was higher in those areas where there had been an attempt to reintroduce the *Verwaltungsgemeinschaft.* It appeared that couples resorted to contracts in an attempt to exclude the disruptive effects of unfavorable systems of marital property as seen, most notably, in Baden and the Rhineland. Despite the laws, which awarded husbands substantial rights to their wives' property, women were still able to maintain independent property rights by forcing would-be husbands to sign away administrative rights in prenuptial agreements.

Women's Wealth and Local Courts

The increased independence of women in marital property relations, as exhibited in the state reports, corresponded to an increase in women's wealth and social status. As André Burguière and François Lebrun have illustrated, girls came to constitute the essential trump card for great families 'seeking to extend their influence by means of illustrious alliances, and they demanded comfortable dowries in order to play this role'.[67] As a result, noble women were often financially better off than their male siblings and cousins.[68] As cash became more important in Europe, women's cash dowries proved to be more valuable resources than the economically troubled great *Grundbesitze* that their male siblings were likely to inherit. Indeed, by the eighteenth century, in some parts of continental Europe, a girl from the middle-ranking nobility could receive a dowry as large as three or four years of a family's income.[69] The increased importance of cash resulted in the elevation of women's political and social position within German society.[70]

At the same time, just as increased wealth for women led to an elevation in their position, shrinking property value, for men, resulted in the devaluation of their political and social position. Judith Hurwich has shown effectively that social mobility among the south-west German nobility took place primarily through the marriage of men of lower rank to women of higher rank.[71] Men were very often forced to seek marriages with propertied women in order to maintain their class standing, a compromise that very often came at a cost to their decision-making power within the family, as I mentioned earlier.

In this highly competitive marriage environment, it was not long before gender conflict was reflected in Central European courts. Women, it seems, did not simply turn over their wealth to men, but increasingly demanded male accountability and equal property rights in the courts. In the second decade of the nineteenth century, married women's property rights emerged as a major source of liberal discontent—a point that was reiterated at the *Germanisten* conferences. As women's share of family wealth increased substantially, family authority could no longer be determined on the basis of sex. Despite the musing of the Germanists, women not only contributed land, homes, businesses and substantial amounts of cash to their marriages, but demanded a participatory place in family financial decisions.[72] The increased economic status and authority of wives in the family had a leveling effect on sexual inequality in the society at large, and local courts increasingly confirmed basic rights for propertied women. Courts were flooded with civil claims filed by wives, demanding a say-so in family finances, particularly in the instance of their husband's bankruptcy. Just as prominent, however, and bound up with liberal concerns about property rights in general, was a debate on women's rights to execute negotiable instruments, take oaths and distribute wealth. These were the very areas of law that absorbed Germanists' attention.

In 1826, the second of a series of articles titled 'Kann nach gemeinen Rechten von den Weibern die Bürgschaft gültig in einem Privat-Instrumente bestellt und darin auf die weiblichen Rechtswohlthaten verzichtet werden oder nicht' appeared in Hanover's *Juristische Zeitung.*[73] The author of this article, Dr. Freundentheilin, underscored recent legal changes that confirmed women's rights to execute negotiable instruments. He explained that under the 'age-old' law, personal guarantees by a woman were only valid in negotiable instruments if they were accompanied by the signature of three witnesses.[74] As he pointed out, however, in the eighteenth century, these restrictions had been relaxed, progressively. The unfortunate result, from Freundentheilin's perspective, was that, in customary legal practice, negotiable instruments executed by women were accepted as valid.[75]

These changes were hotly contested in Hanover's courts. While local courts tended to sanction women's newly won rights, appeals courts rigorously tried to uphold traditional norms. The case of a professional woman, Doctorin R, which was cited in Freundentheilin's article, provides an excellent example of the conflict over the position of women in Hanover. In this case, Doctorin R had been permitted to swear an oath and to assume guardianship of a minor child.[76] Soon after, the matter was contested before the Municipal Civil Court in Stade in 1825. The court upheld not only Doctorin R's right to swear an oath, but also gave its legal seal of approval to her guardianship of the minor child. Only a year later, the Court of Appeals in Celle chastised the Stade court and overturned its ruling. Indeed, the Appeals

Court went so far as to state that such things 'are not to be respected: Rather, your judgement of 31 January 1826 is itself invalid'.[77] Moreover, it denied Doctorin R the right to appeal and file additional process in the matter.[78]

While the doctor's case was a striking harbinger of the strident discrimination women would face in the liberal court system after the introduction of the BGB, bankruptcy cases filed in the early nineteenth century also showed that women demanded the right to exercise independent control over their property. In 1826, the wife of a bankrupt farmer submitted a sworn declaration on the amount of her dowry *(Brautschatz)* to the Stade Municipal Court. She subsequently filed a claim, as a creditor, for the restitution of her property, which she won.[79] On appeal, the appellant, who was the primary creditor, argued that wives did not possess *Rückforderungsrecht* in the instance of their husband's bankruptcy.[80] The supporting brief cited a number of legal sources, including customary law and Ottersberg's local law.[81]

More important, however, was the question of ownership with regard to marital property. Apparently, the couple had opted for Roman *Dotalrecht* and the appellant, who was the creditor, argued that under Roman law, 'the *dos* becomes the husband's property' and could not be restored to the wife even in the instance of his death.[82] This position, the brief pleaded, was supported by a decision of the Celle Court of Appeals. In 1823, it had ruled that the death of a husband did not entitle the wife to reclaim her property. Therefore, the appellant argued that it followed that wives were not entitled to the restitution of their property in the instance of their husbands' bankruptcy. Interestingly, the Celle Appeals Court's decision was not based on an interpretation of Roman law, but rather the customary legal notion, expressed in a mere phrase: *'Langst Leib, langst Gut'*.[83] Here we see not only the discrimination against women that characterized the Appeals Court's decisions, but also how even the dubious legal antiquarian pronouncements of Grimm and others, which derived law from mere phrases, fairy tales and the like, had an impact on court decisions. However much liberals effected constitutional transformation and demanded political revision in the name of legal security against arbitrary acts, where women were concerned any justification that blocked their property rights would be accorded the sanction of the gavel, as seen in the decision of the Celle Appeals Court.

Nevertheless, particularism remained strong; it was still only 1828, and the Hanover *Prozessordnung* and a central legal system were merely figments of liberal imagination. Local norms still set precedent, and neither local officials nor local courts were obliged by the upper court's decisions. Despite the Court of Appeals decision, the Municipal Court in Stade simply refused to recognize its jurisdiction and did not demur to its decision. Instead, the Stade court issued a decision, invoking that marital property relations in Ottersberg were not based on the phrase *'Langst Leib, langst Gut'*.[84] Rather, it confirmed its earlier decision and upheld the wife's position, finding that 'under customary law, the wife's authority *(Befugnis)* to reclaim her dowry cannot be barred in the instance of her husband's bankruptcy'.[85] Local jurisdiction remained strong and, in reality, local court officials still had to live and walk amongst the other members of their community. This, in the end, was a stronger imperative in the decision-making process than liberal sociopolitical machinations.

In another matter, a wife filed a complaint directly before the Court of Appeals in Celle.[86] Recently married, she had contributed a sizeable cash dowry to her marriage. Apparently, soon after the marriage, the husband took an interest in the guesthouse business. The wife complained that, without her knowledge or consent, the husband had used her dowry to purchase his first cottage. *'Häuslicher Unfrieden',* as the article colourfully recounted, ensued and it was not long before the husband had to move in with his widowed sister. The wife subsequently filed a civil action, demanded the restitution of her property and argued that she was not consulted before her husband disposed of her property. Interestingly, the Celle Court of Appeals threw the case out on a technicality, claiming improper venue, but it still chose to exercise disciplinary jurisdiction over the wife. The court chastised the wife for filing a claim against her husband and ordered her to pay the cost of the suit.[87] While municipal court decisions confirmed the basic property rights of women, the Appeals Court, rigorously, tried to legislate sex guardianship from the bench. This practice also contradicted the politics of Germanist legal scholarship, which laid claim to the people as the source of law.

Women in other areas of Central Europe seemed to have found new independent rights as well. In Thuringia and Anhalt, similar legal questions on the status of women arose in the courts. In a matter put before the Weimar Court in 1857, a wife sued and won a claim against her husband. The court awarded the wife damages because the husband had mismanaged a guesthouse that she had contributed to the marriage.[88] An 1858 article in the *Blätter für Rechtspflege in Thüringen und Anhalt* reported that, as a result of decrees from 1729 and 1730, the right of married women to administer their own property was sanctioned 'once and for all time', restoring their rights and capacity.[89] The article pointed out that court decisions upheld women's rights to bequeath assets to their biological children even over the objections of their husbands.[90] In 1867, courts in Saxony upheld married women's rights to swear oaths as to their contributed property and to demand its removal from the bankruptcy estate of their husbands.[91] An 1880 article took up the question of a married woman's right to sue her husband for repayment of money she loaned him to start a business.[92]

Private property had emerged in the systems of Mittermaier, Eichhorn, Grimm, Beseler and others as the cornerstone of all other rights of public participation society. It was the prerequisite on which *vollkommene Freiheit,* in Eichorn's word, rested. It was not only that liberal political thought appealed to history to justify excluding women, but that this body of thought in fact was a reaction against the reality of women's considerable private property and property rights. Essentially, courts upheld the rights of women to execute testamentary instruments, which as readers will recall was a pillar of the idea of legislative revolution handed down from Niebuhr and others. The demand for male rights and participation must also be understood against the fact that women may have been considerably farther along in this regard than their male peers, and liberals may have felt that they were being swamped by women.

Women's Economic and Professional Expectations

Women's sense of economic and social independence, which was confirmed in lower court decisions, was also evident in their changing labor choices. German women, over the course of the nineteenth century, increasingly pursued careers that required special skills. The entrepreneurial spirit and the promise of the market economy had an impact on this sector of the population as well. In what I have called the century of promise, women no longer thought of themselves as secondary personalities, but as full persons in their own right. A good example of this spirit was reflected in the popular middle-class women's magazine, *Die Frau.*

In response to women's growing demand for economic independence and interest in both professional careers and independent business options, the magazine carried a section titled *Erwerbsthätigkeit der Frau.* For the years 1893 and 1894, alone, *Die Frau* carried nineteen articles that addressed business options for women. Honey cultivation, interior decorating, horticulture and bookstore proprietorship were suggested as promising business options for women. An article titled 'Die Kunst- und Handelsgärtnerinnen' appeared in the October 1893 edition, urging that horticulture was 'rapidly fashioning into an exceptional profession well suited for women'.[93] It was a growing field that offered women independent business proprietorship as florists, landscapers and produce suppliers.[94] In the same issue, 'Die Photographin' identified photography as another possible option for '*Mädchen und Frauen*'.[95] 'In photography studios', the article pointed out, 'under the title "*Photographin*" fall different branches of the profession', including retoucher, copier and studio manager.[96] Income, the article reported, was comparatively high, 45 to 100 Marks per month for copiers, 50 to 160 for retouchers and 200 to 300 for receptionists, but it also suggested that women consider opening their own studios.[97]

In this same section, *Die Frau* also provided information about various trade schools that were open to women. The article 'Die Kunst- und Handelsgärtnerinnen' recommended the gardening school, owned and operated by Frau Kommerzienrat Heyl in Berlin. The degree requirement involved some two years of course studies and practical work. The cost ranged between ten to fifteen marks per month. The article also suggested similar schools in Karlsruhe, Kiel and Neuenkirch.[98] In 'Die Photographin', a number of photography schools in Berlin, Munich, Breslau and Vienna were suggested—some of which were owned and operated by women. A year of study cost between one hundred and two hundred marks.[99] There were also trade schools that offered training in a variety of trades, including the Altoner Mädchen-Gewerbeschule, the Malerinnenschule in Karlsruhe and the Handels- und

Gewerbeschule für Frauen und Töchter in Stettin.[100] In Dresden, the Frauenerwerbsverein (Women's Professional Association), which was operated by women and had been in operation for twenty-three years, offered training in the 'white-blouse' professions, including tailoring, bookkeeping, typing and stenography. It also operated a business design school for women. As many as six hundred students enrolled annually, and the school was the recipient of considerable financial support from local officials. The mayor of Dresden donated five hundred marks annually, and the queen of Saxony was a regular donor as well.[101]

As I have tried to suggest in this chapter, the liberal anxiety over the position of women in society reacted against major changes in gender relations that had resulted from the decline of sex guardianship in the eighteenth century. In the nineteenth century before the introduction of the BGB, women contributed substantial sums of wealth to their marriages and they demanded the institution of marital property systems that allowed them to protect their wealth. German municipal courts upheld not only women's property rights, but their right to take oaths, bequeath their property and have guardianship of minor children. Moreover, women sought careers that required special skills and were more visible than ever in the business community. In her article 'Die Ehefrage und der Beruf', Henriette Fürth reported that, in the thirteen years between 1882 and 1895, the number of women in the trade and service industries had risen 94.3 percent from 298,110 to 579,608.[102] The rise of women's trade schools and women's interest in professional options offered strong evidence that women felt a sense of economic and social independence. Even the *Handelsgesetzbuch* (1897) acknowledged the rising numbers of businesswomen. Paragraph 1 reads: 'In the sense of this code, a *Kaufmann* is one who operates a business'.[103] In a footnote, it specifically stated that the definition also included 'married women with or without the approval of their husbands'.[104] These economic, social and political changes of the time created an atmosphere of promise for German women and, during the nineteenth century, women increasingly exercised basic property rights inside and outside the home.

At the same time, liberal, codified law was on the rise, and the political, social and economic gains women made in German society were lost when the BGB was introduced in 1900. For the first time, women were faced with a national unified system of marital property relations and the denial of contractual freedom. The BGB reintroduced the *Verwaltungsgemeinschaft* and denied contractual liberty, forcing Germans to adhere to its provisions on marital property relations. The Code's denial of women's property rights had an adverse impact on the entire range of basic rights women had won over the course of the nineteenth century. Because the institution of sex guardianship was part and parcel of the liberal agenda of constitutional transformation, the paradox is that, for this reason, it emerges as one of the key sociopolitical indicators of the *Bürgerliche Revolution* that occurred in 1896. Nevertheless, the BGB would become one of the major sources of discontent in German society after

1900. It was not just that German women were denied rights under the *bürgerliche* sociopolitical arrangements, but that they, indeed, experienced legislated regress rather than progress.

Notes

1. Jacob Grimm, *Deutsche Rechtsalterthümer* (1828), p. 557.
2. Stephan Buchholz, 'Ehe- und Familienrecht', in Helmut Coing (ed.), *Handbuch der Quellen und Literatur der neueren europäischen Privatrechtsgeschichte,* vol. 3, *Das 19. Jahrhundert,* vol. 2 (1982), p. 1663.
3. Joan Scott, *Gender and the Politics of History* (1988), pp. 1–11.
4. Rudolf Nieberding, 'Erste Berathung des BGB im Plenum des Reichstags' (1896), in Benno Mugdan (ed.), *Die gesammten Materialien zum Bürgerlichen Gesetzbuch für das Deutsche Reich* (1899).
5. Ibid.
6. Ibid.
7. Ibid.
8. Ibid.
9. Richard Schroeder, *Geschichte des ehelichen Güterrechts in Deutschland: Die Zeit der Volksrechte* (1863), pt. 1, p. vi.
10. Buchholz, 'Ehe- und Familienrecht', pp. 1627–73.
11. Rudolf Hübner, *Principles of Germanic Private Law,* Francis S. Philbrick (trans.) (1918), p. 23.
12. 'Bayerns Partikularrechte', *Münchener Neueste Nachrichten* (4 March 1894).
13. Richard Evans, *The Feminist Movement in Germany 1894–1933* (1976), pp. 12–13.
14. Nieberding, 'Erste Berathung des BGB'.
15. Ernest Benz, *Fertility, Wealth, and Politics in Three Southwest German Villages: 1650–1900* (1999), pp. 54–5.
16. Ibid.
17. Ibid.
18. Ibid.; and Jack Goody, 'Inheritance, Property and Women: Some Comparative Considerations', in Jack Goody, Joan Thirsk and Edward Thompson (eds), *Family and Inheritance: Rural Society in Western Europe 1200–1800* (1976).
19. Heide Wunder, *He Is the Sun, She Is the Moon: Women in Early Modern Germany* (1998), p. 202.
20. Ibid., p. 89.
21. Ibid., p. 203.
22. David Sabean, *Property, Production and Family in Neckarhausen, 1700–1870* (1990), p. 174.
23. Ibid.

24. Dieter Grimm, 'Die Zeit der Begründung von Verfassungsstaat und Bürgerlichem Recht, 1789–1815', in Coing (ed.), *Handbuch,* p. 17.
25. Kathleen Canning, *Gender History in Practice: Historical Perspectives on Bodies, Class and Citizenship* (2006), pp. 145–63.
26. Ibid., p. 153.
27. Rudolf Jhering, *Der Kampf ums Recht* (1872).
28. Geyer, 'Der Kampf ums Recht', *Der Gerichtssaal,* 25 (1873), pp. 1–38.
29. Hübner, *Germanic Private Law,* pp. 591–2.
30. The notion of the 'age of the folk laws' was derived from Jacob Grimm's mythological musings about an ancient German free epoch and should be considered in this light.
31. Hübner, *Germanic Private Law,* p. 623.
32. Ibid.
33. Ibid.
34. Ibid.
35. Ibid., pp. 623–4.
36. Ibid., pp. 626–7.
37. Ibid.
38. Ibid.
39. Ibid., p. 627.
40. Ibid.
41. Ibid., pp. 627–8.
42. Ibid.
43. Ibid.
44. Ibid.
45. Ibid., p. 629.
46. Ibid., pp. 629–30.
47. Ibid., p. 630.
48. Georg Beseler, *Ueber die Stellung des römischen Rechts zu dem nationalen Recht der germanischen Völker* (1836).
49. Ibid.
50. Hübner, *Germanic Private Law,* p. 622.
51. Ibid.
52. Gottlieb Planck's letter was not in the file; however, it is referenced in all of the responses. See, for example, the cover letter for the Prussian report: Adolf Leonhardt to Herr Reichkanzler Fürst von Bismarck (30 August 1876), in Acta Betreffend: Die Mittheilung der Bundes Regierungen ueber das eheliche Gueterrecht (January 1876–April 1877), Bundesarchiv Berlin file no. 30.01 4009. All of the state reports on marital property relations are in this file, and henceforth only the report and not the file will be referenced.
53. See, for example, the cover letter for the Kingdom of Saxony's report from the Dresden office to the Reichskanzler Amt, dated 12 June 1876, in ibid.
54. Evans, *Feminist Movement in Germany,* p. 12.

55. For more on Leonhardt see Werner Schubert, *Entstehung und Quellen der Civilprozessordnung von 1877* (1987).
56. Adolf Leonhardt to Herr Reichskanzler Fürst von Bismarck (30 August 1876), in Bundesarchiv file no. 30.01 4009.
57. Hübner, *Germanic Private Law,* p. 634.
58. Ibid.
59. Adolf Leonhardt to Herr Reichskanzler Fürst von Bismarck (30 August 1876), in Bundesarchiv file no. 30.01 4009.
60. My discussion of Westphalia in the context of Prussian law deserves some qualification. The Herzogtum Westphalen had been a part of Hesse-Darmstadt (1803–1816), but was renamed Königreich Westphalen when it became a French satellite, under the leadership of Napoleon's notorious brother Jèrôme between 1807 and 1813. The *Code civil* was early, but in 1816 it became a Prussian province and subject to the ALR.
61. Adolf Leonhardt to Herr Reichskanzler Fürst von Bismarck (30 August 1876), in Bundesarchiv file no. 30.01 4009.
62. Ibid.
63. Ibid.
64. See *Darstellung des im Königreiche Bayern bestehenden ehelichen Güterrechts* (1877) in Bundesarchiv file no. 30.01 4009.
65. *Bericht des Gross Badische Staatsministerium in Carlsruhe zu dem Reichskanzler-Amt* (1 February 1876), in Bundesarchiv file no. 30.01 4009.
66. Ibid.
67. André Burguière and François Lebrun, 'The One Hundred and One Families of Europe', in André Burguière (ed.), *A History of the Family,* vol. 2, *The Impact of Modernity* (1996), pp. 70–1.
68. Ibid.
69. Ibid.
70. Sabean, *Property, Production and Family.*
71. Judith Hurwich, 'Marriage Strategy among the German Nobility, 1400–1699', *Journal of Interdisciplinary History,* 29/2 (1998), pp. 169–95.
72. For more on how women's changing economic position in Central Europe affected the balance of power in the family see Sabean, *Property, Production and Family*; Benz, *Fertility, Wealth and Politics*; Wunder, *He Is the Sun*; and Goody, 'Inheritance, Property and Women'.
73. 'Kann nach gemeinen Rechten von den Weibern die Bürgschaft gültig in einem Privat-Instrumente bestellt und darin auf die weiblichen Rechtswohlthaten verzichtet werden oder nicht', *Juristische Zeitung für das Königreich Hannover,* 4 (1 April 1826).
74. Ibid.
75. Ibid.
76. Ibid.
77. Ibid.

78. Ibid.
79. 'Kann die Ehefrau eines in bäuerlichen Verhältnissen lebenden Stellwirthes, eines Meyers oder Erberens, ihr Eingebrachtes in dessen Concurse zurückfordern', *Juristische Zeitung für das Königreich Hannover,* 9 (1 November 1826).
80. Ibid.
81. Ibid.
82. Ibid.
83. Ibid.
84. Ibid.
85. Ibid.
86. Ibid.
87. Ibid.
88. Rückert, 'Character der fortgesetzten Gütergemeinschaft nach Koburger statuarischem Recht', *Blätter für Rechtspflege in Thüringen und Anhalt* (1858).
89. Ibid.
90. Heumann, 'Über die Verpflichtung des Ehemannes zur Ertheilung des ehemännlichen Consenses in einem von seiner Ehefrau mit ihrem Sohne über ihr eigenthümliche Immobilien abgeschlossenen Kaufvertrag', *Blätter für Rechtspflege in Thüringen und Anhalt* (1857).
91. 'Die Ehefrau kann einen Eid über den eigenthümlichen Erwerb von in die Ehe gebrachten und von ihr der Concursmasse ihres Ehemannes abgeforderten Gegenständen ohne Beitritt des Ehemannes ableisten', *Blätter für Rechtspflege in Thüringen und Anhalt* (1867).
92. 'Unter welchen Voraussetzungen kann eine Ehefrau, welche während der Ehe ihrem Manne ein Darlehn gegeben, die von ihrem Manne ihr dafür in solutum überlassenen Mobilien als ihr Eigenthum in Anspruch nehmen', *Blätter für Rechtspflege in Thüringen und Anhalt* (1880).
93. 'Die Kunst- und Handelsgärtnerinnen', *Die Frau* (October 1893).
94. Ibid.
95. A. Hautzinger, 'Die Photographin', *Die Frau* (October 1893).
96. Ibid.
97. Ibid.
98. 'Die Kunst- und Handelsgärtnerinnen'.
99. Hautzinger, 'Die Photographin'.
100. 'Die Erwerbsthaetigkeit der Frau', *Die Frau,* 1–12 (October 1893–September 1894).
101. Ibid.
102. 'Die Ehefrage und der Beruf', *Die Frau* (late 1890s).
103. Julius Basch (ed.), *Handelsgesetzbuch und Wechselordnung: sowie Nebengesetze und Auszug aus dem Bürgerlichen Gesetzbuch* (1931), p. 1.
104. Ibid.

—6—

Last Bastion

The *Bürgerliches Gesetzbuch* and the Transformation of German Society

> Presently, our conditions indeed are different: It will not be determined by war and powerful weapons, but the substance of our struggle against each other is no less great. Only the historic law, what we can all struggle to extract from it, remains and it will remain [witness to our free spirit]. The law: no greater idea can be used to reach the victory.[1]
>
> —Gottlieb Planck, Speech in Hanover Landtag, 1853

> So far as the laws of the Empire or of the states' statutes are referred to, which by the *Bürgerliches Gesetzbuch* or by this Act are declared as of no force, the corresponding provisions of the Code or of this Act take their place.[2]
>
> —Article 4, BGB *Einführungsgesetz,* 18 August, 1896

Slow *Bürgerliche Revolution* did not just happen in Germany; it was made to happen. By no measure an accident of history, this legislative revolution reached its apex with the enactment on 18 August 1896 and introduction on 1 January 1900 of the *Bürgerliches Gesetzbuch für des Deutsche Reich* and accompanying *Einführungsgesetz.* Comparing the English Revolution with that of his own time and referring specifically to Charles I, Gottlieb Karl Georg Planck (1824–1910), known to contemporaries as the Father of the Code, issued these considered words on the calculating perseverance of Germany's own political struggle at the height of the mid-century constitutional conflicts in Hanover. His words show the continuity of liberal political strategy with the ideas of the first half of the century and help us to catch sight of a German Revolution. In just shy of twenty years, he would sit on both BGB drafting commissions and play a vital role in the constitutional transformation of the nation.

Under the Reich Constitution of 1871, the King of Prussia held the *Präsidium* of the *Bund,* and his authority depended not only on Prussia retaining jurisdiction and supremacy vis-à-vis the other states, but on a sustained confederate structure. Every act of legislation that transferred jurisdiction from the states to the Reich declined the sphere of jurisdiction of states, eroded the confederate structure and, accordingly, legislated away Prussian supremacy and the power of the throne of Prussia itself. 'Since imperial statutes took precedence over state laws,' as Otto Pflanze noted, 'the importance of the Reich grew and that of Prussia and the other states shrank with the passage of every major bill through the Reichstag and Bundesrat.'[3] Despite Bismarck's shifting political alliances and rising modern conservatism, once the *Kompetenz-Kompetenz* of the Reichstag and Bundesrat was set in motion in 1873, legislated revolution was almost a *fait accompli* as Rudolf Bennigsen and others confidently believed.[4] Through a process of constitutional transformation, the crisis of the states in German-speaking Europe and, after 1871, the Reich, was remedied, and such remedy involved widespread popular mobilization and the reconstitution of political relations. The office of the kaiser, which increasingly found itself sharing executive power with a competitive chancellery, was already severely hemmed in by 1896 as a result of the onslaught of civil legislation. The *Einführungsgesetz,* which accompanied the BGB, however, undermined the last vestiges of personal rule in domestic affairs. This was Germany's bourgeois revolutionary moment. It was the point at which the transfer of domestic sovereignty from personal jurisdiction of personal rulers to the institutions of the Reich occurred. There was no Bastille or Guillotine in German history, but there was also no Terror.

The Father of the Code

As Wieacker acknowledged some years ago, Gottlieb Planck should be 'rated the true intellectual father of the BGB'.[5] Planck's life spanned those critical years when liberal idealism captured the imagination of German liberal youth. His liberalism was, however, also a reflection of his background. He was born into a well-established Göttingen family, which was defined above all by education. His great-grandfather, a professor of theology, married Veronica Schwiegersohn, the daughter of a third-generation civil servant in Nürtingen. His grandfather and namesake, Gottlieb Jacob Planck (1751–1833), attended Nürtingen's famous *Lateinschule* in his early years. He was a professor of theology at the University of Göttingen and a leading reformer of church history. In his position as vice-chancellor of the university, he received the government's ban on Caroline and Friedrich Schlegel in 1800. Professor Planck's twin boys, Heinrich and Wilhelm, are of particular interest. Heinrich became a professor of theology and married Johanne Wagemann. Their son Julius Wilhelm was a professor of German law and father of the famous physicist Max Planck, as well as a chief justice of the *Reichsgericht,* Hugo Planck. Wilhelm became an influential Hanoverian jurist, specializing in French civil procedure. His political leanings are clear as early as 1835, when he drafted procedural legislation based on German customary law. He would later work with Adolf Leonhardt on the *Bürgerliche Processordnung für das Königreich Hannover* (1850). Amongst his friends were prominent liberal figures such as Karl Welcker. Wilhelm also practiced law before the infamous High Court of Appeals in Celle. He married late in life to Doris Osterley, sister of the famous liberal Georg Osterley. They had one child, Gottlieb Karl Georg Planck.[6]

Although Planck's lineage virtually predestined him to liberalism, signs of his political awakening came during his early university years and legal studies between the universities of Göttingen and Berlin. At the University of Berlin in 1842–1843, Planck studied Pandects and inheritance law with Georg Putcha. He also studied Roman legal history and private law, with emphasis on the laws of feudal tenure, peasant farmers and commerce. In addition to these law courses, Planck studied Aristotle's rhetoric and Plato's theory, as well as logic and metaphysics. Returning to Göttingen in 1843, he studied Roman law, civil procedure and the construction of civil society, in addition to constitutional law under Zächariae's direction. Finally, Planck studied politics and European international law in light of national economy and the modern history of European states.[7] The courses that had the most significant impact on his drafting of German family law, however, were those in German private law taken with the Germanist Wilhelm Kraut. Kraut was famous for his three volumes of *Die Vormundschaft nach den Grundsätzen des deutschen Rechts* (1835–59). This work was a classic example of Germanist scholarship, in which the family functioned as the metaphor for the state.[8]

In terms of extracurricular activities, Planck joined a prestigious fraternity in 1843. In 1844, he played an active role in the movement for democratic equality amongst students and the improvement of academic manners through the restriction of dueling. In this capacity, he helped found an arbitration organization, called Progress. The chief target here was the notorious Corps. Dueling continued to play an active role relative to male honor on German university campuses throughout the nineteenth century, reflecting a *bürgerliche* cult of manhood. 'Manly dignity', as the president of the Berlin Supreme Court, Adolf von Kleist, noted in 1864, 'requires above all else manliness, that is, the consciousness of personal courage', and he suggested that 'the demonstration of this characteristic seems to us to be the principal aim of the duel.'[9] In dueling, middle-class men were not aping the norms of the aristocracy, but rather derived meaning that increasingly reflected a bourgeois cult of individuality.[10] The goal of the Göttingen student movement was not the end of dueling, but rather reforming access to the sport through the extension to bourgeois commoners. To serve this end, the fraternity called Hildeso-Cellensen was founded by both bourgeois and noble students. Fraternity social engagements provided an important meeting place for the liberal student body to express these values and interact as equals. It is in this environment that Planck developed a lifelong friendship and political alliance with Rudolf von Bennigsen.[11]

The generation of Planck, Bennigsen, Lasker and so many others was the generation behind the powerful movement of institutional change and modern state-building, which had a major importance for the place of the bourgeoisie in German society. Their legal education came after the Germanists had established themselves in universities, and it shaped the legislation they enacted. It was they who came into possession of Grimm's misplaced keys and, as they enacted legislation, unlike the earlier generation, they could look to German historical sources to justify their demands for liberal political, social and economic arrangements. Legal training also meant that this generation was more calculating and methodical in their approach to constitutional transformation. In the fateful days of March 1848, Planck wrote to his parents: 'Once again we are in a time where history hastens forward on the double, when what was wished for and striven after for decades is attained in a few days or even hours.'[12] 'Often earlier I had wished to have lived during the time of the first French Revolution', he continued 'so that I could have seen and taken part in the experience of the magnificent drama of a people wakening to the consciousness of their Rights and the Freedom.'[13] While the *'liberté, égalité, fraternité'* of the French Republic captured his soul and political imagination, he wished 'it could be repeated ... without the excess and terrorism that contaminated the first Revolution and laid to waste its best fruits'.[14] 'The best hope for the German people', he concluded, was to undermine the Confederation from within.'[15]

These sentiments were expressed by Planck's other liberal contemporaries. 'The mere expansion of borders was not the *deutsche* aim of the wars', Eduard Lasker wrote to Bismarck in August of 1870, 'and the nation will not be satisfied with this as its prize' as he suggested the need to create structural unification after the war.[16] Lasker's letter clarified that liberals would not be sidetracked from their demands for equal civil rights. 'Famous victories and dazzling external successes', as Rudolf Gneist also made clear in 1871, 'will not turn us away from the unchanging demands for a secure legal system and for political participation in the reconstruction of the law.'[17]

Lasker's life was a struggle up from the margins of Prussian society. Born Eisak Lasker into a Jewish family of decidedly humble origins in Posen, Lasker refused to convert and, thus, his liberalism was also driven by his own exclusion from the Prussian civil service because of his faith. In 1848, Lasker was a member of the Academic Legion, which joined Robert Blum's battle in the streets of Vienna. When the revolution was put down in 1849, he had no real option but to lead a life of exile in England. It was here that he developed an expertise in English law and became an adherent of John Stuart Mill's writings as well as Gladstone's reforms.[18] His place as one of the most important National Liberal figures of his time was also a testament to the significant progress of religious tolerance and diversity in German society by the late nineteenth century. The gaps in the constitution, which Lasker incidentally had a hand in drafting, left significant room for later political transformation, and the *Lex Miquel-Lasker* was the most significant amendment to that constitution and extended the competency of the Reich to the whole range of civil law.

Like so many of his liberal contemporaries, Planck packed off for Frankfurt in the summer of 1849. As a result of his activities, he lost his court clerk position in the city of Hanover and received the first of several disciplinary transfers. Exiled to

Osnabrück, here again he met Bennigsen and Johann Struve, both also suffering disciplinary transfer. His founding of the National Association with Bennigsen resulted in another disciplinary transfer to Aurich in 1852, a place Bennigsen described as the worst possible post for a civil servant.[19] Undaunted, as the constitutional debate reached full steam, Planck's continuing liberal agitation included a speech, published in the *Landtagsblatt,* in which he openly criticized noble privilege and demanded 'equality and freedom of all the people in every way'.[20] Condemning it as a 'the chamber of privilege', Planck reported that he was 'no admirer of the composition of the First Chamber'.[21] Here, 'a small sector of the people, with great privileges, has separated themselves from the rest of the people, and as a result, encounters hostility and hatred'.[22] 'Their interest is to create a more favorable environment for the preservation of their existing privileges and this is the essence of the conservative element in the First Chamber.'[23] Comparing the struggle of the German people to the English Revolution, Planck issued the warning that opened this chapter, and it is worth repeating here.

> Presently, our conditions indeed are different: It will not be determined by war and powerful weapons, but the substance of our struggle against each other is no less great. Only the historic law, what we can all struggle to extract from it, remains and it will remain [witness to our free spirit]. The law: no greater ideal can be used to reach the victory.[24]

The speech bore for him the immediate fruit of yet another disciplinary transfer to Dannenberg, where he would remain until 1857.

It was in not until 1857 that Planck returned to the city of Hanover, which was again a lively legal community and one with many returning liberal lawyers, including Bennigsen. This, however, was not the end of his disciplinary transfers, and he continued to be active in the liberal movement, as I discussed in Chapter 4. A year after the founding of the North German Confederation in 1867, Planck was appointed judge of the Superior Court in Göttingen and in 1868, judge of the Appeals Court in Celle. From Celle in 1869, he narrowly defeated the Social Democratic candidate for a seat in the North German Reichstag. It was during this period that he worked on the commission to draft a procedure code for the North German Confederation with Gneist, Leonhardt, Lasker, Johannes Miquel and others.[25] In 1871 he was elected to the national Reichstag, and it was his active support that helped carry the *Lex Miquel-Lasker* motion in 1873, which formally amended the constitution to extend full legislative competency to the Reich in civil law.[26]

In 1874, Planck was appointed to the first BGB drafting commission and chief editor of the family law. Of the other members of the commission, Planck was the most public figure and the only person who would sit on the second commission as well. It was Planck who defended the first draft against Otto v. Gierke's fiery criticism. By 1890, he emerged as the most influential editor on the second commission, expanding his reach well beyond family law to become the Code's lead editor. Through the formidable figure of Planck, despite the ups and downs of National Liberal representation in the Reichstag, and the aging or death of Lasker (d. 1884), Miquel (d. 1901) and Bennigsen (d. 1902), the liberal ideal of legislative revolution was carried through to its final completion. Planck, who was blind by the time the BGB was passed, died in 1910. He had outlived not only his fellow National Liberals, but indeed the other original members of the first commission. This was pure luck, but in the same way that Mittermaier, Grimm and Savigny lived a good long time and were around to see constitutional transformation through its theoretical development, Planck saw it through its practical development.

The Lay of the Imperial Land

The vital importance of giving close scrutiny to language and the grammatical arrangement of words in order to decipher the deep meaning of law and legislation cannot be emphasized enough. Legal language, even where claim is made to the vernacular of the people, remains highly technical, and any analysis, historical or otherwise, must necessarily begin with what the law says, although its full meaning may only become apparent in its life of adjudication. Equally as important as what the law says is what the law does not say; its silences or gaps may be as important as its written words. In this regard, at least, the Bismarckian constitution was an open-ended masterpiece.

As early as 1868, Bismarck expressed to Eulenburg his opinion that the Reichstag was a parliamentary body 'whose reinforcement is at present the most important task of Prussian policy'.[27] 'Toward this end', as Pflanze suggested, 'he permitted and even encouraged the expansion of its legislative competence and the exploitation of that competence in the first decade of its existence'.[28] As the Saxon envoy in Berlin, Koennerizt soon observed from Bismarck's actions, 'Prussia will eventually merge into Germany and not the reverse'.[29] Prussian ministers complained that Bismarck was 'ruining the entire Prussian state', and the Hessian minister-president wrote that they were seething with dissatisfaction.[30] As for the Kaiser, Bismarck remarked to Hohenlohe that he 'must above all become accustomed to seeing that he is more important as Kaiser than as King of Prussia'.[31]

In German historiography, to some degree, Bismarck's legacy has shared a similar fate as that of Savigny, but here, also, there is some indication of conservative liberalism. Pflanze, for example, suggested that he equated republicanism with parliamentary rule and monarchism with the constitutional system of mixed powers. 'Of all the experiments that have taken place in the sphere of politics since Montesquieu and others,' as Pflanze cites Bismarck's comments in 1884, 'the only truly useful result is the [concept of the separation of powers] between the executive, legislature, and judiciary.'[32] No more fundamental articulation of the modern conception of the state could be uttered, and there was no ideological requirement that such branches be equal, as their functions were not equal, but different. Bismarck was fascinated by the English parliamentary system, and it offered an example of separation of powers. Given Bismarck's hand in the growth of conservatism, there is cause for caution, but it is worth keeping in mind that in the face of an obstinate Wilhelm II, Bismarck wrote that 'after experiencing how difficult ruling monarchs made it for their ministers to serve the country, one could almost become a republican'.[33]

Whether or not Bismarck was transformationist-minded or not, constitutional transformation was aided by his early cooperation with National Liberals in installing the constitutional and legal avenues for the gradual formation of a representative state. The key to transformation was the Bundesrat and Reichstag's acquisition of *Kompetenz-Kompetenz,* as noted, in the early twentieth century, by Paul Laband and Heinrich Triepel amongst others.[34] Accordingly, the only distinction the constitution made between ordinary legislation and constitutional amendments was that the latter could be defeated by fourteen negative votes in the Bundesrat. *Kompetenz-Kompetenz* allowed that no statute passed by the Bundesrat and the Reichstag could later be pronounced unconstitutional whether or not it conformed to, altered or amended the constitution. The Bundesrat and the Reichtag held the power to extend the competence of the Reich by simple legislation, and as a result there were significant changes to the constitution over time. While some of these changes were 'formally written into the constitution' such as the *Lex Miquel-Lasker,* 'most were not'.[35] This is where Jellinek drew the distinction between constitutional amendment, a 'change in the text through a purposeful act of will', and constitutional transformation, 'a change that allows the text to remain formally unchanged and is caused by facts that need not be accompanied by an intention or awareness of the change'.[36]

As Reichstag deputies and members of the Bundesrat were no doubt well aware, the 1871 Constitution of the German Empire was flexible, and it did not confirm the supremacy of the monarchical principle. An indication of this was discernible in the written Constitution's silences and the order of priority of its construction. It first sought to establish the Reich's geographical boundaries and, then, in the discussion of legislation, essentially the Reich's jurisdiction. It also addressed the realm of the Bundesrat, and not until section four did the question of the imperial office become the main subject. Article 11 specifically stated that 'the King of Prussia shall hold the *Präsidium* (presidency) of the *Bund,* and shall have the title of German Emperor'.[37] Even a strict constructionist interpretation would have held that the King of Prussia was only the president of the confederation. His kingship was tied to Prussia alone and emperor was merely a name devoid of any constitutional authority. 'The Reich Constitution of 1871 did not renew the universal *imperium* of the Holy Roman Empire'; rather, as Ernst Huber wrote some time ago, the old notion of the 'Emperor of the Germans' evolved into a conception of an imperial office as a symbol of national integration and 'an institution whose legitimacy and authority was based on the common consciousness of the nation'.[38] 'The Reich', as such, 'was a democracy and monarchy at the same time'.[39] It aimed to install the democratical, aristocratical and monarchical components.[40] In other words, the Reich Constitution assumed that there would be continuing transformation. This was evident in Article 35, which held that the states of the confederation shall 'endeavor to bring about uniform legislation regarding the taxation of these articles', and Article 45.1, which called for 'uniform regulations to be speedily introduced on all German railway lines'.[41] For these reasons, the final form of the German constitution remained an open question in 1871, and the answer to that question was wholly dependent, not only on the character and content of the laws, but on the spirit of the people. This in turn contributed a latent primacy of legislation in the constitutional transformation of the Reich.

For these reasons, almost from the moment of its inception, the imperial title suffered from a progressive decline, which began slowly in 1871 and then sped up sharply in the mid-1890s. 'The Prussian King', as Laband suggested, was conceived as 'an organ of the member states'.[42] As even these comments written in 1906 indicate, the Prussian crown was besieged by devolutionary forces laterally, from above and below, from within and without, and by social and economic transformations that it could not control. Despite the fact that many public celebrations of the persons of the Kaiser filled calendars, these only hid the daunting reality of constitutional weakness, sinking fortunes and public humiliation, all of which were indicators of a progressive obsolescence. By the 1890s any pretentious hopes for personal rule were figments of Wilhelm II's imagination. Mirroring his marriage, Wilhelm II was by then a kaiser in name only. He was, at least as Ludwig Fulda's *Der Talisman* (1892) lampooning portrayal implied, 'freezing in solitary greatness'.[43]

Perhaps a fate worse than the swift end at the guillotine, 'Wilhelm the Sudden', as south Germans not so adoringly called him, was left alive, besieged by financial insecurity, humiliating public ridicule and disrespect, *causes célèbres* of a Duke of Buckingham order, social rejection and wanting prestige not to mention the dismissive flattery and circumvention of his attempted personal rule even by his closest advisors. Save for a speedy influx of cash from the Hamburg shipping magnate Albert Ballin, Wilhelm II scarcely would have been able to cover the costs for celebrations associated with the opening of the Kiel Canal in 1895.[44] Published the same year that he reluctantly oversaw the opening of the new Reichstag building, Ludwig Quidde's *Caligula* (1894) compared him to the infamous Roman emperor and went into several editions, selling more than 150,000 copies. Indicted for *Majestätsbeleidigung,* Quidde received a light sentence of only three months in the *Gefängnis.* Even the penalty of jail time failed to stem the tide of public criticism, however. 'As many years of imprisonment', mocked a contemporary source, are 'annually meted out as there are days of the year ... for the heinous crime of impeaching the Kaiser's aptitude.'[45] The *Vossische Zeitung,* usually more supportive, ran an article in 1895 excoriating his absences in 1894: 156 days hunting, at sea or visiting, 27 days with the army, and 16 dedicated to official duties.[46] Wilhelm found himself lampooned regularly in the international and national press, for which there was gradually less police protection for him in an era of *bürgerliche* legalism.

The Eulenburg-Moltke scandal (1907), followed shortly by the Daily Telegraph Affair (1908) and then the notorious Zabern Affair (1913) were late on the scene in a long string of disgraces, which found receptive coverage in the German press. Kaiser Wilhelm II's reputation suffered from scandal after scandal in the 1890s, including the Kotze, Schiller Prize and Kruger telegram uproars, to name a few.[47] In 1896 Bismarck delivered a blow of his own. He published the secret Reinsurance Treaty with Russia and criticized Wilhelm's decision not to renew it. The Emperor 'completely lost control' and threatened to have Bismarck arrested, until he was convinced to reconsider.[48] This change of heart, perhaps, had little to do with Bismarck's celebrity status and more to do with the fact that there were no legal grounds for such an arrest or prosecution as a result of the vast legal changes in the constitution of Germany. The Prussian monarch no longer possessed the authority simply to order out the police.

Unlike in the area of civil law, where competency required an amendment, the original constitution granted the Reich legislative competency in the area of criminal and procedural law. The *Reichsstrafgesetzbuch* (RStGB) went into effect in 1871, but the *Strafprozessordnung* (StPO) only came into effect later as part of the sweeping procedural legislation discussed in chapter four. It went into effect on 1 October 1879 alongside the *Gerichtsverfassungsgesetz* (GVG), *Zivilprozessordnung* (ZPO), *Rechtsanwaltsordnung* (RAO) and lawyers' *Gebührenordnung.* Again, here the criminal codes were heavily influenced by earlier state-level reforms. It owed its theoretical heritage to the writings of Feuerbach and other south German liberals, and was an adaptation of the Bavarian Criminal Code of 1813, which had in turned shaped the Prussian Criminal Code of 1851. The *Strafgesetzbuch* abolished flogging, and, after strenuous debate, the death penalty was retained only in cases of premeditated murder, embodying 'a degree of liberalization' unknown in Britain.[49] The combination of the GVG and StPO affirmed the basic rights of litigants and in cases of criminal prosecution, the rights of defendants to legal counsel (state funded where necessary), public trials, *Schöffengericht* and jury trials in serious cases. These measures also eradicated the last vestiges of the early modern judicial monopoly by also establishing the independent office of the state prosecutor. 'The judicial power', Paragraph 1 of the GVG read clearly, 'is to be exercised by the independent courts subject only to the statutes'.[50] The role of Germany's very active press corps also cannot be discounted in keeping the public aware of any discrepancies between law and practice. By the 1890s, as Benjamin Hett points out, judges who showed bias or marked disregard for proper court procedures became the subjects of unflattering editorial attention.[51]

Recent scholarship has pointed out that these measures established the independence of the judiciary.[52] What has not been emphasized, however, is that understood within the frame of *Kompetenz-Kompetenz,* procedural legislation fundamentally transformed the constitution, creating separate branches of the modern Reich government. The *Reichskanzleramt für die Reichsjustiz Angelegenheiten,* which had fallen under the chancellery, became the self-standing *Reichsjustizamt* in 1876 just prior to the introduction of the procedural reforms in 1879.[53] This was a vital development, because not only did it place ordinary citizens beyond the immediate arbitrary reach of the government, it also meant that the courts were in a position to exercise a checking and balancing function on the government, especially the imperial branch. The more laws that were passed through the Bundesrat and the Reichstag, the broader the reach and power of the courts. This also meant that the government scandals, certainly by the 1890s, quite often played out in the public courts with the full attention of the free press.

The courts, therefore, also provided an excellent measure of the political pulse of German society in the critical political years between 1888 and 1914 and in and around the enactment of the BGB. Cases of *Majestätsbeleidigung* offer a good example. Upon the accession of Wilhelm II, there was a marked increase in requests to the Berlin police to investigate libel against the Kaiser. While there had been only 18 requests in 1887, that number jumped to 60 in 1888. Whereas the average had been 10.2 cases annually from 1882 to 1887, it jumped to 82.5 for the years 1889–1899. As Hett's examination shows, judges and juries alike rejected politically driven prosecutions, and, we might add, so long as they were driven by government forces. Rates of acquittal in trials involving *Majestätsbeleidigung* were high and increased significantly. In 17.9 percent of cases, defendants were acquitted in Germany as a whole in 1882. In 1888, with the accession of Wilhelm II, that number rose to 20.9 percent, and by 1890 shot up to 26 percent and then leveled off at about 25 percent to 1900. In Berlin, convictions for libel against the Kaiser fell from 24 in 1898 to 14 in 1899, down to 4 in 1900 and hovered between 0 and 2 after 1904. These trends were at the same time punctuated by high-profile acquittals. The 'gadfly journalist' Maximillian Harden, who regularly broke the news of scandals in the Kaiser's entourage, was acquitted by a Berlin court in 1893. He walked again in 1907 and 1909, and attempts to convict other journalist and editors also failed. The cases confirmed the principles of freedom of the press and speech. What is more, bills, such as the *Umsturzvorlage* (Sedition Bill) and *Zuchthausvorlage* (Hard Labor Bill for strikers and advocates of a strike), which tried to exploit the courts for political ends, failed in the Reichstag in the late 1890s, or, like the moral legislation of the *lex Heinze,* emerged in such watered-down form that they were but a useless shadow of what Wilhelm hoped for.[54] These matters, not to mention the fact that members of Wilhelm's entourage faced convictions in the courts, give a sense of how severely the Kaiser was hemmed in by law and legal structures on the eve of the BGB.

The Kaiser's prestige, on which he was dependent to sustain the monarchy, also was wanting. This was evident in the fact that prominent members of the European nobility, many of whom were his blood relatives, increasingly pushed him aside. Despite what he thought was a close friendship, he did not attend the funeral of Alexander III of Russia in 1894, feeling 'cut by [his] rude comments which Bismarck vindictively revealed to him'.[55] In 1896, Nicholas II declined his official invitations, and, when Wilhelm traveled to Hessen, the Tsar Nicholas II and the Grand Duke, Ernst Ludwig, brushed him off. After this failure, Eulenburg reported that the Kaiser 'looked frightful'.[56] Nicholas later sent word that he 'no longer wished to receive letters of a political nature from him', and declined additional invitations in 1899 and 1903.[57] Ernst Ludwig was instructed by his grandmother, Queen Victoria, as soon as he ascended the throne in 1892: 'For God's sake's do not let Wilhelm interfere in your affairs—and in family affairs'.[58] Wilhelm was excluded from the Queen's eightieth birthday celebration in May of 1899; the royal family apparently regarded receiving him as a 'purgatory rather than a pleasure'.[59] Utterly humiliated, Kaiser Wilhelm II was without pride when he wrote to Ernst Ludwig about his social rejection in 1901.

> But how did you treat me? Condescendingly: as an outsider, you kept me at a distance, your sisters considered me loathsome ... The hope that I would find a second true home in Darmstadt ... quickly evaporated, and I was forced to go away greatly upset and full of suffering, because as far as you were concerned I was a 'nuisance'.[60]

Wilhelm's hurt feelings were a mild consequence in comparison to the serious ramifications this type of international rebuff held for his domestic rule in Germany. Although the German people did not face encirclement, the Kaiser was increasingly isolated in the middle of Europe. At least since the 1860s, the British had wanted to see in Germany 'consensual, organic political change leading toward a British-style parliamentary monarchy'.[61] Fritz placed great confidence in his Vicky's anticipated future and ability to foster political reform in Germany. Hope had centred on the crown prince, Frederick III, but this dwindled with his premature death on 15 June 1888, after just three months as Kaiser.[62] Ernst Ludwig stood in clear opposition to Wilhelm's *suprema lex Regis voluntas* pretensions, openly favoring a limited and responsible monarchy as well as the expansion of the power of the other states at Prussian expense.[63]

In the political environment of the 1890s, it was not difficult to fathom a constitutional alteration that would allow other princes in the Reich to hold the *Präsidium*. Anti-Prussian feeling amongst the state princes focused on Wilhelm II and, increasingly, was articulated in the language of constitutionalism. Here Ernst Ludwig was only one voice in a chorus. In 1895, although somewhat eccentric in his own right, Prince Ludwig of Bavaria criticized Prussian leadership in a speech for the coronation of Nicholas in Moscow. In a clear reference to constitutional arrangements, he reminded his audience that the princes were 'not vassals but allies of the German Emperor'.[64] There was no doubt a good bit of domestic and international political jockeying behind the scenes, and we should not underestimate the place of princely political ambition and interest to knock off Wilhelm II, regardless of blood ties. After the abdication of Kaiser Wilhelm II, Ernst Ludwig 'told the Prussian Minister in Darmstadt in 1919 that he believed that the German monarchies could eventually be restored, but that the King of Prussia should never again become German Kaiser, and that the German capital should be transferred from Berlin to Kasel, in the interests of the Reich's political and geographical equilibrium'.[65] Surely, this betrayed an earlier ambition and did not simply crop up in the aftermath of the First World War.

By the 1890s, the regime was in trouble. Junkers had been routed from the top jobs even in Prussia, and worse, landowners also were holding up Wilhelm's bills in the Reichstag.[66] The Kaiser's rift with the Bundesrat and the Reichstag also cost him diplomatically, which turned out to be his last card in the end. Edward VII of England's dynastic diplomacy was successful because it was supported by the government's (Parliament's) policy, in an era when the international differences could only be overcome on the basis of vital interests. Wilhelm II handicapped himself in this regard and was left with only personalistic diplomacy. As Moltke observed, it was vital interests that determined the policies that states adopted, and no longer the exchange of visits between royal families.[67] Behind the scenes, chancellors wrote patronizingly of Wilhelm's character, sentiments that took the form of insincere gush in person. Passing Wilhelm off to Bülow in 1897, Eulenburg wrote: 'Only if you handle the Kaiser psychologically correctly can you be of use to the country'.[68] Of Wilhelm, he emphasized that he needed to be praised, that he loved fame and was jealous; 'he belongs to those who become mistrustful if they do not hear recognition from important people'.[69] 'Above all', Eulenburg wrote in another letter, 'don't forget the sugar.'[70]

Since John Röhl revived research interest in Wilhelm II, scholarship has duly noted his declining prestige and public reputation. In his examination of jubilees, Bernd Sösemann has shown the precipitous loss of monarchical aura and the corrosion of monarchical sociopolitical capital.[71] Roderick McLean has examined the Kaiser's declining prestige amongst the European nobility.[72] Isabel Hull has argued that men like Tirpitz and Ludendorff, who were more loyal to the national state than to the crown and the social order it represented, were 'the advance guard in the triumph of military-cultural actionism over the monarchy' in the years immediately preceding the First World War.[73] This research has, in turn, broadened the scope of our understanding of political culture in turn-of-the-twentieth-century Germany, but, at the same time, has kept the more fundamental transformation of the German constitution hidden deeper by focusing on the person of Wilhelm II. In fact, while it was Wilhelm II's fate, like that of Louis XVI of France, to have the phase of steep monarchical decline occur on his watch, in reality the imperial office was in jeopardy of obsolescence from its somewhat temporary-expedient origins, at least in constitutional terms. More than any other element, that decline resulted not only from tidal waves of *bürgerliche* legislation, but the Kaiser's inability to get his measures through the legislative branch from the mid-1890s onward, including his military spending bills.

The trend toward civil legislation that began in the states and led to the formation of *Rechtskreise* gained steam in the North German Confederation, and the constitutional practice of adopting and adapting state reformations into the Reich constitution was magnified onto the national stage after the founding of the Reich in 1871. As it did in 1866, geographical unification resulted in liberal control of structural unification, and this meant more liberal *ius civile,* which in no small measure was not derived from Prussian sources. It was not simply unification *(Vereinigung)* that liberals and a broad sector of the German population desired, but unity *(Einheit).*[74] By the 1870s, civil law was perceived as something fundamental to any modern nation, and leading National Liberals, notably Lasker and Planck, manipulated 'the power of the spirit' by keeping the liberal press cranked up with articles on the merit of civil law.[75] In the early years of the Reich, National Liberals had a powerful ally in Bismarck. Law was seen as 'intrinsically good and as necessary to create a better, more rational society'.[76] By 1874, nobody wanted to be responsible for the failure to enact unified civil law.[77] There was no question that a civil code would be enacted and introduced in Germany, and this could lead to nothing other than the treasured victory. As Gottlieb Planck's biographer, Frensdorff, portentously commented on the BGB's political significance: *'Die Krönung sollte das Bürgerliche Gesetzbuch bringen'.*[78]

Legislating the *Gemeinwesen*

The BGB and *Einführungsgesetz* were the apex of a process of constitutional transformation that had been in the making since the founding of the Reich in 1871. With the BGB came the final transfer of sovereignty, constituting an expansion of the basic rights of German citizens. Article 2 of the *Einführungsgesetz* stated clearly that 'Law in the meaning of the *Bürgerliches Gesetzbuch* and of this Act is every principle of Right *(Rechtsnorm).*'[79] The BGB comprised 2,385 paragraphs of law when it was introduced on 1 January 1900, divided into five books, namely the General Part, Obligations, Things (Property), Family Law and Inheritance. While it would be impossible to examine the entire Code, its sheer size offers an indication of its major transformative impact on German society. While there was no pronouncement of fundamental rights in the Reich Constitution, such fundamental rights as freedom of travel, some measure of religious equity, penal reform, freedom of industry, privacy of the post, freedom of the press, basic judicial rights, rights of possession and rights of association (1908) were filled through regular legislation.[80] Rights were again confirmed, but also expanded in the BGB. 'Never fading youth', even Otto Gierke wrote in January 1900, 'in these changing times, our people will only be successful in winning cultural renewal and inner peace again and again if we hold true to our own laws.'[81] 'With the achievement of legal unity', he encouraged, 'we can abandon the last century, because the new law—a truly German *Volksrecht*—will stand up to the great task of the dawning century.'[82]

Of fundamental importance to the modern representative polity was, of course, the bestowing of citizenship. In the BGB, this was delineated first in the General Part, under the title of Natural Persons. 'The legal status *(Rechtsfähigkeit)* of a man', according to Paragraph 1, 'begins with his (successful) birth.'[83] 'The age of Majority', Paragraph 2 followed, 'begins upon the completion of the twenty-first year.'[84] The key word here is *majority,* which, as it had come to be defined in Germanist scholarship, emerged as the alter ego of full citizenship. While superficially it may have seemed as if this referred only to coming of age, majority was identified with a state of being fully *geschäftsfähig,* or the point at which, specifically, a boy became a man with full disposing capacity, the right to engage in juristic acts (to contract) and to take his place as a man in public society. It was this aspect that gave majority *(Mündigkeit)* its deeper political meaning.

What appeared as law in 1900 had its roots in Germanist theory of state. The concept of majority expressed German legal revolutionaries' rejection of *väterliche Gewalt* in the same sense that French revolutionaries rejected *la puissance paternelle.*[85] In *Rechtsalterthümer,* Grimm had identified *Fähigkeit* with *Manneskraft.* Examining fragments of *Städterecht,* he focused on the capacity of the *Bürger* and *Bauer.* To have *Manneskraft* was to possess the right to manage and dispose of property, and, under the Lombardian ordinance, this was a right reserved for men who bore arms. Following Grimm's example, Kraut, who was Planck's professor and who had participated in both *Germanisten* conferences, examined ancient German culture, from the so-called free epoch, and then drew a line of continuity to his own time. In his discussion of *Altersvormundschaft,* he argued that *Mündigsprechung* symbolized the termination of the father's guardianship over his son and the son's investment with his entitlement to *'unbezweifeltes Souverainitätsrecht',* rights granted to all members of the *'Deutscher Bund'.*[86] While fathers originally declared their sons' emancipation, Kraut wrote, it became a public matter attached to the management and distribution of property.[87] Sons became equals to their fathers, owing them only respect, but no longer obedience. *Mündigsprechung,* or majority, signified the son's acquisition of an equal level of membership in the fraternal brotherhood of the tribe, and, as an equal member, he possessed certain rights, the most important of which was full *Geschäftsfähigkeit.* All other rights stemmed from majority, including the right to marry, because marriage entailed the management of a wife's property. According to Paragraph 1303 of the BGB men could not marry before attaining the all-important majority.[88]

The construction of majority symbolized the renunciation of *väterliche Gewalt* within the family, and this served as a metaphor for renunciation of the absolute monarchial principle or a king as the public father and head of the sociopolitical body. In *Rechtsalterthümer,* Grimm explained that the *Herrschende* did not stand above the people, but rather ruler and ruled were equals. 'Where the free temper of the people was concerned', he wrote, '[the *Herrschende*] was without a doubt severely restricted.'[89] The symbolism contained in Grimm's legal myths, when viewed as political constructions, revealed a civil society of men held together by bonds of mutual respect rather than deference. Following Grimm's lead, in the first volume of his *Die Vormundschaft,* Kraut described a progression from an age of a monarch to a higher stage of human political development, in which the monarch is no longer sovereign, but equal to others in a society of *Mündigsprechungen.*[90] Under Roman law, he argued that sons never attained majority. The *pater familias* retained control over his children's wealth as head of the family.[91] It was the higher stage of human political development that liberals effected in the BGB.

The legal right to majority challenged the old order. Inherently, the concept of majority involved the extension of rights to a much broader sector of the population, and property rights determined public rights. The emancipation of sons and their property from their fathers within the family served as a metaphor for the transition to civil society and the emancipation of economic capital from the arbitrary regulation of the monarchical state. To reach majority was to become sovereign and master of one's own fate, to become equal to other men in society and, most importantly, to possess the right to progress (happiness), chiefly economic progress, according to one's own rational will and capacity. Tearing down filial devotion was a part of the process of creating a modern nation, because it tore down the willingness of the subject to obey and vested him with control over his own affairs; in effect, it involved the bestowing of full citizenship. The new basis for political consent was now derived from the fraternal bond of the majority or, in effect, citizens of the nation.

These principles of a representative polity, in which political consent was based on the collective will of the majority, found confirmation in the Second Title of the General Part on Juristic Persons. Here again, while it may seem that the section was only conceived with associations in mind, in fact it housed significant constitutional principles, which it set out to ingrain in German culture. Wilhelm Albrecht, writing in 1837, had conceived of the state as a juristic person offering a constitutional understanding that was directed against the patrimonial idea of state. 'Prince, minister, and civil servant' were made into 'organs' of this legal person, and 'this meant a binding of the prince to the constitutionally established state'.[92] In the second half of the nineteenth century, the understanding of the state as a legal person, as Stolleis writes, placed the monarchical principle in a greatly changed context. The imperial branch 'was forced to be more legally aware and thus became more predictable due to the triumph of the central postulates of the *Rechtsstaat* and, above all, of the administrative judiciary'.[93]

The BGB's title on Juristic Persons was also transformative insofar as the conceptualization of the state as a juristic person had triumphed in these years. It not only provides a measure of the Reich's constitutional precepts, but was a medium by which constitutional culture was earthed in German society. Under Paragraph 25, all associations had to have a constitution, and Paragraph 26 mandated the existence of a governing body. 'The governing body represents the association in court and out of court,' and as Paragraph 26 read, 'the extent of its power may be limited by the laws of the association.'[94] 'The appointment of the governing body', under Paragraph 27, was to be 'effected by resolution at a meeting of the members'.[95] Such appointment could be impeached at any time, however, and the revocation could be 'limited by laws of the association to cases where an important reason for such revocation exists;

such important reasons are especially: grave violation of duty or inability to conduct the business in an orderly manner'.[96] The matter of conducting business found further legal definition in the Second Book on Laws of Obligations. According to Paragraph 662, 'by acceptance of a mandate the mandatory obliges himself to attend gratuitously to the business committed to him by the mandate'.[97] In any instance involving a change of laws, 'the assent of a majority of two thirds of the members present is requisite'. Paragraph 33 reads, 'for the adoption of a resolution which contains a change in the laws of the association'.[98] These measures and others enshrined constitutional principles at every level of German society. It was not only that Germans were just practicing democracy.[99] They were rather exercising their ever-increasing guaranteed legal rights, and they engaged in the practice of their constitution.

The interdependence of dynamic virtue and civic participation also found legal expression in the BGB. Majority, as it appeared in the BGB, also reflected exclusive liberal values of citizenship. One had to be fully *geschäftsfähig* to be capable of sovereign civic participation, a point made particularly clear in the BGB's delineation of incompetence in the General Part. 'The following persons', under Paragraph 6, 'may be adjudged incompetent':

(1) those, who by reason of mental illness or mental feebleness are incapable of attending to their affairs;
(2) those, who by reason of extravagance expose themselves or their families to want;
(3) those, who by reason of habitual drunkenness are incapable of attending to their affairs or expose themselves or their families to the danger of poverty or who endanger the safety of another.[100]

A determination of incompetence held serious ramification for a person's majority, as it resulted in a loss of *Geschäftsfähigkeit,* which was the legal basis for participation. 'A declaration of will', as Paragraph 105 read, 'is void when made by an incompetent person', and under Paragraph 114, those who had been 'declared incompetent by reason of mental feebleness, or wastefulness or drunkenness, or who have been placed under temporary guardianship under Paragraph 1909 have the same legal business capacity as minors who have completed their seventh year'.[101]

Rising constitutional transformation in the form of enacted *bürgerliche* laws meant that the ramifications of criticism against the Kaiser, particularly with regard to purported incompetence, was far more serious than it would have been at mid century. After 1900, what had been little more than perhaps attacks on his honour were potentially actionable charges. Grimm had written that a vote for a new monarch could be taken if the *'Herrschende untüchtig war'*.[102] After Wilhelm II's accession, there was a marked rise of research on the legal history of *Königsabsetzung,* and, if the earlier history of the Germanists is any guide, this certainly meant that the writing was on the wall.[103] Although dripping with what had become insincere flattery by 1896, in legal terms, Article 57 of the *Einführungsgesetz* also did not appear to offer immunity here: 'Respecting the Sovereigns and the members of the families of Sovereigns, as well as the members of the princely family of Hohenzollern, the provisions of the Civil Code are only so far applicable, as the House Constitutions or State laws do not provide others'.[104] It is not likely that there were provisions covering incompetence in age old *Familienverträge*, and, thus, the BGB provisions would have applied. What is more, there was precedent for removal of an executive from office due to incompetence. In the 1880s, Heilbronn's mayor, Paul Hegelmaier, 'had made himself the object of hatred because of his strong-arm tactics, and opposition to him fed into liberal critiques of Württemberg's anachronistic system of lifelong mayoral appointments'.[105] Although there was a public outcry, opponents had him removed from office by having the Württemberg medical board declare him insane.[106]

Conceivably, thus, the Kaiser was also hemmed in by the fact that Paragraph 6 may well have offered a means for his removal from office. Certainly, the criticism of the Kaiser at the height of the Daily Telegraph Affair was articulated in the language of legal incompetence at a time when Harden forcefully called for his abdication.[107] In the international press, he was seen as a 'distinctly unreliable member of the international brotherhood of princes'.[108] At home, indignation mounted and there was the feeling of 'inadequate rule at the top'.[109] Even Bülow, before the Reichstag, confirmed sentiments that 'the Kaiser had acted in a manner damaging to the interests of the country'.[110] It also did not help that Wilhelm II remained away, or when the spectacle of the chief of the Military Cabinet, Count Dietrich von Hülsen-Haeseler, dressed up as a ballerina and performed pirouettes to distract the Kaiser made it into the papers. The impression in Berlin was of an 'irresponsible ruler away enjoying himself', while Bülow had 'to keep the ship of state afloat'.[111]

Finally, in addition to the BGB's impact at the top of German society, the great mass of the population experienced this *Bürgerliche Revolution* in their homes, as a transformation of gender relations at the grass roots of society. The political meaning of legislated gender inequality is that it is also one of the significant indicators of the *Bürgerliche Revolution* in 1896. From its earliest beginning, the *bürgerliche* family was conceived as a metaphor for the state, and gender relations as a metaphor for power. 'The home', Gierke felt, 'is still the head of and articulation of the existing union, the organizational foundation of the social body, the strong pillar of the moral and economic order.'[112]

In the first instance, the BGB solidified separation of church and state by confirming the primacy of the state in the regulation of civil marriage. 'The expression *êwa,* shortened to *êa,* which in *alterthümliches Deutsch* meant law, union *(Bund),* association', according to Grimm, was 'not matrimony'.[113] In his *Materialien zum Familienrecht,* Planck specifically wrote that 'only the closing of [civil] marriage' secures the effects of marriage, 'not the *consummatio matrimonii*'.[114] The new law would effect both rights and obligations; in particular, the responsibility of the couple 'to be true to each other, to stand by each other's side, to live together and to strive for the attainment of marital duty'.[115] It would 'bind' the couple to the *'eheliche Lebens-gemeinschaft'*.[116] As a result of its moral nature, marriage had 'a legal side', which justified state regulation.[117]

> But marriage is also a legal relationship; it is the basis of the family and our entire social order. That is why the State has the right and the duty to lay down the legal rules for marriage. However, in this respect, it will at all times have to consider the moral and religious character of marriage, as it may not establish any legal rules which conflict with the moral nature of marriage; on the contrary, the legal rules should as far as possible serve to fulfill the moral obligations which are established by marriage. In any event, it is the State's duty to establish the legal rules.[118]

In the first instance, marriage formed the primary union of those who cannot live without each other. The beginning of the family was thus society's most basic social unit. As such, the private matter of marriage became a public matter of state. This is where civil law was not simply private law, but had public consequences. When marriage and the family became the microcosmic reflection of the social order, in reality it ceased to be totally private. The legal procedure surrounding the closing of marriage was public and oral. As Paragraph 1316 of the BGB read, a 'public summons should precede the celebration of marriage', and the vows had to be given orally and before a civil servant of the state.[119]

The *bürgerliche* family was conceived as an oppositional model to practices of the hereditary nobility as we have seen. These conceptions were also carried over into the BGB. Paragraph 1310 prohibited marriages between first, second or even third cousins as well as others. 'A marriage', Paragraph 1310 read, 'cannot be concluded between relatives by blood in the direct line, nor between brothers and sisters of full or half-blood, nor between relatives by marriage in the direct line ... [or] between persons one of whom has had sexual intercourse with parents, grandparents, or descendants of the other.'[120] Paragraphs 1589 and 1590 took this proscription even further, broadly defining relatives as 'persons of whom one is descended from the other are relatives by blood in the direct line', and 'persons who are not related by blood in the direct line, but are descended from one and the same third person, are related by blood in the collateral line'.[121] Paragraph 1590 specifically declared that '[r]elatives by blood of a spouse are related to the other spouse by marriage ... [and the] relationship by marriage continues even if the marriage whereby it was created has been dissolved'.[122]

The modern constraints on marriage between relatives derived in part from the political writings of Grimm and the Germanists. Under the ancient Germans, he wrote, marriages between 'close relatives *(nahe Verwandtschaft)* between parents, children and siblings', relatives by marriage and 'spiritual relatives' were forbidden.[123] The practice of marriage between relatives began with the nobility: '*Fürstliche Kinder* of tender ages *(zarteste Alter)* were engaged and married to each other', and he cited a myth regarding Elisabeth and Ludwig of Thüringia.[124] In his *Entwurf eines Familienrechts für das Deutsche Reich,* Planck justified the proscription of cousin marriage on chiefly moral grounds, but also on scientific grounds: 'Marriage between close relatives is forbidden [because]', he wrote 'the moral sense demands the maintenance of chastity in the family and, on physiological grounds, the advance of healthy fertilization and breeding between married persons, which is jeopardized in the unity of the blood.'[125] His comments also show how the growing influence of biological sciences, which quite often only sustained pre-existing *bürgerliche* conceptions of society.

As rigorously as the Germanists defined who was *Mündigsprechung,* women were identified with *Unmündigkeit.* According to the Germanist theory of civil society, women were released from their father's authority only to fall under the guardianship of their husbands. Grimm wrote that 'the wife fell under the power of the husband like the child under his father.'[126] This opinion was confirmed by Kraut, who, citing Grimm, wrote that the term *Mündigsprechung* was never 'feminine, but in all German dialects, only appears as masculine'.[127] He flatly declared that 'according to the codes of German laws, women only become free from *Altersvormundschaft* through marriage ... [but] naturally not in the sense of a *Mündigsprechung.*'[128] 'Yes', he wrote 'they never become *Mündig.*'[129]

The BGB actively disenfranchised German women in every way, reversing women's prior gains in the century of promise. 'The right to decide in all matters affecting the common conjugal life', under Paragraph 1354, belonged 'to the husband; he determines especially the place of abode and the dwelling'.[130] In a speech delivered to the Göttingen Women's Club, Planck justified Paragraph 1354 on the basis of the historical morality and tried to placate women with references to Christian principles: 'To conduct the community of married life', he said, 'it is necessary for one party to have the decisive vote, and the BGB takes up the opinion of Christian and German views of marriage, according to which the husband is head *(Haupt)* of the marriage'.[131]

Designed to support and reinforce the power of majority rule, marriage was seen as playing a vital role in the security of the constitution of the nation. This explains why Paragraph 1354 granted the husband sole decision-making authority and made him head of his wife and family. Conversely, the BGB bound women and their property to their husbands. Paragraph 1356, for example, required wives 'to work in the household and in the business of the husband, where such activity is customary according to the circumstances in which the couple lives'.[132] Reversing the nineteenth-century court standards, Paragraph 1362 annulled the right of a wife to file as a creditor in the case of her husband's bankruptcy and specifically made her property liable for his debts: 'It is presumed in favor of the creditors of the husband that all movables which are in the possession of one of the spouses or of both of the spouses belong to the husband.'[133]

The BGB awarded women what may only be characterized as paper rights. A classic example of this comes in the much celebrated *Schlüsselgewalt.* Paragraph 1356 continued, 'the wife is ... entitled to and bound to conduct the joint household.'[134] According to Paragraph 1357, 'the wife is entitled, within the sphere of her domestic activity, to manage the husband's affairs for him and to represent him,' and 'juristic acts which she enters into within such sphere or activity are deemed to be entered into in the husband's name, if it does not appear otherwise from the circumstances.'[135] While Grimm argued that the *Schlüssel* was the 'symbol of the power of the housewife *(hausfrauliche Gewalt)*', he emphasized that women were only the *Schlüsselträgerinnen* of their husbands.[136] *Hausfrauliche Gewalt* was not independently held, but was given by the husband, who could rescind it at any time by simply retrieving the keys.[137] Some years later, Gierke explained that wives 'did not represent the marital community, but rather acted only as "the representative of the husband",' who could limit or rescind the *Schlüsselgewalt* at any time.[138] When Planck turned his attention to the position of women within the marriage in his *Motives*, he opened by pointing out that other modern codes obliged women to do housework.[139] According to the German view and morality, 'it is not only her obligation, but her right to manage the household.'[140] 'The *Hauptberuf* of the wife', he declared 'relates to the inner life of the home and related matters.'[141] The *Motives* of the BGB editors came into force as law along with the Code in 1900. The final version of the BGB reflected Planck's influence, and Paragraph 1357 further declared that 'the husband may limit or exclude the right of the wife.'[142] The *Schlüsselgewalt* was not a right, but was rather a privilege that women enjoyed at the discretion of their husbands.

The clearest legislated expression of the exclusive male citizenship and majority rule came in the BGB's regulation of marital property relations. No other area of law as actively reinforced male dominion in public matters and disenfranchised German women as the BGB's statutory regime of marital property relations. The notorious Paragraph 1363 declared 'by the conclusion of a marriage the property of the wife becomes subject to the management and usufruct by the husband—contributed property includes also the property which the wife acquires during the marriage.'[143] This measure did not stand alone but its effects, as Gierke noted, came 'out of the elaborate joining of disparate elements into a complicated complex of norms'.[144] No one paragraph would have alerted German women that they would be disenfranchised after 1900; it is only by cross-referencing that this reality became clear.

A good example of this comes in the underlying gender distinction between contributed property and separate property. Paragraph 1365 appeared to leave women with independent property rights, declaring 'the management and usufruct by the husband does not extend to the separate property.'[145] Separate property is defined as the wife's property, while contributed property clearly belonged to the husband. Technically, separate property included personal effects, i.e. clothing, ornaments, etc. (Paragraph 1366), property acquired as a result of the wife's labor or separate business (Paragraph 1367), property specified in a marriage contract (Paragraph

1368) and inheritance (Paragraph 1369). In reality, this separate property did not exist for women in any significant form. These paragraphs did not take precedence over Paragraph 1362, for example, that 'presumed in favor of the creditors ... [that property] in possession of one of the spouses or both of the spouses belong to the husband'.[146] Under the title of 'Rights of Management and Usufruct', Paragraph 1373 declared that the husband was 'entitled to take possession of all things forming part of the contributed property'.[147] Under Paragraph 1376, the husband could 'without the consent of the wife ... dispose of money and other fungible things belonging to the wife'.[148] Planck's *Motives* set forth the intent of the law in clear terms. All the property of the wife, he wrote, was 'presumed to be contributed property', until the contrary can be shown.[149] The problem here is that 'showing the contrary' involved filing legal process, which required that one be fully *rechtsfähig,* one of many independent rights where women were severely limited as a result of Paragraph 1363 and the fact that they never obtained majority.

The direct link between the early Germanist writers and the BGB's family law comes in the scholarly writings and political consulting of Richard Schroeder. By 1874, when work on the first draft began, he was the leading scholar on the history of marital property relations in Germany. His volumes, titled *Geschichte des ehelichen Güterrechts* (1863 to 1874), remained the leading work into the twentieth century. A member of the new generation of Germanist scholars, Schroeder's inaugural dissertation, the first volume of *Geschichte,* was directed by Georg Beseler, and he received considerable counsel from the aging Jacob Grimm. It should not come as a surprise that the publications are dedicated to Grimm and his *theurer Lehrer,* Georg Beseler. Well known for his work, in 1874 Planck commissioned Schroeder as a consultant to the committee on family law. It is this interlocutory nature of legal scholarship and politics that allowed the new generation of German liberals, like Planck and Bennigsen, to wage their genteel insurgency on the ancient regime.

In his introduction, he wrote that his secondary sources for Germany include Karl Eichhorn's legal history, Grimm's *Rechtsalterthümer* and 'particularly the writings of Beseler, Gaupp, Kraut and Rive'.[150] At the same time, he relied on the more developed French law, noting that 'only the French, particularly Ginoulhiac, Koenigswarter, Laboulaye and Pardessus' had thoroughly examined the evolution of marital property relations.[151] Schroeder wanted 'to bring the confused and complicated property relations of German married couples into light and clarity'.[152] 'No other branch of German law', he wrote, 'has suffered so much under the particularism of our people.'[153] Yet despite this, there existed a 'curious harmony' that allows one to make out 'a complete system of common German marital property relations'.[154]

The underlying politics of liberal gender inequality pervaded *Geschichte.* The first volume opens with a familiar discussion of *Geschlechtsvormundschaft.* 'The governing position of women, the universal weakness of her sex and incapacity in legal matters [extending from her inability to bear arms],' Schroeder wrote, 'under German law, from the beginning left her under the guardianship of the stronger and more prudent men in the public life.'[155] In his analysis, he relied very heavily on Kraut's *Vormundschaft* as well as on Grimm and the French scholars. 'Every lawfully wedded wife falls under the guardianship of her husband. He is her *Haupt,* her *Herr* and master; he establishes his home and its law, and as she finds herself, her entire property is also under his guardianship power *(vormundschaftliche Gewalt),* everything is in his hand.'[156]

It is, however, through Schroeder's relationship with Planck that we are offered a clear and decisive example of how Germanist scholarship influenced legislation. By 1875, only a year after he was enlisted for Planck's committee, Schroeder made the leap from scholar to scholarly lobbyist for the BGB. In that year, he published the pamphlet *Das eheliche Güterrecht Deutschlands in Vergangenheit, Gegenwart und Zukunft* (1875), in which he not only offered a condensed version of the past, but suggested what form of marital property relations should be enacted under the BGB. He opened with the familiar attack on the independent control of property that contemporary Roman law allowed German women. 'It is known', he writes, 'that the marital property relations of the Romans moved in two contradictory legal extremes.'[157] Under Justinian's law as it was received in Germany, marriage was 'formless and free' with the 'absolute separation of property and independent property rights of the wife'.[158] The husband only controlled the wedding gift and, at the same time, was responsible for the burdens of the marriage. In contrast to Justinian's Code from the period of Roman decline, under the law of the Republic, the wife and her entire property stood under the 'hand of her husband'.[159] This latter system was the most similar to the ancient German order, where the wife and her entire property fell under the *Mundium* of her husband.[160] The essential difference he identified between the law of the Roman Republic and German law was the distinction between *Gütereinheit* and *Verwaltungsgemeinschaft.* Under the Roman system, the property of the wife actually became the property of the husband, whereas, under the German system, the wife's property remained vested in her person, but the husband retained management and usufruct rights 'for the good of the marriage'.[161]

As for the *zukünftige* aspect of Schroeder's analysis, it seems that Planck had a hand in shaping his final opinion and, after the publication of the first draft and the criticism that followed, Schroeder faced increasing pressure from Planck to provide scholarly legitimacy for the proposed law. In a 15 June 1875 letter to Planck, Schroeder did not suggest the reintroduction of the *Verwaltungsgemeinschaft,* and it appears that the pamphlet on *eheliches Güterrecht* was produced at Planck's direction. He wrote that 'the entire work, and hopefully to your satisfaction, should be in your hands by late August.'[162] While he did suggest the *Verwaltungsgemeinschaft* in the pamphlet, in his letter, he emphasized that *'ein Mittelweg'* should be taken. He also suggested the legislation of *Errungenschaftsgemeinschaft* and the *allgemeine Gütergemeinschaft* along with the *Verwaltungsgemeinschaft.* Moreover, he suggested that the existing right of couples to contract alternative arrangements should be permitted under the new law. In this way, he urged that the German people's longing for legal unity could be brought into existence in harmony with the history of the legitimate legal particularism of the German *Stämme.*[163]

By 1889, Schroeder was pressured into offering a different opinion. In a letter to Planck during the second commission, Schroeder wrote that he 'was earlier of the opinion that one should allow all three systems within certain geographical boundaries to remain in place, but I have been persuaded on the basis of national legislative politics for legal unity', to offer a different opinion.[164] With great reluctance and with a clear preference for the *allgemeine Gütergemeinschaft,* Schroeder concedes that either the *Verwaltungsgemeinschaft* or the *allgemeine Gütergemeinschaft* should be enacted as the statutory regime. It is doubtful whether Schroeder viewed references to *Mundium* and *Schlüsselgewalt* as anything other than a humorous means of discussing family life. On 23 November 1880, he wrote to Planck that he was unable to follow through on Planck's request because his wife was still in bed after the birth of a child and that, 'as the paterfamilias of a half dozen ... he had taken over the *Regiment der Schlüssel*'.[165] Nevertheless, in his commentaries on the BGB, Planck frequently cited Schroeder's *Geschichte* as scholarly justification for the reintroduction of an administrative community.

Paragraph 1363 reversed German women's progress, and its effect on their condition in society extended well beyond the private sphere of the family. No other paragraph more actively disenfranchised German women. Lack of full control over their property after marriage left them limited in their *Geschäftsfähigkeit,* and left them in a legal state of *defacto* incompetence. Only those who were fully *geschäftsfähig* could vote and serve as *Schöffen* and jurors in German society. As a result of the *beschränkte Geschäftsfähigkeit,* women were also *rechtsunfähig;* they no longer possessed the right to file process without the consent of their husbands. A 1901 article in *Das Recht,* titled "Die Stellung der Ehefrau im Civilprocess bei bestehender Verwaltungsgemeinschaft," is particularly enlightening in this regard. The article described the case of a woman who, in accord with her perceived right under the BGB, filed a civil complaint against her husband for the mismanagement and restitution of her property. The court found that the husband had mismanaged the wife's property and that her complaint was legitimate. However, the wife's complaint was thrown out on the technicality that she did not obtain her husband's consent before filing against him.[166]

Articles of Introduction

Little attention has been paid to the introductory laws that accompanied almost every major piece of legislation. These measures, however, were constitutional amendments in many respects. In the case of the *Einführungsgesetz* to the BGB, an indicator of this is that in contrast to the BGB, its paragraphs appear under the title 'article'. The content and constitutional significance of the *Einführungsgesetz* cannot be emphasized enough. The *Einführungsgesetz* installed the supremacy of the Reich over the state bodies. Unless specifically stated otherwise, the BGB became the precedent for all law in the empire after 1900. The articles of the *Einführungsgesetz* extended the Reich's reach well beyond the geographical limitations of competency provided under the Constitution. Alsace-Lorraine, which, under Article 5 of the Reich Constitution, had been the private domain of the Kaiser, was 'deemed to be a State within the meaning of the BGB and of the present Act'.[167] A good many of the imperial acts were either modified or repealed. Article 43 repealed the Act of 31 March 1873 relating to the legal relations of imperial officials, and Article 45 repealed portions of the Imperial Military Act of 2 May 1874.[168] Articles 48, 49 and 51 repealed the acts of 1881, 1887 and 1895, respectively, relating to the 'Care of Widows and Orphans' of imperial officers, army and navy persons, and persons serving in the imperial army or navy above the rank of sergeant-major.

The BGB, moreover, did not come into effect alone on 1 January 1900. Rather, several other legislative reforms that were designed to dismantle the monarchical state and geared to the BGB went into effect as well. A new Civil Procedure Ordinance (1898), the new Bankruptcy Ordinance (1898), the Law of Forced Sales and Executions (1897), and a new Commercial Code (1897) all went into effect on 1 January 1900. Other legislation was closely coordinated with the BGB, including the Ordinance on the *Grundbuch* and the Law on Arbitration (1898). It was, therefore, not just the BGB that went into effect on 1 January 1900, but an entirely reform legal regime of *bürgerliche* law.

The year 1896 marked a watershed in German history, because liberals achieved the legal revolution they had sought over the long course of the nineteenth century. With the Kaiser under *Der Hammer* of the law, many noble privileges undone, and women confined to the home, Germany turned the corner to a representative state. Following the path of legalism, liberals gradually restructured Germany into the *Gemeinwesen* they desired. The reform impulse that began at the academic level culminated in the enactment of the BGB. The BGB was given the highest regulatory position in private law, but through its *Einführungsgesetz,* it transformed public law also. There may well be no Madame de Guillotine in German history, but a Herr von Reichsgericht, seated in Leipzig, did emerge, and the old order was slowly declining behind a mass of *bürgerliche* law. It was this that made modern Germany's revolutionary moment.

Notes

1. Gottlieb Planck, 'Speech in Second Chamber of Hanover Landtag', in Ferdinand Frensdorff, *Gottlieb Planck: Deutscher Jurist und Politiker* (1914), p. 141.
2. Chung Hui Wang (trans.), *The German Civil Code* (1907).
3. Otto Pflanze, *Bismarck and the Development of Germany: The Period of Consolidation 1871–1880,* vol. 2 (1990), p. 153.
4. Adolf Kiepert, *Rudolf von Bennigsen: Rückblick auf das Leben eines Parlamentariers* (1903); Hermann Oncken, *Rudolf von Bennigsen: Ein deutscher liberaler*

Politiker nach seinen Briefen und hinterlassenen Papieren (1910); and Dietrich Sandberger, *Die Ministerkandidatur Bennigsens* (1929).

5. Franz Wieacker, *A History of Private Law in Europe (with Particular Reference to Germany),* Tony Weir (trans.) (1995), p. 372 fn.
6. Frensdorff, *Gottlieb Planck,* pp. 1–39.
7. Ibid., pp. 45–6.
8. Wilhelm Kraut, *Die Vormundschaft nach den Grundsätzen des deutschen Rechts,* 3 vols (1835–1859).
9. Ute Frevert, 'Bourgeois Honor: Middle-class Duellists in Germany from the Late Eighteenth to the Early Twentieth Century', in David Blackbourn and Richard Evans (eds), *The German Bourgeoisie: Essays on the Social History of the German Middle Class from the Late Eighteenth to the Early Twentieth Century* (1991), p. 270.
10. Ibid.
11. Frensdorff, *Gottlieb Planck,* pp. 46–8.
12. Ibid., p. 81.
13. Ibid.
14. Ibid.
15. Ibid.
16. Lasker to Bismarck (15 August 1870), cited in Richard Dill, 'Der Parlamentarier Eduard Lasker und die parlamentarische Stilentwicklung der Jahre 1867–1884: Ein Beitrag zur Geistesgeschichte des politischen Stils in Deutschland', PhD thesis, Erlangen (1956), p. 59.
17. Gneist, in *Verhandlungen des Neuesten Deutschen Juristentages* (1871), cited in Michael John, *Politics and the Law in Late Nineteenth Century Germany: The Origins of the Civil Code* (1989), p. 43.
18. Dill, *Eduard Lasker,* p. 105; and Veit Valentin, 'Bismarck and Lasker', *Journal of Central European History* (Jan. 1944), pp. 41–64.
19. Frensdorff, *Gottlieb Planck,* p. 116.
20. Ibid., p. 134.
21. Ibid.
22. Ibid., p. 137.
23. Ibid.
24. Ibid., p. 141.
25. Werner Schubert, *Entstehung und Quellen der Civilprozessordnung von 1877,* vol. 1, bk. 1 (1987), p. 36.
26. John, *Politics and the Law,* p. 44.
27. Pflanze, *Bismarck,* p. 153.
28. Ibid.
29. Ibid., p. 140.
30. Ibid.
31. Ibid., p. 144.

32. Ibid., p. 156.
33. Ibid.
34. Heinrich Triepel, *Die Kompetenzen des Bundesstaats und die geschriebene Verfassung* (1908); Paul Laband, *Staatsrecht* (1906); and Paul Laband, 'Die geschichtliche Entwicklung der Reichsverfassung seit der Reichsgründung', *Jahrbuch des öffentlichen Rechts,* 1 (1907), pp. 1–46.
35. Pflanze, *Bismarck,* pp. 149–50.
36. Georg Jellinek, *Verfassungsänderung und Verfassungswandlung* (1906), in Arthur Jacobson and Bernhard Schlink (eds), *Weimar: A Jurisprudence of Crisis* (2000), p. 54.
37. 'The 1871 Constitution of the German Empire', in Elmar Hucko (ed.), *The Democratic Tradition: Four German Constitutions* (1987).
38. Ernst Huber, *Deutsche Verfassungsgeschichte seit 1789: Bismarck und das Reich,* vol. 3, 3rd ed. (1988), p. 773.
39. Ibid., p. 774.
40. Ibid.
41. '1871 Constitution'.
42. Laband, *Staatsrecht,* cited in Huber, *Deutsche Verfassungsgeschichte,* vol. 3, p. 814.
43. Cited in Giles MacDonogh, *The Last Kaiser: William the Impetuous* (2000), p. 199.
44. MacDonogh, *Last Kaiser,* p. 208.
45. Ibid., pp. 197–8.
46. Ibid.
47. Ibid., pp. 186 and 224.
48. Ibid., pp. 186–8 and 224–5.
49. Benjamin Hett, 'The "Captain of Köpenick" and the Transformation of German Criminal Justice 1891–1914', *Central European History,* 36/1 (2003), p. 6.
50. Ibid.
51. Ibid., p. 9.
52. Kenneth Ledford, 'Lawyers, Liberalism and Procedure: The German Imperial Justice Laws of 1877–79', *Central European History,* 26 (1993); and Hett, "Captain of Köpenick".
53. Huber, *Deutsche Verfassungsgeschichte,* vol. 3, p. 841.
54. For this paragraph I am indebted to the important work of Hett, "Captain of Köpenick", pp. 10–15.
55. MacDonogh, *Last Kaiser,* p. 206.
56. Roderick McLean, 'Kaiser Wilhelm II and His Hessian Cousins: Intra-state Relations in the German Empire and International Dynastic Politics 1890–1918', *German History,* 19/1 (2001), pp. 40–1.
57. Ibid.
58. Ibid.

59. Ibid.
60. Wilhelm II to Grand Duke Ernst Ludwig (11 November 1901), cited in ibid., p. 42.
61. James Retallack, 'Something Magical in the Name of Prussia: British Perceptions of German Nation Building in the 1860s', in Ronald Speirs and John Breuilly (eds), *Germany's Two Unifications: Anticipations, Experiences, Responses* (2005), p. 141.
62. Hannah Pakula, *An Uncommon Woman: The Empress Frederick, Daughter of Queen Victoria, Wife of the Crown Prince of Prussia, Mother of Kaiser Wilhelm* (1995), and Patricia Kollander, *Frederick III: Germany's Liberal Emperor* (1995).
63. McLean, 'Kaiser Wilhelm II', p. 49.
64. Prince Ludwig, cited in MacDonogh, *Last Kaiser,* p. 222.
65. McLean, 'Kaiser Wilhelm II', p. 34.
66. MacDonogh, *Last Kaiser,* pp. 205 and 200.
67. Ibid., p. 53.
68. Ibid., pp. 228–9.
69. Ibid.
70. Ibid.
71. Bernd Sösemann, 'Hollow-sounding Jubilees: Forms and Effects of Public Self-display in Wilhelmine Germany', in Annika Mombauer and Wilhelm Deist (eds), *The Kaiser: New Research on Wilhelm II's Role in Imperial Germany* (2003).
72. McLean, 'Kaiser Wilhelm II'.
73. Isabel Hull, 'Military Culture, Wilhelm II, and the End of the Monarchy in the First World War', in Mombauer and Deist (eds), *The Kaiser,* p. 245.
74. James Harris, *A Study in the Theory and Practice of German Liberalism: Eduard Lasker, 1829–1884* (1984), p. 17.
75. John, *Politics and the Law*; Harris, *Study in German Liberalism*; and Frensdorff, *Gottlieb Planck.*
76. Harris, *Study in German Liberalism,* p. 45; Michael John, 'The Peculiarities of the German State: Bourgeois Law and Society in the Imperial Era', *Past and Present,* 119 (1988), pp. 105–31; and Jürgen Kocka (ed.), *Bürgertum im 19. Jahrhundert: Deutschland im europäischen Vergleich* (1988), pp. 340–405; and Blackbourn and Evans, *German Bourgeoisie.* On the importance of legal training for civil servants see W. Bleek, *Von der Kameralausbildung zum Juristenprivileg: Studium, Prüfung and Ausbildung der höheren Beamten des allgemeinen Verwaltungsdienstes in Deutschland im 18. und 19. Jahrhundert* (1972).
77. John, *Politics and the Law,* p. 206.
78. Frensdorff, *Gottlieb Planck,* p. 308.
79. Wang, *German Civil Code.*
80. Michael Stolleis, *Public Law in Germany, 1800–1914* (2001), p. 347.

81. Otto Gierke, 'Wünsche hervorragender Juristen für das neue Jahrhundert', *Das Recht* (25 January 1900).
82. Ibid.
83. Wang, *German Civil Code.*
84. Ibid.
85. For more see Lynn Hunt, *The Family Romance of the French Revolution* (1992).
86. Kraut, *Vormundschaft,* vol. 2, p. 168.
87. Ibid., p. 169.
88. Wang, *German Civil Code.*
89. Jacob Grimm, *Deutsche Rechtsalterthümer* (1828), p. 339.
90. Kraut, *Vormundschaft,* vol. 1, pp. 63–97.
91. Kraut, *Vormundschaft,* vol. 2, p. 175.
92. Stolleis, *Public Law in Germany,* pp. 344–5.
93. Ibid.
94. Wang, *German Civil Code.*
95. Ibid.
96. Ibid.
97. Ibid.
98. Ibid.
99. Margaret Anderson, *Practicing Democracy: Elections and Political Culture in Imperial Germany* (2000).
100. Wang, *German Civil Code.*
101. Ibid.
102. Grimm, *Deutsche Rechtsalterthümer,* pp. 318–19.
103. Paul Scheffer-Boichorst, *Kleinere Forschungen zur Geschichte des Mittelalters 6: Über den Plan einer Thronumwälzung in den Jahren 1254 und 1255* (1885); Victor Domeier, *Zur Absetzung Adolfs von Nassau* (1887); Heinrich Finke, *Ein Gutachten Zabarellas über die Absetzung des römischen Königs Wenzel* (1890); and Wilhelm Eberhard, *Ludwig III. Kurfürst von der Pfalz und das Reich, 1410–1427* (1896). See the bibliography in Ernst Schubert, *Königsabsetzung im deutschen Mittelalter: Eine Studie zum Werden der Reichsverfassung* (2005), pp. 563–91.
104. Wang, *German Civil Code.*
105. Ann Goldberg, 'A Reinvented Public: Lunatics' Rights and Bourgeois Populism in the Kaiserreich', *German History,* 21/2 (2003), p. 172.
106. Ibid.
107. Sösemann, 'Hollow-sounding Jubilees', p. 59.
108. Terence Cole, 'The *Daily Telegraph* Affair and Its Aftermath: The Kaiser, Bülow and the Reichstag 1908–1909', in J. Röhl and N. Sombert (eds), *Kaiser Wilhelm II: New Interpretations* (1982), p. 254.
109. Ibid.

110. Ibid., p. 255.
111. Ibid., pp. 255–6.
112. Otto Gierke, *Der Entwurf eines bürgerlichen Gesetzbuchs und das deutsche Recht* (1889), p. 394.
113. Grimm, *Deutsche Rechtsalterthümer,* p. 578.
114. Planck, in Werner Schubert (ed.), *Die Vorlagen der Redaktoren für die erste Kommission zur Ausarbeitung des Entwurfs eines Bürgerlichen Gesetzbuches: Die Vorentwürfe der Redaktoren zum ... und Wirkungen der Ehe, Eheverträge* (1983), p. 250.
115. Ibid.
116. Ibid.
117. Ibid.
118. Gottlieb Planck, *Die rechtliche Stellung der Frau nach dem Bürgerlichen Gesetzbuch* (1899), p. 5.
119. Wang, *German Civil Code.*
120. Ibid.
121. Ibid.
122. Ibid.
123. Grimm, *Deutsche Rechtsalterthümer,* pp. 602–3.
124. Ibid.
125. Gottlieb Planck, *Begründung des Entwurfs eines Familienrechts für das Deutsche Reich* (1880), in Schubert (ed.), *Vorlagen der Redaktoren,* p. 100.
126. Grimm, *Deutsche Rechtsalterthümer,* p. 598.
127. Kraut, *Vormundschaft,* vol. 1, p. 6.
128. Kraut, *Vormundschaft,* vol. 2, p. 179.
129. Ibid.
130. Wang, *German Civil Code.*
131. Planck, *Rechtliche Stellung der Frau,* p. 11.
132. Wang, *German Civil Code.*
133. Ibid.
134. Ibid.
135. Ibid.
136. Grimm, *Deutsche Rechtsalterthümer,* p. 214.
137. Ibid.
138. Gierke, *Entwurf,* p. 405.
139. Planck, in Schubert (ed.), *Vorlagen der Redaktoren,* p. 260.
140. Ibid.
141. Ibid.
142. Wang, *German Civil Code.*
143. Ibid.
144. Gierke, *Entwurf,* p. 394.
145. Wang, *German Civil Code.*

146. Ibid.
147. Ibid.
148. Ibid.
149. Planck, in Schubert (ed.), *Vorlagen der Redaktoren,* p. 250.
150. Richard Schroeder, *Geschichte des ehelichen Güterrechts in Deutschland: Die Zeit der Volksrechte,* pt. 1 (1863), p. xi.
151. Ibid.
152. Ibid., p. vi.
153. Ibid.
154. Ibid.
155. Ibid., p. 1.
156. Ibid., p. 126.
157. Ibid.
158. Ibid.
159. Ibid.
160. Ibid., p. 4.
161. Ibid., pp. 4–5.
162. Schroeder to Planck (15 June 1875), in Gottlieb Planck records at the Niedersächsische Bibliothek in Göttingen.
163. Richard Schroeder, *Das eheliche Güterrecht Deutschlands in Vergangenheit, Gegenwart und Zukunft* (1875).
164. Undated letter from Schroeder to Planck (posted 1889), in Gottlieb Planck records at the Niedersächsische Bibliothek in Göttingen.
165. Schroeder to Planck (23 November 1880), in Gottlieb Planck records at the Niedersächsische Bibliothek in Göttingen.
166. 'Die Stellung der Ehefrau im Civilprozess bei bestehender Vewaltungsgemeinschaft', *Das Recht* (10 February 1901).
167. Wang, *German Civil Code.*
168. Ibid.

–7–

Discontent in the *Bürgerliche* Society 1900–1933
Exclusion and Popular Resentment

> It hardly seems necessary to point out how many passages in ancient writings, how many phenomena of matriarchal cultures were illuminated ... by Tacitus' remarks about the far-reaching implications of sisterhood as the basis of the Germanic family.[1]
>
> —Johann Bachofen, *Das Mutterrecht,* 1861

In the January 1900 issue of *Das Recht,* celebrating the BGB, Heinrich Dernberg was quoted encouraging Germans to 'hold on to the continuity of the civil law' because 'under its umbrella and protection, the German people will be liberated to grow free and powerful, effecting social progress'.[2] 'Never fading youth', as Gierke extolled, 'in these changing times, our people will only be successful in winning cultural renewal and inner peace again and again if we hold true to our own laws'. 'With the achievement of legal unity', he was quoted, 'we can abandon the last century, because the new law—a truly German *Volksrecht*—will stand up to the great task of the dawning century.'[3] No comments were more telling of the BGB's political implications, however, than those that appeared in the *Deutsche Juristen-Zeitung* on 1 January 1900: 'On this New Year's Eve, Germany's old laws depart from our lives and the new *Bürgerliches Gesetzbuch* comes into its rule. *Le roi est mort, vive le roi!* Celebrating we will welcome the new sovereign of our legal life'.[4] In the popular press, a New Year's Eve ball held by the Munich Bar Association in honor of the BGB's introduction was covered by the *Münchener Neueste Nachrichten.*[5] 'The great day on which German legal unification shall take place is standing before the door,' the *Hannoverische Rundschau* reported enthusiastically, and 'now we will possess a unified German Civil Code ... written in the German language for the whole German nation.'[6] 'By means of legal unity', read the *Hamburger Nachrichten,* 'the work of the German people for political unification has found its essential completion.'[7]

However much these voices of jubilation dominated the national press coverage, they did not echo the sentiments of the many Germans who found themselves facing discrimination and exclusion under the new majority rule constitution of the Deutsche Reich, namely women, workers, gays and the 'mad'. As even Planck was aware, most women viewed the BGB as 'a system of tyrannical male despotism over women'.[8] August Bebel saw it as the '*Götterdämmerung* of the bourgeois world', and following his leadership Social Democrats voted unanimously against the BGB's enactment.[9] In 1887 the *Wissenschaftlich-humanitäre Kommittee* was founded in Berlin to agitate for repeal of Paragraph 175 of the *Strafgesetzbuch,* under which 'unnatural fornication' was punished by imprisonment and/or the loss of competence.[10] By 1909, the *Bund für Irrenrecht und Irrenfürsorge* formed and was 'largely led by the "mad"' in response to the skyrocketing rates of declarations of incompetence.[11]

The lofty celebration that was expressed in the popular press was soon tempered by these voices, which increasingly demanded the redistribution of power and property in the years following 1900. Once the legislated realities of the *Bürgerliche Revolution* were etched in black and white, it fueled the political fires that were simmering on the Left and Right. These groups began to offer an alternative basis of sociopolitical organization and the distribution of power in the first republic. This chapter examines the rise of *gegenpolitische* sentiments, and how the redefinition of gender operated as a metaphor in the agitation against legislated discrimination and demands for equal personality before the law and within the nation. Bachofen's comments which open this chapter aimed at a radical reorganization by displacing the Germanist assumptions of original patriarchy and replacing it with original matriarchy. In the context of the German legal world and the history of German constitutional transformation, Bachofen's insistence on 'Tacitus' remarks about the far-reaching implications of sisterhood as the basis of the Germanic family' housed radical political implications.

In this chapter, I also hope to offer a sense of how the legal revolution reached into the lives of ordinary Germans. In addition to the reaction against the consolidation of majority rule that was ushered in by the legislated *Bürgerliche Revolution,* the BGB produced widespread alienation at the grassroots of German society. For those that the BGB excluded from full participation, New Year's 1900 was not a day for celebration; the latest transformation of the German constitution and the new sovereign of the legal life were altogether unwelcome. For this reason, the BGB not only marked the *Bürgerliche Revolution* and the exclusive society it inaugurated, but the rise of counter-revolutionary action from above and below. The BGB etched in stone the supremacy of industrial interest over all others and exclusive liberal notions of dynamic virtue as a prerequisite for civic participation. To achieve the sociopolitical values of the revolution, the BGB jammed exclusive liberalism down the throats of ordinary Germans and, more than any other element, this reality was revealed after its introduction. In particular, family law touched every German household, sparking bitter resentment and discontent across gender and class lines. Paragraph 6 of the General Part, effectively, provided a convenient means to get rid of agitators who resisted toeing the line on the new order. While the political Left was able to fill its ranks with the discontented, in reality, the Weimar Constitution failed to relieve the stresses of German society at the grassroots because it left the BGB intact, a reality which, when combined with economic downturn, left German society ripe for Nazism, in a discontented society where the law itself could be made a scapegoat for society's ills.

The Politics of Matriarchy

The 'axial age' of anthropological science involved what Thomas Trautman called the 'invention of kinship'.[12] Even more important than the publication of Darwin's *Origin of the Species* (1859) and *Descent of Man* (1871) was the discovery of human fossils in the 1860s. This discovery expanded time, freeing human history from biblical chronology and the tutelage of the classics.[13] The expansion of time ushered in by the discovery of fossils allowed antiquarian-minded legal scholars to locate immemorial prescriptive rights in epochs even more remote than the ancient German free epoch. Many of the leading supporters of anthropology were also legal scholars, including Johann Bachofen, Lewis Morgan, Henry Sumner Maine and John McLennan. The emerging anthropological community defined itself around the debate over patriarchal theory and the desire to develop alternatives. 'The issue was far from antiquarian', as was the case with Germanist scholarship, and 'it had political resonance and a very direct bearing upon relations between the sexes'.[14]

Freed from the biblical timetable, the *Rechtsalterthumswissenschaftler* and Savigny student, Johann Jakob Bachofen (1815–1887), precipitated another split in the German legal world with the publication of *Das Mutterrecht* in 1861. Although his research was dismissed almost immediately by the dominant historical school of law, *Das Mutterrecht* was revived and promptly put to social-democratic ends in the face of the increasing consolidation of majority rule. Despite Bachofen's major influence on figures like Lewis Morgan, Friedrich Engels and August Bebel, he has remained an obscure figure, and his influence overlooked by historians.[15] Nevertheless, he was one of the most controversial and influential scholars between 1861 and 1887. Eyeing the social and class strife of the 1840s, he broke with the exclusively masculine conception of participation in Grimm's *Rechtsalterthümer.* In his *Confessions,* he wrote that he went to Rome in 1848 'a republican who wished to hear no more of the seven kings, as an unbeliever who respected no tradition, as an adventurer bent on entrusting his ship to the high seas instead of steering cautiously along the shore and keeping the solid ground in sight'.[16] After witnessing the fall of Rossi and the 'disorder of all sorts', however, 'all this I left behind in Italy'.[17]

Das Mutterecht undermined the exclusive conception of participation that was at the foundation of political thought in Mittermaier, Eichhorn and Grimm's systems, amongst others, by arguing that the original civilization of mankind in the family and state was matriarchal. 'In the times antedating classical antiquity where an older world of ideas totally different from those with which we are familiar' existed, the organization of the family was characterized by gynaecocracy, a society ruled by women.[18] The interdependency of gender, the family and the state, as well as the need to redevelop their origins and relationships, were the essence of Bachofen's interest in gynaecocracy. In seeking to develop a new basis of *ius civile* for transformation to a new *civitas,* Bachofen set out to locate prescriptive social-democratic rights in an immemorial primordial epoch, in effect, an epoch prior to that which served as the historical foundation for majority rule. Ancient myth, tradition and mortuary symbolism formed the data for a universal law of mankind—a new *ius gentium.*

> Multiform and shifting in its outward manifestation, myth nevertheless follows fixed laws, and can provide as definite and secure results as any other source of historical knowledge. Product of a cultural period in which life had not yet broken away from the harmony of nature, it shares with nature that unconscious lawfulness which is always lacking in the works of free reflection.[19]

Myth, which replaced fairy tales, housed remnants of law, but from a primordial rather than an ancient epoch. Myth, like the remnants of law it contained, showed the underlying system; 'everywhere there is system, everywhere cohesion, in every detail the expression of a great fundamental law.'[20] In this primoridial epoch, Bachofen was free to construct an immemorial alternative anthropology of social and political organization. It was his profoundest conviction that 'without a return to ancient simplicity and health of soul, one cannot gain the merest intimation of the greatness of those ancient times and their thinking, of those days when the human race had not yet, as it has today, departed from its harmony with creation and the transcendent creator.'[21] Whereas the Germanists were interested to vest basic rights in a period predating the first king, in opposition to this, Bachofen developed a theory of universal prescriptive social-democratic rights by locating their origins in a primordial age. 'I see more and more that one law governs all things', he wrote, 'and that primordial man planned and regulated his earthly life with the regularity, as it were, of animal instinct'.[22]

This primordial epoch, according to Bachofen, was marked by three stages of development and struggles between the sexes. The best example of this comes in his discussion of the ancient Lycians and the gradual transformation from the legal organization of the *ius naturale* to a *ius civile.* The most elementary difference between the two systems was the change of power between the sexes. *Ius naturale* existed first in a pure stage of 'undifferentiated sexual union', but in its later development was characterized by exclusive marriage and matriarchy.[23] This later stage may be defined as a *ius gentium.* It was followed by the *ius civile,* where the juridical formulation of marriage was derived from patriarchy. Under the *ius gentium,* the essential factors of the material *ius naturale* were retained; the predominance of the material principle, matriarchal lineage and the exclusive inheritance rights of daughters. In contrast, *ius civile* was defined by patriarchal family authority derived from masculine principles; it represented the stage when women and their property fell under the authority of men.[24] *Ius civile,* Bachofen wrote, 'found its purest expression amongst the Romans [i.e. the Republic]. No other people so fully developed the idea of *potestas* (authority) over women and children; and consequently no other people so consciously pursued the corresponding idea of imperium.'[25]

Transition from one stage to the next was the result of primordial struggles between the sexes. The lowest stage was characterized by hetaeric sexuality and instability in the male line of descent. 'Man's sexual life', Bachofen explained, was 'promiscuous and public.'[26] To symbolize his sexual uniting with a woman, man 'thrust his staff in the earth, an image of his own act'.[27] Women, 'wearied by continuous cohabitation' and the male tyranny it represented, revolted against men.[28] 'The staff', accordingly was 'wrenched from the male and the woman became his master.'[29] Marriage and matriarchy resulted from the revolt of women against unregulated sex and gave the mother domination over the family and state.[30]

The construction of the original basis of heterosexual relations should be understood by its oppositional political value. Sex-labor exploitation, in Bachofen's analysis, was interpreted as the earliest form of labor, a labor and exploitation which had its roots in the oldest profession. Here Bachofen cited the Greek physician, Sextus Empiricus, from the third century on the meaning of the *dos* (dowry). Sextus' observation of sex exploitation as the origin of the *dos* (dowry), was supported by Plautus' mythical address to an Etruscan woman: 'You earn your dowry with your body'.[31] In Bachofen, accordingly, the dowry was originally a payment for the labor of sex, by which women earned their keep.

This sex-labor exploitation precipitated a primordial struggle between the sexes. By means of revolution, according to Bachofen, women raised primordial mankind to a higher stage of development by instituting marriage and founding the family. The beginning of marriage was linked to women's higher moral consciousness and revolt against sex-labor exploitation by men. 'The very word matrimony or mother-marriage', Bachofen argued, 'was based on the fundamental idea of mother right; one said *matrimonium,* not *patrimonium* (father-marriage)'.[32] '*Familia*', he continued, related 'at first only to the mother'.[33] Once conquered by women, men were forced to submit to monogamous sexual relationships in the confines of marriage. 'Matriarchy [was] necessary to the education of mankind and particularly of men', and the rigorous law of marriage was upheld by women who checked intemperate manhood.[34] 'It is the woman's vocation', Bachofen argued, 'to tame man's primordial strength and to guide it into benign channels.'[35]

The final primordial stage, according to Bachofen, was characterized by amazonianism, an unnatural exaggeration of matriarchy that resulted in another struggle between the sexes.[36] As the story went, the primordial women of Lemnos murdered all the males and resorted to an amazonian life when their men begin cohabiting and marrying Thracian girls they captured in war. Soon bands of warlike maidens poured victoriously across Asia Minor, Greece, Italy and Gaul. 'The Amazons', Bachofen wrote, 'renounced marriage and founded a society which not only played an outstanding part in the history of our race through the devastation which it brought on the world, but also contributed more than anything else to the downfall of the matriarchate.'[37] This extreme militarism of amazonianism compelled men to band together and defeat what had become female tyranny.[38]

Although Bachofen's theory of law clearly challenged the exclusive liberalism of the historical school of law, including the work of the Germanists, he nevertheless was not able to escape the grip of classical political thought. He essentially adopted into his own theory the Aristotelian model of dichotomous formations of virtue and vice, healthy and sick *polis* (monarchy vs. tyranny, aristocracy vs. oligarchy, democracy vs. mob rule) along with the Polybian ideal of the cycle of constitutions (monarchy, tyranny, aristocracy, oligarchy, democracy, mob rule). Bachofen delineated a cycle of constitutions passing from hetaerism to male heterosexual promiscuity to marriage and family to amazonianism to patriarchy and then to articulation. The idea was to formulate a legal theory for social democracy that would be capable of standing in opposition to exclusive liberalism. Here again there was the idea, however, that unless prevented society would pass through each of these cycles returning from articulation of hetaerism. Bachofen's system also offered a vision of a representative system, but on a social democratic basis. Accordingly, he theorized that it was first women's defeat of the male tyranny of sex-labor exploitation, and then men's defeat of the female tyranny of amazonianism, that led mankind into the peace of exclusive marriage.[39] Marriage, thus, appears as a metaphor of sorts for a secure mixed constitution on a democratic basis.

When Bachofen's sex narratives are understood as an expression of political theory, their social-democratic colourings become clear. The sex-labor exploitation of primordial women was a metaphor for the exploitation of labor that was emerging rapidly with the capitalist economy in mid-century Central Europe. The narrative of gender evolution revealed a society passing through a kind of dialectical development. Bachofen traced this evolution from hataerian tyranny to the revolt of women, which led to the concord of marriage and matriarchy. Above all else this should be seen as a metaphor for the regulation of capital and industry. Yet, it also housed a warning in showing that continuing male promiscuity in the gynaecocracy resulted in the absolute exclusion in amazonianism, which in turn caused the revolt of men and led to patriarchal marriage under the *ius civile.* The dialectical evolutionary element was contained in these shifts between balanced form and degeneration that led to corruption of the form.

In his analysis of the role of women and religion, Bachofen identified women as the bearers of the requisite virtue for civic participation, temperance (education), valor, prudence and justice. Aware of the broad gulf between his views and the 'current theories', he urged that 'there is only one mighty lever of all civilization and that is religion.'[40] His own decadent age, he felt, was in need of rejuvenation, and for this he looked to the simplicity of the primordial as well as the celestial laws that governed all mankind. Religion was woman's great *Otium,* which led her to the *negotium;* 'at all times woman has exerted a great influence on men and on education and culture of nations through her inclination toward the supernatural and divine, the irrational and miraculous'.[41] 'Prophecy began with women', and women were the great 'keeper[s] of religion'. Although not the preferred method of resolution, women were capable even of military valor, or swinging of the spear. 'Women played the most active part in the propagation of most religions,' and as Bachofen wrote, 'sometimes engaging in active warfare' to preserve religion.[42]

Nevertheless, even in Bachofen we find confirmation of the German idea of law as a means to political transformation and a continuing emphasis of nonviolent means. Female temperance emerged as the avenue to prudent *reformatio* and exercise of justice. 'Endowed with such [religious] powers, the weaker sex can take up the struggle with the stronger and emerge triumphant,' he wrote.[43] 'To man's superior physical strength woman opposes the mighty influence of her religious consecration,' and as a result, 'she counters violence with peace, enmity with conciliation, hatred with love; and thus she guides the wild, lawless existence of the earliest period toward a milder, friendlier culture, in whose center she sits enthroned as the embodiment of the higher principle, as the manifestation of the divine commandment.'[44] 'Herein', Bachofen argued, 'lies the magic power of the feminine figure, which disarms the wildest passions, parts battle lines, making woman the sacrosanct prophetess and judge, and in all things gives her will the prestige of supreme law.'[45]

Having established the requisite dynamic virtue in women, Bachofen identified 'the civil primacy of womanhood' in pre-Hellenistic culture.[46] Accordingly, 'the Lycians, Herodotus reports, did not name their children after their fathers like the Hellenes, but exclusively after their mothers; in their genealogical records they dealt entirely with the maternal line, and the status of children was defined solely in accordance with that of the mother.'[47] 'Only the daughters possessed the right to inherit,' he wrote, and this custom among the Lycians had its 'parallel in the obligation of [daughters in Egypt] alone to provide for aged parents'.[48] Primordial conditions were the inverse of patriarchy; in Cantabri, 'the sisters provided their brothers with dowries.'[49] 'The prestige of womanhood among these peoples', Lycinians, Egyptians, Locrians, Leleges, Carians, Aetolians, Pelasgians, Caucones, Arcadians, Epeisians, Minyae and Teleboeans, 'was a source of astonishment to the ancients, and gives them all, regardless of individual colouration, a character of archaic sublimity that stands in striking contrast to Hellenic culture.'[50] Bachofen then turned his attention the lost poems of Hesiod, which dealt with the mythical and legendary genealogy of the Greek peoples, and the *Catalogues* support his argument. 'Here' there could be discerned 'the basic ideal form which sprang the genealogical system ... the unions of immortal mothers wedded to mortal fathers, the emphasis on maternal property and the name of the maternal line, the closeness of maternal kinship, which gave rise to the term 'mother country', the appellation *'Mutterland'*.[51]

This *ius gentium,* moreover, was not confined to Mediterranean peoples. On the contrary, Bachofen argued that 'all these traits join to form a single picture and lead to the conclusion that mother right is not confined to any particular people but marks a cultural stage.'[52] It was universal; the basis of *ius genitium.* Accordingly, matriarchy represented the *Ausgangspunkt* of the Germanic family structure as well. 'The significance of sisterhood among the Germanic people' Bachofen wrote 'is disclosed by an observation of Tacitus, and a corresponding statement from Plutarch about Roman customs proves that this is no accidental local notion, but a consistent and fundamental idea.'[53]

> It hardly seems necessary to point out how many passages in ancient writings, how many phenomena of matriarchal cultures, were illuminated and made available for this work by Tacitus' remarks about the far-reaching implications of sisterhood as the basis of the Germanic family. The greater love for the sister leads us into one of the noblest aspects of matriarchal culture.[54]

Once dynamic virtue was located in the symbol of the feminine, Bachofen was free to describe an alternative society based on matriarchal principles. Whereas the 'paternal principle' was inherently restrictive and implied limitation of definite groups, the 'maternal principle' was universal and 'like the life of nature itself, knows no barriers'.[55] 'Every woman's womb, the mortal image of the earth mother Demeter', he wrote, 'will give brothers and sisters to the children of every other woman; the homeland will know only brothers and sisters until the day when the development of the paternal system dissolves the undifferentiated unity of the mass and introduces a principle of articulation.'[56] In matriarchal society, the 'universal freedom and equality' of the people was evident in their 'aversion to restrictions of all sorts'.[57] Law was 'rooted [in] the admirable sense of kinship and fellow feeling which knows no barriers or dividing lines and embraces all members of a nation alike'.[58] 'Hence', Bachofen wrote on the distribution of wealth, 'the equal right of all to the sea, the seashore, the air; and the *communis omnium possessio* (common property) may be traced back to the *ius naturale.*'[59] These ideas and principles found their expression in the concept of *'Mutterland'*.[60] Published in 1861, the year Savigny passed on, *Das Mutterrecht* was none other than a call for the study of the *mutterländisches Recht* in contrast to Savigny's earlier summons to the *vaterländisches Recht* that had produced exclusive liberalism. It represented the first major attempt to offer a foundation for the development of a theory of social democratic constitutionalism and conceptions of inclusive citizenship and extended participation.

While Bachofen's theory of law offered a powerful support to social-democratic constitutionalism, both were swimming upstream against the rapid advance of *bürgerliche* constitutional transformation in the nineteenth century. This project dominated the law faculties and legislative practice and as a result, social-democratic constitutionalism remained underdeveloped. It did not develop the great mass of literature as then existed in Germanist scholarship and, therefore, was not in a position to develop a basis for the structural transformations of procedural, criminal or civil law that would have to accompany any constitution. This underdevelopment would prove to be one of the key factors in the failure of the Weimar experiment after the First World War.

Mutterrecht and the Foundations of Social Democratic Constitutionalism

Bachofen's thesis had a considerable impact on a number of significant scholars and political figures, such as his colleagues at the University of Basel, Jakob Burckhardt and Friedrich Nietzsche. The theoretical proposition on the origins of marriage shaped John McLennan's *Primitive Marriage* (1865), as he acknowledged in his work.[61] His most significant disciple was Lewis Henry Morgan. *Ancient Society* (1877) bore the influence of *Das Mutterrecht* on all sides, but was reflected particularly in his discussion of matriarchy amongst the Native American Iroquois.[62] Indeed, he took on Bachofen's propositions about the evolution of ancient society wholesale as his many references to *Das Mutterrecht* indicate.[63]

Morgan's influence on the development of socialist political theory in the German context was significant. During the winter months of 1880–1881, two years before his death, Karl Marx took some ninety pages of notes based on his reading of *Ancient Society,* with particular interests in collective forms of property holding and the collective living arrangements of the Iroquois.[64] After Marx's death, Engels used his notes to centrally position the new anthropology in socialist thought. The fruit of this labor was his famous *The Origin of the Family, Private Property and the State, in the Light of the Researches of Lewis H. Morgan* (1884), which in many respects was a restatement of Morgan for the Germanic context.

Engels specifically emphasized the tremendous influence of Bachofen, not only on his own work, but on Morgan's as well. 'Until the beginning of the sixties', he wrote in the preface to the fourth edition published in 1891, 'there was no such thing as a history of the family'.[65] 'In this sphere historical science was still completely under the influence of the Five Books of Moses', and, he argued, 'the patriarchal form of the family, described there in greater detail than anywhere else, was not only implicitly accepted as the oldest form of the family, but also—after excluding polygamy—identified with the present day bourgeois family, as if the family had really undergone no historical development at all.'[66] He went on to specifically note that the history of the family dated 'from 1861, from the publication of Bachofen's *Mutterrecht*'.[67]

> This rediscovery of the primitive matriarchal gens as the earlier stage of the patriarchal gens of civilized peoples has the same importance for anthropology as Darwin's theory of evolution has for biology and Marx's theory of surplus value for political economy ... The matriarchal gens has become the pivot on which the whole science turns; since its discovery we know where to look and what to look for in our research, and how to arrange the results.[68]

The influence of Bachofen and the destruction of patriarchy appealed to socialists, and they embraced the matriarchal ideal. It provided the theoretical foundation for socialist constitutionalism. Engels directly contradicted Grimm's philological findings on the meaning of the term 'woman', writing: 'among Langobards and Burgundians we find ... the term *fara,* which Grimm derives from the hypothetical root *fisan,* to beget'.[69] In opposition to this view, *fara* was linked to the 'more obvious root, *faran, fahren*'.[70] This, in his reasoning, was essentially the equivalent of the Greek *genos* and the Latin *gens,* an indication of the existence of *genealogiae,* characterized by the collective living and communal ownership of property.

From Engels and Marx, Bachofen's theory of law permeated the rise of social democratic political thought in Germany. Eduard Bernstein, Karl Kautsky, Rosa Luxembourg, Clara Zetkin, Lily Braun, Wilhelm Liebknecht and August Bebel were all well versed on the importance of Bachofen. In his pamphlet *Socialism,* Liebknecht identified prostitution as the contemporary example of sex-labor exploitation. 'Thanks to the wrong conditions of society and the State', he wrote, 'woman is today without rights and in countless cases is condemned to wedded and unwedded prostitution'.[71] The politics of sex, however, was explicitly clear in *Socialism.* 'The intercourse of the sexes is unnatural and immoral', he wrote, and 'socialism will bring the emancipation of woman as well as of man.'[72] 'It', he stated, 'insists on her complete political and social equality and equal position with man,' and 'it will destroy prostitution, whether it walk ashamed under the mantle of marriage for wealth or convenience, or whether it run shameless painted and naked upon the street.'[73] While prostitution in socialist ideology was seen as the modern manifestation of sex-labor exploitation, as we see in Liebknecht, civil marriage was also seen as a form of property ownership of women and sex-labor exploitation. Sex was exploitative because it was a right of men and an obligation of women.

Kautsky, who was recognized as the intellectual heir to Engels, was also the founder of the leading Marxist journal, *Die Neue Zeit.* In the spring of 1881, he also undertook a detailed study of the works of both Bachofen and Morgan.[74] These works very much influenced his *Die Entstehung der Ehe und der Familie,* which appeared two years later in 1883. Clara Zetkin's essay 'Die Arbeiterinnen- und Frauenfrage der Gegenwart' (1889) was based on her reading of Bachofen as well as Morgan and Engels.[75] Developed from her reading of *Das Mutterrecht,* her work showed a dialectical view of evolution and the likening of matriarchy with primitive communism.[76] Following the work of Morgan and Engels, however, Bachofen figured most prominently in August Bebel's *Die Frau und der Sozialismus* (1879).

August Bebel's political history as the leader of the Social Democratic Party has been duly considered by scholars. My interest here is in the ideological connection between Bachofen and Bebel as a means of explaining the centrality of gender in German social democracy as metaphor for the redistribution of property and power. Richard Evans has described *Die Frau und der Sozialismus* as Bebel's 'lifework', but scholars of German history have clearly struggled with the pivotal place gender occupied in his book.[77] Traditional intellectual historians tend to divide Bebel's political development into pre-Marxist and Marxist periods, arguing that *Die Frau und der Sozialismus* showed his underdevelopment as a Marxist. Evans found that the work could not be counted as a part of the canon, because it had 'origins outside the Marxist tradition'.[78] 'The historical picture presented in this book', he reasoned, was 'more liberal than socialist'.[79] In the same spirit, Moira Donald argued that it 'revealed an incomplete understanding of Marxism'.[80] In this interpretation, the central position of women in *Die Frau und der Sozialismus* was set aside as a curious oddity, while scholars searched for the true Marxism in Bebel's political thought. These interpretations suffered from an incomplete understanding of the centrality of gender in the development of German political ideology on the whole.

Since the 1980s, alternative methodologies have been employed to interpret Bebel's work within the German feminist movement, positing the existence of Marxist feminism. Jean Quataert focused not on political ideology, but on the activities of what she termed 'socialist feminists', and identified Bebel as a feminist.[81] In his analysis of the feminist movement, Evans also viewed Bebel as a feminist.[82] The most recent analysis, *Men's Feminism,* by Anne Lopes and Gary Roth, has subjected Bebel to a Foucauldian analysis. They argue that many of his ideas were *'eigenartig',* and that a Foucauldian genealogical analysis will make sense of 'the out rightly trivial and provides explanations for the sudden shifts in his views'.[83]

The feminist interpretation, however, does not adequately capture the deep politics of the place of gender in Bebel's writing and social democratic constitutionalism. *Die Frau und der Sozialismus* continued the gendered political discourse established by Grimm and Bachofen in German political thought. Indeed, Bachofen's influence was revealed not only in the content of the work, but in its very construction. The first and second chapters are entirely dedicated to the evolution of the *'Urgesellschaft',* namely the transitions from *'Promiskuität'* to *'Mutterrecht'* to the dissolution of the gens with the rise of patriarchy.[84] Accordingly, in the opening paragraphs of the chapter, 'Die Stellung der Frau in der Urgesellschaft', Bebel clearly indicated the symbolic meaning of the feminine in socialist ideology. He wrote that the condition of women and workers had very much in common, but that 'she was the first in human existence to be enslaved'.[85] The origin of exploitation extended from the hetaeric primordial epoch. He then described the changed conditions under *Mutterrecht* with the rise of the gens, and that 'property remained [collectively held] in the gens'.[86] 'One spoke', as he wrote of '*matrimonium* instead of *patrimonium,* of *mater familias* instead of *pater familias,* and the homeland was called, lovingly, *Mutterland.*'[87] With the rise of patriarchy, however, '*Mutterrecht* disappeared and patriarchy emerged in its place ... man as the owner of the private property legitimated and looked after the interests of the children.'[88]

Die Frau und der Sozialismus was one of the most influential works of the period. Despite the tremendous role it played in awakening women to feminism, Bebel should not be classified as a feminist. Rather, his theoretical ideals about gender were derived from Bachofen and rest squarely within the legal anthropological tradition of socialist political thought. The place of gender in his thinking was not peculiar, but represented an important normative element in developing a theory of socialist constitutionalism, which in the first instance was concerned with the civic participation of working-class men. The interplay and inversion of patriarchy and matriarchy was pure political symbolism rather than feminism. The redevelopment of gender relations, particularly the public position of women, should be seen as a central feature of socialist political ideology. The two are interlocutory, and the imposition of an artificial separation misses the much larger significance for how we think about gender and its place in the history of politics. Nevertheless, this body of constitutionalist thought remained underdeveloped, as discussed earlier. Thus, when social democracy came to Germany in 1919, it was handicapped by the underdeveloped state of its constitutional theory and was unable to effect the transformations, particularly, in civil law that would have given it sustainability in German society.

Mutterrecht and Motherhood

As Joan Scott noted in *Gender and the Politics of History,* scholars have tended to interpret the history of women into broader existing theoretical positions.[89] In the case of German women's history, Evans set a tone some years ago that has continued to shape interpretations of the women's movement. His decidedly critical view depended heavily on the *Sonderweg* thesis, and he saw in the feminist movement a lack of bourgeois virtues that led to their eventual espousal of right-wing doctrines. 'Like the liberalism to which it was so closely bound', he argued that the women's movement 'retreated from the radicalism of 1848', like liberalism itself.[90] In the decades that followed, it was 'stunned by the successive blows of 1866, 1871 and 1878', until it finally 'withdrew even further and compromised more and more with the existing order, the General Association followed suit'.[91] Obviously, this study challenges this interpretation of German liberalism. Nevertheless, German liberalism was exclusive and the conception of the representative state as it found expression in the writings of the historical school called for male participation based on the exclusion of women. In this way, the BGB signaled regress and not progress for German women. Although Evans noted that it worsened the condition of women in many ways, he was not aware of the important place of the code in constitutional transformation.[92] Neither the German women's movement nor feminism could be closely bound to liberalism, because liberalism rejected the participation of women and built property-based male participation around their exclusion.

Despite more recent research, scholars have continued to view the women's movement as a part of liberalism, rather than a reaction against liberalism.[93] Ute Frevert accused the leaders of the women's movement of arguing tentatively and timidly, conceiving only of 'extended motherliness *(Mütterlichkeit)*'—a concept that was founded on the very preconceptions and assumptions that restricted their options and kept them in the home.[94] 'Motherhood' was a reflection of an 'anti-modernist ideal of culture'.[95] Considered in light of the Germanist ideology that was at the heart of constitutional transformation, motherhood was more radical than these scholars have considered.[96]

In reality, motherhood opposed the exclusive liberalism of majority rule at its ideological foundation. The publications, protests and general orientation of the women's movement, beginning in 1865 and gaining speed in 1896, were characterized by their repudiation of these ideals, particularly in their codified form. This becomes particularly clear when the ideology of motherhood is juxtaposed against the philosophical writings of the Germanists and is understood as an outgrowth of Bachofen's work.

The ideology of motherhood should be understood in light of the politicization of private life that marked the course of the *Bürgerliche Revolution.* During the French Revolution, in sometimes surprising ways, family romances, both conscious and unconscious, helped to organize the political experience of the revolution; revolutionaries and counterrevolutionaries alike confronted issues of paternal authority, female participation, and fraternal solidarity.[97] Grimm referred only to wives and girls. He did not develop equivalent conceptions to *Bruderschaft,* such as *Schwesterschaft, Weiberkraft, Mutterschaft,* or, more applicable to the women's movement, *Mütterlichkeit.* Indeed the suffixes *'-schaft',* which implied guardianship, and *'-kraft',* which implied power, were not attached to feminine words. It was only in Bachofen's work that these philological constructions of power and public identity were applied to women. Matriarchy was diametrically opposed to exclusive liberalism. Bachofen made women virtuous and thus capable of full citizenship, and their public participation was essential to the common good. Theories of motherhood drew on these principles and the anthropological findings, following Bachofen in the 1880s, but also remained underdeveloped.

In Grimm's analysis of the household, he described a patriarchal social order in which power in the home formed the prerequisite for power in public society. Only 'the *Hausherr* is free and unrestricted' and 'the wife, his sisters and children fell under his guardianship *(Schutz* or *Mund)*'.[98] He cited Tacitus' *Germania* when he described the position of the *Hausherr* as 'like a king on the throne, the judge on the highest chair, so is the *Hausvater* in his pride of place *(Ehrensitz).*'[99] The ideology of motherhood undermined the exclusive basis of participation in liberal political thought. It claimed female virtue, even the capacity for valor, and thus demanded full citizenship for women. Indeed, Helene Lange spoke in 1899 of women's 'struggle for existence' and their *'Wettkampf mit der Männerwelt'.*[100] She called for the energetic 'solidarity of women from all classes'.[101]

Nevertheless, National Liberals controlled the introduction of civil law, and Germanist theory was reflected in the BGB's provisions on *elterliche Gewalt.* The first striking point is that the section on parental power was divided into two sections, 'Parental Power of the Father' and 'Parental Power of the Mother'. Paragraph 1627 legislated that 'a father has, by virtue of his parental power, the right and the duty to take care of his child's person and property.'[102] Paragraph 1684, on the other hand, specifically stated that 'parental power belongs to the mother' only in the instance of the father's death or forfeiture of his rights accompanied by the dissolution of the marriage.[103] The protest article, 'Aufruf!', that appeared in *Die Frauenbewegung* duly noted that the BGB 'spoke of *elterliche Gewalt* but that the exercise of this power is vested solely in the father; he alone will control and decide all of the children's life and educational questions'.[104]

Moreover, it was necessary again to pay attention to the fine print in the other paragraphs. While there was no such provision for male parents, in the case of a father's death or absence, Paragraph 1687 provided for the appointment of a 'supplementary guardian', if for example the father requested the same at the 'time of his death', (Paragraph 1777) or 'special reasons', (Paragraph 1687.3) such as the management of property.[105] Paragraph 1688 made the Guardianship Court's authority over women absolute: 'the supplementary guardian may be appointed for all kinds of affairs, for certain kinds of affairs, or for special affairs.'[106] 'The supplementary guardian', according to Paragraph 1689, 'shall, within the scope of his authority, assist and supervise the mother in her exercise of the parental power.'[107] Moreover, Paragraph 1697 decreed that 'the mother loses the parental power if she remarries'; in effect, she would lose her children.[108] No such penalty was meted out against the rights of fathers to remarry. Indeed, under the BGB only the *Hausherr* was free and unrestricted, and even in the instance of the father's death, parental authority did not transfer to the mother.

It is worth noting also that the BGB placed considerable limitations on fathers relative to their children's property and held them accountable to the Guardianship Court, yet another manifestation of exclusive *bürgerliche* rule. Indeed, under Paragraph 1668, the court could require fathers to put up security for the property subjected to his management.[109] If a father failed to comply with any order of the Guardianship Court, his rights could be rescinded and, what is more, under Paragraph 1674, even the judge of the Guardianship Court could be held liable for negligence in the protection of a child's property.[110] The property of children, therefore, was far more secure than the property of their mothers. Indeed, they seemed to have been somewhat better positioned, insofar as a father's management and usufruct rights could be revoked for mistreatment of the child.

The BGB depended heavily on Germanist principles, and the obligations that accompanied guardianship over children entailed the exercise of considerable public civil rights, especially the management and usufruct of property. Under Paragraph 1630 in the fathers' section, 'the care of the child's person and property [included] the right to represent him.'[111] In the case of his right to management and usufruct, this involved the representation of child before the state, whether in the execution of negotiable instruments or in a court of law, which, in turn, required the right to swear oaths. Mothers were not construed as guardians under the BGB, but rather only as statutory agents. Under Paragraph 1676, 'the right to take care of the person of the child belongs to both the father and the statutory agent (i.e., the mother if her marriage with the father still subsists) of the child.'[112] The proscription on independent guardianship by mothers, therefore, was tied to the denial of women's civil rights more generally, particularly the right to property. The exercise of full guardianship rights would have made women, if not as persons or wives, then as mothers, fully *geschäftsfähig* and this, of course, was the key to the political participation that they were denied.

By examining the relationship between the feminist concept of motherhood and Bachofen's theory of ancient *Mutterrecht,* and by comparing it with Germanist political ideology and the legislated expression of that ideology in the BGB, the full political implications of the concept become clear and reveal the radicalism of the women's movement's political engagement. The ideology of motherhood was deeply political and struck at the heart of German liberalism and the exclusive liberal order that came into existence with the BGB. Motherhood challenged the legitimacy of patriarchy in both the historical and contemporary context and, thus, challenged the legal foundation of the *bürgerliche* society and the majority rule that was the basis of the *bürgerliche Gemeinwesen.* It denied the validity of exclusive *väterliche Gewalt* and the *eheliches Güterrecht* of the BGB. Moreover, it redefined the political organization of the state in such a manner that it gave women exclusive control of matters such as education, social welfare and the general moral common good.

Discontent in the Republics: A Continuity in German History

In addition to the discontent in high culture, the constitutional transformation of Germany into an exclusive *bürgerliche Gemeinwesen* produced both organized and individual popular discontent at the grassroots of German society. Liberals tried to legislate into existence a sociopolitical order designed to sustain majority rule. The BGB, particularly its family law, left no German untouched. As soon as it became law, the state, rather than the National Liberal Party, became the target of resentment and protest. Liberal ideals of creating happiness and good for the people fell flat when far too many Germans found themselves trapped in unhappy unions, and the state became the target of personal discontent.

The legal revolution in Central Europe that began with procedural reform in Hanover slowly eroded the gains women had made during a century of promise and denied women equal civil rights under *bürgerliche* law. As Beatrix Geisel suggests: 'The women's movement cannot be understood without its foundation in the reaction to mounting civil legislation.'[113] Ute Gerhard has written that the chief instrument used to consolidate paternalistic gender relations in *bürgerliche* society was the law.[114] The introduction of the Civil Code of Saxony (BGBS) in 1865 offered an important harbinger for what would occur at the national level in 1896. The *Allgemeiner Deutscher Frauenverein* (ADF) was founded the same year, partially in response to the enactment of the BGBS, and the founding of the *Frauenrechtschutzverein* by Marie Stritt, Marianne Menzer and others in Dresden soon followed. As early as

1876, the ADF published *Einige deutsche Gesetzes Paragraphen über die Stellung der Frau,* which called for the introduction of civil legislation to protect the rights of women, particularly relative to marriage and guardianship laws.[115]

Only two decades later, it was the impending denial of civil rights under the BGB that spurred the founding of the *Bund Deutscher Frauenvereine* (BDF) in 1894. The BDF's legal commissions were set up the same year. The first organized strike of women workers occurred in the confection industry, not surprisingly in 1896. As Geisel points out, the strike in 1896 was tied to a protest against the BGB. Unlike other strikes, however, these women were joined on the picket lines by some five hundred middle class women.[116] Indeed, the BDF's final petition to the Reichstag calling for a revision of the family law in 1899 clearly stated the resolve of German women: 'The unusual request for a change in the law after its promulgation, but before its introduction, is justified by the deeply injured feelings of German women, whose conscience will never reconcile with these laws'.[117] It went on to state that women regarded the BGB's *Mundium* over women as 'an unjust limitation of their human rights'.[118] Grassroots discontent with the Code's denial of women's rights extended well beyond the ranks of women, however. The petition was signed by some fifty thousand men and women across class lines. Paradoxically, *bürgerliche* law was perhaps the greatest unifying force for the Left in Germany after 1900.

The bitterness of German women was stoked by the Reichstag's arrogant refusal even to consider the complaints of women. Gottlieb Planck resolutely, and without reservation, told members of *Göttingen Frauenverein* that, despite demands to change the draft from radical as well as moderate representatives of the women's movement, 'the legislators finally decided against taking the women's demand into consideration, and the Code was based on the draft.'[119] Planck 'did not have any illusions about reaching an agreement with the representatives of the women's movement'.[120] He simply laid down the law to his female audience, pointing out in a clear reference to social discipline powers of Paragraph 6 that 'incurable mental disease was grounds for divorce'.[121] 'The *Bürgerliches Gesetzbuch*', he explained, 'sets out the following rules about the personal relationship between the spouses: cohabitation is a marital duty for the spouses; in matters regarding the conjugal life, the vote of the husband is decisive. Irrespective of this right of the husband, the wife is entitled and obligated to manage the domestic affairs.'[122] As a consolation for the loss of their property to men, Planck told German women 'the wife can buy her household necessities, food and drink from the butcher, baker or *Kolonialwaarenhändler* on credit and only the husband will be responsible.'[123]

Many men registered their complaints about the BGB's family law, only to be dismissed as well. In the Reichstag, August Bebel and the SPD demanded the modification of the marriage law to reflect full equality between husbands and wives and the full economic freedom of women.[124] The SPD was the only faction to vote unanimously against the Code's introduction. The conservative Baron von Stumm-Halberg demanded equal rights for women, specifically the right to manage their property, equal guardianship over their children and independent testamentary rights over their estates: 'I believe it is false, as many have said, that a nation's civilization is measured best by the position of women.'[125] 'If the German nation is to march forward towards a higher civilization', he suggested that 'German women must have a better position in society like women in other nations.'[126] Hostility toward the family law was echoed in the complaints of left-wing liberals like Albert Träger and Eugen Richter of the Liberal People's Party. Träger satirically commented:

> Let us admit that women have shown themselves everywhere to be of equal ambition and equal worth to men. And how many marriages have we seen in all classes of society in which, gentlemen, it is the wife who bears the real burden of the marriage, not just with her property, but also, gentlemen, with her earnings, with her work! And how is it, gentlemen that you then want to place such a wife under the unconditional control of her husband?[127]

In the meantime, couples in the west of the Reich resorted to the same prenuptial measures they had relied on to escape the ill effects of the earlier *Code civil* and Civil Code of Baden. There was much less contractual liberty under the BGB, and it strictly defined the alternative forms of marital property relations in such a manner that women were still left powerless. In addition to this, the state discouraged prenuptial agreements through a host of red-tape measures. Couples had to provide marriage officials with a detailed list of their holdings and choose between one of the allowed forms under the BGB. In addition, such agreements had to be registered before the time of marriage in the local *Güterrechtsregister* and couples had to give public notice of their property holdings and alternative arrangements through publication in the newspaper. The whole community thus knew if a woman was worth more than her mate and knew if she chose to deprive him of control over her property.

Nevertheless, couples still tried to opt for the forms that appeared under the old names even though the substance of the alternative forms was changed under the BGB. As the records for the regions of Gießen and Fürth show, women married with sizeable sums of personal wealth. According to the notice in the *Darmstädter Zeitung,* in the *Güterrechtsregister* for the Fürth region, Eva Schneider married with some 77,000 RM in hand in 1911.[128] A female photographer, worth more than 10,000 RM, married in 1910 only after her husband agreed to accept *Gütertrennung.*[129] In 1910, a couple from Birkenau where the wife's property was worth 9,349 RM and the husband's 5,100 RM opted for *Errungenschaftsgemeinschaft.*[130] In addition, the *Güterrechtsregister* also recorded detailed information about the couples' professional life, and it is clear from the records that even the working-class penniless were going through the trouble to file prenuptial agreements. A similar pattern was evident in the *Güterrechtsregister* for Gießen. Regina Schmieg made her intentions absolutely clear in her agreement with her husband, setting down *'völlige Gütertrennung'*.[131]

In addition to women, workers also perceived the negative effects of the Code. An article, 'Curiosités juridiques le nouveau code allemand', which appeared in the 1 February 1901 edition of *Indépendence Belge* offered a telling expose on the BGB. It echoed the sentiments of many when it pointed out that the Code favored the interests of the commercial sector and employers over the interests of others. In particular, the author explained that employers 'could demand that an employee sign a written contract *(Engagementvertrag)* as to the duration and quality of his (or her) services'.[132] Moreover, concerning associations, the Code hindered the organization of the very groups and persons it rigorously discriminated against. The article complained that commercial associations were granted 'juristic capacity' and 'civil personality' on the basis of simple application, while all others faced considerable measures designed to discourage membership, such as the requirement to provide the state with the names of their members.[133] Association discrimination remained a reality until the passage a new associations law in 1908.

Articles in the German press spoke out against these provisions and others, pointing out that the Code produced new quarrels in German society. Only seven months after the BGB's introduction, the *Kölnische Zeitung* reported, 'a certain legal insecurity has beset, not only the public, but also the legal advisors to the public.'[134] The Code, it reported, 'has already produced dozens of new *Streitfragen,*' including dissatisfaction with divorce and associations laws as well as the regulation of service relationships.[135] 'We hope that this painful period of transition we find ourselves in the middle of,' the article closed 'if at all possible, is nearing its end and we can delight without reservation in our legal unity.'[136] The *Allgemeine Zeitung* also reported that the BGB's introduction was the source of considerable *Streitigkeiten* over the regulation of tenancy and the rights of workers and service people.[137] The *Berliner Neueste Nachrichten* followed suit, reporting that there was particular dissatisfaction with marital property relations, the denial of *mütterliche Gewalt* and the divorce provisions, which reinstated fault as the basis for divorce.[138] In the matter of divorce, the article complained that the BGB represented regression to the days before the ALR, a 'set-back *(Rückschritt)* of over a century'.[139]

'Curiosité juridiques' also captured the fact that the BGB created new categories of disaffected persons. 'According to the classic conception', it reported, 'marriage is a petite reflection of an absolute monarchy; today, the woman is not situated any better as the companion of the man.'[140] Anita Augsburg's reaction published in *Die Frauenbewegung* offered a stinging criticism of the Code as well. It read:

> On the one hand, it effects legal discrimination against every single woman as a person, which finds expression in the family and marriage laws. On the other hand, it is not only

discrimination, but a direct denial of rights, making all women a sex-class and *Partei*. It imposes political duties on women, but denies them every political right.[141]

The denial of civil rights under the BGB became the rallying cry for the German women's movement. As Augsburg acknowledged in her remarks, the code created a new class of discontents composed of Germany's many women. It pushed middle-class women, temporarily at least, into closer union with their similarly situated working-class compatriots on the rapidly expanding political Left.

While high on the list of those who were denied full citizenship and subjected to civil social control, women and workers were not alone, and it seems that there was considerable dissatisfaction with the extension of minority. Wilhelmine Germany witnessed the rise of socialist and radical youth organizations that rebelled against abuse, oppression and labor exploitation.[142] The feminist Lily Braun was an outspoken supporter of children's liberation, and some members of the SPD encouraged the party leadership to incorporate the demands of youth.[143] But youth would face much the same plight as women when psychologists, such as G. Stanley Hall, constructed a so-called new stage of life, adolescence.[144] This was the period, as John Gillis and others note, when the concept developed and was used to draw a distinction between the dependence of the teen years and the independence of the twenties.[145] The state responded to organized youth with an increasing array of laws and methods of social control.[146]

It was this tremendous change that was reflected in the 'Curiosités juridiques' complaint that 'even young men over the age of sixteen will be classified as children and, in a similar social position to their mothers, will remain under the guardianship of their fathers.'[147] As Jürgen Reulecke suggests, in the mid-1890s, a cult of youth began to flourish in Germany.[148] Arthur van den Bruck stated in 1904 that 'the nation needs a change of blood, an uprising of the sons against the father, the replacement of old age by youth'.[149] Reulecke argues that behind this attack on the fathers there lay some doubts about the order of the *bürgerliche* family model, which vested the father with absolute authority and rigidly delineated roles in the family.[150] While there were other measures in the late nineteenth century, the BGB was the most comprehensive, setting the age of majority at twenty-one. The rise of youth movements during the late nineteenth century also reflected the reaction against mounting civil legislation that increasingly demanded conformity to the liberal model of society. This reality also helps to explain why women's groups agitated on behalf of 'children' they were now expected to rear for even longer periods of time.

Finally, the article in the *Indépendence Belge* aptly identified the new parameters of discontent and offered a foreboding comment that was a harbinger for the political and social concerns that emerged after the First World War. 'Economically', it concluded, the Code 'necessarily adapted to modernity; socially, it enforces the guardianship of the feeble and incapable: women, bastards, workers.'[151] This very telling comment underscored the changed nature of the debate on Germany's laws and political organization. The emerging demand for reform of the marriage laws was a demand for the redistribution of rights on more democratic terms. Many men had signed the BDF's petition and registered their demands for revision of the draft's family. Ignoring the protests of women, therefore, ignored the complaints of men, who, unlike women, possessed the right to vote. The public expression of discontent with the marriage laws was an increasing feature of post-1900 Wilhelmine society.

Just as the noble family structure had embodied all that was wrong under the absolutist system in the minds of liberals, the paternalistic bourgeois family structure came to symbolize all that was wrong under majority rule. To the rising numbers of cultural critics, the legislated *bürgerliche* family structure personified the dominion of capital. This sentiment was echoed by the lawyer Herr Bleicken in his protest treatise *Unser Deutsches Volksrecht! Eigenthum oder Ehe?* He viewed the BGB's marriage law as *'Unersättlichkeit des Egoismus'* and *'Heiligkeit des Eigenthums'*.[152] From 1896 until 1933, Bleicken continued his criticism of the BGB.[153] Although his interpretation was perhaps a bit misinformed, his discontent offers a window into the widespread alienation that was the ultimate product of the *Bürgerliche Revolution.*

Whereas the complaints of women and bitter unhappiness in marriage grew out of the hated sex guardianship, men appeared to be particularly disgruntled about the Code's divorce provisions. The BGB installed very strict fault-based provision for divorce, as I have discussed. However, it was the character of the legal procedure for obtaining a divorce that no doubt discouraged even severely unhappy couples. Because divorce was based on fault, local courts actually sent an assessor into the community to investigate the validity of claims. Assessors interviewed for the public record, not only family members, but neighbours, co-workers and virtually anyone of their choosing who had a relationship with the parties. This meant that the actual charges in a divorce, no matter how intimate the nature of these charges, were exposed to the couple's social and professional world. It was a terribly humiliating process, which could only discourage divorce. What is more, even after subjecting oneself to such public humiliation, it was often the case that a judge could decide that there were no grounds for divorce and force couples to remain married.

Letters to the *Reichjustizministerium* attest to the realities of popular marital suffering. There were bitter complaints and raw demands for reform of the divorce provisions. In 1903, Alexander Richard wrote that, after his wife left their common home in 1902, he secured a court order to have her returned home.[154] Apparently, his wife opted to flee to *'Amerika'* in January of 1903 rather than return to his home.[155] This left Herr Richard in a difficult situation, because the BGB required a three-year waiting period before he could even file for a divorce. As a result, when Richard filed for divorce in 1903, as he wrote, the court denied his motion under the provisions of law.[156] Making matters worse, his letter was forwarded to a clerk in the *Reichjustizministerium,* who simply replied on 8 December that they could not get involved.[157] The BGB was accompanied with new procedural amendments, which left judges little room for flexibility, even in extreme cases like Richard's. He was stuck for three years before he could even file for divorce and was left bearing the binding legal effects of a marriage to a woman who had taken flight across the Atlantic Ocean with no legal remedy or relief.

Stories like Richard's are abundant in the numerous letters that were sent to the *Reichjustizministerium.* The BGB's strict divorce provisions left many Germans trapped in unhappy unions and often desperate circumstances. These conditions were noted frequently in the German press. An article in the *Kölnische Zeitung* reported of a 16-year-old student who committed suicide after being caught in the middle of her parents' nasty divorce proceedings.[158] Blame for this tragedy was placed, not on the couple, but on the fault provisions of the BGB.[159] Fault, as the basis of divorce, necessarily involved the character assassination of the other spouse, which meant that divorces were rarely, if ever, amicable. As Dirk Blasius shows, the divorce rate in Germany dropped sharply after the introduction of the BGB.[160] What is clear from the correspondence to the *Justizministerium,* as well as newspaper articles, is that widespread dissatisfaction with the divorce provisions embodied the rejection of civil law's intrusion and regulation of very private relationships. These tales of *häusliche* woe nourished rising discontent in German society, by raising the specter of hypocrisy in liberal law. Instead of the BGB leading to the happiness of the *Volk* as liberals promised, it had produced unhappiness in many sectors of the German population, leading people to take desperate measures. The charge was increasingly levied that the law was out of sync with the people, particularly on the political Right, a strategy for attacking existing law that had been inaugurated by German nationalists in the years following the *Freiheitskriege*. The new edifice of civil law was increasingly seen as un-German on the Right and inhumane on the Left as many Germans were forced to live in *unglückliche Ehen.*

By the beginning of the First World War, the BGB's divorce provisions had become a leading source of discontent. The divorce laws were increasingly viewed as tyranny. In 1914, Dr. A. Kolbe published his 'Hilferuf an den Kaiser und die deutsche Öffentlichkeit: Unglaubliches Prozessmartyrium in einem Ehescheidungsverfahren'. No other area of legislation, he wrote, so deeply affected every single citizen, 'with such grave consequences to their natural rights', than the regulation of marriage and the marital relations of the spouses.[161] The code adhered to the 'stiff principle of continuing unhappy marriages'.[162] 'It is a well known fact', he wrote, 'that the German legislation of the new BGB represented a scandalous chapter [in our history], bringing into existence legal insecurity as a result of its defectiveness and inadequacy rather than positive legal norms.'[163] 'Nowhere', he continued, 'is the gap between the legal consciousness and sense of the people and that of the law deeper and wider than in the severity of family life produced by the stringency of the marriage law.'[164] Entering into marriage under the existing laws was 'a monstrous peril'.[165] The BGB had turned marriage into 'a plague, a torment [and] a repulsive immorality'.[166] At the height of the war effort in 1916, Kolbe forwarded a petition to the Bundesrat and Reichstag, tellingly titled *No Taxation without Democratic Marriage Laws.*[167]

Despite the major rupture of 1918 and the Weimar Constitution of 1919, the BGB remained on the books and continued to serve as the basis of law along with the entire legal edifice, which was the fruit of the *Bürgerliche Revolution.* Ordinary Germans, therefore, found no relief from these conditions under the new constitution and political arrangements. In a November 1921 letter, Paul Breuning wrote of the desperate suffering of his brother Max, who had owned a small bicycle and engine shop in Berlin. In 1909, Max married and lived for one year in a 'very bad marriage' until he decided to leave his wife in 1910.[168] His wife of one year filed a motion for support against him in a Berlin court, and the court ordered him to pay a monthly sum of 40 Marks, a sizeable amount in 1910. 'This crime', Paul Breuning wrote 'led to my brother's flight.'[169] 'Now', he bitterly reported, 'my brother lives in Russia and writes me more and more letters of despair ... and I must help him out.'[170] He respectfully requested help for the 'poor German in Russia'.[171] Again, the state offered no recourse, and the reply letter merely suggested that he consult the *'Bürgerliches Gesetzbuch'.*[172]

In 1918, Anton Linder wrote with resentment of the dissolution of his own marriage, placing blame squarely on the BGB's divorce provisions. For twenty-three years he was married to a 'completely penniless' woman, contributing his entire income to the welfare of his family and the upbringing of their four children. 'The wife', he wrote 'quarrelsome and argumentative, made demands incessantly that exceeded my income and I could never catch up.'[173] Making matters worse, he had to take responsibility for his mother-in-law, and he complained that his children refused him respect and obedience. All of this became the source of conflict and unpleasant scenes, and his wife simply left him without notice. The court later denied his petition for restoration of the marital community and slapped him with a bill of 950 Marks for the cost of the suit. Moreover, the court obliged him to pay the cost of living for, not only his wife, but all four of his children. 'Now', he wrote grievously, 'in my old age, I have earned in substance only disappointments and ingratitude.'[174] Linder pointed out that these conditions made remarriage impossible for him, which he perceived as the loss of a basic right. Fault as the basis of divorce, he demanded, should be done away with, so that people in 'unhappy marriages' may more easily obtain divorce.[175]

Herr A. Wilken recounted the difficulties of obtaining a divorce in his letter to the *Justizministerium* of 5 December 1921. 'In a few words', he wrote, 'married in 1893 for the sake of decency.'[176] There was 'permanent discord' between the spouses, with a *'totale Ehezerrüttung'* in 1910 and separation in 1912. After ten years of divorce proceedings, what he referred to as *'der Kriegszeit',* the couple was still not permitted to divorce. 'Shattered marriages', he protested, 'are no longer marriages and [people] should be allowed to divorce on legal as well as moral grounds!'[177] 'In my opinion', he closed, 'a ten year separation of the couple should constitute grounds alone.'[178]

Kolbe was not alone in producing written protest against the BGB's marriage laws. In 1919, Dr. Kurt Erhardt wrote a short piece for popular consumption titled *Ein neues Ehescheidungsrecht!*[179] Amongst other things, he cited the detrimental effects *unglückliche Ehen* had on children. By 1920, the dissatisfaction with family law turned into organized resistance, and the *Verband Eherechtreform* was founded in Cologne. 'The basis for the union', according to its first petition to the Reichstag, 'is the deep and great misery of the people who must live their lives in shattered marriages.'[180] In 1921, associations were founded in other cities, and the *Verband Eherechtreform* in Berlin began the publication of a monthly newsletter. In the years leading to the Weimar Constitution, the BGB had bred organized resistance against the organization of the basic foundational structures of society so long envisioned by liberals. It is also likely that the basic alienation brought on by the BGB was a source of discontent in German society, and not lingering Prussianization or even the aftermath of the First World War alone.

The most potent critique that emerged from disgruntled veterans after the First World War reflected the radicalization of continuing discontent over prewar social realities. Veterans underscored the fact that they were 'workers and soldiers' and that they fought alongside the *'Heldentot'*.[181] In January of 1919, J. Bügsen wrote of his friend's troubles in the Rhineland. Before the war, he had a 'happy family life' with his 'young wife and their children'.[182] In 1914, however, he had been called to 'the Flag, and, in his absence, another young soldier was quartered in his home with his young wife.[183] At war's end, he returned home 'to find his home violated—his wife and children indifferent'.[184] 'The happiness of my friend is now destroyed,' Bügsen lamented. 'Who is responsible for this unhappiness', he closed, 'the war and the State that started the war'.[185] Moreover, one must remember that many Germans continued to live in small towns, where not only individuals, but entire communities felt and witnessed the effects of individual personal tragedy. A resident of the same town as Bügsen, Carl Schmidt wrote of the same tragedy, but he went further, protesting that the war had 'destroyed many marriages'.[186] 'Many women', he wrote, have forgotten their place.'[187] The state, he protested, had an obligation to help its 'workers and soldiers'; they should not be expected to remain in unhappy family relationships.[188]

The *Bürgerliche Revolution* was made visible not only by the triumph of *bürgerliche* law, but by the widespread discontent it produced at every level of German society and across class lines. It was not just industrialization or modernity that produced unrest in German society, but the tangibility of the BGB, which, in reality, etched the supremacy of property over the everyday happiness of ordinary Germans. The attempt to force people into a liberal sociopolitical mold proved disastrous in the end and implanted the seeds for the undoing of the liberal power and cultural consolidation. While at a high cultural level, Social Democrats and the women's movement rejected the Code's marriage law for ideological reasons, the great mass of men and women were disaffected by the realities of their family life, leaving them perhaps miserable in the factory and at home. In the case of women, this involved complete submission to the *Vormundschaft* of their husbands, including the loss of control over their property and children. Ordinary men were disgruntled over the BGB's provisions for divorce, which, in reality, made divorce impossible, as well as binding obligation to provide for wives and children whether they were present or not. This widespread unhappiness in marriage, which liberals had long viewed as the beginning of the family—the basic foundation of society—alongside unhappy family life, contributed to instability at the grassroots and did not bode well for the future. These conditions, aggravated by the stress brought on by the First World War, also contributed to the stormy demise of the Kaiserreich.

The potency of *Gegenpolitik* came in the fact that so many people were disaffected by the BGB, and the fact that discontent was held in common at all levels of German society, from Conservatives to Social Democrats, to Left Liberals, to a great mass of women and ordinary German men. The problem, however, was that these groups never coalesced into a united front. *Gegenpolitik* was marked by atomization, with every excluded group taking its own road to inclusion.

While the Weimar Constitution changed some of these conditions on paper, its provisions were somewhat empty, because the BGB remained in effect.[189] The Weimar Republic was a social democratic republic wobbling on top of the structures of the *bürgerliche* republic. Moreover, there existed a lingering, exclusive liberalism in the official areas of the legal bureaucracy. As the files of the *Justizministerium* reveal, bureaucrats continued the practice of ignoring letters from women. Frau Käte Edlich wrote a total of eight letters to the *Justizministerium* on the question of divorce between 1929 and 1930.[190] Herr Oegg, who had worked on the family law committee with Gottlieb Planck, replied only once with a two-sentence letter.[191] In contrast, he seemed very eager to aid the *Kaufmann,* Hans Petersen, in his bid for control of his wife's property. In November of 1928, Emil Petersen wrote in on behalf of his brother, Hans. Apparently, Hans had married while out of the country and had signed a prenuptial agreement, giving up any rights to the management and usufruct of his wife's property. Emil inquired as to whether there was any way for his brother to get out of the prenuptial agreement.[192] Oegg promptly replied and explained that the agreement was not valid unless it was registered in a *Güterrechtsregister* of the *Amtsgericht* of the husband's residence. 'If the husband does not have a residence in Germany, as in the case at hand', he wrote, 'the contract cannot be registered.'[193] Although he said that he could not predict the outcome in court, in so many words, he explained that the contract was not valid.[194] Hans Petersen later wrote to Oegg directly and their correspondence continued as Oegg, basically, walked him through gaining the rights of management and usufruct he had originally signed away.[195] It was this type of underhanded social control and sociopolitical hypocrisy that also contributed to the decline of Weimar in the end and left Germany open to Nazism in 1933.

Notes

1. Johann Bachofen, *Das Mutterrecht: Eine Untersuchung über die Gynaikratie der alten Welt nach ihrer religiösen und rechtlichen Natur* (1861).
2. Heinrich Dernberg, 'Wünsche hervorragender Juristen für das neue Jahrhundert', *Das Recht* (25 January 1900).
3. Otto Gierke, 'Wünsche hervorragender Juristen für das neue Jahrhundert', *Das Recht* (25 January 1900).
4. Article in *Deutsche Juristen-Zeitung* (1 January 1900).
5. 'Die Feier der Münchener Juristischen Gesellschaft anläßlich der Einführung des neuen Bürgerlichen Gesetzbuches', *Münchener Neueste Nachrichten* (1 January 1900).
6. 'Das neue Recht', *Hannoverische Rundschau* (12 December 1899).
7. 'Die Einheit des deutschen Rechts', *Hamburger Nachrichten* (3 January 1900).
8. Gottlieb Planck, *Die rechtliche Stellung der Frau nach dem Bürgerlichen Gesetzbuch* (1899).
9. August Bebel, quoted in Michael John, *Politics and the Law in Late Nineteenth Century Germany: The Origins of the Civil Code* (1989), p. 237. See also August Bebel, 'Das Bürgerliche Gesetzbuch und die Sozialdemokratie', *Neue Zeit,* 2 (1895–1896), pp. 554–9 and 577–85.
10. Claudia Bruns, 'The Politics of Masculinity in the (Homo-)Sexual Discourse 1880–1920', *German History,* 23/3 (2005), p. 308.
11. Ann Goldberg, 'A Reinvented Public: Lunatics' Rights and Bourgeois Populism in the Kaiserreich', *German History,* 21/2 (2003), p. 160.
12. Thomas Trautman, *Lewis Henry Morgan and the Invention of Kinship* (1987), p. 4.
13. Ibid., p. 3.
14. Ibid., p. 245.
15. For more on Bachofen see Jonathan David Fishbane, *Mother-Right, Myth and Renewal: The Thought of Johann Jakob Bachofen and Its Relationship to the Perception of Cultural Decadence in the Nineteenth Century,* vols 1–3 (1981); Susanne Lanwerd, *Mythos, Mutterrecht und Magie: Zur Geschichte religionswissenschaftlicher Begriffe* (1993); Beate Wagner-Hasel (ed.), *Matriarchatstheorien der Altertumswissenschaft* (1992). For brief discussions see Lionel Gossman, *Basel in the Age of Burckhardt: A Study in Unseasonable Ideas* (2000); and Thomas Trautman, *Lewis Henry Morgan.*
16. Johann Jakob Bachofen, *Myth, Religion and Mother Right: Selected Writings of J. J. Bachofen*, Ralph Mannheim (trans.) (1992), p. 13.
17. Ibid., pp. 13–15.
18. Ibid., p. 69.
19. Ibid., p. 76.
20. Ibid.

21. Ibid.
22. Ibid.
23. Ibid., pp. 146–7.
24. Ibid., p. 147.
25. Ibid.
26. Ibid., p. 134.
27. Ibid., p. 135.
28. Ibid., p. 141.
29. Ibid., p. 142.
30. Ibid.
31. Ibid., p. 136.
32. Ibid., p. 133.
33. Ibid.
34. Ibid., p. 144.
35. Ibid.
36. Ibid., p. 153.
37. Ibid., p. 144.
38. Ibid.
39. Ibid., p. 153.
40. Ibid., pp. 84–5.
41. Ibid.
42. Ibid.
43. Ibid., pp. 85–6.
44. Ibid.
45. Ibid.
46. Ibid., p. 87.
47. Ibid., p. 70.
48. Ibid., pp. 70–1.
49. Ibid., p. 71.
50. Ibid.
51. Ibid.
52. Ibid.
53. Ibid., p. 78.
54. Ibid., pp. 78–9.
55. Ibid., p. 80.
56. Ibid.
57. Ibid.
58. Ibid.
59. Ibid., p. 189.
60. Ibid., p. 79.
61. Susanne Lanwerd, *Mythos, Mutterrecht und Magie*; and Trautman, *Lewis Henry Morgan.*

62. Ibid.
63. Lewis Henry Morgan, *Ancient Society, or, Researches in the Lines of Human Progress from Savagery through Barbarism to Civilization* (1877).
64. Lawrence Krader (ed.), *The Ethnological Notebooks of Karl Marx: Studies of Morgan, Phear, Maine, Lubbock* (1974).
65. Friedrich Engels, *The Origin of the Family, Private Property and the State, in the Light of the Researches of Lewis H. Morgan* (1972), p. 9.
66. Ibid.
67. Friedrich Engels, *Origin of the Family,* pp. 9–10.
68. Friedrich Engels, cited in Trautmann, *Lewis Henry Morgan,* p. 254.
69. Ibid., p. 133.
70. Ibid.
71. Wilhelm Liebknecht, 'Socialism', reprinted in William Pelz (ed.), *Wilhelm Liebknecht and German Social Democracy: A Documentary History,* Erich Hahn (trans.) (1994), p. 229.
72. Ibid.
73. Ibid.
74. John H. Kautsky, *Karl Kautsky: Marxism, Revolution and Democracy* (1994), p. 224.
75. Jean H. Quataert, *Reluctant Feminists in German Social Democracy, 1885–1917* (1979), p. 69.
76. Ibid., p. 70.
77. Richard Evans, *Sozialdemokratie und Frauenemanzipation im deutschen Kaiserreich* (1984), p. 42.
78. Ibid., pp. 43–4.
79. Ibid.
80. Moira Donald, 'Introduction', in August Bebel, *Women in the Past, Present and Future,* Adams Walther (trans.) (1988), p. iii.
81. Quataert, *Reluctant Feminists,* p. 16.
82. Richard Evans, *The Feminist Movement in Germany 1894–1933* (1976).
83. Anne Lopes and Gary Roth, *Men's Feminism: August Bebel and the German Socialist Movement* (2000), pp. 46–7.
84. August Bebel, *Die Frau und der Sozialismus* (1980), pp. 45–78.
85. Ibid., p. 45.
86. Ibid., p. 61.
87. Ibid., p. 57.
88. Ibid., p. 61.
89. Joan Scott, 'Gender: A Useful Category of Historical Analysis', in Joan Scott, *Gender and the Politics of History* (1988).
90. Evans, *Feminist Movement in Germany,* p. 24.
91. Ibid.
92. Ibid., p. 13.

93. Nancy Reagin, *A German Women's Movement: Class and Gender in Hanover 1880–1933* (1995).
94. Ute Frevert, *Women in German History: From Bourgeois Emancipation to Sexual Liberation* (1989), p. 126.
95. Ibid., pp. 126–7.
96. Renate Bridenthal, Claudia Koontz and Susan Stuard (eds), *Becoming Visible: Women in European History* (1987).
97. Lynn Hunt, *The Family Romance of the French Revolution* (1992).
98. Jacob Grimm, *Deutsche Rechtsalterthümer* (1828), p. 557.
99. Ibid., p. 557, n. 1.
100. Helene Lange, 'Frauentage', *Die Frau* (November 1899).
101. Ibid.
102. C. Wang, *The German Civil Code* (1907).
103. Ibid.
104. 'Aufruf!: Deutsche Frauen und deutsche Männer!', *Die Frauenbewegung,* 2/12 (1896).
105. Wang, *German Civil Code.*
106. Ibid.
107. Ibid.
108. Ibid.
109. Ibid.
110. Ibid.
111. Ibid.
112. Ibid.
113. Beatrix Geisel, *Klasse, Geschlecht und Recht: Vergleichende sozialhistorische Untersuchung der Rechtsberatungspraxis von Frauen- und Arbeiterbewegung 1894–1933* (1997), p. 35.
114. Ute Gerhard, 'Patriarchatskritik als Gesellschaftsanalyse: Ein nicht erledigtes Projekt', in Arbeitsgemeinschaft Interdisziplinäre Frauenforschung und -studien (eds), *Feministische Erneuerung von Wissenschaft und Kunst* (1990), p. 77.
115. Geisel, *Klasse, Geschlecht und Recht,* p. 38.
116. Ibid., pp. 102–5.
117. BDF, *Begleitschrift zu der Petition des Bundes Deutscher Frauenvereine an den Reichstag betreffend das Familienrecht des neuen bürgerlichen Gesetzbuchs für das Deutsche Reich* (1899).
118. Ibid.
119. Ibid.
120. Planck, *Rechtliche Stellung der Frau.*
121. Ibid.
122. Ibid.
123. Ibid.

124. Evans, *Feminist Movement in Germany,* p. 15; and John, *Politics and the Law,* pp. 231–8.
125. Baron von Stumm-Halberg, 'Erste Berathung im Plenum des Reichstages' (1896), in Benno Mugdan (ed.), *Die gesammten Materialien zum Bürgerlichen Gesetzbuch für das Deutsche Reich* (1899).
126. Ibid.
127. Albert Träger, cited in ibid.
128. File G28 Fürth: *Eheverträgen vor dem Grossherzoglichen Amtsgericht Fürth,* file no. 129, Hessisches Staatsarchiv in Darmstadt.
129. Ibid., file no. 132.
130. Ibid., file no. 115.
131. G 28 Gießen F 402/1: Eheverträge 1908, file no. 235, Hessisches Staatsarchiv in Darmstadt.
132. Georges Waterlot, 'Curiosités juridiques le nouvelle code allemande', *Indépendence Belge* (1 February 1901).
133. Ibid.
134. 'Ein halbes Jahr Bürgerliches Gesetzbuch', *Kölnische Zeitung* (9 July 1900).
135. Ibid.
136. Ibid.
137. 'Das erste Halbjahr des Inkraftseins des Bürgerlichen Gesetzbuches', *Allgemeine Zeitung* (3 July 1900).
138. 'Ein Jahr einheitliches Recht', *Berliner Neueste Nachrichten* (31 December 1900).
139. Ibid.
140. Waterlot, 'Curiosités juridiques'.
141. Anita Augsburg, 'Gebt acht, solange noch Zeit ist!', *Frauenbewegung: Revue für die Interessen der Frauen,* 1/1 (1895).
142. Alex Hall, 'Youth in Rebellion', in Richard Evans (ed.), *Society and Politics in Wilhelmine Germany* (1978).
143. Alfred Meyer, *The Feminism and Socialism of Lily Braun* (1985), pp. 146–59.
144. G. Stanley Hall, *Adolescence: Its Psychology and Its Relations to Physiology, Anthropology, Sociology, Sex, Crime, Religion and Education* (1911).
145. John R. Gillis, *Youth and History: Tradition and Change in European Age Relations, 1770–Present* (1981), pp. 95–131; Jacques Donzelot, *The Policing of Families* (1980); Lutz Roth, *Die Erfindung des Jugendlichen* (1983); and Peter Dudek, *Jugend als Objekt der Wissenschaft: Geschichte der Jugendforschung in Deutschland und Oesterreich 1880–1933* (1990).
146. Thomas Nipperdey, 'Jugend und Politik um 1900', in Thomas Nipperdey, *Gesellschaft, Kultur, Theorie: Gesammelte Aufsätze zur neueren Geschichte* (1976), pp. 338–59; Jürgen Reulecke, 'Bürgerliche Sozialreformer und Arbeiterjugend im Kaiserreich', *Archiv für Sozialgeschichte,* 22 (1982), pp. 299–329;

Detlev Peukert, *Grenzen der Sozialdisziplinierung: Aufstieg und Krise der deutschen Jugendfürsorge 1878–1932* (1986); and Derek Linton, *'Who Has the Youth Has the Future': The Campaign to Save Young Workers in Imperial Germany 1870–1914* (1991).

147. Waterlot, 'Curiosités juridiques'.
148. Jürgen Reulecke, 'The Battle for the Young: Mobilizing Young People in Wilhelmine Germany', in Mark Roseman (ed.), *Generations in Conflict: Youth Revolt and Generation Formation in Germany 1770–1968* (1995), p. 97.
149. Quoted in ibid.
150. Quoted in ibid., pp. 97–8.
151. Georges Waterlot, 'Curiosités juridiques'.
152. See for example the treatise by the lawyer B. Bleicken, *Unser Deutsches Volksrecht!, Eigenthum oder Ehe?: Ein Wort aus dem deutschen Volke an den deutschen Erb-Kaiser Wilhelm II* (1896).
153. B. Bleicken, *Schreiben an Sr. Excellenz den Herrn Justizminister Schönstedt betreffend Unsere nationale Rechtsentwicklung auf dem sozialen Lebensgebiete* (1897); B. Bleicken, *Schreiben an Sr. Excellenz den Herrn Staatsekretair Dr. Nieberding betreffend Unsere nationale Rechtsentwicklung auf dem sozialen Lebensgebiete* (1898); B. Bleicken, *Der Zusammenhang zwischen Gesellschafts-Verfassung und Heeres-Verfassung* (1899); and B. Bleicken, *Vom neuen Deutschen Volksrecht,* in Bundesarchiv file no. 30.01 625, Eingaben zum Bürgerlichen Gesetzbuch, 1896–1933.
154. Alexander Richard to Fürst von Bülow (1 December 1903), in Bundesarchiv file no. 30.01 1355 Acta betreffend: Eingaben in Familienrecht.
155. Ibid.
156. Ibid.
157. Reich-Justizministerium to Alexander Richard (8 December 1908), in Bundesarchiv file no. 30.01 1355.
158. 'Ein jugendlicher Selbstmörder', *Kölnische Zeitung* (8 December 1910).
159. Ibid.
160. Dirk Blasius, *Ehescheidung in Deutschland im 19. und 20. Jahrhundert* (1992).
161. Dr. A. Kolbe, *Hilferuf an den Kaiser und die deutsche Öffentlichkeit: Unglaubliches Prozessmartyrium in einem Ehescheidungsverfahren* (1914), pp. 1–3.
162. Ibid.
163. Ibid.
164. Ibid.
165. Ibid.
166. Ibid.
167. *Petition an den hohen Bundesrat und Reichstag zur Märztagung 1916: Keine Steuerbewilligung ohne freiheitlichere Ehegesetze!* in Bundesarchiv file no. 30.01 1355.

168. Paul Breuning to Reichjustizministerium (25 November 1921), in Bundesarchiv file no. 30.01 1357: Eingaben in Familienangelegenheiten, 1921–1923.
169. Ibid.
170. Ibid.
171. Ibid.
172. Reichjustizministerium to Paul Breuning (12 December 1921), in Bundesarchiv file no. 30.01 1357: Eingaben in Familienangelegenheiten, 1921–1923.
173. Anton Linder to Reichjustizministerium (17 November 1918), in Bundesarchiv file no. 30.01 1355, Acta Betreffend: Eingaben zum Familienrecht, vol. 1, March 1869–February 1920.
174. Ibid.
175. Ibid.
176. A. Wilken to Herr Minister (5 December 1921), in Bundesarchiv file no. 30.01 1357.
177. Ibid.
178. Ibid.
179. Kurt Erhardt, *Ein neues Ehescheidungsrecht!* (1919).
180. *An den Deutschen Reichstag,* in Bundesarchiv file no. 30.01 1357.
181. J. Bügsen to Reich (20 January 1919), in Bundesarchiv file no. 30.01 1355.
182. Ibid.
183. Ibid.
184. Ibid.
185. Ibid.
186. Carl Schmidt to Reichjustizministerium (20 January 1919), in Bundesarchiv file no. 30.01 1355.
187. Ibid.
188. Ibid.
189. Franz Wieacker, *A History of Private Law in Europe (with Particular Reference to Germany),* Tony Weir (trans.) (1995).
190. See letters in Bundesarchiv file no. 30.01 1388.
191. Oegg to Frau Käte Edlich (28 May 1929), in Bundesarchiv file no. 30.01 1388.
192. Emil Petersen to Reichjustizministerium (20 November 1928), in Bundesarchiv file no. 30.01 1388.
193. Ibid.
194. Ibid.
195. Ibid.

–8–

Conclusion
The German Idea of Revolution: Some Final Thoughts

> The King of Prussia has the constitutional right to rule autocratically ... If now the Kaiser steps forward as a personal ruler, he has every right to do so, the only question is whether the consequences can be borne in the long run. There is above all the question: who will win the game? I am afraid that only a successful war will provide the necessary prestige for this [domestic] conflict.[1]
>
> —Letter from Eulenburg to Holstein, circa 1898

The game, in fact, had already been won and the Prussian monarchy lost. As Frensdorff's double entendre implied, the BGB brought down the crown.[2] Germany's slow revolution reached its first apex in 1896. From 18 August of that year, the monarchy was on borrowed time pending good constitutional behavior and everybody, except perhaps for Wilhelm II, knew it. More than anything else, Eulenburg's strident insistence that the Kaiser could step forward as an autocrat underscored the anxieties of the hour. By 1914, the Kaiser's domestic authority had been stripped away, and he was hemmed in by law and a declining prestige in the diplomatic sphere as well. At least where the Reich was concerned, the majesty of the Prussian monarchy was diminished, and, increasingly, the only hope for its survival was seen in a risky roll of the dice, in Eulenburg's words 'a successful war'. The answer to the fundamental political question is, yes, there was a *Bürgerliche Revolution* in Germany, but it produced many discontents at the grassroots of German society; and worse, at the top. The Kaiser was the very dangerous discontent number one. When all else failed on the domestic front, he could still take Germany to war and unleash the terrible violence and bloodshed that followed in 1914. It was, as Prince Albert had written, 'a morally unjustified undertaking'.[3]

This book has sought to argue that the gradual consolidation of law, especially civil law, in Germany during the last quarter of the nineteenth century was the chosen means to a fundamental constitutional transformation, and that by liberal design, this process was both slow and nonviolent. The Constitution of 1871, in fact, was changeable, and it left many matters to be settled through the legislative process, a process that for a while Bismarck himself used adeptly. In making this argument, this study has drawn on the *Staatslehre* thought of Jellinek, Laband

and Triepel. Jellinek's *Verfassungsänderung und Verfassungswandlung* (1906) is particularly instructive. He drew a distinction between constitutional amendment, 'change in the text of the constitution through a purposeful act of will', and constitutional transformation, which 'allows the text to remain formally unchanged and is caused by facts that need not be accompanied by an intention or awareness of the change'.[4] Closely connected with constitutional transformation was this idea of filling 'gaps in the constitution'. The historical experience, Jellinek wrote, 'leads to the realization that every constitution is fraught with gaps, which often become evident only after a long time', and with 'such unexpected discoveries', the task of the legislature may lead to constitutional transformation.[5]

> Incomparably more instructive than all the constitutional transformations discussed, which take on one or another part of the constitution, are those that, without any sudden disruption of the state itself, completely destroy the existing state system and have as their ultimate result the complete rebuilding of the state. Long periods of time and the effect of great historical forces are necessary to give rise to something like this. If we look backwards through history we must grant, in astonishment, how even the most solid foundations of a state entity upon which it rested, apparently unshakably, for many centuries can crumble, shake, collapse, without the hand of a purposeful legislature having shaken them. The doctrine of such slow death of a constitution has been little cultivated. It could die because the value of its institutions sinks so low that no one desires them anymore—that ultimately none can be found to place their wills in the service of such institutions.[6]

Several points in Jellinek's commentary stand out in the context of this study. Most notable is that fact that he perhaps was only able to recognize constitutional transformation because it had happened in his lifetime. The attributes of constitutional transformation he describes bear striking resemblance to the ideas articulated in Gaetano Filangieri's *La Scienza della Legislazione* (1784–1791), which shaped Savigny's theory of politics and modern legislation articulated in *Vom Beruf unserer Zeit für Gesetzgebung und Rechtswissenschaft* (1814). Filangieri wrote:

> 'The first step to be taken is to create in the public a wish for the proposed reformation. A change in the constitution of a country is not the work of a moment, and to prepare the way for it, the inclinations of the people should be gradually led towards it.' 'They', he continued, 'should be made fully sensible of the inefficacy of their established laws, and be convinced their hardships and oppression are owing to them. The ablest writers should be employed to state the errors and inconveniences of the old system, and the propriety as well as the necessity of abolishing it, and adopting a more advantageous one.'[7]

It was from here that Filangieri went on to offer an important alternative conception of revolution: 'A decline of the legislative system is a political revolution, but a revolution affected slowly, which advances by sensible steps, and takes up ages to reach its termination. It is not, therefore, instantaneous in its nature ... the process of a revolution in a legislative system is slow, and consequently there is opportunity for its reformation.'[8] Filangieri's theory of legislative revolution and Jellinek's constitutional transformation represent two sides of the same coin, and, by linking the two together through Savigny's theory of politics and modern legislation, we are able to detect the German idea of revolution and follow its path.

In intellectual historical perspective, the fathers of the idea of making nonviolent *Bürgerliche Revolution* in Germany drew on and rationalized specifically age-old, German political traditions and modes of resistance. Accordingly, in the first instance, delineating the German idea of revolution has involved making the uniquely German conception of sovereignty and its identification with local *iurisdictio* visible. The conception of sovereignty, as it developed in German-speaking Europe, centred on the power to make and effect law, a *rechtliche Weltanschauung* and consciousness that had its roots not in ideas, but in the practices of the many German city-states and autonomous regions. The practice of local jurisdiction was not organized on a theoretical basis until it was challenged by the competing suzerain ambitions of popes and princes alike during the period of urbanization and *Verdorfung* between the twelfth and thirteenth century. Local communities faced the need to fend-off the legal effects of both classical canon law, which was used to effect the Papal Revolution, and the Reception of Roman law, which princes claimed as a basis of secular authority. In the midst of this, the development of urban law and inter-city *Rechtskreise*, particularly amongst the Hansa cities, emerged from local practice and in opposition to would-be authority imposed from outside. It was the Bolognese glossator Azo who offered the first rationalization of local *iurisdictio*. His views shaped the conception of sovereignty that was handed down through Bartolus to key political thinkers in the German world, including Conrad Celtis. Indeed, even before the Reformation, the use of the technical element of Roman law to gradually effect a rationalization, systematization, professionalization and scientization of German law was well underway. The aim of municipal *reformatio* was to nullify the influence of classical canon law, and this was not only a harbinger of the Reformation to come, but shows that legal conflict was at the heart of the Reformation.

Continuing identification of jurisdiction as the basis of sovereignty was again a significant factor in the development of Herman Conring's civic consciousness and principles of right to self-governance. His *Discursus novus* (1642) exploded the myth of Roman imperium in German-speaking Europe and with it the legitimacy of Roman law. Here again, it was a matter of time before, by the second half of the eighteenth century, the proto-rationalization of the German law served as a basis for resistance to would-be absolutism in Württemberg and elsewhere. The strength of self-governing practice was evident in Johann Jakob Moser's publication of his *Communal Ordinance* (1758), which was a handbook on self-governance, according to the local constitutional arrangements and laws. This traditional and continuing

German identification of sovereignty with jurisdiction formed a vital prelude to modern German constitutional theory as it began to emerge in the wake of the French revolutionary wars.

The strength of the traditions of local jurisdiction and self-governance, which found their clearest representation in discourses on law, meant that legalism as a traditional mode of civic consciousness was bound to be a distinguishing characteristic of what Margaret Anderson identifies as practicing democracy.[9] In addition to what has been shown in this study, demands for local jurisdiction were the alter ego of demands for popular sovereignty, and these demands served as the basis for resistance to the imposition of French law on German soil and Prussianization alike. When Württemberg's constitutional arrangements (including the *Tübinger Vertrag*) were abrogated during the Napoleonic rule in 1806, a Waiblingen petition demanded the restoration of 'Württembergers' Magna Charta', and under the leadership of Heinrich Bolley, the continuing struggle between prince and people resulted in the formation of an *Altrechtlicher* party of popular resistance.[10] This not only showed an identification of sovereignty with jurisdiction, it also expressed a popular notion of a basic inviolate law and customary law constitutionalism.[11] Later, Reyscher's *Vollständige, historisch und kritisch bearbeitete Sammlung der württembergischen Gesetze* (1828) would keep knowledge of the Württemberg constitution alive in liberal circles.[12] 'First and foremost,' patriotic Hamburgers and members of the resistance to the French occupation, as Katherine Aaslestad writes, 'sought to recover the city's republican constitution, independence, and autonomy.'[13] In the aftermath of unification, Hamburgers rejected Prussianization and increasingly saw its self-governing constitution as a model for the Reich. 'Hamburg, Lübeck and Bremen,' as a popular children's song went, 'do not have to be ashamed, because they are free cities where Bismarck has no say.'[14] Recent scholarship has also shown that the demand for local self-governance formed the basis for political mobilization, sometimes violent mobilization, in the *Vormärz* Prussian Rhineland.[15]

Accordingly, when Savigny repudiated Thibaut's call for immediate philosophical codification, he did so with the full knowledge that the imposition of French law was one of the major impulses behind resistance to Napoleonic rule in Hamburg, resistance that gave way to the *Freiheitskriege* themselves. In no way should Savigny's response be seen as a reaction against a purported revolutionary element in Thibaut's treatise. His concern was that a hasty imposition of codified law might incite still more violence in the aftermath of nearly a quarter century of warfare on German soil, and there was also the concern not to offer legal support to the reactionary consolidation of power emerging at the Congress of Vienna. While interest in the technique of Roman law continued to be a source of learning, the study of Roman law itself, more and more, confirmed the view that the rules of Roman law belonged to the people of a bygone Roman epoch. Indeed, even the articles on Roman law that appeared in the *Zeitschrift für geschichtliche Rechtswissenschaft* were marked by interest in the constitutionalism of the Roman Republic rather the practice of the *ius commune.*

Savigny's call for the study of the *vaterländisches Recht* responded to popular civic culture, and he realized that if any codification was ever to take place in Germany, it would have to occur on a foundation of German customary law arrangements. The idea of *ius civile* as a formative element in the creation of the *civitas* (city-state) was *combined* with Filangieri's conception of legislative revolution by Savigny to formulate a modern theory of nonviolent revolution as an alternative path for political reformation in Central Europe. 'And when the spirit of these violent revolutions die down,' he wrote to Constantin von Neurath in 1798, 'as I hope and I pray, this higher standpoint will be no less necessary as we ourselves nurture and refine our own norms and bring about tranquil reform without the high costs of blood, which is slower but safer and more certain.'[16] By 1814, Savigny's theory of politics and modern legislation, along with his comments in 'Ueber den Zweck dieser Zeitschrift' (1815), clearly articulated a course of nonviolent revolution, which would be obtained through a process of constitutional transformation. This was the slower path, but it was one that also found broad support in liberal circles. Barthold Niebuhr's *Römische Geschichte* and his lectures, which showed that the free constitution of the Roman Republic had resulted from a process of legislative rogations associated with the introduction of civil laws, seemed to confirm the efficacy of legislative revolution.[17]

The notion of constitutional transformation had its roots in the early-nineteenth-century development of private law scholarship. Particularly in the systems of private law produced by Eichhorn, Grimm and others, a programmatic political discourse was evident, and these works offer a window into the sociopolitical arrangements that liberals wanted to realize in German-speaking Europe. What is more, the restrictive realities of the reactionary years following 1819 pushed constitutionalism and public law scholarship underground, and as a result, private law became the mainstay of German political science. It is for this reason that I argue it forms a vital artery of German political thought or *Privatrechts-Staatslehre.* This concept allows scholars to appreciate not only the subtleties of German constitutionalism, but the deeply political character of the construction of 'private' relationships. Just as the discussion of private law was never separated from constitutional concerns, the 'private space,' especially the bourgeois family model, was never really distinct from public arrangements and constitutional organization. For this reason also, the very sharp distinctions that scholars have drawn between the public and private space may need to be reconsidered.

It can also be said that the tremendous expansion of private law scholarship, particularly the work of the Germanists, was not purely 'scientific', but was connected to the broader production of romantic art that developed in these years. Where scholars have seen romanticism as merely a mode of artistic expression, it is now necessary to see this entire production as part and parcel of liberal mobilization. George Williamson has argued that the construction of national mythology in 1848 shows how romanticism was bound up with notions of liberty and constitutionalism.

Here, he has emphasized the recovery of the *Nibelungenlied* and the importance of the Grimm brothers' fairy tales.[18] Germanist scholarship embodied nothing less than a modern process of rationalization, systematization, professionalization and scientization of German customs as a basis for German rules of laws, none other than the political element. At the same time, there was a strong creative, almost *künstlich* dimension in the development of envisioning a German *Gemeinwesen*. The mobilization and drive for constitutional transformation was sustained at the popular level by German fairy tales, which Grimm believed contained the remnants of ancient German law and customs from the free epoch. This critical detail leaves one with an understanding that the moral of the Grimm's brothers' stories impressed liberal sociopolitical and constitutional values in the popular mind.

Nowhere is the link between constitutionalism and art made clearer than in the consideration of the formidable influence of Jacob Grimm on the development of *Privatrechts-Staatslehre*, namely the growth of legal antiquarianism. He also emphasized the primacy of the people as the source of law, but called for greater consideration of the *sinnliche element.* In poetry, language, and fairy tales, Grimm claimed to find remnants of private law, from the so-called ancient German free epoch. He argued that a *Lebendigkeit,* or organic relationship, existed between contemporary folklore and ancient German law, and, as I have argued, this marked the growth of a German common law constitutionalism. His *Rechtsalterthümer* proved to be one of the most influential texts in German legal development and offered a glimpse of the imagined *Gemeinwesen.* While he clearly outlined the structure of a German public space in a free society, his descriptions of social relations defined the parameters of that public space in such a way that it depended on dichotomous formations, which made inclusion and exclusion interdependent.

The organization of the family—and particularly gender relations—was a central feature in the Germanists' writings. Gender relations became the central metaphor for power relations in public society, and here the capacity for the independent ownership and distribution of property was a principal concern. A significant portion of *Rechtsalterthümer* was concerned with private relationships, yet these relationships were politically significant. This pattern of political development continued to be evident in the writings of important liberal legal scholars, such as Karl Mittermaier, A. L. Reyscher, Friedrich Dahlmann, and Georg Beseler, and it reemerged in the platforms of the *Germanisten* conferences that were held in 1846 and 1847. Constitutional transformation, for these reasons, was as concerned about the social question as it was about political transformation. As a result, social transformations, such as the reorganization of family relations, also emerged as an important measure of revolution; installing the *bürgerliche* family as the basis of society was a part of the revolutionary strategy from the outset.

By the late 1840s constitutional transformation had emerged as a programatic strategy for political revision. Georg Gervinus wrote to Friedrich Dahlmann in 1847 that it would be their place 'to achieve the advantages of political revision without violent movement, wisely to learn from the sufferings and errors of foreign countries and gradually, following the path of legalism and through the power of the spirit, to gain what other nations have achieved by means of sudden attacks and by violence'.[19] Similar views were echoed by the editor of the BGB, Gottilieb Planck, in an 8 March 1848 letter to his parents: 'Once again we are in a time where history hastened forward on the double, when what has been hoped and striven after for decades is attained in a few days or even hours. Earlier I often had wished to have lived during the time of the first French Revolution', he continued, 'so that I could have seen and taken part in the experience of the magnificent drama of a people awakening to the consciousness of their rights and freedom,' but wished 'it could be repeated ... without the excess and terrorism that contaminated the first Revolution and laid to waste its best fruits.' 'The best hope for the German people' is by undermining the confederation from within.[20] This strategy did not change when the challenge became the would-be personal rule of Wilhelm II.

I have tried to highlight how what was developed in theory before 1848 was increasingly introduced as positive law between 1850 and 1900. It is significant that perhaps one of the last major works on public law prior to the Restoration appeared in the first two editions of the *Zeitschrift für geschichtliche Rechtswissenschaft.* Karl Eichhorn's lengthy articles *Ueber den Ursprung der städtischen Verfassung in Deutschland* (1815–1816) not only offered an account to the autonomous *iurisdictio* of the city constitutions as a basis of liberty, but also offered some indication of a development of *Rechtskreise* over time.[21] In practice this was widely evident at the state level after 1848, where procedural reforms modeled on the Hanover legislation were passed in Oldenburg (1857), Baden (1862), Württemberg (1868) and Bavaria (1869). In his *Lehrbuch* (1887) on the new code of civil procedure in Germany, Johann Planck, who was Max Planck's father, acknowledged that the 'powerful impulse' for the legislation had come from 'the political movement of the year 1848', and he viewed 'the *Civilprozessrecht* as part of the public laws'.[22] Lothar Seuffert opened his own commentary by quoting §64 of the constitutional document of 1849. 'The constitution did not come to pass,' but he continued, the construction of material legal unity through the states 'was the only road open', and there was already the example of *'des Wechselrechts und des Handelsrechts'*.[23]

In addition, nineteenth-century gender conditions on the ground were examined in order to offer a measure of how the *Bürgerliche Revolution* transformed ordinary life in German society. In particular, I examined marital property relations and indicated that women, perhaps, were far more prominent as property owners and breadwinners in Central Europe than previously thought. Indeed, they contributed substantial sums of wealth to their marriages, and, what was even more striking, was that they retained independent management and usufruct rights. The trend in marital property relations, as the state reports indicated, was toward the separation of property. Moreover, German municipal courts increasingly upheld not only women's property rights, but public rights, such as the right to swear oaths, bequeath property and be guardians of minor children. Beneath what appeared to be a century of promise, however, regressive tendencies were evident in private law scholarship and in appeals courts' decisions, courts that increasingly fell into the hands of liberal judges.

One of the remarkable aspects of the making of revolution in Germany is that constitutional transformation was carried forward across generations. Gottlieb Planck, for example, was an important link in the chain of constitutional transformation and he clearly articulated his commitment to legislative revolution in the 1848 letter to his parents. More than this, however, Planck was a liberal veteran of mid-century constitutional conflicts. He was born into a liberal family of Hanoverian scholars; indeed, his father, Wilhelm Planck, had been an influential jurist, who worked on the Hanover procedural legislation with Adolf Leonhardt. In addition, the significant influence of the Planck family must be taken into consideration. They were originally from Württemberg. Gottlieb Planck's uncle was Julius Planck and the famous physicist, Max, and his brother, Hugo were his first cousins. Considering that Hugo Planck was Chief Justice of the *Reichsgericht,* one can see that Gottlieb Planck's ability to influence, not only the making, but the interpretation of the law was far reaching.

The influence of liberalism was already apparent in Planck's education. At the University of Göttingen, he formed important political friendships, such as that with Rudolf von Bennigsen. Amongst a collection of courses with clearly liberal orientation, Planck studied German private law with the Germanist, Wilhelm Kraut. By mid century, he suffered from disciplinary transfer after disciplinary transfer for his liberal agitation, a road he often shared with his good friend Bennigsen. Their generation no longer viewed themselves as *Fürstendiener;* rather they were the people behind the powerful movement of institutional change and modern state-building, which had a major importance for the place of the bourgeoisie in German society.[24] Unlike the earlier generation of liberal legal scholars, the second generation had been encouraged to seek careers in the civil service and represented a second phase in Gervinus's path of legalism. This is an important point, because some historians have persisted in viewing the bureaucracy as a conservative force in Central European society.[25] At the same time, Werner Conze, James Retallack and others have found that at the local and town level, the liberal spirit survived during the Restoration and that the bourgeoisie was more powerful than had been assumed.[26]

The key to constitutional transformation after the founding of the Reich was the Bundesrat's and Reichstag's acquisition of *Kompetenz-Kompetenz.*[27] Indeed, this might just as well be termed jurisdiction-jurisdiction. No statute passed by the Bundesrat and Reichstag could later be pronounced unconstitutional, whether or not it conformed to, altered or amended the constitution. The Bundesrat and the Reichtag held the power to extend the competence of the Reich by simple legislation, and as a result there were significant changes to the constitution over time. There were important formal amendments, such as the *Lex Miquel-Lasker,* but most of the transformation was informal.[28] The constitution was flexible, and it did not cement the supremacy of the monarchical principle. Article 11 specifically read that 'the King of Prussia shall hold the *Präsidium* (presidency) of the *Bund,* and shall have the title of German Emperor,' and over time this was legislated into reality. The final form of the German constitution remained an open question in 1871, and how that question was answered was wholly dependent, not only on the character and content of the legislation, but also on public opinion. This in turn contributed to a latent primacy of the legislative branch in German politics and constitutional formation.

Although the Kaiser attempted to reassert personal rule in the 1890s, this position in the Reich was in progressive decline almost from its inception and decline sped up as soon as Wilhelm II ascended the throne of Prussia. In addition, with public relations nightmare after public relations nightmare, every major piece of legislation that passed the Bundesrat and Reichstag clipped away at his domestic authority. By the time public criticism mounted against him in the 1890s, his ability to act was limited by the *Reichsjustizgesetze,* the leniency of the *Strafgesetzbuch* on *Majestätsbeleidigung* and, above all, by the reluctance of jurors and judges to hold defendants accountable. Increasingly, criticism of the Kaiser took on the language of legalism and held dire consequences for his position, particularly under §6 of the BGB. No doubt the memory of King Frederick Wilhelm IV having been declared insane and removed from the throne loomed large. More than the BGB, however, its *Einführungsgesetz* fundamentally deprived the Kaiser of traditional realms of power. Alsace-Lorraine became a state and its citizens were given the full benefits of *bürgerliche* legal protections, giving the Reichstag and Bundesrat some measure of jurisdiction. This certainly became apparent during the notorious Zabern Affair, when the offenders were hauled before the Reichstag and the army's constitutional transgressions were redressed.[29]

It is no accident of history that Tirpitz was brought on board in 1897, and that it is directly in the aftermath of the BGB that we may locate the beginning of Weltpolitik. It was precisely a 'feeling of suffering a loss of power' which aroused the Kaiser's 'determination to defend his [monarchical] right, if necessary by force'.[30] Yet, historians have generally pointed toward the rise of this sentiment in the years immediately prior to the First World War. In fact, however, the Kaiser's and his entourage's rising anxiety about his domestic power may be located in the immediate aftermath of the enactment of the BGB, as Eulenburg's comments that open this conclusion clearly indicate. As one scholar has noted: 'By 1913 the question of civil war and foreign war had indeed become the two sides of the same coin in the minds of the Kaiser and his advisers.'[31]The crisis of the monarchy reached the breaking point in 1896, when the BGB and *Einführungsgesetz* severely clipped the kaiser's wings.

After 1896 there was one—and only one—loophole in the constitutional system that might be exploited as an avenue for personal rule, and this was through the imminent threat provisions of Article 68. It read: 'The Emperor shall have the power, if the public security of the Empire demands it, to declare martial law in any part thereof. Until the publication of a law regulating the grounds, the form of announcement and the effect of such declaration shall be regulated under the provisions of the Prussian law of 4 June 1851.' This, in effect, allowed all the civil structures of the state to be immediately subsumed under military administration, and it also dramatically increased the position of Prussia vis-à-vis the other states. What is more, to deal with domestic social problems that might arise, there was an unfortunate clause in the *Einführungsgesetz zum Strafgesetzbuch* that allowed for a ratcheting-up of summary arrests in the event of wartime.[32] The power to make defensive war was one of a very few constitutional cards that the Kaiser had left to play, and his advisors were keenly aware of the need to make the war appear as a defensive measure against Russian aggression. In the excited climate of July and August 1914, as Michael Stolleis points out, 'the fact that the constitution was circumvented and violated in a number of ways during the internal events that led to the German decision to go to war was hardly noticed by contemporaries'.[33] In the face of this lingering, untransformed constitutional flaw, the Enabling Act of 4 August 1914 was the civil twin of two evils. As for the *Burgfrieden*, one must consider this against the fact that the Military Code also came into effect for most men of recruiting age. While they had enjoyed greater protection of their civil rights under *bürgerliche* laws, this protection evaporated as soon as they were enlisted in the armed services. These measures taken together, in effect, left German citizens under the personal rule of the Prussian King.

Michael John argues that the BGB was the product of a liberal-conservative alliance. In particular, he emphasized that preparation of the BGB was consigned to the ministerial bureaucracy, and that effective control continued to rest in the hands of the bureaucracy and professional lawyers, even on the second drafting commission.[34] As I have tried to indicate here, by the late nineteenth century, it seems that in terms of the legal bureaucracy, liberals and the bourgeoisie were a powerful force at the national level as well.[35] The *Reichjustizministerium* was stacked successively with powerful liberal figures, such as Adolf Leonhardt, Rudolf Nieberding and Heinrich Gustav Struckmann, who was one of Planck's former court clerks on the Court of Appeals in Celle, and who had worked on the family law committee. Moreover, John points out that the editors of each section of the Code were given a free hand with regard to the content of their sections.[36]

The General Part of the BGB defined citizenship and the rights of citizens. At the same time, its definition of majority was clearly indebted to the exclusive liberalism of the Germanists. This was also apparent in the family law, which rigorously disenfranchised German women. While it showed that the *Bürgerliche Revolution* was able to transform the social fabric to meet the needs of the new state, as we have seen this also created significant discontent at the grassroots of German society. Most Germans experienced the transformation in their homes. While the state reports for Planck's committee plainly showed that the existing trend in marital property relations was toward separate property rights and wives' independent management and usufruct rights, the BGB reinstated the ancient *Verwaltungsgemeinschaft,* which scholars freely acknowledged had been in decline for centuries. Paragraph

1354 granted the husband sole decision-making authority, while §1363 declared that 'by the conclusion of a marriage the property of the wife becomes subject to the management and usufruct by the husband.' Moreover, this system was instituted despite the fact that existing particularism, combined with the contract rate, indicated that the overwhelming majority of German couples, in the regions of French law where it was in effect, rejected this system. The Baden report showed that there were marital agreements in 48 percent of all marriages, which abandoned outright the statutory regime of the Civil Code of Baden.

The rigid *bürgerliche* social precepts of the BGB soon gave rise to *Gegenpolitik.* Here the work of Johann Bachofen proved to be as influential on the development of legal anthropology as that of Savigny, Eichhorn, Mittermaier, Grimm, Beseler and others had been on legal history. *Das Mutterrecht* grew out of Bachofen's rejection of the exclusive doctrine of participation, and, as suggested, his work opposed the theoretical propositions of the Germanists in important ways. Where Grimm and the Germanists argued that the *Ausgangspunkt* of the Germanic family was characterized by patriarchy, Bachofen argued that this era had been preceded by an earlier epoch characterized by gynaecocracy. Here, he identified a special moral and social function of women in society, which supported the public participation of women.

Bachofen's work had a significant impact on the development of German socialism and Lewis Henry Morgan's *Ancient Society.* Karl Marx and Friedrich Engels relied heavily on Morgan and Bachofen in the development of a Marxist position on the family. From Engels and Marx, Bachofen's theory of law shaped the ideological character of social democracy. Prominent socialist figures, such as Karl Kautsky, Clara Zetkin, Lily Braun and Wilhelm Liebknecht, were well versed on the importance of Bachofen's theory. His influence was most apparent, however, in Bebel's *Die Frau und der Sozialismus.* Despite the growth of social-democratic constitutionalism, however, this sphere of legal thought was swimming upstream against the *Bürgerliche Revolution,* which was brought about through major legislations of *bürgerliche* law. The historical school remained firmly entrenched in German legal education for some time. As a result, even when social democracy came to Germany in the form of the Weimar Republic, this democratic experiment only penetrated the surface of German society. There was no corresponding great body of scholarship to sustain social democracy as there had been for *Bürgerliche Revolution* and this left the Weimar Republic teetering on top of *bürgerliche* laws and judicial institutions. It was, therefore, unable to effect reform in German society beyond the paper of the Constitution, and the pre-war basis of social discontent in German society lingered on to become one of the major causes of the second republic's failure.

In addition to the discontent that was reflected at the intellectual level in German society, popular dissatisfaction with the Code's family law appears to have been significant. Scholars of German history have argued that the rise of alternative cultures intensified during the period of bourgeois cultural consolidation.[37] The BGB etched in stone the supremacy of majority rule and the interest of capital in society, including exclusive liberal notions of political participation by denying full citizenship to large sectors of the population. Indeed, the demands of the economic life were a consistent theme expressed by National Liberals in favor of the BGB's introduction. In his opening speech to the Reichstag debates, Rudolf Nieberding stated: 'The second commission worked in ... association with the great interest groups that our economic life demands.'[38] Whereas Nieberding confirmed the interest of industry, Planck confirmed the demand for the people to conform their social relations to those interests. In his speech before the Reichstag, he linked 'social weakness' to 'economic weakness' and argued that regulation of private relations was necessary to sustain economic prosperity.[39]

More than any other element, the social consequences of the *Bürgerliche Revolution* were revealed to ordinary Germans with the introduction of the BGB. It made bourgeois rule tangible and, in this way, created discontent and large numbers of newly disaffected people. It was not simply a coincidence of history that the strongest criticism of German society emerged during the decades that witnessed the introduction of civil measures. To the growing number of cultural critics, whether literary or political figures, the rise of civil law was met with skepticism. The discontent expressed by *fin-de-siècle* thinkers, such as Paul de Lagarde and Julius Langbehn, perhaps was not based solely on an abstract sense of modern culture, but emerged because modernity was increasingly given shape in the form of civil legislation.[40]

Nowhere did the *bürgerliche* rule of law pierce into the lives of more Germans than in the area of family law. For the many average Germans who were unhappy with the new society, the bourgeois family organization, as ordered under civil law, became a metaphor for all that was wrong in German society. The BGB's statutory regime of marital property relations symbolized a society that was unequal from the core. The emerging demand for reform of the marriage laws was a demand for the redistribution of rights on democratic terms. Many men had signed the BDF's petition and registered their demands for revision of the draft's family law. Ignoring the protests of women, therefore, ignored the complaints of men, who, unlike women, possessed the right to vote. Whereas the complaints of women and bitter unhappiness in marriage grew out of the hated sex guardianship, men appeared to be particularly disgruntled about the Code's divorce provisions. By the beginning of the First World War, the BGB's divorce provisions had become a leading source of discontent, not least amongst men.

In conclusion, it seems clear that there was a bourgeois revolution in German history. The fact that revolution was brought about through legislation means that the evidence is circumstantial. There is little reason to be surprised by this, however, given that it was brought about by a number of shrewd lawyers, skilled, above all else, in the arts of fine legal print. The German idea of revolution, from its origins in the aftermath of the *Freiheitskriege,* centred on obtaining national *iurisdictio,* defined as sovereignty. The *ius civile* was seen as a tool in the formation of the national *civitas.* In point of fact, the tremendous constitutional transformation that occurred cannot be denied, and the responses at both the highest, as well as the lowest, levels of German society clearly mark a major sociopolitical shift. Revolution happened, but any trend toward optimistic research must be tempered by the fact that Germany's *Bürgerliche Revolution* was one wrought with significant international and domestic sociopolitical consequences, namely, the twin realities of the First World War and widespread social discontent on the ground. Despite tremendous constitutional transformation, there was one very significant *lex imperfecta* in the constitution: Article 68 of the *Reichsverfassung.*

Notes

1. Eulenburg to Holstein, circa 1898, cited in Giles MacDonogh, *The Last Kaiser: William the Impetuous* (2000), p. 205.
2. Ferdinand Frensdorff, *Gottlieb Planck: Deutscher Jurist und Politiker* (1914), p. 308.
3. Patricia Kollander, *Frederick III: Germany's Liberal Emperor* (1995), p. 15.
4. Georg Jellinek, *Verfassungsänderung und Verfassungswandlung* (1906), in Arthur Jacobson and Bernhard Schlink (eds), *Weimar: A Crisis of Jurisprudence* (2000), p. 54.
5. Ibid., p. 56.
6. Ibid., p. 57.
7. Gaetano Filangieri, *The Science of Legislation, from the Italian of Gaetano Filangieri* , R. Clayton (trans.) (1806), p. 57.
8. Ibid., pp. 66–7.
9. Margaret Anderson, *Practicing Democracy: Elections and Political Culture in Imperial Germany* (2000).
10. Ian McNeely, *The Emancipation of Writing: German Civil Society in the Making, 1790s–1820s* (2003), pp. 96–164.
11. Ibid., p. 124.
12. August Ludwig Reyscher, *Vollständige, historisch und kritisch bearbeitete Sammlung der württembergischen Gesetze* (1828).
13. Katherine Aaslestad, 'Remembering and Forgetting: The Local and the Nation in Hamburg's Commemorations of the Wars of Liberation', *Central European History,* 38/3 (2005), p. 390. For more on political thought in Hamburg see also Katherine Aaslestad, 'Old Visions and New Vices: Republicanism and Civic Virtue in Hamburg's Print Culture 1790–1810', in Peter Hohendahl (ed.), *Patriotism, Cosmopolitanism and National Culture: Public Culture in Hamburg 1700–1933* (2003), pp. 143–65.
14. Aaslestad, 'Remembering and Forgetting', pp. 403–5.
15. James Brophy, 'Violence between Civilians and State Authorities in the Prussian Rhineland 1830–1846', *German History,* 22/1 (2004), pp. 1–35; and

Walter Rummel, 'Motive staatlicher und dörflicher Gewaltanwendung im 19. Jahrhundert. Eine Skizze zum Ende der frühneuzeitlichen Sozialkultur in der preußischen Rheinprovinz', in Magnus Eriksson and Barbara Krug-Bichter (eds), *Streitkulturen: Gewalt, Konflikt und Kommunikation in der ländlichen Gesellschaft (16.–19. Jahrhundert)* (2003), pp. 157–78.

16. Savigny to Constantine von Neurath (end 1798), in Adolf Stoll, *Savigny: Ein Bild seines Lebens mit einer Sammlung seiner Briefe*, vol. 1, *Der junge Savigny* (1927), p. 70.
17. Barthold Niebuhr, *Römische Geschichte,* 3 vols (1811–1812).
18. George Williamson, *The Longing for Myth in Germany: Religion and Aesthetic Culture from Romanticism to Nietzsche* (2004), pp. 72–120.
19. Georg Gervinus to Friedrich Dahlmann, cited in R. Hinton Thomas, *Liberalism, Nationalism and the German Intellectuals: An Analysis of the Academic and Scientific Conferences of the Period* (1951), p. 125.
20. Gottlieb Planck to Parents, cited in Frensdorff, *Gottlieb Planck,* p. 81.
21. Karl Eichhorn, 'Ueber den Ursprung der städtischen Verfassung in Deutschland', *Zeitschrift für geschichtliche Rechtswissenschaft,* 1 (1815), pp. 147–247; and Karl Eichhorn, 'Ueber den Ursprung der städtischen Verfassung in Deutschland', *Zeitschrift für geschichtliche Rechtswissenschaft* 2 (1816), pp. 165–237.
22. Johann Planck, *Lehrbuch des Deutschen Civilprozessrechts* (1887), pp. 11 and 17.
23. Lothar Seuffert, *Kommentar zur Civilprozessordnung für das Deutsche Reich zum Einführungsgesetze* (1895), p. ix.
24. David Blackbourn and Richard Evans (eds), *The German Bourgeoisie: Essays on the Social History of the German Middle Class from the Late Eighteenth to the Early Twentieth Century* (1991).
25. H. Beck, *Origins of the Authoritarian Welfare State in Prussia: Conservatives, Bureaucracy and the Social Question 1815–70* (1995).
26. Werner Conze, 'Das Spannungsfeld von Staat und Gesellschaft im Vormärz', in Werner Conze (ed.), *Staat und Gesellschaft im deutschen Vormärz* (1962), pp. 207–69; and Larry Eugene Jones and James Retallack (eds), *Elections, Mass Politics and Social Change in Modern Germany: New Perspectives* (1992).
27. Heinrich Triepel, *Die Kompetenzen des Bundesstaats und die geschriebene Verfassung* (1908); Paul Laband, *Staatsrecht* (1906); and Paul Laband, 'Die geschichtliche Entwicklung der Reichsverfassung seit der Reichsgründung', *Jahrbuch des öffentlichen Rechts,* 1 (1907), pp. 1–46, cited in ibid., p. 150.
28. Otto Pflanze, *Bismarck and the Development of Germany: The Period of Unification 1815–1871* (1990), pp. 149–50.
29. David Schoenbaum, *Zabern 1913: Consensus Politics in Imperial Germany* (1982), pp. 175–83.
30. Volker Berghahn, *Germany and the Approach of War in 1914* (1993), p. 36.
31. Ibid.

32. Achim Kurz, *Demokratische Diktatur? Auslegung und Handhabung des Artikels 48 der Weimarer Verfassung 1919–25* (1992), pp. 17–18.
33. Michael Stolleis, *A History of Public Law in Germany 1914–1945* (2004), p. 20.
34. Michael John, *Politics and the Law in Late Nineteenth Century Germany: The Origins of the Civil Code* (1989), pp. 243–5.
35. See also Kenneth Ledford, 'Lawyers, Liberalism and Procedure: The German Imperial Justice Laws of 1877–79', *Central European History,* 26 (1993), pp. 165–94.
36. John, *Politics and the Law,* p. 79.
37. See for example Vernon Lidtke, *The Alternative Culture: Socialist Labor in Imperial Germany* (1985); Lynn Abrams, *Worker Culture in Imperial Germany: Leisure and Reaction in the Rhineland and Westphalia* (1992); and Gerhard Ritter, *Arbeiterbewegung, Parteien und Parlamentarismus: Aufsätze zur deutschen Sozial- und Verfassungsgeschichte des 19. und 20. Jahrhunderts* (1976).
38. Rudolf Nieberding, 'Erste Berathung des BGB im Plenum des Reichstags' (1896), in Benno Mugdan (ed.), *Die gesammten Materialien zum Bürgerlichen Gesetzbuch für das Deutsche Reich* (1899), p. 846.
39. Gottlieb Planck, 'Erste Berathung des BGB im Plenum des Reichstags' (1896), in Benno Mugdan, *Die gesammten Materialien zum Bürgerlichen Gesetzbuch für das Deutsche Reich* (1899), pp. 883–90.
40. Fritz Stern, *The Politics of Cultural Despair: A Study in the Rise of Germanic Ideology* (1961).

Bibliography

Aaslestad, K., 'Old Visions and New Vices: Republicanism and Civic Virtue in Hamburg's Print Culture 1790–1810', in P. Hohendahl (ed.), *Patriotism, Cosmopolitanism and National Culture: Public Culture in Hamburg 1700–1933,* Amsterdam and New York: Rodopi, 2003.

Aaslestad, K., 'Remembering and Forgetting: The Local and the Nation in Hamburg's Commemorations of the Wars of Liberation', *Central European History*, 38/3 (2005), pp. 384–416.

Abrams, L., *Workers' Culture in Imperial Germany: Leisure and Reaction in the Rhineland and Westphalia,* London and New York: Routledge, 1992.

Ahcin, C., *Zur Entstehung des bürgerlichen Gesetzbuchs für das Königreich Sachsen von 1863/65*, Frankfurt am Main: V. Klostermann, 1996.

Alfonso, I., Kennedy, H., and Escalona, J. (eds), *Building Legitimacy: Political Discourse and Forms of Legitimacy in Medieval Societies*, Leiden and Boston: Brill, 2004.

Allgemeine Deutsche Biographie (1875–1912).

Amman, 'Über den Proceß gegen Gustav von Struve und Karl Blind aus Mannheim, wegen Hochverraths: Die erste Verhandlung vor einem Badischen Schwurgerichte', *Der Gerichtssaal*, 1/2 (1849), pp. 201–13.

An den Deutschen Reichstag, Bundesarchiv file no. 30.01 1357: Eingaben in Familienangelegenheiten, 1921–1923.

Anderson, M., *Practicing Democracy: Elections and Political Culture in Imperial Germany*, Princeton: Princeton University Press, 2000.

Anonymous, 'Aufruf!: Deutsche Frauen und deutsche Männer!', *Die Frauenbewegung*, 2/12 (1896), Bundesarchiv file no. 30.01 Fb23440, Reichs-Justizamt, Äußerungen der Presse über das Familienrecht von 1896 bis 1919.

Anonymous, *Durch welche Bedingungen ist das System der Handelsfreiheit ausführbar?*, 1834.

Anonymous, 'Die Ehefrage und der Beruf', *Die Frau* (late 1890s).

Anonymous, 'Die Ehefrau kann einen Eid über den eigenthümlichen Erwerb von in die Ehe gebrachten und von ihr der Concursmasse ihres Ehemannes abgeforderten Gegenständen ohne Beitritt des Ehemannes ableisten', *Blätter für Rechtspflege in Thüringen und Anhalt* (1867).

Anonymous, 'Die Einheit des deutschen Rechts', *Hamburger Nachrichten* (3 January 1900), Bundesarchiv file no. 30.01 Fb23440, Reichs-Justizamt, Äußerungen der Presse über das Familienrecht von 1896 bis 1919.

Anonymous, 'Das erste Halbjahr des Inkraftseins des Bürgerlichen Gesetzbuches', *Allgemeine Zeitung* (3 July 1900), Bundesarchiv file no. 30.01 Fb23440, Reichs-Justizamt, Äußerungen der Presse über das Familienrecht von 1896 bis 1919.

Anonymous, 'Die Erwerbsthaetigkeit der Frau', *Die Frau*, 1–12 (October 1893–September 1894).

Anonymous, 'Die Feier der Münchener Juristischen Gesellschaft anläßlich der Einführung des neuen Bürgerlichen Gesetzbuches', *Münchener Neueste Nachrichten* (1 January 1900), Bundesarchiv file no. 30.01 Fb23440, Reichs-Justizamt, Äußerungen der Presse über das Familienrecht von 1896 bis 1919.

Anonymous, *Gewerbefreiheit für Nürnberg*, 1846.

Anonymous, 'Ein halbes Jahr Bürgerliches Gesetzbuch', *Kölnische Zeitung* (9 July 1900), Bundesarchiv file no. 30.01 Fb23440, Reichs-Justizamt, Äußerungen der Presse über das Familienrecht von 1896 bis 1919.

Anonymous, 'Ein Jahr einheitliches Recht', *Berliner Neueste Nachrichten* (31 December 1900), Bundesarchiv file no. 30.01 Fb23440, Reichs-Justizamt, Äußerungen der Presse über das Familienrecht von 1896 bis 1919.

Anonymous, 'Ein jugendlicher Selbstmörder', *Kölnische Zeitung* (8 December 1910), Bundesarchiv file no. 30.01 Fb23440, Reichs-Justizamt, Äußerungen der Presse über das Familienrecht von 1896 bis 1919.

Anonymous, 'Die Kunst- und Handelsgärtnerinnen', *Die Frau* (October 1893).

Anonymous, 'Das neue Recht', *Hannoverische Rundschau* (12 December 1899), Bundesarchiv file no. 30.01 Fb23440, Reichs-Justizamt, Äußerungen der Presse über das Familienrecht von 1896 bis 1919.

Anonymous, 'Die Stellung der Ehefrau im Civilprozess bei bestehender Verwaltungsgemeinschaft', *Das Recht* (10 February 1901).

Anonymous, 'Unter welchen Voraussetzungen kann eine Ehefrau, welche während der Ehe ihrem Manne ein Darlehn gegeben, die von ihrem Manne ihr dafür in solutum überlassenen Mobilien als ihr Eigenthum in Anspruch nehmen', *Blätter für Rechtspflege in Thüringen und Anhalt* (1880).

Applet, H., 'Frederick Barbarossa und das römische Recht', *Römische historische Mitteilungen*, 5 (1961/62).

Arndt, E., *Reisen durch einen Theil Teutschlands, Italiens und Frankreichs in den Jahren 1798 und 1799*, 1803.

Arnswaldt, A. von, *De Vicariatus controversia: Beiträge Hermann Conrings in der Diskussion um die Reichsverfassung des 17. Jahrhunderts*, Berlin: Duncker & Humblot, 2004.

Augsburg, A., 'Gebt acht, solange noch Zeit ist!', *Frauenbewegung: Revue für die Interessen der Frauen*, 1/1 (1895).

Bachofen, J., *Das Mutterrecht: Eine Untersuchung über die Gynaikratie der alten Welt nach ihrer religiösen und rechtlichen Natur*, Stuttgart: Krais & Hoffman, 1861.

Bachofen, J., *Myth, Religion and Mother Right: Selected Writings of J. J. Bachofen*, R. Mannheim (trans.), Princeton: Princeton University Press, 1992.

Bachrach, D., 'Making Peace and War in the "City-state" of Worms, 1235–1273', *German History*, 24/4 (2006), pp. 505–25.

BDF, *Begleitschrift zu der Petition des Bundes Deutscher Frauenvereine an den Reichstag betreffend das Familienrecht des neuen bürgerlichen Gesetzbuchs für das Deutsche Reich*, 1899, Bundesarchiv file no. 30.01 1350.

Bebel, A., 'Das Bürgerliche Gesetzbuch und die Sozialdemokratie', *Neue Zeit*, 2 (1895/96).

Bebel, A., *Die Frau und der Sozialismus*, London: Zwan, 1980.

Beck, H., *Origins of the Authoritarian Welfare State in Prussia: Conservatives, Bureaucracy and the Social Question 1815–70*, Ann Arbor: University of Michigan Press, 1995.

Bekker, E., 'Über das gemeine deutsche Recht der Gegenwart und dessen Behandlung', *Jahrbuch des gemeinen deutschen Rechts*, 1 (1857), pp. 1–23.

Benz, E., *Fertility, Wealth, and Politics in Three Southwest German Villages: 1650–1900*, Leiden and Boston: Brill, 1999.

Berghahn, V., *Germany and the Approach of War in 1914*, New York: St. Martin's Press, 1993.

Berkowitz, R., *Gift of Science: Leibniz and the Modern Legal Tradition*, Cambridge: Harvard University Press, 2005.

Beseler, G., *Die Lehre von den Erbverträgen*, 1837–1840.

Beseler, G., *System des gemeinen deutschen Privatrechts*, 1847–1855.

Beseler, G., *Ueber die Stellung des römischen Rechts zu dem nationalen Recht der germanischen Völker*, 1836.

Beseler, G., *Volksrecht und Juristenrecht*, 1843.

Billich, C., *Das württembergische Gewerbe-Recht*, 1852.

Birtsch, G., 'Reform Absolutism and the Codification of Law: The Genesis and Nature of the Prussian General Code', in J. Brewer and E. Hellmuth (eds), *Rethinking Leviathan: The Eighteenth Century State in Britain and Germany*, Oxford: Oxford University Press, 1999.

Blackbourn, D., *The Long Nineteenth Century: A History of Germany 1780–1918*, New York: Oxford University Press, 1997.

Blackbourn, D., and Eley, G., *The Peculiarities of German History: Bourgeois Society and Politics in Nineteenth-Century Germany*, Oxford: Oxford University Press, 1984.

Blackbourn, D., and Evans, R. (eds), *The German Bourgeoisie: Essays on the Social History of the German Middle Class from the Late Eighteenth to the Early Twentieth Century*, London and New York: Routledge, 1991.

Blackstone, W., *Commentaries on the Laws of England*, 1767.

Blanning, T., *The French Revolution in Germany: Occupation and Resistance in the Rhineland 1792–1802*, Oxford: Oxford University Press, 1983.

Blasius, D., *Ehescheidung in Deutschland im 1794–1945: Scheidung und Scheidungsrecht in historischer Perspektive*, Göttingen: Vandenhoeck & Ruprecht, 1987.

Bleibtreu, L., *Die Lehre von den Wechseln mit Hinweisung auf bestehende Gesetze*, 1860.

Bleicken, B., *Schreiben an Sr. Excellenz den Herrn Justizminister Schönstedt betreffend Unsere nationale Rechtsentwicklung auf dem sozialen Lebensgebiete* (1897), Bundesarchiv file no. 30.01 625, Eingaben zum Bürgerlichen Gesetzbuch, 1896–1933.

Bleicken, B., *Schreiben an Sr. Excellenz den Herrn Staatsekretair Dr. Nieberding betreffend Unsere nationale Rechtsentwicklung auf dem sozialen Lebensgebiete* (1898), Bundesarchiv file no. 30.01 625, Eingaben zum Bürgerlichen Gesetzbuch, 1896–1933.

Bleicken, B., *Unser Deutsches Volksrecht!, Eigenthum oder Ehe?: Ein Wort aus dem deutschen Volke an den deutschen Erb-Kaiser Wilhelm II* (1896), Bundesarchiv file no. 30.01 625, Eingaben zum Bürgerlichen Gesetzbuch, 1896–1933.

Bleicken, B., *Vom neuen Deutschen Volksrecht* (n.d.), Bundesarchiv file no. 30.01 625, Eingaben zum Bürgerlichen Gesetzbuch, 1896–1933.

Bleicken, B., *Der Zusammenhang zwischen Gesellschafts-Verfassung und Heeres-Verfassung* (1899), Bundesarchiv file no. 30.01 625, Eingaben zum Bürgerlichen Gesetzbuch, 1896–1933.

Blickle, P., *From the Communal Reformation to the Revolution of the Common Man*, B. Kümin (trans.), Leiden and Boston: Brill, 1998.

Bock, G., Skinner, Q., and Viroli, M. (eds), *Machiavelli and Republicanism*, Cambridge: Cambridge University Press, 1990.

Bödeker, H., 'Debating the *respublica mixta*: German and Dutch Political Discourses around 1700', in M. van Gelderen and Q. Skinner (eds), *Republicanism: A Shared European Heritage*, Cambridge and New York: Cambridge University Press, 2002.

Bodemer, H., *Zur Beurtheilung des Entwurfs einer Gewerbe-Ordnung für das Königreich Sachsen*, 1859.

Bodungen, F., *Das königlich-hannoverische Wechselrecht in alphabetischer Ordnung*, 1824.

Breuning, P., to Reichjustizministerium (25 November 1921), Bundesarchiv file no. 30.01 1357, Eingaben in Familienangelegenheiten, 1921–1923.

Brewer, J., and Hellmuth, E. (eds), *Rethinking Leviathan: The Eighteenth Century State in Britain and Germany*, Oxford: Oxford University Press, 1999.

Bridenthal, R., Koontz, C., and Stuard, S. (eds), *Becoming Visible: Women in European History*, Boston: Houghton Mifflin, 1987.

Brockhaus, F. *Conversations-Lexikon* (1820), cited in W. Mager, 'Republik', in Otto Brunner, Werner Conze and Reinhart Koselleck (eds.), *Geschichtliche Grundbegriffe: Historisches Lexicon*. p. 619.

Brophy, J., 'Salus publica suprema lex: Prussian Business Men in the New Era and Constitutional Conflict', *Central European History*, 28 (1995), pp. 125–52.

Brophy, J., 'Violence between Civilians and State Authorities in the Prussian Rhineland 1830–1846', *German History*, 22/1 (2004), pp. 1–35.

Bruns, C., 'The Politics of Masculinity in the (Homo-) Sexual Discourse 1880–1920', *German History*, 23/3 (2005), pp. 306–20.

Buchholz, S., 'Ehe- und Familienrecht', in H. Coing (ed.), *Handbuch der Quellen und Literatur der neueren europäischen Privatrechtsgeschichte*, vol. 3, *Das 19. Jahrhundert*, vol. 2, Munich: Beck, 1982.

Buchka, G. von, 'Erste Berathung des BGB im Plenum des Reichstags', in B. Mugdan (ed.), *Die gesammten Materialien zum Bürgerlichen Gesetzbuch für das Deutsche Reich*, Berlin: Decker, 1896.

Bügsen, J., to Reich (20 January 1919), Bundesarchiv file no. 30.01 1355, Eingaben zum Familienrecht, vol. 1, March 1869–February 1920.

Burgdorf, W., *Reichskonstitution und Nation: Verfassungsreformprojekte für das Heilige Römische Reich Deutscher Nation im politischen Schrifttum von 1648 bis 1806*, Mainz: P. von Zabern, 1998.

Burguière, A. (ed.), *A History of the Family*, vol. 2, *The Impact of Modernity*, Cambridge, UK: Polity Press, 1996.

Burke, E., *Reflections on the Revolution in France*, 1790.

Burke, E., *Speech on the Reform of Representation of the Commons in Parliament*, 1782.

Burns, J. (ed.), *The Cambridge History of Political Thought 1450–1700*, Cambridge: Cambridge University Press, 1991.

Bush, M., *Noble Privilege*, Manchester: Manchester University Press, 1983.

Canadian Society for Eighteenth-Century Studies, *Man and Nature: Proceedings of the Canadian Society for Eighteenth-Century Studies*, London, Ont.: Faculty of Education, University of Western Ontario, 1982.

Canning, K., *Gender History in Practice: Historical Perspectives on Bodies, Class and Citizenship*, Ithaca: Cornell University Press, 2006.

Carter, F., 'Gustav Radbruch and Hermann Kantorowicz: Two Friends and a Book—Reflections on Gnaeus Flavius' *Der Kampf um die Rechtswissenschaft* (1906)', *German Law Journal*, 7/7 (2006), pp. 657–700.

Chen, Y.-C., 'Civil Law Development: China and Taiwan', *Stanford Journal of East Asian Affairs*, 2 (Spring 2002), pp. 8–14.

Clarke, P., 'The Interdict and Popular Resistance', in F. Andrews, C. Egger and C. Rousseau (eds), *Pope, Church and City*, Leiden and Boston: Brill, 2004.

Coing, H. (ed.), *Handbuch der Quellen und Literatur der neueren europäischen Privatrechtsgeschichte*, vol. 3, *Das 19. Jahrhundert*, Munich: Beck, 1982.

Cole, T., 'The *Daily Telegraph* Affair and Its Aftermath: The Kaiser, Bülow and the Reichstag 1908–1909', in J. Röhl and N. Sombert (eds), *Kaiser Wilhelm II: New Interpretations*, Cambridge: Cambridge University Press, 1982.

Conring, H., *Hermann Conring's New Discourse of the Roman-German Emperor*, C. Fasolt (trans.), Tempe: Arizona Center for Medieval and Renaissance Studies, 2005.

Conze, W. (ed.), *Staat und Gesellschaft im deutschen Vormärz 1815–1848*, Stuttgart: E. Klett, 1962.

Coupe, W. (ed.), *German Political Satires from the Reformation to the Second World War: Part II 1849–1918*, White Plains, NY: Kraus International Publications, 1987.

Crosby, M., 'The Civil Code and the Transformation of German Society: The Politics of Gender Inequality 1814–1919', PhD thesis, Brown University, Providence, 2001.

Curren, V., 'The Critique of Classicism', in A. Riles (ed.), *Rethinking the Masters of Comparative Law*, Oxford and Portland, OR: Hart Publishers, 2001.

Dahrendorf, R., *Society and Democracy in Germany*, Garden City, NY: Doubleday, 1965.

Daniels, H., *Grundsätze des Wechselrechts*, 1827.

Davies, J., *Irish Reports*, 1612.

Deflers, I., 'Melanchthon und die Rezeption des römischen Rechts in Sachsen und im Alten Reich', in A. Schmidt-Recla, E. Schumann and F. Theisen (eds), *Sachsen im Spiegel des Rechts*, Cologne: Böhlau, 2001.

Dernberg, H., 'Wünsche hervorragender Juristen für das neue Jahrhundert,' *Das Recht* (25 January 1900).

Deutsche Juristen-Zeitung (1899–1936).

Dill, R., 'Der Parlamentarier Eduard Lasker und die parlamentarische Stilentwicklung der Jahre 1867–1884: Ein Beitrag zur Geistesgeschichte des politischen Stils in Deutschland', PhD thesis, University of Erlangen, Erlangen, 1956.

Dolinger, J., and Rosenn, K. (eds), *A Panorama of Brazilian Law*, Miami: University of Miami, Iberian Studies Institute, 1992.

Dollinger, P., *The German Hansa*, London and New York: Routledge, 1999.

Donald, M., 'Introduction', in August Bebel, *Women in the Past, Present and Future*, A. Walther (trans.), 1988.

Donzelot, J., *The Policing of Families*, Baltimore: Johns Hopkins University Press, 1980.

Dreitzel, H., 'Hermann Conring und die politische Wissenschaft seiner Zeit', in M. Stolleis (ed.), *Hermann Conring: Beiträge zu Leben und Werk*, Berlin: Duncker & Humblot, 1983.

Dudek, P., *Jugend als Objekt der Wissenschaft: Geschichte der Jugendforschung in Deutschland und Oesterreich 1880–1933*, Opladen: Westdeutscher Verlag, 1990.

Eichhorn, K., *Einleitung in das deutsche Privatrecht mit Einschluß des Lehenrechts*, 1829.

Eichhorn, K., 'Ueber das geschichtliche Studium des deutschen Rechts', *Zeitschrift für geschichtliche Rechtswissenschaft*, 1 (1815), pp. 124–46.

Eichhorn, K., 'Ueber den Ursprung der städtischen Verfassung in Deutschland', *Zeitschrift für geschichtliche Rechtswissenschaft*, 1 (1815), pp. 147–246.

Eichhorn, K., 'Ueber den Ursprung der städtischen Verfassung in Deutschland', *Zeitschrift für geschichtliche Rechtswissenschaft*, 2 (1816), pp. 165–237.

Eley, G., and Palmowski, J. (eds), *Citizenship and National Identity in Twentieth-century Germany*, Stanford: Stanford University Press, 2007.

Engels, F., *The Origin of the Family, Private Property and the State, in the Light of the Researches of Lewis H. Morgan*, New York: International Publishers, 1972.

Erhardt, K., *Ein neues Ehescheidungsrecht!*, (1919) Bundesarchiv file no. 30.01 1355: Eingaben zum Familienrecht, March 1869–February 1920.

Evans, R., *The Feminist Movement in Germany 1894–1933*, London and Beverly Hills: Sage, 1976.

Evans, R. (ed.), *Society and Politics in Wilhelmine Germany*, London: Croom Helm, 1978.

Evans, R., *Sozialdemokratie und Frauenemanzipation im deutschen Kaiserreich*, Bonn: Dietz, 1984.

Eyck, F., *Frankfurt Parliament 1848–1849*, London: Macmillan, 1968.

Eyck, F., *The Prince Consort: A Political Biography*, Portway: Chivers, 1975.

Fehrenbach, E., *Verfassungsstaat und Nationsbildung 1815–1871*, Munich: Oldenbourg, 1992.

Feuerbach, A., *Betrachtungen über das Geschworenengericht*, 1813.

Fiedler, W., *Sozialer Wandel, Verfassungswandel, Rechtsprechung*, Freiburg: K. Alber, 1972.

Filangieri, G., *The Science of Legislation, from the Italian of Gaetano Filangieri*, R. Clayton (trans.), 1806.

Finke, H., *Ein Gutachten Zabarellas über die Absetzung des römischen Königs Wenzel*, 1890.

Fischer, F., *Preußens kaufmännisches Recht*, 1856.

Freiburg, R. von, 'Civic Humanism and Republican Citizenship in Early Modern Germany', in M. van Gelderen and Q. Skinner (eds), *Republicanism: A Shared European Heritage*, Cambridge and New York: Cambridge University Press, 2002.

Frensdorff, F., *Gottlieb Planck: Deutscher Jurist und Politiker*, Berlin: J. Gutentag, 1914.

Frevert, U., 'Bourgeois Honor: Middle-class Duelists in Germany from the Late Eighteenth to the Early Twentieth Century', in D. Blackbourn and R. Evans (eds), *The German Bourgeoisie: Essays on the Social History of the German Middle Class from the Late Eighteenth to the Early Twentieth Century*, London and New York: Routledge, 1991.

Frevert, U., *Women in German History: From Bourgeois Emancipation to Sexual Liberation*, Oxford: Berg, 1989.

Gall, L., *Bismarck: Der weisse Revolutionär*, Frankfurt am Main: Propyläen, 1980.

Gall, L. (ed.), *Bürgertum, liberale Bewegung und Nation: Ausgewählte Aufsätze*, Munich: Oldenbourg, 1996.

Geisel, B., *Klasse, Geschlecht und Recht: Vergleichende sozialhistorische Untersuchung der Rechtsberatungspraxis von Frauen- und Arbeiterbewegung 1894–1933*, Baden-Baden: Nomos, 1997.

Gelderen, M. van, 'Aristotelians, Monarchomachs and Republicans: Sovereignty and *respublica mixta* in Dutch and German Political Thought, 1580–1650', in

M. van Gelderen and Q. Skinner (eds), *Republicanism: A Shared European Heritage*, Cambridge and New York: Cambrige University Press, 2002.

Gelderen, M. van, and Skinner, Q. (eds), *Republicanism: A Shared European Heritage*, Cambridge and New York: Cambridge University Press, 2002.

Gerhard, U., 'Die Rechtsstellung der Frau in der bürgerlichen Gesellschaft des 19. Jahrhunderts: Frankreich und Deutschland im Vergleich', in J. Kocka (ed.), *Bürgertum im 19. Jahrhundert: Deutschland im europäischen Vergleich*, Munich: DTV, 1988.

Gerhard, U. 'Patriarchatskritik als Gesellschaftsanalyse: Ein nicht erledigtes Projekt', in Arbeitsgemeinschaft Interdisziplinäre Frauenforschung und -studien (eds), *Feministische Erneuerung von Wissenschaft und Kunst Pfaffenweiler:* Centaurus, 1990.

Gerlach, L. von, *Die Civilehe und der Reichskanzler*, 1874.

Germanistentag, *Verhandlungen der Germanisten zu Frankfurt am Main*, 1846.

Germanistentag, *Verhandlungen der Germanisten zu Lübeck*, 1847.

Geyer, 'Der Kampf ums Recht', *Der Gerichtssaal*, 25 (1873), pp. 1–38.

Gierke, O., *Der Entwurf eines bürgerlichen Gesetzbuchs und das deutsche Recht*, 1889.

Gierke, O., 'Wünsche hervorragender Juristen für das neue Jahrhundert', *Das Recht* (25 January 1900).

Gilbert, A. (trans.), *Machiavelli: The Chief Works and Others*, Chapel Hill: Duke University Press, 1989.

Gillis, J., *Youth and History: Tradition and Change in European Age Relations, 1770–Present*, New York: Academic Press, 1981.

Goldberg, A., 'A Reinvented Public: Lunatics' Rights and Bourgeois Populism in the Kaiserreich', *German History*, 21/2 (2003), pp. 159–83.

Goldschmidt, L., *Gutachten über den Entwurf eines deutschen Handelsgesetzbuchs nach den Beschlüssen zweiter Lesung*, 1860.

Goldschmidt, L., *Das Handbuch des Handelsrechts*, 1864.

Goldschmidt, L., *Kritik des Entwurfs eines Handelsgesetzbuchs für die Preussischen Staaten*, 1857.

Goldschmidt, L., *System des Handelsrechts*, 1887.

Goody, J., Thirsk, J., and Thompson, E. (eds), *Family and Inheritance: Rural Society in Western Europe 1200–1800*, Cambridge: Cambridge University Press, 1976.

Göschen, J., 'Einige Bemerkungen in Beziehung auf das ältere Recht der Freylassung bey den Römern', *Zeitschrift für geschichtliche Rechtswissenschaft*, 3 (1817), pp. 242–88.

Gossman, L., *Basel in the Age of Burckhardt: A Study in Unseasonable Ideas*, Chicago: University of Chicago Press, 2000.

Greig, J.Y.T. (ed.), *The Letters of David Hume*, Oxford: Clarendon, 1932.

Grimm, D., 'Die Grundrechte im Entstehungszusammenhang der bürgerlichen Gesellschaft', in J. Kocka (ed.), *Bürgertum im 19. Jahrhundert: Deutschland im europäischen Vergleich*, Munich: DTV, 1988.

Grimm, D., 'Die Zeit der Begründung von Verfassungsstaat und Bürgerlichem Recht, 1789–1815', in H. Coing (ed.), *Handbuch der Quellen und Literatur der neueren europäischen Privatrechtsgeschichte*, vol. 3, *Das 19. Jahrhundert*, Munich and New York: Prestel-Verlag, 1982.

Grimm, J., *Briefe der Brüder Grimm an Savigny*, W. Schoof (ed.), Berlin: E. Schmidt, 1953.

Grimm, J., *Deutsche Rechtsalterthümer*, Leipzig: T. Weicher, 1828.

Grimm, J., *Jacob Grimm: Selbstbiographie*, Munich: Deutscher Taschenbuch Verlag, 1984.

Grimm, J., 'Recht von Hiesfeld', *Jahrbuch des gemeinen deutschen Rechts*, 1 (1857).

Grimm, J., 'Ueber eine eigene altgermanische Weise der Mordsühne', *Zeitschrift für geschichtliche Rechtswissenschaft*, 1 (1815), pp. 323–37.

Grimm, J., 'Von der Poesie im Recht', *Zeitschrift für geschichtliche Rechtswissenschaft*, 2 (1816), pp. 27–99.

Grimm, J., *Weisthümer*, Göttingen: Dieterich, 1840–1842.

Gross Badische Staatsministerium, *Bericht des Gross Badische Staatsministerium in Carlsruhe zu dem Reichskanzler-Amt* (1 February 1876), Bundesarchiv file no. 30.01 4009, Die Mittheilung der Bundes Regierung ueber das eheliche Güterrecht, January 1876–April 1878.

Gruchot, J., 'Vorwort', *Beiträge zur Erläuterung des preußischen Rechts durch Theorie und Praxis*, 1 (1857), p. i.

Gründler, C., *Polemik des germanischen Rechts, Land- und Lehnrecht: Nach den Systemen des Herrn Geheimrat Prof. Dr. Mittermaier und Geheimrat Prof. Dr. G. L. Böhmer*, 1832–1839.

Guterman, S., *The Principle of Personality of the Law in the Germanic Kingdoms of Western Europe from the Fifth to the Eleventh Century*, New York: P. Lang, 1988.

Hagemann, K., 'Of "Manly Valor" and "German Honor": Nation, War, and Masculinity in the Age of the Prussian Uprising against Napoleon', *Central European History*, 30/2 (2001), pp. 187–220.

Haimerl, F., *Anleitung zum Studium des Wechselrechtes*, 1855.

Hale, M., *A History of the Common Law of England* (1713), C. Gray (ed.), Chicago: University of Chicago Press, 1971.

Hall, A., 'Youth in Rebellion', in R. Evans (ed.), *Society and Politics in Wilhelmine Germany*, London: Croom Helm, 1978.

Hall, G., *Adolescence: Its Psychology and Its Relations to Physiology, Anthropology, Sociology, Sex, Crime, Religion and Education*, New York: D. Appleton & Company, 1911.

Harris, J., *A Study in the Theory and Practice of German Liberalism: Eduard Lasker, 1829–1884*, Lanham, MD: University Press of America, 1984.

Haskins, C., *The Renaissance of the Twelfth Century*, Cambridge: Harvard University Press, 1927.

Hautzinger, A., 'Die Photographin', *Die Frau* (October 1893).

Hemholz, R. H., *The Spirit of Classical Canon Law*, Athens: University of Georgia Press, 1996.

Hett, B., 'The "Captain of Köpenick" and the Transformation of German Criminal Justice 1891–1914', *Central European History*, 36/1 (2003), pp. 1–43.

Heumann, 'Über die Verpflichtung des Ehemannes zur Ertheilung des ehemännlichen Consenses in einen von seiner Ehefrau mit ihrem Sohne über ihr eigenthümliche Immobilien abgeschlossenen Kaufvertrag', *Blätter für Rechtspflege in Thüringen und Anhalt* (1857).

Hoeflich, M., *Roman and Civil Law and the Development of Anglo-American Jurisprudence in the Nineteenth Century*, Athens: University of Georgia Press, 1997.

Hoffmann, J., *Die Befugniss zum Gewerbbetriebe zur Berichtigung der Urtheile über Gewerbefreiheit und Gewerbezwang*, 1841.

Hohendahl, P. (ed.), *Patriotism, Cosmopolitanism and National Culture: Public Culture in Hamburg 1700–1933*, Amsterdam and New York: Ropodi, 2003.

Huber, E., *Deutsche Verfassungsgeschichte seit 1789: Bismarck und das Reich*, vol. 3, Stuttgart: Kohlhammer, 1988.

Hübner, R., *A History of Germanic Private Law*, Boston: Little, Brown, 1918.

Hucko, E. (ed.), *The Democratic Tradition: Four German Constitutions*, Oxford: Berg, 1987.

Hugo, G., 'Ueber den Plan, die Absicht und die Grenzen dieses Journals', *Civilistisches Magazin*, 1 (1790), pp. 1–22.

Hull, I., 'Military Culture, Wilhelm II, and the End of the Monarchy in the First World War', in A. Mombauer and W. Deist (eds), *The Kaiser: New Research on Wilhelm II's Role in Imperial Germany*, Cambridge: Cambridge University Press, 2003.

Hull, I., *Sexuality, State and Civil Society in Germany 1700–1815*, Ithaca: Cornell University Press, 1995.

Hunt, L., *The Family Romance of the French Revolution*, Berkeley: University of California Press, 1992.

Hunt, M. (ed.), *Grimm's Household Tales*, London, 1884.

Hurwich, J. 'Marriage Strategy among the German Nobility, 1400–1699', *Journal of Interdisciplinary History*, 29/2 (1998), pp. 169–95.

Jacobson, A., and Schlink, B. (eds), *Weimar: A Jurisprudence of Crisis*, Berkeley: University of California Press, 2000.

Jagemann, L., 'Der Uebergang vom alten zum neuen Rechte: Zugleich als Prospect der Zeitschrift', *Der Gerichtssaal*, 1/1 (1849), pp. 3–16.

Jagemann, L., 'Zur deutschen Nationalgesetzgebung', *Der Gerichtssaal*, 3/1 (1851), pp. 272–4.

Jellinek, G., *Allgemeine Staatslehre: Das Recht des modernen Staates*, Berlin: O. Häring, 1900.

Jellinek, G., *Verfassungsänderung und Verfassungswandlung* (1906), in A. Jacobson and B. Schlink (eds), *Weimar: A Jurisprudence of Crisis*, Berkeley: University of California Press, 2000.

Jenks, E., *Law and Politics of the Middle Ages*, 1897.

Jhering, R., *Der Kampf ums Recht*, 1872.

John, M., 'Between Estate and Profession: Lawyers and the Development of the Legal Profession in Nineteenth-Century Germany', in D. Blackbourn and R. Evans (eds), *The German Bourgeoisie: Essays on the Social History of the German Middle Class from the Late Eighteenth to the Early Twentieth Century*, London and New York: Routledge, 1991.

John, M., *Politics and the Law in Late Nineteenth Century Germany: The Origins of the Civil Code*, Oxford: Clarendon, 1989.

Johnston, D., 'The General Influence of Roman Institutions of State and Public Law', in D. Miller and R. Zimmerman (eds), *The Civilian Tradition and Scots Law: Aberdeen Quincentenary Essays*, Berlin: Duncker & Humblot, 1997.

Jones, L., and Retallack, J. (eds), *Elections, Mass Politics and Social Change in Modern Germany: New Perspectives*, Cambridge: Cambridge University Press, 1992.

Jong, J. de, '"The Principles of Steam": Political Transfer and Transformation in Japan 1868–1889', *European Review of History*, 12/2 (2005), pp. 269–90.

Kadel, H. (ed.), *Paul Johann Anselm Feuerbach and Friedrich Carl von Savigny: Zwölf Stücke aus dem Briefwechsel*, Lauterbach: Officinum Libroum, 1990.

Kaiser, T., 'From Austrian Committee to Foreign Plot: Marie-Antoinette, Austrophobia and the Terror', *French Historical Studies*, 26/4 (2003), pp. 579–617.

Kantorowicz, H., *Dictatorships: A Sociological Study*, 1935.

Kantorowicz, H., *The Spirit of British Policy and the Myth of the Encirclement of Germany*, W. H. Johnston (trans.), 1932.

Kantorowicz, H., *Rechtswissenschaft und Soziologie*, 1911.

Kantorowicz, H., 'Savigny and the History School', *Law Quarterly Review*, 53 (1937).

Kantorowicz, H., *Volksgeist und historische Rechtsschule*, 1912.

Kantorowicz, H., *Was ist uns Savigny?*, 1911.

Kautsky, J., *Karl Kautsky: Marxism, Revolution and Democracy*, New Brunswick: Transaction, 1994.

Kehr, E., *Economic Interest, Militarism, and Foreign Policy*, G. Craig (ed.), G. Heinz (trans.), Berkeley: University of California Press, 1977.

Keither, H., *Ideal wird was Natur war: Abhandlungen zur Privatrechtsgeschichte des späten 18. und des 19. Jahrhunderts*, Stockstaat am Main: Keip, 1997.

Kelley, J., *A Short History of Western Legal Theory*, Oxford: Oxford University Press, 1992.

Kiepert, A., *Rudolf von Bennigsen: Rückblick auf das Leben eines Parlamentariers*, Hanover: C. Meyer, 1903.

Kirshner, J., 'Civitas Sibi Faciat Civem: Bartolus of Sassoferrato's Doctrine on the Making of a Citizen', *Speculum*, 48/4 (1973), pp. 694–713.

Kleinschmidt, 'On the Customary Measures of Hildesheim', *Juristische Zeitung für das Königreich Hannover*, 1 (1826).

Kleinschrod, C., *Beiträge zu einer Deutschen Gewerbeordnung mit Rücksicht auf die bayerische Gewerbsgesetzgebung*, 1840.

Koch, A., 'C.J.A. Mittermaier and the 19th Century Debate about Juries and Mixed Courts', *Revue internationale de droit pénal*, 72 (2001), pp. 347–53.

Kocka, J. (ed.), *Bürgertum im 19. Jahrhundert: Deutschland im europäischen Vergleich*, Munich: DTV, 1988.

Kocka, J., *Industrial Culture and Bourgeois Society: Business, Labor and Bureaucracy in Modern Germany*, 1999.

Kohn, H., *The Mind of Germany: The Education of a Nation*, New York: Scribner, 1960.

Kolbe, A., *Hilferuf an den Kaiser und die deutsche Öffentlichkeit: Unglaubliches Prozessmartyrium in einem Ehescheidungsverfahren* (1914), Bundesarchiv file no. 30.01 1355, Eingaben in Familienrecht, March 1869–February 1920.

Kollander, P., *Frederick III: Germany's Liberal Emperor*, Westport, CT: Greenwood, 1995.

Königreich Bayern, *Darstellung des im Königreich Bayern bestehenden ehelichen Güterrechts* (1877), Bundesarchiv file no. 30.01 4009, Die Mittheilung der Bundes Regierung ueber das eheliche Güterrecht, January 1876–April 1878.

Koselleck, R., *Preussen zwischen Reform und Revolution: Allgemeines Landrecht, Verwaltung und soziale Bewegung von 1791 bis 1848*, Munich: Klett-Cotta, 1989.

Krader, L. (ed.), *The Ethnological Notebooks of Karl Marx: Studies of Morgan, Phear, Maine, Lubbock*, New York: Irvington, 1974.

Kraut, W., *Grundriss zu Vorlesungen über das deutsche Privatrecht mit Einschluss des Lehns- und Handelsrechts nebst beigefügten Quellen*, 1859.

Kraut, W., *Die Vormundschaft nach den Grundsätzen des deutschen Rechts*, 1835–1859.

Kreuzer, M., 'Parliamentarization and the Question of German Exceptionalism: 1867–1918', *Central European History*, 36/3 (2003), pp. 327–57.

Krieger, L., *The German Idea of Freedom: A History of a Political Tradition*, Boston: Beacon, 1957.

Krieger, L., and Stern, F. (eds), *The Responsibility of Power: Historical Essays in Honor of Hajo Holborn*, London: Macmillan, 1968.

Kuntze, J., *Der Wendepunkt der Rechtswissenschaft*, 1857.

Kurz, A., *Demokratische Diktatur? Auslegung und Handhabung des Artikels 48 der Weimarer Verfassung 1919–25*, Berlin: Duncker & Humblot, 1992.

Laband, P., 'Die geschichtliche Entwicklung der Reichsverfassung seit der Reichsgründung', *Jahrbuch des öffentlichen Rechts*, 1 (1907).

Landau, P., 'Schwurgerichte und Schöffengerichte in Deutschland im 19. Jahrhundert bis 1870', in A. Schioppa (ed.), *The Trial Jury in England, France, Germany 1700–1900*, Berlin: Duncker & Humblot, 1987.

Lando, O., and Beale, H., *Principles of European Contract Law*, Boston: Kluwer Law International, 2000.

Lange, H., 'Frauentage', *Die Frau* (November 1899).

Langewiesche, D. (ed.), *Liberalismus im 19. Jahrhundert: Deutschland im europäischen Vergleich*, Göttingen: Vandenhoeck & Ruprecht, 1988.

Lanwerd, S., *Mythos, Mutterrecht und Magie: Zur Geschichte religionswissenschaftlicher Begriffe*, Berlin: Dietrich Reimer, 1993.

Ledford, K., 'Formalizing the Rule of Law in Prussia: The Supreme Administrative Law Court, 1876–1914', *Central European History*, 37/2 (2004), pp. 203–24.

Ledford, K., *From General Estate to Special Interest: German Lawyers 1878–1933*, Cambridge and New York: Cambridge University Press, 1996.

Ledford, K., 'Lawyers, Liberalism and Procedure: The German Imperial Justice Laws of 1877–79', *Central European History*, 26 (1993), pp. 165–94.

Le Goff, J., *The Birth of Europe*, Malden, MA: Blackwell, 2005.

Leonhardt, A., to Herr Reichkanzler Fürst von Bismarck (30 August 1876), Bundesarchiv file no. 30.01 4009, Die Mittheilung der Bundes Regierung ueber das eheliche Güterrecht, January 1876–April 1877.

Leuch, J., *Vollständiges Handelsrecht*, 1822.

Lidtke, V., *The Alternative Culture: Socialist Labor in Imperial Germany*, New York: Oxford University Press, 1985.

Liebel-Weckowicz, H., 'The Revolt of the Württemberg Estates, 1764–1770', in Canadian Society for Eighteenth-Century Studies, *Man and Nature: Proceedings of the Canadian Society for Eighteenth-Century Studies*, London, Ont.: Faculty of Education, University of Western Ontario, 1982.

Liebknecht, W., *Wilhelm Liebknecht and German Social Democracy: A Documentary History*, W. Pelz (ed.), E. Hahn (trans.), Westport, CT: Greenwood, 1994.

Linder, A., to Reichjustizministerium (17 November 1918), Bundesarchiv file no. 30.01 1355, Eingaben zum Familienrecht, vol. 1, March 1869–February 1920.

Linton, D., *'Who Has the Youth Has the Future': The Campaign to Save Young Workers in Imperial Germany 1870–1914*, Cambridge and New York: Cambridge University Press, 1991.

MacDonogh, G., *The Last Kaiser: William the Impetuous*, London: Weidenfeld & Nicolson, 2000.

Machiavelli, N., *Machiavelli: The Chief Works and Others*, A. Gilbert (trans), Durham, NC: Duke University Press, 1989.

Machiavelli, N., *The Prince and The Discourses*, M. Lerner (ed.), New York: Modern Library, 1950.

Mann, V., and Cohen, R. (ed.), *From Court Jews to the Rothchilds: Art, Patronage and Power 1600–1800*, Munich and New York: Prestel-Verlag, 1996.

Matzerath, J., 'Die Familienverträge des sächsischen Adels vom 16. bis zum 19. Jahrhundert', in K. Keller and J. Matzerath (eds), *Geschichte des sächsischen Adels*, Cologne: Böhlau, 1997.

McLean, R., 'Kaiser Wilhelm II and His Hessian Cousins: Intra-state Relations in the German Empire and International Dynastic Politics 1890–1918', *German History*, 19/1 (2001), pp. 28–53.

McManus, B. J., 'The Ecclesiology of Laurentium Hispanus (c. 1180–1248) and His Contribution to the Romanization of Canon Law Jurisprudence', PhD thesis, Syracuse University, Syracuse, 1991.

McNeely, I., *The Emancipation of Writing: German Civil Society in the Making, 1790s–1820s*, Berkeley: University of California Press, 2003.

Mehren, A. von, and Gordley, J., *The Civil Law System: An Introduction to the Comparative Study of Law*, Boston: Little, Brown, 1977.

Meinecke, F., *Die deutsche Katastrophe*, Wiesbaden: E. Brockhaus, 1946.

Meißner, W., *Beleuchtung des Entwurfs einer Gewerbe-Ordnung für das Königreich Sachsen*, 1857.

Meyer, A., *The Feminism and Socialism of Lily Braun*, Bloomington: Indiana University Press, 1985.

Miller, D., and Zimmerman, R. (eds), *The Civilian Tradition and Scots Law: Aberdeen Quincentenary Essays*, Berlin: Duncker & Humblot, 1997.

Mittermaier, K., 'Beiträge zur Geschichte der ehelichen Gütergemeinschaft, des Erbrechts und der Freiheit zu testiren im Mittelalter', *Zeitschrift für geschichtliche Rechtswissenschaft*, 2 (1816), pp. 318–61.

Mittermaier, K., *Der gemeine deutsche bürgerliche Prozeß in Vergleichung mit dem preußschen und französischen Civilverfahren*, 1820.

Mittermaier, K., *Grundsätze des gemeinen deutschen Privatrechts*, 1823.

Mittermaier, K., 'Das Indossament nach dem Verfalltage: Erläuterung des §16 der Deutschen Wechselordnung', *Archiv für deutsches Wechselrecht*, 1 (1850), pp. 10–31.

Mittermaier, K., *Die künftige Stellung des Advokatenstandes*, 1832.

Mittermaier, K., *Lehrbuch des deutschen Privatrechts*, 1821.

Mittermaier, K., *Die neuesten Gesetzgebungsarbeiten auf dem Gebiete der Civilgesetzgebung mit besonderer Beziehung auf die neueren Civilgesetzbücher oder Entwürfe für das Königreich Sachsen, für das Grossherzogthum Hessen, für das Herzogthum Modena und die Schweizer Gesetzbücher oder Entwürfe für Zürich, Slothurn, Freiburg, Thurgau, Wallis, Aargau, mit Entwicklung der Rücksichten, welche die Prüfung dieser neuen Arbeiten leiten müssen*, 1853.

Mittermaier, K., *Ueber die Bestimmungen einer zweckmässigen Gerichtsverfassung und Processordnung*, 1831.

Mittermaier, K., 'Ueber den Einfluß höherer Gewalt auf die Regreßklage im Falle der Unterlassung wechselrechtlicher Pflichten nach der deutschen Wechselordnung', *Archiv für deutsches Wechselrecht*, 1 (1850), pp. 147–64.

Montesquieu, *The Spirit of the Laws*, T. Nugent (trans.), New York: Hafner, 1949.

Morgan, L., *Ancient Society, or, Researches in the Lines of Human Progess from Savagery through Barbarism to Civilization*, Chicago: C. H. Kerr, 1877.

Moser, J., *Teutsches Staats-Recht*, 1737–1757.

Mugdan, B. (ed.), *Die gesammten Materialien zum Bürgerlichen Gesetzbuch für das Deutsche Reich*, Berlin: Decker, 1899.

Nauert, C., *Humanism and the Culture of Renaissance Europe*, Cambridge and New York: Cambridge University Press, 1995.

Nieberding, R., 'Erste Berathung des BGB im Plenum des Reichstags' (1896), in B. Mugdan, *Die gesammten Materialien zum Bürgerlichen Gesetzbuch für das Deutsche Reich*, Berlin: Decker, 1899.

Niebuhr, B., *The History of Rome*, J. Hare and C. Thirlwall (trans.), Philadelphia: Thomas Wardle, 1835.

Niebuhr, B., *Lectures on History of Rome*, L. Schmidtz (ed.), London: Taylor, Walker and Maberly, 1844.

Niebuhr, B., 'Nachricht von einem Breviarum des Justinianischen Codex: (Aus einem Schreiben an Savigny)', *Zeitschrift für geschichtliche Rechtswissenschaft*, 3 (1817), pp. 389–96.

Niebuhr, B., 'Notizen über Handschriften in der Vaticana: Erster Brief', *Zeitschrift für geschichtliche Rechtswissenschaft*, 3 (1817), pp. 408–20.

Nipperdey, T., *Deutsche Geschichte 1866–1918*, Munich: C. H. Beck, 1990.

Nipperdey, T., *Germany from Napoleon to Bismarck 1800–1866*, Dublin: Gill & Macmillan, 1996.

Nipperdey, T., *Gesellschaft, Kultur, Theorie: Gesammelte Aufsätze zur neueren Geschichte*, Göttingen: Vandenhoeck & Ruprecht, 1976.

Nürmberger, G., *Sammlung einiger nürnbergischen Handelsrechts-Gewohnheiten*, 1846.

Nürmberger, G., *Sammlung von Beiträgen und andern Anmerkungen zur praktischen Erläuterung der Nürnberger Handelsgerichtsordnung*, 1846.

Nürmberger, G., *Sammlung von Beiträgen und Anmerkungen zu praktischer Erläuterung der Nürnberger Wechselordnung*, 1846.

Oegg to Frau Käte Edlich (28 May 1929), Bundesarchiv file no. 30.01 1388, Eheliches Güterrecht, 1928–1934.

Ogorek, R., 'Individueller Rechtsschutz gegenüber der Staatsgewalt: Zur Entwicklung der Verwaltungsgerichtsbarkeit im 19. Jahrhundert', in J. Kocka (ed.), *Bürgertum im 19. Jahrhundert: Deutschland im europäischen Vergleich*, Munich: DTV, 1988.

Oncken, H., *Rudolf von Bennigsen: Ein deutscher liberaler Politiker nach seinen Briefen und hinterlassenen Papieren*, 1910.

Pakula, H., *An Uncommon Woman: The Empress Frederick, Daughter of Queen Victoria, Wife of the Crown Prince of Prussia, Mother of Kaiser Wilhelm*, New York: Simon & Schuster, 1995.

Palmowski, J., *Urban Liberalism in Imperial Germany: Frankfurt am Main 1866–1914*, Oxford: Clarendon, 1999.

Pape, E., 'Ueber die Organisation und Zuständigkeit der gerichtlichen Behörden', *Der Gerichtssaal*, 3 (1851), pp. 1–12.

Peltonen, M., *Classical Humanism and Republicanism in English Political Thought 1570–1640*, Cambridge: Cambridge University Press, 1995.

Pestalutz, J., *Abhandlung über das Züricherische Wechselrecht, mit Vergleichung der Augsburger, Sct. Galler und Basler Wechselordnung*, 1827.

Petersen, E., to Reichjustizministerium (20 November 1928), Bundesarchiv file no. 30.01 1388, Eheliches Güterrecht, 1928–1934.

Petition an den Hohen Bundesrat undReichstag zur Märztagung 1916: Keine Steuerbewilligung ohne freiheitlichere Ehegesetze!, Bundesarchiv file no. 30.01 1355, Eingaben in Familienangelegenheiten, 1921–1923.

Peukert, D., *Grenzen der Sozialdisziplinierung: Aufstieg und Krise der deutschen Jugendfürsorge 1878–1932*, Cologne: Bund-Verlag, 1986.

Pfeiffer, W., *Ideen zu einer neuen Civil-Gesetzgebung für Teutsche Staaten*, 1815.

Pitz, E., *Bürgereinung und Städteeinung: Studien zur Verfassungsgeschichte der Hansestädte und der deutschen Hanse*, Cologne: Böhlau, 2001.

Pflanze, O., *Bismarck and the Development of Germany: The Period of Unification 1815–1871*, Princeton: Princeton University Press, 1990.

Pflanze, O. 'Juridical and Political Responsibility in Nineteenth-Century Germany', in L. Krieger and F. Stern (eds), *The Responsibility of Power: Historical Essays in Honor of Hajo Holborn*, London: Macmillan, 1968.

Planck, G., *Begründung des Entwurfs eines Familienrechts für das Deutsche Reich* (1880), in W. Schubert (ed.), *Die Vorlagen der Redaktoren für die erste Kommission zur Ausarbeitung des Entwurfs eines Bürgerlichen Gesetzbuches: Die Vorentwürfe der Redaktoren zum ... und Wirkungen der Ehe, Eheverträge,* Berlin and New York: W. de Gruyter, 1983.

Planck, G., *Kommentar zum Bürgerlichen Gesetzbuch nebst Einführungsgesetz*, 1901.

Planck, J., *Lehrbuch des Deutschen Civilprozessrechts*, 1887.

Planck, G., *Die rechtliche Stellung der Frau nach dem Bürgerlichen Gesetzbuch*, 1899.

Planck, G., *Die Rechtswidrigkeit des in Hannover bestehenden Verfassungszustandes*, 1861.

Planck, G., *Zur Kritik des Entwurfs eines Bürgerlichen Gesetzbuchs für das deutsche Reich*, 1889.

Pocock, J., *The Machiavellian Moment: Florentine Political Thought and the Atlantic Republican Tradition*, Princeton: Princeton University Press, 1975.

Pöggeler, W., *Die deutsche Wissenschaft vom englischen Staatsrecht: Ein Beitrag zur Rezeptions- und Wissenschaftsgeschichte 1748–1914*, Berlin: Duncker & Humblot, 1995.

Postema, G., *Bentham: Moral, Political and Legal Philosophy*, Aldershot, UK: Ashgate. 2002.

Puchta, G., *Gewohnheitsrecht*, 1828.

Puchta, G., *Pandekten*, 1844.

Puhle, H. (ed.), *Bürger in der Gesellschaft der Neuzeit: Wirtschaft, Politik, Kultur*, Göttingen: Vandenhoeck & Ruprecht, 1991.

Quataert, J., *Reluctant Feminists in German Social Democracy, 1885–1917*, Princeton: Princeton University Press, 1979.

Reagin, N., *A German Women's Movement: Class and Gender in Hanover 1880–1933*, Chapel Hill: University of North Carolina Press, 1995.

Rehberg, A., *Ueber den Code Napoleon und dessen Einführung in Deutschland*, 1814.

Reichs-Gesetzblatt (1871–1945).

Reichjustizministerium to Alexander Richard (8 December 1908), Bundesarchiv file no. 30.01 1355, Eingaben zum Familienrecht, vol. 1, March 1869–February 1920.

Reichjustizministerium to Paul Breuning (12 December 1921), Bundesarchiv file no. 30.01 1357, Eingaben in Familienangelegenheiten, 1921–1923.

Renaud, A., *Lehrbuch des allgemeinen deutschen Wechselrechts*, 1857.

Renouard, Y., *The Avignon Papacy 1305–1403*, Hamden, CT: Archon Books, 1970.

Rentzsch, H., *Die Gewerbefreiheit und Freizügigkeit*, 1861.

Retallack, J., 'Something Magical in the Name of Prussia: British Perceptions of German Nation Building in the 1860s', in R. Speirs and J. Breuilly (eds), *Germany's Two Unifications: Anticipations, Experiences, Responses*, New York: Palgrave Macmillan, 2005.

Reulecke, J., 'The Battle for the Young: Mobilizing Young People in Wilhelmine Germany', in M. Roseman (ed.), *Generations in Conflict: Youth Revolt and Generation Formation in Germany 1770–1968*, Cambridge and New York: Cambridge University Press, 1995.

Reulecke, J., 'Bürgerliche Sozialreformer und Arbeiterjugend im Kaiserreich', *Archiv für Sozialgeschichte*, 22 (1982), pp. 299–329.

Reyscher, A., *Beiträge zur Kunde des deutschen Rechts*, 1833.

Reyscher, A., *Ueber die Bedürfnisse unserer Zeit in der Gesetzgebung*, 1828.

Reyscher, A. 'Ueber den Zweck dieser Zeitschrift', *Zeitschrift für deutsches Recht und deutsche Rechtswissenschaft*, 1 (1839), pp. 1–10.

Reyscher, A. *Vollständige, historisch und kritisch bearbeitete Sammlung der württembergischen Gesetze*, 1828.

Richard, A., to Fürst von Bülow (1 December 1903), Bundesarchiv file no. 30.01 1355, Eingaben zum Familienrecht, vol. 1, March 1869–February 1920.

Riles, A. (ed.), *Rethinking the Masters of Comparative Law*, Oxford and Portland, OR: Hart Publications, 2001.

Ritter, G., *Arbeiterbewegung, Parteien und Parlamentarismus: Aufsätze zur deutschen Sozial- und Verfassungsgeschichte des 19. und 20. Jahrhunderts*, Göttingen: Vandenhoeck & Ruprecht, 1976.

Röhl, J., and Sombart, N. (eds), *Kaiser Wilhelm II: New Interpretations: Corfu Papers*, Cambridge and New York: Cambridge University Press, 1992.

Roseman, M. (ed.), *Generations in Conflict: Youth Revolt and Generation Formation in Germany 1770–1968*, Cambridge and New York: Cambridge University Press, 1995.

Rosenberg, H., *Bureaucracy, Aristocracy, and Autocracy: The Prussian Experience 1660–1815*, Cambridge: Harvard University Press, 1958.

Roth, L., *Die Erfindung des Jugendlichen*, Munich: Juventa, 1983.

Rothschildt, H., *Die bei dem Verkehre mit Wechseln zu beobachtenden Formen nach gemeinem Rechte und der Braunschweigschen Wechselordnung*, 1841.

Rückert, 'Character der fortgesetzten Gütergemeinschaft nach Koburger statuarischem Recht', *Blätter für Rechtspflege in Thüringen und Anhalt* (1858).

Rückert, J., *Idealismus, Jurisprudenz und Politik bei Friedrich Carl von Savigny*, Ebelsbach: R. Gremer, 1984.

Rudorff, A., 'Friedrich Karl von Savigny: Erinnerungen an sein Wesen und Wirken', *Zeitschrift für Rechtswissenschaft*, 2 (1863), pp. 1–68.

Rummel, W., 'Motive staatlicher und dörflicher Gewaltanwendung im 19. Jahrhundert. Eine Skizze zum Ende der frühneuzeitlichen Sozialkultur in der preußischen Rheinprovinz', in E. Eriksson and B. Krug-Bichter (eds), *Streitkulturen: Gewalt, Konflikt und Kommunikation in der ländlichen Gesellschaft (16.–19. Jahrhundert)*, Cologne: Böhlau, 2003.

Sabean, D. *Property, Production and Family in Neckarhausen, 1700–1870*, Cambridge and New York: Cambridge University Press, 1990.

Sandberger, D., *Die Ministerkandidatur Bennigsens*, 1929.

Savigny, F. von, 'Beytrag zur Geschichte der Römischen Testamente', *Zeitschrift für geschichtliche Rechtswissenschaft*, 1 (1815), pp. 78–95.

Savigny, F. von, *History of the Roman Law in the Middle Ages*, E. Cathcart (trans.), Edinburgh: E. Black, 1829.

Savigny, F. von, *Juristische Methodenlehre nach der Ausarbeitung des Jacob Grimm*, (1803), G. Wesenberg (ed.), 1951.

Savigny, F. von, 'Neu entdeckte Quellen des Römischen Rechts', *Zeitschrift für geschichtliche Rechtswissenschaft*, 3 (1817), pp. 129–72.

Savigny, F. von, *Of the Vocation of Our Age in Legislation and Jurisprudence*, A. Hayward (trans.), Kitchener, Ont.: Batoche, 1999.

Savigny, F. von, *Politik und neuere Legislationen: Materialien zum 'Geist der Gesetzgebung'*, H. Akamatsu and J. Rückert (eds), Frankfurt am Main: Klostermann, 2000.

Savigny, F. von, *Das Recht des Besitzes: Eine civilistische Abhandlung*, 1803.

Savigny, F. von, 'Ueber den Zweck dieser Zeitschrift', *Zeitschrift für geschichtliche Rechtswissenschaft*, 1 (1815), pp. 1–17.

Savigny, F. von, 'Wesen und Werth der deutschen Universitäten', *Historisch-politische Zeitschrift*, 1/4 (1832), reprinted in F. von Savigny, *Vermischte Schriften*, 1850.

Scherner, K. (ed.), *Modernisierung des Handelsrechts im 19. Jahrhundert*, Heidelberg: Verlag Recht und Wirtschaft, 1993.

Schilling, H., *Religion, Political Culture and the Emergence of Early Modern Society: Essays in German and Dutch History*, Leiden and New York: Brill, 1992.

Schleiermacher, F.,'Gelegentliche Gedanken über Universitäten in deutschem Sinn', *Heidelberger Jahrbücher für Philologie, Historie, Literatur und Kunst*, 3 (1808), reprinted in F. Savigny, *Vermischte Schriften*, 1850.

Schlosser, J., 'Ueber das Studium der reinen Römischen Jurisprudenz', *Civilistisches Magazin*, 1 (1791), pp. 72–108.

Schmidt, C., to Reichjustizministerium (20 January 1919), Bundesarchiv file no. 30.01 1355, Eingaben zum Familienrecht, vol. 1, March 1869–February 1920.

Schmidt-Recla, A., Schumann, E., and Theisen, F. (eds), *Sachsen im Spiegel des Rechts*, Cologne: Böhlau, 2001.

Schoenbaum, D., *Zabern 1913: Consensus Politics in Imperial Germany*, London and Boston: George Allen & Unwin, 1982.

Schroeder, R., *Das eheliche Güterrecht Deutschlands in Vergangenheit, Gegenwart und Zukunft*, 1875.

Schroeder, R., *Geschichte des ehelichen Güterrechts in Deutschland: Die Zeit der Volksrechte*, 1839–1863.

Schroeder, R., Letter to G. Planck (23 November 1880). Gottlieb Planck Records, Niedersächsische Bibliothek, Göttingen.

Schroeder, R., Letter to G. Planck (posted 1889). Gottlieb Planck Records, Niedersächsische Bibliothek, Göttingen.

Schroeder, R., Letter to G. Planck (15 June 1875). Gottlieb Planck Records, Niedersächsische Bibliothek, Göttingen.

Schubert, E., *Königsabsetzung im deutschen Mittelalter: Eine Studie zum Werden der Reichsverfassung*, Göttingen: Vandenhoeck & Ruprecht, 2005.

Schubert, W. (ed.), *Vorlagen der Redaktoren für die erste Kommission zur Ausarbeitung des Entwurfs eines Bürgerlichen Gesetzbuchs*, Berlin and New York: W. de Gruyter, 1980–1986.

Schubert, W., *Entstehung und Quellen der Civilprozessordnung von 1877*, Frankfurt am Main: Klostermann, 1987.

Schudnagies, C., *Der Kriegs- oder Belagerungszustand im Deutschen Reich während des Ersten Weltkrieges: Eine Studie zur Entwicklung und Handhabung des deutschen Ausnahmezustandsrechts bis 1919*, Frankfurt am Main and New York: P. Lang, 1994.

Schulze (ed.), *Allgemeine deutsche Wechselordnung nebst Einführungsgesetz für das Königreich Hannover*, 1849.

Schwerhoff, G., 'Die goldene Freiheit der Bürger in Köln', in K. Schreiner and U. Meier (eds), *Stadtregiment und Bürgerfreiheit: Handlungsspielräume in deutschen und italienischen Städten des späten Mittelalters und in der frühen Neuzeit*, Göttingen: Vandenhoeck & Ruprecht, 1999.

Schreiner, K., and Meier, U. (eds), *Stadtregiment und Bürgerfreiheit: Handlungsspielräume in deutschen und italienischen Städten des späten Mittelalters und in der frühen Neuzeit*, Göttingen: Vandenhoeck & Ruprecht, 1999.

Scott, J., *Gender and the Politics of History*, New York: Columbia University Press, 1988.

Seuffert, L., *Kommentar zur Civilprozessordnung für das Deutsche Reich zum Einführungsgesetze*, 1895.

Sheehan, J., *German Liberalism in the Nineteenth Century*, Chicago: University of Chicago Press, 1978.

Siebenhaar, E. (ed.), *Das Bürgerliche Gesetzbuch für das Königreich Sachsen*, 1883.

Silberg, S., *Hermann Kantorowicz und die Freirechtsbewegung*, Berlin: Logos, 2004.

Souchay, E., *Anmerkungen zu den Wechsel-Gesetzen der Freien Stadt Frankfurt, mit besonderer Bezugnahme auf die offizielle Ausgabe der Wechselordnung vom Jahre 1845*, 1845.

Stein, P., *Roman Law in European History*, New York: Cambridge University Press, 1999.

Stern, F., *The Politics of Cultural Despair: A Study in the Rise of Germanic Ideology*, Berkeley: University of California Press, 1961.

Stern, J. (ed.), *Thibaut und Savigny: Ihre programmatischen Schriften*, Munich: Valen, 1973.

Stern, S., *The Court Jew: A Contribution to the History of the Period of Absolutism in Central Europe*, Philadelphia: Jewish Publication Society of America, 1950.

Stobbe, O., 'Die Grundsätze der deutschen Rechtsquellen des Mittelalters über den Gerichtsstand', *Jahrbuch des gemeinen deutschen Rechts*, 1 (1857), pp. 427–62.

Stobbe, O., *Die Juden in Deutschland während des Mittelalters*, 1866.

Stoll, A., *Savigny: Ein Bild seines Lebens mit einer Sammlung seiner Briefe*, Berlin: C. Heyman, 1927.

Stolleis, M. (ed.), *Hermann Conring: Beiträge zu Leben und Werk*, Berlin: Duncker & Humblot, 1983.

Stolleis, M., *A History of Public Law in Germany 1914–1945*, Oxford and New York: Oxford University Press, 2004.

Stolleis, M., *Public Law in Germany, 1800–1914*, New York: Berghahn Books, 2001.

Stumm-Halberg, C. von, 'Erste Berathung im Plenum des Reichstages', in B. Mugdan (ed.), *Die gesammten Materialien zum Bürgerlichen Gesetzbuch für das Deutsche Reich*, Berlin: Decker, 1896.

Sydow, R. (ed.), 'Gerichtsverfassungsgesetz', in *Reichs-Justizgesetze*, 1878.

Taylor, A.J.P., *Course of German History: A Study in the Development of Germany since 1815*, London: H. Hamilton, 1945.

Thatcher, O., and McNeal, E. (eds), *Source Book for Medieval History*, New York: C. Scribner's Sons, 1905.

Thibaut, A., *System des Pandekten-Rechts*, 1803.

Thibaut, A., *Über die Notwendigkeit eines allgemeinen bürgerlichen Rechts für Deutschland*, 1814.

Thöl, H., *Das Handelsrecht: Als gemeines in Deutschland geltendes Privatrecht mit Berücksichtigung des ausserdeutschen Handelsrechts*, 1841.

Thöl, H., *Das Transportgewerbe*, 1880.

Thöl, H., *Das Wechselrecht*, 1847.

Thomas, R., *Liberalism, Nationalism and the German Intellectuals: An Analysis of the Academic and Scientific Conferences of the Period*, Cambridge: W. Heffer & Sons, 1951.

Thompson, A., *Left Liberals, the State, and Popular Politics in Wilhelmine Germany*, Oxford and New York: Oxford University Press, 2000.

Trautman, T., *Lewis Henry Morgan and the Invention of Kinship*, Berkeley: University of California Press, 1987.

Triepel, H., *Die Kompetenzen des Bundesstaats und die geschriebene Verfassung*, 1908.

Triepel, H., *Die Reichsaufsicht: Untersuchungen zum Staatsrecht des Deutschen Reichs*, 1917.

Triepel, H., *Unitarismus und Föderalismus im Deutschen Reich: Eine staatsrechtliche und politische Studie*, 1907.

Unterholzner, K., 'Ueber die Rede des Cicero für den Schauspieler Q. Roscius, und über die litterarum obligatio insbesondere', *Zeitschrift für geschichtliche Rechtswissenschaft*, 1 (1815), pp. 248–69.

Unterholzner, K., 'Ueber die Stelle der zwölf Tafeln, Si in jus vocat', *Zeitschrift für geschichtliche Rechtswissenschaft*, 2/3 (1816), pp. 432–40.

Valentin, V., 'Bismarck and Lasker', *Journal of Central European History* (January 1944), pp. 41–64.

Vico, G., *New Science: Principles of the New Science Concerning the Common Nature of Nations*, D. Marsh (trans.), London: Penguin, 1999.

Vogel, U., 'Patriarchale Herrschaft, bürgerliches Recht, bürgerliche Utopie: Eigentumsrechte der Frauen in Deutschland und England', in J. Kocka (ed.), *Bürgertum im 19. Jahrhundert: Deutschland im europäischen Vergleich*, Munich: DTV, 1988.

Wagner-Hasel, B. (ed.), *Matriarchatstheorien der Altertumswissenschaft*, Darmstadt: Wissenschaftliche Buchgesellschaft, 1992.

Walker, M., *German Home Towns: Community, State, and General Estate 1648–1871*, Ithaca: Cornell University Press, 1971.

Walker, M., *Johann Jakob Moser and the Holy Roman Empire of the German Nation*, Chapel Hill: University of North Carolina Press, 1981.

Wang, C. (trans.), *The German Civil Code*, London: Stevens, 1907.

Waterlot, G., 'Curiosités juridiques le nouveau code allemand', *Indépendance Belge* (1 February 1901), Bundesarchiv file no. 30.01 Fb23440, Reichs-Justizamt, Äußerungen der Presse über das Familienrecht von 1896 bis 1919.

Wehler, H., *Deutsche Gesellschaftsgeschichte*, Munich: C. Beck, 1987.

Weiler, J., *The Constitution of Europe: Do the New Clothes Have an Emperor? And Other Essays on European Integration*, Cambridge and New York: Cambridge University Press, 1999.

Wentzcke, P., and Klötzer, W. (eds), *Deutscher Liberalismus im Vormärz: Heinrich von Gagern, Briefe und Reden 1815–1848*, Göttingen: Musterschmidt, 1959.

Wieacker, F., *A History of Private Law in Europe (with Particular Reference to Germany)*, T. Weir (trans.), Oxford: Clarendon, 1995.

Wigmore, J., Borchard, E., and Pollock, F., *The Progress of Continental Law in the Nineteenth Century*, Boston: Little Brown & Co., 1918.

Wilda, W., *Das Strafrecht der Germanen*, 1842.

Wilken, A., to Herr Minister (5 December 1921), Bundesarchiv file no. 30.01 1357, Eingaben in Familienangelegenheiten, 1921–1923.

Williamson, G., *The Longing for Myth in Germany: Religion and Aesthetic Culture from Romanticism to Nietzsche*, Chicago: University of Chicago Press, 2004.

Wilson, P., *War, State and Society in Württemberg, 1677–1793*, Cambridge and New York: Cambridge University Press, 1995.

Witte, J., *Law and Protestantism: The Legal Teachings of the Lutheran Reformation*, Cambridge and New York: Cambridge University Press, 2002.

Worden, B., 'English Republicanism', in J. Burns (ed.), *The Cambridge History of Political Thought 1450–1700*, Cambridge: Cambridge University Press, 1991.

Wrobel, H., 'Rechtsgeschichte, Wirtschaftsgeschichte, Sozialgeschichte: Die Thibaut-Savigny-Kontroverse', *Kritische Justiz*, 6 (1973), pp. 149–57.

Wunder, H., *He Is the Sun, She Is the Moon: Women in Early Modern Germany*, Cambridge: Harvard University Press, 1998.

Zachariä, H., 'Ueber den Zweck dieser Zeitschrift', *Kritische Zeitschrift für Rechtswissenschaft und Gesetzgebung des Auslandes*, 1 (1829), pp. 1–27.

Ziegler, J., *Ueber Gewerbefreiheit und deren Folgen*, 1819.

Index

Printed in the United States
128427LV00001B/105/A

9 781859 738122